At the Vanishing Point in History

Also available from Bloomsbury

Philosophical Thought in Russia in the Second Half of the Twentieth Century
Edited by Vladislav A. Lektorsky and Marina F. Bykova

At the Vanishing Point in History

Critical Perspectives on the Russia-Ukraine War

Edited by
Marina F. Bykova

BLOOMSBURY ACADEMIC
LONDON • NEW YORK • OXFORD • NEW DELHI • SYDNEY

BLOOMSBURY ACADEMIC
Bloomsbury Publishing Plc
50 Bedford Square, London, WC1B 3DP, UK
1385 Broadway, New York, NY 10018, USA
29 Earlsfort Terrace, Dublin 2, Ireland

BLOOMSBURY, BLOOMSBURY ACADEMIC and the Diana logo are
trademarks of Bloomsbury Publishing Plc

First published in Great Britain 2025

Copyright © Marina Bykova and contributors 2025

Marina Bykova has asserted her right under the Copyright, Designs and
Patents Act, 1988, to be identified as Author of this work.

For legal purposes the Acknowledgments on p. xiii constitute
an extension of this copyright page.

Cover design by Studio Auto

All rights reserved. No part of this publication may be reproduced or transmitted
in any form or by any means, electronic or mechanical, including photocopying,
recording, or any information storage or retrieval system, without prior
permission in writing from the publishers.

Bloomsbury Publishing Plc does not have any control over, or responsibility for,
any third-party websites referred to or in this book. All internet addresses given
in this book were correct at the time of going to press. The author and publisher
regret any inconvenience caused if addresses have changed or sites have ceased
to exist, but can accept no responsibility for any such changes.

A catalogue record for this book is available from the British Library.

A catalog record for this book is available from the Library of Congress.

ISBN:	HB:	978-1-3504-3832-3
	PB:	978-1-3504-3831-6
	ePDF:	978-1-3504-3830-9
	eBook:	978-1-3504-3833-0

Typeset by Integra Software Services Pvt. Ltd.
Printed and bound in Great Britain

To find out more about our authors and books visit www.bloomsbury.com
and sign up for our newsletters.

Contents

List of Contributors   vii
Acknowledgments   xiii

Introduction

At the Edge of the Abyss: The Countdown Begins   3
Marina F. Bykova

Prologue

Doors of Hell: New Russian Apocalypticism   15
Mikhail Epstein

Part 1   Unlearned Lessons from Russia's Bloody History

1. The War on Progress and the Missed Opportunities of Russian Enlightenment   45
   Marina F. Bykova
2. Between Nationalism and Universalism: The Imperial Imagination from Vladimir Solovyov to Alexandre Kojève   79
   Boris Groys
3. The Defeated Judge the Victors, or Bolshevism in Post-October Russian Thought   107
   Alexander L. Dobrokhotov
4. War in Ukraine and the Ethics of Pragmatism   125
   Dmitri N. Shalin
5. Against the West: The Weimar Republic and Post-Soviet Russia in the Yeltsin Era as Aggrieved Powers   149
   Leonid Luks

Part 2   The War of Obsession

6. The "End of History" or the End of the Human Race? Rereading Fukuyama and Huntington During Russia's War Against Ukraine   169
   Mikhail Sergeev

7	Point of Madness and the Search for History's Meaning *Mikhail Blumenkranz*	191
8	Nostalgia, Trickster, and the War *Mark Lipovetsky*	201
9	The Return of the Grand Inquisitor *Maja Soboleva*	219
10	The Viscosity of Russian Space: An Essay in Structural Analysis *Helen Petrovsky*	235

Part 3 Does Russia Have a Future?

11	Cyclical Progress: The Eternal Return of Modernity *Vladimir Marchenkov*	251
12	Being Guilty, Feeling Guilty: Right and Morality in Russia in the Shadow of the Current War *Michail Maiatsky*	273
13	Russian Ouroboros *Mikhail P. Shishkin*	291
14	Defederating Russia *Alexander Etkind*	311

Index 327

Contributors

Mikhail Blumenkranz is a philosopher specializing in cultural philosophy and the philosophy of history. He obtained his PhD in 1991 from Kharkov State University (formerly in the USSR, now Ukraine), where he later served as an Associate Professor at the Department of Cultural History and Philosophy of Science from 1991 to 2001. Since 2001, he has resided in Munich, Germany. He has authored several books, including *Vvedenie v Filosofiiu Podmeny: (Legenda v Istoriko-filosofskoy Perspektive)* [*Introduction to the Philosophy of Substitution*] (Moscow, 1994), *V Poiskakh Imeni i Litsa* [*In Search of Name and Face*] (Kiev-Kharkov, 2007), and *Obshchestvo Mertvykh Velosipedistov* [*Society of Dead Cyclists*] (Kharkov, 2017), as well as over 50 articles and essays. Since 1997, he has been the Chief Editor of the annual philosophical-cultural almanac, *Vtoraiia Navigatsiia* [*Second Navigation*], which publishes articles on various philosophical, historical, socio-political, and literary topics, with a particular emphasis on analyzing the spiritual landscape of the contemporary Western world and the post-Soviet space.

Marina F. Bykova is a Professor of Philosophy at North Carolina State University (USA) and the Editor-in-Chief of *Studies in East European Thought*. Her main area of specialization is the history of the nineteenth-century Continental philosophy, with a focus on German idealism, especially on Fichte and Hegel. Her most recent books include *The German Idealism Reader: Ideas, Responses and Legacies* (2019), *Hegel's Philosophy of Spirit: A Critical Guide* (ed., 2019), *The Bloomsbury Handbook of Fichte* (ed., 2020), and *The Palgrave Hegel Handbook* (co-ed. with K. Westphal; 2020). She has also published books on Russian intellectual tradition, including *Philosophical Thought in Russia in the Second Half of the 20th Century: A Contemporary View from Russia and Abroad* (co-ed. with V.A. Lektorsky; 2019) and *The Palgrave Handbook of Russian Thought* (co-ed. with M. Forster and L. Steiner; 2021). Her new book, *Hegel's Philosophy of Nature: A Critical Guide*, is forthcoming in early fall 2024.

Alexander L. Dobrokhotov is currently a Visiting Senior Research Fellow at the King's Russia Institute at King's College London (UK) and a Researcher at the Independent Institute of Philosophy (IPHI) in Paris (France). Previously, he held the position of Ordinary Professor of Philosophy at the National Research University Higher School of Economics in Moscow, Russia.

Dobrokhotov specializes in the history of Russian culture, philosophy of culture, and the history of philosophy, with a broad interest in ancient and medieval philosophy, philosophy in Russia, as well as Kant and German idealism. He has authored six books and more than 200 articles and essays. His most recent publications include *Filosofiia kultury* [*Philosophy of Culture*] (Moscow, 2016), *Teleologiia kultury* [*Teleology of Culture*] (Moscow, 2016), and *Dante* (Moscow, 2017).

Mikhail Epstein is a philosopher and a cultural and literary scholar. He is the Samuel Candler Dobbs Emeritus Professor of Cultural Theory and Russian Literature at Emory University (USA). He served as a professor at Emory University from 1990 to 2023. From 2012 to 2015, he also served as professor and founding director of the Centre for Humanities Innovation at Durham University (UK). His research interests include new directions in the humanities, contemporary philosophy and religion, the poetics and history of Russian literature, postmodernism, and the evolution of language. He has authored fifty books and over 1,000 articles and essays. His works have been translated into twenty-six languages. Among his latest books are *The Transformative Humanities: A Manifesto* (2012); *The Irony of the Ideal: Paradoxes of Russian Literature* (2017); *The Phoenix of Philosophy: Russian Thought of the Late Soviet Period, 1953–1991* (2019); and *Ideas Against Ideocracy: Non-Marxist Thought of the Late Soviet Period (1953–1991)* (2021). He is a recipient of the Andrei Bely Award (St. Petersburg, 1991), the prize of the London Institute of Social Inventions for intellectual creativity (1995), the Liberty Prize (New York, 2000), and the Modern Language Association Aldo and Jeanne Scaglione Prize for the best book in Slavic studies (US, 2023).

Alexander Etkind is a Professor at the Department of International Relations, Central European University in Vienna (Austria), and Director of the Open Society Hub for the Politics of the Anthropocene. He previously taught at the European University Institute in Florence (2013–2022), the University of Cambridge (2004–2013), and the European University in St. Petersburg (1999–2004). He defended his PhD in cultural history in Helsinki (1998), and since then supervised more than thirty PhD students. His interests include global decarbonization, cultural memory, European intellectual history, and various aspects of Russian history. A Fellow of King's College Cambridge, Etkind was the leader of a European research project "Memory at War: Cultural Dynamics in Poland, Russia and Ukraine" (2010–2013). He is the author of *Eros of the Impossible. The History of Psychoanalysis in Russia* (1996); *Internal Colonization: Russia's Imperial Experience* (2011); *Warped Mourning: Stories of the Undead in the Land of the Unburied* (2013); *Roads not Taken. An*

Intellectual Biography of William C. Bullitt (2017); *Nature's Evil: A Cultural History of Natural Resources* (2021), and *Russia against Modernity* (2023).

Boris Groys is a philosopher, essayist, art critic, and media theorist, internationally renowned for his expertise on Soviet-era art and literature, particularly the Russian avant-garde. He serves as a Professor of Philosophy at the European Graduate School in Saas-Fee (Switzerland). Additionally, he is a member of the Association Internationale des Critiques d'Art (AICA) and has held positions as a senior scholar at the Courtauld Institute of Art in London, a fellow at the International Research Center for Cultural Studies (IFK) in Vienna, and at institutions such as Harvard University Art Museum, the University of Pittsburgh, and New York University. His contributions span philosophy, politics, history, and art theory and criticism, with numerous books, research articles, and literary essays to his credit. Among his latest books are *Philosophy of Care* (2022) and *Becoming an Artwork* (2022).

Mark Lipovetsky is a Professor at the Department of Slavic Languages, Columbia University (USA). Among his many publications are books on Russian postmodernism, New Drama, Dmitry Prigov, and post-Soviet literature. Lipovetsky is also one of four co-authors of *History of Russian Literature* (2018). He is a winner of the Andrei Bely Prize for his contribution to literary studies (2019).

Leonid Luks is a historian specializing in East Europe. He serves as the managing editor of two scholarly journals: *Forum für osteuropäische Ideen- und Zeitgeschichte* and *Forum noveishei vostochnoevropeiskoi istori i kul'tury*. From 1995 to 2012, he held the position of Professor of Central and Eastern European Contemporary History at the Catholic University of Eichstätt-Ingolstadt in Germany, and from 2011 to 2015, he acted as the Director of the Institute for Central and Eastern European Studies at the same university. His primary research interests encompass the history of Polish Catholicism, Bolshevism, and the history of Russian ideas and the Eurasian movement. He has published over thirty books and numerous scholarly articles; his most recent books include *K stoletiiu "filosofskogo parokhoda." Mysliteli "pervoj" russkoj emigratsii o russkoj revolutsii i o totalitarnykh soblaznakh 20 veka* [*To the 100th Anniversary of the "Philosophical Steamship": Thinkers of the "First" Russian Emigration on the Russian Revolution and the Totalitarian Temptations of the 20th Century*] (2023) and *The "Offended Great Power?" Post-Soviet Russia in Search of a Lost Empire. Essays* (2023).

Michail Maiatsky holds a Master's degree in Philosophy from the Rostov-on-Don State University, USSR (1984) and PhD in Ancient Philosophy from the University of Fribourg, Switzerland (2005). He worked as Lecturer at the Universities of Fribourg and Lausanne (Switzerland). He is the author of numerous books that have been published in French: *Platon penseur du visuel* (2005), *Europe-les-Bains* (2007), and in Russian: *Vo-vtorykh* [*Secondly*] (2002), *Spor o Platone*. *Khrug Shtefana George i nemetskij universitet* [*Controversy over Plato: Stefan George's Circle and the German University*] (2012), *Dekoratsii / Zavisimosti. Ommazh Zhaku Derrida* [*Decorations (of) Dependence. Hommage to Jacques Derrida*] (2019), *Ad hominem i obratno* [*Ad hominem and back*] (2020).

Vladimir Marchenkov is a Professor of Philosophy of Art at the Ohio University School of Interdisciplinary Arts (USA). He is the author of *The Orpheus Myth and the Powers of Music* (2009), translator of Aleksei Losev's *Dialectics of Myth* (2003), and author as well as consulting editor on Russian philosophy for the award-winning *Encyclopedia of Philosophy*, Second Edition (2006). Marchenkov edited two volumes of essays: *Between Histories: Art's Dilemmas and Trajectories* (2013), and *Arts and Terror* (2014), and co-edited with Stefan Bird-Pollan a collection of essays on *Hegel's Political Aesthetics: Art in Modern Society* (2020). He also served as an Associate Editor of *Studies in East European Thought* from 2018 to 2022. He has published essays, articles, and chapters in a wide range of academic venues in the US, Russia, UK, France, Germany, Italy, the Netherlands, Sri Lanka, and Kazakhstan. He teaches courses on the philosophy of art, history of aesthetics, world aesthetic ideas, and art and morality and is currently writing a book on *Three Borises: Poetic Truth against the Will to Power*.

Helen Petrovsky is Head of the Department of Aesthetics at the Institute of Philosophy of the Russian Academy of Sciences in Moscow (Russia). She is currently employed by Université Sorbonne Nouvelle. Her major fields of interest are contemporary philosophy, visual studies, and North American literature and culture. She has authored ten books, including *Vozmushchenie znaka: Kul'tura protiv transtsendentsii* [*Disturbance of the Sign: Culture against Transcendence*] (Moscow, 2019, 2022) and *Zhan-Liuc Nansi. Lektsii o Kante (po konspektam Eleny Petrovskoi)* [*Jean-Luc Nancy. Lectures on Kant (Based on Notes Taken by Helen Petrovsky)*] (Moscow, 2023). Since 2002 she has been Editor-in-Chief of the theoretical and philosophical journal *Sinii divan*. She is laureate of the Andrei Bely Prize (2011), the Innovation Prize (2012), and the Alexander Piatigorsky Literary Prize (2020–2021).

Mikhail Sergeev is a historian of religion, philosophy, and modern art. He served as an editor of the book series "Contemporary Russian Philosophy" (2016–2019) and as Chair of the Department of Religion, Philosophy, and Theology at the Wilmette Institute (2017–2021). He teaches courses in humanities at the University of the Arts, Philadelphia, and the Graduate Theological Union in Berkeley, California (USA). He is also an Affiliate Professor at the United Theological Seminary of the Twin Cities in New Brighton, Minnesota. He has authored more than 200 scholarly, literary, and journalistic articles published in the United States, Canada, Great Britain, the Netherlands, Poland, the Czech Republic, Greece, Slovakia, Russia, Ukraine, Japan, Kyrgyzstan, Uzbekistan, and Azerbaijan. He is the author and contributing editor of fifteen books, including his latest, *The Crucifixion in Painting: From the Middle Ages to Post-Modernism* (2023), for which he received the silver medal in the category "Education" at the American Illumination Book Awards.

Dmitri N. Shalin is a Professor of Sociology and Director of the Center for Democratic Culture at the University of Nevada, Las Vegas (USA). He is coordinator of the Justice & Democracy Forum series, editor of *The Social Health of Nevada* report, director of the Erving Goffman Archives and International Biography Initiative, and organizer of international forums on Russian politics and culture. His research interests and publications are in the areas of biohermeneutics, pragmatism, democratic culture, emotional intelligence, and Russian culture and society. Among his books and edited volumes are *Pragmatism and Democracy: Studies in History, Social Theory, and Progressive Politics* (2017); *Russian Culture at the Crossroads: Paradoxes of Postcommunist Consciousness* (2018); *Russian Intelligentsia in the Age of Counterperestroika: Political Agendas, Rhetorical Strategies, Personal Choices* (2019); *Contemporary Autobiographical Prose Writing* (Special Issue of *Avtobiografija. Journal on Life Writing and the Representation of the Self in Russian Culture*, 2021); and *Erving Manuel Goffman: Biographical Sources of Sociological Imagination* (2024).

Mikhail P. Shishkin is a writer and one of the most prominent names in contemporary Russian literature. He is the only author to have received all the most prestigious Russian literary awards, such as the Russian Booker Prize (2000), the National Bestseller Prize (2006), and the Big Book Prize (2011), among many others. His work has recently been recognized with the Italian Strega Prize (2022). He has authored over ten books of fiction and non-fiction translated into thirty-five languages, as well as numerous articles and essays. His essays have been published in the *New York Times*, *Wall Street*

Journal, *The Guardian*, *Le Monde*, and media outlets. Since 1995, he has lived and worked in Switzerland.

Maja Soboleva is an extra-ordinary professor of philosophy at the Philipps-University of Marburg (Germany). Her areas of specialization are epistemology, hermeneutics, philosophy of language, and the history of philosophy, in particular German and Russian philosophy. She is the editor of nine collections of articles, as well as the author of nine books and more than a hundred articles. Her recent publications include "Das Schöne in der kritisch-philosophischen Poetik Ingeborg Bachmanns," *Colloquium: New Philologies*, 9 (1–2) (2024), Special issue: Ingeborg Bachmann und Philosophie, 128–41; "Paul Celan and Leo Schestow, "Philosophie des Überlebens und Philosophie der Überlebenden," in Bernd Auerochs, Friederike Felicitas Günter, Markus May, Anne Fleig and Susanne Zepp-Zwirner (eds) *Celan-Perspektiven 2022* (Universitätsverlag Winter, 2023), 21–37; "Kantianism: Schools and Directions," *RUDN Journal of Philosophy*, 27 (3) (2023), 499–512; "Knowledge, Self-Knowledge and Self-Identity: Transcendental and Empirical Arguments," Giuseppe Motta, Dennis Schulting and Udo Thiel (eds), *Kant's Transcendental Deduction and the Theory of Apperception* (2022), 597–611; "Marxism as Spinozism? One Episode in the History of Soviet Philosophy," *Studies in East European Thought* 74 (3), 319–32.

Acknowledgments

This volume is indebted to the support and assistance of numerous individuals who generously contributed their time, expertise, and encouragement.

I extend my deepest gratitude to the authors of this collection. While I wish the circumstances prompting our project were different, and that we never had to confront our home country for perpetuating acts of aggression against an independent neighboring nation, I am truly grateful for the honor of working with such a distinguished group of intellectuals. Their willingness to critically engage with the tragic experience of the ongoing Russia-Ukraine war and their commitment to truth, however painful it may be, is matched only by their generosity toward those seeking to understand the roots and real causes of the unfolding catastrophe.

I am also deeply thankful to the reviewers for their invaluable feedback, constructive comments, and suggestions, which have helped enhance the quality and rigor of the volume. Their expertise and insights have been instrumental in shaping the content of this collection.

The completion of this volume would not have been possible without the guidance and support of the Philosophy Editor at Bloomsbury, Colleen Coalter, and her editorial assistants, Suzie Nash and Aimee Brown. Their professionalism and commitment to excellence have been instrumental in bringing this project to fruition. I am also grateful to the production team for their tremendous efforts and hard work in giving life to this book.

In my editorial work, I have been greatly aided by my Research Assistants at North Carolina State University, Kerry Synowiez and Sean MacKay. I wish to thank Kerry and Sean for their invaluable help with copyediting essays, and Sean specifically for his assistance in compiling the index for this book.

Lastly, I would like to express my gratitude to my husband and soulmate, Andrey, for his love, understanding, patience, and encouragement during the preparation of this collection and beyond. His unwavering support has been a constant source of inspiration.

Thank you to everyone who contributed to the realization of this project. Our collective efforts have made this book possible.

Introduction

At the Edge of the Abyss: The Countdown Begins

Marina F. Bykova

When Francis Fukuyama declared the "end of history" in 1989, confidently asserting the triumph of the "Western *idea*" and liberal democracy in the great ideological battles between East and West, the world responded with hesitant relief and hope (Fukuyama, 1989, 3, 4; see also Fukuyama, 1992). The fall of communism in Eastern Europe and the dissolution of the Soviet Union, which marked the end of the Cold War, seemed only to confirm such predictions until global protests and demonstrations in the early 2010s brought the reality of the relentless march of history back into focus. Then-current social and political developments in the West prompted Alain Badiou to speak of "the rebirth of history" and to contemplate "the advent of a different world" with the potential to usher in a new political order (Badiou, 2012, 6, 1; see also 15, 85). The challenges Badiou and others pose to Fukuyama's thesis are underscored by the intensification of geopolitical antagonism between the West and Russia in recent decades, which has led to open political-ideological clashes and military confrontation.

February 24, 2022, marked a tragic division in contemporary history, demarcating a "before" and an "after." The darkest scenarios now unfold before our eyes. By launching a brutal full-scale invasion of Ukraine, Putin's Russia has ignited the largest military conflict in Europe since World War II, resulting in immense loss of life and widespread devastation in the neighboring country. The invasion has also sent shockwaves worldwide. Its immediate global consequences are profound; the conflict has already displaced millions of refugees, created tensions in geopolitics and diplomacy, and instilled persistent fears of political and economic instability around the globe.

Undoubtedly, the primary and immediate victims of the conflict, the ones bearing the brunt of all the hardships and deprivations, are the heroic people of Ukraine. The devastating impact of Russia's war of aggression against Ukraine is difficult to fathom and cannot be justified in any way. But the war unleashed by the Putin regime against Ukraine also has dramatic implications for Russia itself. The question of whether Russia has a future is no longer merely a polemical question. In the wake of its full-scale invasion of Ukraine, it finds itself at a critical juncture in history, reaching a vanishing point where its future becomes uncertain.

The guiding metaphor for the present collection, the notion of a "vanishing point," originates in the visual arts, referring to the point on the horizon where parallel lines seem to converge and objects seem to disappear from view. In the context of historical inquiry, this concept takes on metaphorical meaning, suggesting a threshold beyond which events, ideas, and civilizations may fade into obscurity or undergo profound shifts in meaning and significance. This metaphor prompts reflection on the impermanence and transience of human endeavors and the temporal dimensions of human civilization. It invites contemplation of the ephemeral character of empires, ideologies, and cultural paradigms, highlighting the fleeting nature of power, influence, and legacy.

The vanishing point on the horizon also invokes the image of a boundary of history, inviting us to contemplate the elusive lines dividing the past, present, and future. While historians can shed light on the past by reconstructing historical narratives, and while we may believe we have access to the present, the future remains an enigmatic prospect. Moreover, at turning points in history—like the ongoing Russia-Ukraine conflict—the pursuit of the future intensifies, gaining crucial existential significance. Russia's dangerous regression into barbarism exposes the fragility of the societal structures and norms that uphold civilization. Furthermore, the path ahead for Russia is obscured by an air of uncertainties surrounding its political direction. In February 2022, Russia entered another dark period in its troubled history, and it might be even bloodier, with far more severe consequences for the country and its people than any other social experiment Russia has undergone thus far.

Despite the Kremlin's attempts to paint Russia's current situation in a positive light, the war has inflicted significant damage on the country, causing political, economic, and cultural ruin and exposing a moral collapse. The geopolitical repercussions for Moscow have been disastrous. Putin's initial endeavor to frame Russia's invasion as a response to NATO expansion, with the aim of limiting NATO's presence near Russian borders and in Europe, suffered a serious defeat. Instead of containment, this resulted in two additional countries—Finland and Sweden—joining NATO. Similarly, efforts to validate Putin's "firm belief" that Russians and Ukrainians "are one people" (Putin, 2021) not only failed, but led to a rare consolidation of all political and social forces during the war, uniting the Ukrainian nation, fortifying the country's spirit, and making the defense of its independence a shared goal.

Apart from these counter-results, which demonstrate the inadequacy of Russia's agenda in Europe and Ukraine, the war has strained Russia's relationships with Western nations, leading to its growing alienation in some key arenas on the global stage. To be sure, this alienation is far from being a wholesale isolation. We are witnessing an increasing realignment of allegiances, with Russia strengthening its influence in Asia and powerfully pushing its agenda of Greater Eurasia.[1] This troubling development signifies the growing split of the global world into two antagonistic parts, divided not merely by geography but by social and political values. The Russia-Ukraine military confrontation is only deepening this rift. However, despite the strengthening of Russia's relationship with countries such as China, India, and Turkey, the war in Ukraine has seriously undermined Russia's position in Central Asia. Nations such as Kazakhstan, Kyrgyzstan, Tajikistan, Turkmenistan, and Uzbekistan—long-standing partners of Russia with deep historical, economic, and military connections—have taken a step back from Moscow amid the conflict.[2] The fate of Russia's relationship with other Asian countries is also uncertain. The escalation of Moscow's aggression against Ukraine has heightened the pressure on developing nations to choose between aligning with the democratic West or with authoritarian powers like Russia and its several allies. However, many countries, including those from the Global South, which have traditionally depended on Russia not only economically but also politically, are reluctant to make this decision. More and more nations challenge the long-term viability of maintaining close association with Russia and pursuing established relations. For by disregarding the established world order and violating established laws, Russia has damaged its standing within the international community. This predicament extends beyond matters of prestige; it also yields tangible effects on trade, alliances, and access to vital resources.

In addition to the serious geopolitical setbacks already suffered by Moscow due to the war, its immediate and enduring domestic consequences are equally, if not more, detrimental. The economic aftermath of the conflict has plunged Russia into a deep abyss. The cost of military operations, coupled with international sanctions, has led to a severe economic downturn. Instead of progressing towards the establishment of a prosperous, post-industrial nation, Russia's economy has become essentially structured around the war. The entire political, economic, ideological, and military apparatus is now focused on expanding the scale of hostilities in Ukraine.

Public discourse is visibly dominated by militant anti-Ukrainianism, nationalistic Russophilia, and anti-Western sentiment, all feeding into the escalating war narrative. Russian nationalism, which has been growing since the fall of the Soviet Union, is omnipresent and increasingly dominant in today's Russia. While previously mostly characterized by "imperial" tendencies, such as pride in a vast, powerful, and multi-ethnic state capable of exerting influence beyond its borders, Russian nationalism now focuses more on ethnic issues. The political system has transitioned beyond mere authoritarianism to dictatorship. The current regime tightens its political and ideological control within the country, imposing serious restrictions on participation in the public sphere and suppressing political opposition while instilling fear among the population. The authorities shut down public debate by cracking down on independent media, restricting access to information online, and persecuting those who attempt to criticize their aggressive policies and actions.

The spread of disinformation and false narratives—ranging from propaganda and historical revisionism to conspiracy theories and open falsehoods about events on the frontline, at home and around the world—has emerged as the Kremlin's official strategy in the information space. A well-designed, powerful propaganda machine manipulates public opinion and cultivates open hostility towards the West. Calls for the cancellation of Russian culture as a response to the war have hindered the development of cultural ties beyond Russia's borders. The suppression of non-conformist intellectual and cultural figures within the country has created impossible conditions for free thought and creativity. The ban on freedom of expression not only violates individual liberties and rights but also prohibits intellectual development and the free pursuit of knowledge. Independent, critically-thinking individuals, primarily belonging to the educated classes, are leaving the country in the thousands. In addition to the lack of political dynamism characteristic of the last decade of Putin's rule, the distinctive feature of contemporary Russia is the absence of social transformation, resulting in the political passivity and conformism that currently dominate Russian society.

One does not need a vivid imagination to recognize that the war against Ukraine is self-destructive, virtually suicidal, for Russia. Now, more than ever, Russia's future is at stake, and Putin, widely perceived as a pragmatic politician, appears willing to risk everything. This reckless behavior underscores the importance of comprehending the underlying motivations and geopolitical calculations propelling such perilous actions.

Framed under the banner of the "Russian world," the invasion is portrayed by Putin's regime as a war of necessity, ostensibly justified by the imperative to respond to an existential threat and ensure the nation's survival. Geopolitical nuances aside, it is evident that this explanation lacks credibility. However, it is insufficient to dismiss it merely on these grounds. Challenging this narrative necessitates a thorough examination of Russia's current political and ideological pursuits and an exploration of the past intellectual, cultural, and social discourses that paved the way for it.

The ongoing war is a far more intricate event than a mere display of Russian power. The multifaceted nature of this aggression cannot be attributed to a single cause; its analysis necessitates careful consideration and thoughtful deliberation—an aspect currently lacking in the existing literature. One-sided perspectives and misguided notions prevalent on social media platforms lead to significant misrepresentations. Similarly, the terminology employed to characterize the current state of Russia-Ukraine relations often misinterprets the historical context. Hence, there is a pressing need for a careful analysis and balanced assessment of the conflict, acknowledging its complexity through accurate historical and contemporary data. Identifying the genuine roots of the ongoing crisis and understanding the intricacies of the unfolding realities are urgent, as navigating a way out without thorough understanding is futile. This task is critical not only for political actors but even more so for intellectuals, especially those well-versed in Russian history, culture, and thought. Intellectuals today bear the responsibility of accurately assessing the current crisis, critically reflecting on its causes, and striving to develop a synthetic understanding of the present situation in connection with the past and the future.

At the Vanishing Point in History is an effort to grapple with the challenges posed by the ongoing Russia-Ukraine military confrontation. It offers a thorough examination of this critical situation, contextualizing it within early and recent Russian history and intellectual development. Furthermore, the volume seeks to stimulate meaningful debate on the future of the nation. Comprising analytical articles, literary essays, and personal reflections, this work is authored by a distinguished group of Russian émigrés, including eminent humanities scholars and prominent novelists, whose influence resonates both within Russia and across the wider world.

The idea of this volume emerged in the wake of Russia's unprovoked invasion. Like many around the world, the contributors were deeply shaken by this unprecedented act of aggression. Yet, the impact was particularly poignant in this case. While most of the authors left Russia decades ago, they have maintained personal and professional relationships with friends and colleagues there, fostering mutually beneficial interactions with their compatriots and the country. The fate of Russia remains close to their hearts.

In response to the 1968 Soviet invasion of Czechoslovakia, a dissident Russian poet and writer, Alexander Galich addressed the nation: "With a lump in the throat, a bullet in the barrel: …. 'Fellow citizens! The homeland is in danger! Our tanks are in a foreign land!'" (Galich 2006, 342-3, trans. mine). This verse eloquently encapsulates the emotions experienced by the authors of this collection in the aftermath of Russia's colossal hostility. When Soviet tanks rolled into Prague, domestic newspapers described the invasion of Czechoslovakia as an act of "friendship." Today, we witness a chilling parallel as Russian tanks trample a peaceful, independent Ukraine. The rhetoric from Russia's current leaders and official media presents this as a "special military operation" aimed at "denazification" and the "liberation" of a neighboring country. The tragedy in Ukraine goes beyond its historical precedents, and it is impossible to remain indifferent to such harrowing events.

This war, with the sorrow it brings, also holds a warning for the global world. To grasp the significance of an impending civilizational catastrophe, a thorough analysis of the experiences of recent decades is imperative. Such an examination holds great importance in today's globalized world, where the frequency of political and cultural calamities is on the rise, and humanistic and liberal-democratic values face open challenges. There is also a critical need to delve into the phenomenon of neo-tyranny, which strangely thrives in modernity. Contemporary Russia stands as the most representative example of the imminent danger tyranny presents to global civilization. In its brutal assault on Ukraine, the hostile Putin regime not only holds Russians hostage but poses a threat to all of humanity. Great power syndrome is treacherous, fostering aggression and military conflict. However, it is a tyranny driven by imperial ambitions and fueled by notions of national supremacy that has made the current tragedy inevitable.

As inhabitants of this shared world, we bear responsibilities towards one another, and it is imperative that each of us recognize the well-being of all humanity as a personal duty. The responsibility to condemn aggression becomes even more crucial in the current context, where Putin's regime is perpetrating atrocities in Ukraine under the guise of defending the Russian nation, claiming to act on behalf of the entire country and all its people. The present volume is the authors' collective effort to confront the grim realities unfolding in Ukraine and critically reflect on the catastrophic crisis into which Russia has plunged itself.

Within the history of Russian social thought, the practice of critical intellectuals articulating a shared position is a well-established tradition. Anyone familiar with the history of social and political thought in Russia will immediately recall such renowned publications as *Vekhi* [*Landmarks* or *The Signposts*] (1909), *Iz Glubiny* [*Out of the Depth* or *De Profundis*] (1918), and *Iz-pod Glyb* [*From Under the Rubble*] (1974). While there are other examples, these three each marked an epoch. Collections of essays (symposiums) authored by prominent Russian intellectuals, all three were composed during the most dramatic crises in Russia's stormy history: *Landmarks*, in the aftermath of the 1905 revolution; *Out of the Depth*, as a reaction to the Bolsheviks coming to power; and *From Under the Rubble*, when Russia found itself "under the rubble" of a human and moral disaster caused by the socialism of the Soviet regime. Although these volumes address different issues, in full accordance with the specific needs of particular historical periods, all three books are meant for the same audience—the Russian intelligentsia, whose predicament is believed to be directly associated with the country itself and whose agency (action or inaction) influenced its future. Deeply concerned with the trajectory of Russia's development and the prospects for its future, contributors to these three symposiums critically discussed Russia's then-present state of affairs, expressing radical views about its past, present, and future.

Conscious of historical continuity and aware of their civic responsibility as intellectuals and people of letters, the authors of this volume have united to respond to the current critical moment in Russia's history by analyzing present conditions and contemplating the country's future prospects. While it may be too ambitious to consider this volume on a par with its historical predecessors, there is a hope that readers familiar with the Russian intellectual tradition will recognize and appreciate the topical similarity between the current collection and the likes of *Landmarks* and others. It is worth noting, however, some significant differences between the present volume and its predecessors. One of the most visible differences concerns the dominant political orientation, explicitly or implicitly expressed by the authors of the collections: largely conservative then, and more liberal-minded now. Another difference is related to language choice. While all previous symposiums were originally written in Russian, primarily targeting a Russian audience, the present volume is composed in English, predominantly aiming at an Anglophone (and more broadly, Western) readership.[3]

Western readers often find themselves in the dark or easily confused about the underlying reasons for Russia's war on Ukraine and the historical, political, and cultural developments that led to the current crisis. This lack of background knowledge is prevalent outside academia, but even those who study Russia often struggle with the paradoxes of the country's social, economic, and political evolution. Authored by intellectuals who are not only experts in their relevant areas of study but also highly versed in the internal workings of Russian society, the essays included in this volume aim to provide the needed background and context for the confrontation unfolding in Eastern Europe.

As I write these lines, the war initiated by Putin's regime continues unabated, tragically claiming the lives of thousands of Ukrainian soldiers and innocent civilians. The memory of their sacrifice will remain a poignant reminder of the ongoing tragedy of this conflict. It is our solemn duty to ensure that this memory endures and that their sacrifices are not in vain.

***

The present volume is organized into three conceptual sections, preceded by a prologue. The prologue draws attention to the perilous realities of contemporary Russia, shedding light on the emergence of a world-threatening form of Russian apocalyptic ideology and underscoring the urgency of comprehending and countering it. By addressing a range of topics explored in-depth in the subsequent essays, the prologue sets the stage for the book, exposing the gravity of Russia's current state and prompting focused consideration. Additionally, it provides readers with a general contemporary context before delving into more specific discussions offered in the volume.

The three conceptual parts of the collection roughly address questions relevant to the "Past" (Part 1: "Unlearned Lessons from Russia's Bloody History"), "Present" (Part 2: "The War of Obsession"), and "Future" (Part 3: "Does Russia Have a Future?").

The essays in the first section draw from early and recent Russian history. The present trend of instrumentalizing and weaponizing the cultural and historical past in the name of the future, routinely employed by the Putin regime and its propaganda, is not only dangerous but also damaging to the image of Russian culture. It often leads to gross exaggerations and falsifications of real culture and history. Historical and cultural events are also commonly referred to without attention to their broader context. The essays in this section of the book largely focus on the history of Russia's last few centuries, analyzing events and movements—from Bolshevism and imperialism to pragmatism and Weimar syndrome—in their specific historical context while searching for clues to explain the current crisis. Additionally, there is a discussion of Russian traditionalism, whose roots extend back to earlier periods in Russia's history and which significantly impeded the country's full engagement with the European Enlightenment. Throughout Russia's history, this traditionalism has constantly resurfaced in various forms of anti-progressivism, particularly evident in today's counter-Enlightenment stance of Putin's Russia.

Building on the historical details provided by the first portion of the book, the second part focuses on the present realities of the war in Ukraine, examining its real objectives, characteristics, and dimensions. By placing current events in the broader context of concepts such as the "end of history," the "global world," and human ideals, the contributors attempt to explain how this war differs from previous conflicts. One issue addressed by the essays in this section is why most Russians appear to support the ongoing aggression against Ukraine and do not protest against Putin's oppressive regime. There is also a discussion of the historical roots of Russian silence and the art of protesting through silence in Russian culture.

The essays included in the third portion of the volume deal with questions relevant to Russia's future. Contrary to political forecasting, the chapters focus on the potential consequences of the war in Ukraine for Russia and its people. The common consensus is that whatever outcome the war itself may have, its aftermath will be severe and long-lasting. Russia will become even more isolated from the rest of the world; its image as a great cultural nation will be destroyed, and the value of its cultural wealth jeopardized. The current crisis will dramatically impoverish its future generations. A discussion of Russia and Russians' collective responsibility and how it should be judged is also part of this section's inquiries.

While not claiming to provide exhaustive coverage of all relevant issues and topics, this volume aims to modestly contribute to the broader goal of gaining a deeper understanding of the historical, political, and cultural causes and consequences of the war. It also aims to expose the suicidal nature of the war for Russia itself. The military confrontation with Ukraine has once again pushed the country to the edge of the abyss. Russia now stands at a crucial juncture in history, teetering on the brink of oblivion; the final countdown has begun. It remains to be seen whether Russia will find the strength to overcome its ultra-nationalistic imperial tendencies and regain its now paralyzed reason.

Notes

1   The Russian project of Greater Eurasia—or, more specifically, the "Greater Eurasian Partnership"—emerged well before February 2022. Originally proposed in June 2016, this geo-economic and geostrategic initiative arose in response to Russia's limited economic maneuverability on the European continent and the sharpening confrontation with the European Union. Over time, it has evolved into a multifaceted social, political, and cultural project that Russia has pursued with differing degrees of success and intensity. The project focuses on Russia's development of a new Asian strategy and the formation of a standard Eurasian political, economic, and security structure through civilization-based cooperation (Köstem, 2019). At the core of this initiative is the idea of promoting Russia as a substantial, resilient

northern Eurasian polity and autonomous power center in a globally diversified environment, characterized by a unique geopolitical posture that incorporates both European and Asian dimensions.
2 These countries have refrained from endorsing Russia's actions in Ukraine and, notably, Kazakhstan and Uzbekistan have openly declared their backing for Ukraine's territorial integrity (Blackwood et al., 2023).
3 A thought-provoking Russian collection of essays, authored by critical humanities scholars from Russia, was published in 2023 by the German publishing house LIT Verlag. The volume's title—*Pered litsom katastrofy* [*In the Face of Catastrophe*]—defines its primary message with great precision (Plotnikov, 2023).

References

Badiou, Alain. 2012. *The Rebirth of History: Times of Riots and Uprisings*. Translated by Gregory Elliott. London: Verso.

Blackwood, Maria A., Ricardo Barrios, Rebecca M. Nelson, and Michael D. Sutherland. 2023. *Central Asia: Implications of Russia's War in Ukraine*. Congressional Research Service (CRS) Report, June 9, 2023. https://sgp.fas.org/crs/row/R47591.pdf

Fukuyama, Francis. 1989. "The End of History?" *The National Interest*, No. 16 (Summer 1989), 3–18.

Fukuyama, Francis. 1992. *The End of History and the Last Man*. New York/Toronto: The Free Press.

Galich, Alexander. 2006. "Bessmertny Kuz'min." In *Stikhotvoreniia i poemy*. Introduction and notes by V.P. Betaki. Sankt Petersburg: Akademichesky Proekt. http://www.bards.ru/archives/part.php?id=4104

Köstem, Seçkin. 2019. "Russia's Search for a Greater Eurasia: Origins, Promises, and Prospects." *Kennan Cable* 40 (February 2019). Publication of the Wilson Center, Kennan Institute. https://www.wilsoncenter.org/sites/default/files/media/documents/publication/kennan_cable_no._40.pdf

Plotnikov, Nikolaj (ed.). 2023. *Pered litsom katastrofy* [*In the Face of Catastrophe*]. Münster: LIT Verlag.

Putin, Vladimir. 2021. "On the Historical Unity of Russians and Ukrainians" (July 12). In *President of Russia, Official Site*. http://en.kremlin.ru/events/president/news/66181

Prologue

Doors of Hell: New Russian Apocalypticism

Mikhail Epstein

Apocalypticism and Nihilism

In the post-Soviet era, a new pseudo-religious ideology has formed in Russia, fraught with the gravest spiritual dangers and political upheavals for both the country and humanity. It has absorbed state-sponsored Orthodoxy, the pagan cult of the soil, the Eurasian hatred of the West, traits of Nazi ideology, and archaic cults of war and the realm of the dead. This is a kind of apocalypticism, inheriting the darkest traits of Gnosticism and cursing all existence, for it lies in evil. Hence the drive to consign the whole world to purifying fire, to arrange a man-made end of the world, relying on the destructive power of nuclear weapons.

Nikolai Berdyaev wrote in *The Russian Idea* (1946):

> We Russians are apocalyptic or nihilistic. We are apocalyptics or nihilists because we are striving for the end and poorly understand the stage of the historical process, hostile to pure form. … In Orthodoxy, the eschatological side of Christianity was most strongly expressed. In Russian nihilism, ascetic and eschatological elements can be distinguished. The Russian people are the people of the end, not the middle of the historical process.
>
> (Berdyaev, 2008)

Nihilism and apocalypticism combine perfectly, like two facets of the same mindset: the denial of all values of this world and the expectation of or even desire for its end.

This latest apocalypticism has various religious, nationalist, and political components. These teachings emerged from occult and sectarian ideas of the early Christian era and the Middle Ages. In Russia, they are rooted in schismatic beliefs that the world has already been captured by the Antichrist, and therefore, must be destroyed to hasten the coming of Christ.

The ideology of the extreme right (R. Guénon, J. Evola), occult and geopolitical aspirations of Italian Fascism and German Nazism, the doctrine of the national spirit of "soil and blood," the recourse to the Aryan "Great Tradition" and caste system, and the contrast of continental, "soil-based" and maritime "mercantile" civilizations had a strong influence on the new apocalypticism. Hence, the Eurasian teachings of the eternal confrontation between Russia and the West, with Russia being considered the heart of Eurasia and the heir to the Horde, historically destined to unite Europe (especially Eastern) and Asia (especially Central) in a geopolitical confrontation with the "Anglo-Saxons" (USA, England, Canada, Australia).

Orthodoxy in Russia has almost always been entirely dependent on the state and did not take deep independent roots in the people; otherwise, in 1917, they would not have renounced it so easily, would not have started destroying churches and turning them into warehouses and toilets, chopping up icons, etc. Before the revolution, there were about 55,000 parishes in the country, by the early 1940s about 200 remained. Then there seemed to be a revival, and now the Russian Orthodox Church is approaching the previous level, with almost 40,000 parishes in Russia. But today it is evident that this tree has been hollowed out, eaten from the inside not only by the atheism of the twentieth century, but also by false churchliness, when the church acts as a tool of the state, a "patriotic" institution, similar to the army or the Russian National Guard. For a long time, this did not prevent Russian Orthodoxy from being part of the global. But in 2018, after the Ecumenical Patriarchate recognized the autocephalous Ukrainian church, the Russian Orthodox Church sharply turned onto the path of schism, decided to separate from the universal Orthodoxy, and became in spirit and jurisdiction "Old Believer." The Russian Orthodox Church moved back from the Nikonian reforms of the seventeenth century, which brought Russian Orthodoxy closer to the Greek, and thus ceased to be "Greek-Catholic" or "Greek-Russian," as it was often officially called. On October 16, 2018, the Synod of the Russian Orthodox Church decided to completely cease Eucharistic communion with the Constantinople Patriarchate. Not only the Western, Catholic-Protestant world but also the modern Orthodox world, and first of all the "fraternal Ukrainian," lie in evil and have given themselves over to the Antichrist. The Russian Church, which split off with the Byzantine from Western Christianity in the eleventh century, has separated even from Western Orthodox brethren a thousand years later, right before our eyes, and has gone on the path of further schism, i.e., a kind of self-immolation of faith.

On the other side, equally severe measures followed. Back in 1872 the Orthodox Council in Constantinople condemned the heresy of ethnophyletism as a form of ecclesiastical racism, or tribalism—the sacrifice of general church interests to national-political, tribal interests. Even then it was obvious that Russian Orthodoxy was obsessed with the idea of subordinating religion to the interests of the state. A century and a half later, in 2022, at the height of Russia's war with Ukraine, Ecumenical Patriarch Bartholomew emphasized the worldwide danger of this heresy and the schismatic policy of the Russian Orthodox Church in his keynote speech at the international conference "For a Reasonably Open World." After the fall of communism

> faith has once again been used for ideological purposes. The Russian Orthodox Church has sided with the regime of President Vladimir Putin, especially after the election of His Beatitude Patriarch Kirill in 2009. It is actively involved in promoting the ideology of the Russian World ... This ideology is a tool to legitimize Russian expansionism and the basis of its Eurasian strategy. The connection with the past of ethnophyletism and the present of the Russian world is obvious. Thus, faith becomes the basis of the Putin regime's ideology.
>
> (Bartholomew, 2022)[1]

This is how the Ecumenical Patriarch labeled the schismatic nature of modern Russian ecclesiastical Orthodoxy as a powerful, politically motivated nationalist sect. Now to the etatism of Russian Orthodoxy has been added militarism, not only political but also apocalyptic, since the church supports the state's desire to prepare its citizens not only to die for their homeland but also, in the event of military defeat, for the death of the entire world.

Thus, a new state religion is being formed, a religion of war and "luminosity," which combines such seemingly difficult ingredients as fascism, Orthodoxy, Old Believers, Eurasianism, Russian nationalism, apocalyptic sectarianism, statehood, imperialism, and Millenarianism.[2] This militaristic apocalypticism is virtually devoid of any connection to the transcendent. If it is religion, it knows nothing and wants to know nothing about the creator God, about the world as God's favorite creation; if it is Christianity, it is silent about Christ, about love, mercy, forgiveness, about the mystery of the human person, about life and resurrection. This essentially anti-Christian apocalypticism addresses the theme of death and the end, is permeated with hatred for the individual, human dignity and freedom, and despises science and technology. It partially envisions its ideal in Plato's utopia of a strictly hierarchical and ideologically controlled state, but it finds an even stronger reflection in Platonov's dystopias, *Chevengur* and *Kotlovan*, which depict the ultimate depletion and denudation of all material substrates of life, culminating in the abolition of life itself.

This apocalypticism is close to Chthonism, with its idea of the power of the earth over man, of the continental soil mass that devours individuals and turns them into weak, soulless, will-less outgrowths of the national body.

Hence the closeness of this apocalypticism to fascism. Umberto Eco, as is well known, distinguished fourteen signs of fascism, but they can be reduced to a unifying formula. Fascism is a collective attempt to heal from the trauma of birth through the experience of symbolic, and potentially physical, death, i.e., the rejection of consciousness, language, individuality, and all the anxieties of a separate, problem-experiencing existence. It is the instinct of liberation from oneself and ecstatic dying in the integral body of the earth, the people, the crowd.

The Antichrist in the Church

What role does the church, which has come out of hiding in the post-Soviet years, play in building the anti-world? In Dostoevsky's chapter about the Grand Inquisitor in *The Brothers Karamazov*, there is a prophecy that we are only now beginning to understand. And we can relate it to the latest reality, to the state role that the church is assuming, which the state encourages as a means of supporting itself.

According to the Inquisitor's logic, there are three stages in the history of Christianity. First, it spreads and conquers the nations. Then a great revolt begins against it in the name of science, materialism and atheism, in the name of satiety and power. The Grand Inquisitor turns to the silent Christ:

> Dost Thou know that the ages will pass, and humanity will proclaim by the lips of their sages that there is no crime, and therefore no sin; there is only hunger? "Feed men, and then ask of them virtue!" that's what they'll write on the banner which they will raise against Thee, and with which they will destroy Thy temple. Where Thy temple stood will rise a new building; the terrible tower of Babel will be built again…
>
> (Dostoevsky 2011, 220)

We have already passed this second stage in the twentieth century: the destruction of the Christian Church and the desire to erect a new tower of Babel in its place, to storm heaven from the earth: communism, materialism, and atheism. Let us recall at least the project of the grandiose Palace of Soviets, almost half a kilometer high, which was to rise in Moscow on the site of the Cathedral of Christ the Savior, which was blown up in 1931. This Tower of Babel, as we know, was not built; the utopia collapsed as it was being realized. In its place was left a huge excavation filled with water of the Moscow River—the "Moscow" swimming pool.

And then begins the most interesting phase, which we have to witness already in the twenty-first century. The very church, persecuted, almost destroyed, is reborn—and already claims to build its own earthly kingdom, to the fullness of worldly power:

> [F]or they will come to us after a thousand years of agony with their tower. They will seek us again, hidden underground in the catacombs, for we shall again be persecuted and tortured. They will find us and cry to us, "Feed us, for those who have promised us fire from heaven haven't given it!" And then we shall finish building their tower, for he finishes the building who feeds them. And we alone shall feed them in Thy name, declaring falsely that it is in Thy name.
>
> (Dostoevsky 2011, 220)

So it is the Church, led by the Grand Inquisitor, that will complete the tower that the atheists and communists failed to build. According to Dostoevsky, the open overthrow of God is only a prologue to the much more refined art of His substitution, when the Tower of Babel will be built on the foundations of the Church itself, by its leaders and primate. The same Cathedral of Christ the Savior was rebuilt in the 1990s on the site of the previous one, as an exact copy of it and as the main temple of post-Soviet Russia, where the church meets the state again and begins to serve it. Atheism is a rebellion against religion, and theocracy is a church-state, an earthly power "in the name and on behalf of" God, when the blatant godlessness is replaced by false piety and reverence for God. The very Pharisaism with which Christ was at enmity now grows on the soil of church-state Christianity itself.

If in Dostoevsky's earlier works, *Notes from the Underground* (1864) and *Devils* (1871), the "crystal palace of the future" appears as a dream of convinced atheists and revolutionaries, such as Nikolay Chernyshevsky, then in *The Brothers Karamazov* Dostoevsky penetrates deeper into the mystery of the coming Antichrist: he will come from the Christian environment, from the logic of the development of the Christian Church and the Christian state and will shepherd the people in the name of Christ. It is striking that in the very legend of the Grand Inquisitor this theocratic consummation of history is attributed to the period following the collapse of socialist ideas. Theocracy, or rather its semblance, will replace atheism. At first the godless revolutionaries will win, but they will not be able to feed the people—that is when the reign of the Grand Inquisitor will come. The Tower of Babel will be completed to the end, when the persecuted Christians will come out of their catacombs and receive from the people full authority to build the kingdom of God on earth.

Indeed, the people, exhausted by the revolutionary frenzy, came to those priests and pastors who had been persecuted for seven decades, called them out from the catacombs and distant countries of dispersion, and cried out: feed us, we will accept spiritual food from you, if you give us earthly food. The moment they begin to be fed, enriched, and build not only temples, but also houses in the name of Christ, the real kingdom of Antichrist, according to Dostoevsky will begin. The godless state of the socialists was only its precursor. Atheism is building a kingdom of violence, open in its hatred of God, but it is not yet a kingdom of lies and substitution, which will be erected precisely as a church, shepherding the nations by the holy name of God—"in thy name, and we will lie that in thy name."

If Satan was the first rebel against God, the Antichrist will appear as His false likeness. The new strategy of the Antichrist, postponed to the end of time, is not rebellion, but likening Himself to God. "A man of iniquity, condemned to destruction. .... He will even take his seat in the temple of God and pretend to be God" (2 Thessalonians 2:4). Power-loving, self-serving, covetousness, avarice, inquisitorialism, all under the guise of the most acerbic and cellular piety.

Then the meaning of the atheistic raving of the peoples becomes clear: not just deception, but deception for the sake of more deception. "This is where Satan is," people will say when they come to their senses from the revolutionary rampage, "it was he who blasphemed the name of God, but we will go to those who glorify Him. And the more surely, cursing their former godlessness, they will trust in the one who now speaks in the name of God."

Reflecting on the "Antichrist" spirit in our days, one cannot help but emphasize the touching commonwealth of the newest clergy with weapons of mass destruction. Russia's nuclear weapons, in particular the R-36M missiles, "Satan" in the NATO classification, are blessed by the Orthodox Church with a heavenly patron—the great Russian Saint Seraphim of Sarov. These are the most powerful of all nuclear-powered intercontinental ballistic missiles and, as the Russian resource threateningly promises, "these Russian missiles will make hell in the vast territories of the United States and Western Europe" (The World's Nuclear Stockpile, 2016). Perhaps not by chance, but "providentially," the Federal Nuclear Center of Russia that produces "Satan" was built on the site of the Sarov Desert where Saint Seraphim asceticized. The main cathedrals of the hermitage were blown up in the early 1950s, but since 2007 the saint himself has been declared the patron saint of nuclear weapons and their host (Patriarchia, 2007). In this connection, the Federal Nuclear Center in Sarov (previously classified under the names "Arzamas-16" and "Kremlev") purchased a large batch of icons with the face of the saint (NN.ru, 2019). This center has a staff of tens of thousands of employees and the most powerful supercomputer in Russia, serving, in particular, the complex of "Satan." So the deep interconnection of theology and the technology of hell is reinforced by the combination of the holy monastery with the nuclear center.

As early as 1891, Konstantin Leontiev predicted that "in a hundred years" Russia would give birth to the Antichrist.[3] It is enough to look at the main temple of the Russian Armed Forces near Moscow (consecrated in 2020) to feel alarmed—is it not the temple of the one who will "take his place in the temple of God?" The sanctuary looks intimidating both inside and outside, in its coloring, gold barely breaks through the dusky green, the color of either drab olive or khaki. High pointed domes on the towers resemble ballistic missiles. There are four aisles in the temple, and each one is dedicated to some saint and at the same time to some kind of weapon. Thus, St. Barbara the Great Martyr is appointed patroness of the Strategic Missile Forces. Why the Great Martyr? Is it not because strategic nuclear forces cause the greatest torment to their victims?[4]

Among the main relics of the museum at the Temple of the Armed Forces, oddly enough, are Hitler's suit and cap.[5] A schizophrenic trait: the Führer's memory is honored in the Temple of Victory over Fascism.

However, the "beast from the abyss," which is now ready to attack the whole world, is stronger than Hitler—he has a nuclear bomb in his hands. And even if he loses the war, he can end not with himself, but with life on earth—with a shot not at himself, but at the planet. At the same time, he seems to be quite a churchman: he stands faithfully at services on major holidays; he piously crosses himself with the cross, embraces the patriarch, visits holy places on Mount Athos and Valaam, and acts as the patron of all "sacred traditions." Yet Putin's solitude in the Kremlin's Annunciation Cathedral at the Christmas service in 2023, a complete contradiction to the tradition of cathedral celebrations, is already prompting Orthodox circles to speak directly about the appearance of the Antichrist.[6]

In his prediction of the building of a new tower of Babel on the foundation of the Christian temple, Dostoevsky resonates with the Epistle of St. Paul which finds a disturbing echo in the ecclesiastical reality of our day. The Antichrist comes *after* the era of godlessness and does not destroy the temples but takes his place in them. One of the most vivid evidences of this substitution is Putin's appearance on November 27-28, 2023, at the jubilee 25th World Russian People's Council held in Moscow, in the main temple of the Russian Orthodox Church, the Cathedral of Christ the Savior, where he made a speech via video link. Before the president's speech, the hall collectively prayed, and since the screen with Putin's image was hanging directly in the center of the stage, it looked as though the assembly was praying to Putin. On both sides of the screen, there were two identical iconographic images of Jesus Christ.

On this matter, many bloggers were unusually unanimous: "We've read the story about one Christ hanging between two criminals. But one criminal hanging between two Christs is something we've never seen before" (Ponomareva, 2023).

Satan Rules the World. Toward a Theology of Terror

Next, we will examine the latest apocalypticism on the basis of the work of writer and historian Vladimir Sharov (1952-2018), who has profoundly revealed the religious and political potential of this movement that runs through both pre-revolutionary and Soviet, and, as it now turns out, post-Soviet history. All of Sharov's works are devoted to the religious meaning of Russian history, which is always pointing toward an eschatological limit, toward the end of history as such. In this projection, Sharov's novels act as grim predictions of the path on which Russia has turned in the twenty-first century, and especially in the last decade. Then we will consider other embodiments of this spirit of "Satanodicea" (*sviatobesiye*) in the mindset of modern Orthodox fundamentalism and in Alexander Dugin's Eurasian ideology, which combines fascism and apocalypticism.

In 2018, a fire broke out in the Zimniia Vishnia shopping and entertainment complex in the city of Kemerovo. Sixty people died, including thirty-seven children. Is there any religion or ideology that could justify and glorify this death of children? It is hard to imagine such a degree of perversion, except for Vladimir Mayakovsky's scandalous line: "I love to watch children die." However, such an ideology and even theology exists; it was expressed, to cite just one example, by Valery Pavlovich Filimonov, editor-in-chief of the newsletter "On Guard of Orthodoxy," academician of the Orthodox Theological Department of the Petrovsky Academy of Sciences and Arts, and expert of the Commission on the Interaction of Church, State and Society of the Intersociety of the Russian Orthodox Church:

> Can we say what would have been the earthly fate of the children who died in the Winter Cherry shopping mall? Especially in our troubled times with the general corruption of many and many. Would they have been saved from sin? Would they have kept themselves pure for the imperishable life of the future century or would they have taken the path of perdition? Would it have been the most convenient time for them to pass on to eternal bliss?

(Filimonov, 2018)

It is unlikely that even the most brutal tyrants and murderers, like Stalin or Hitler, would have thought of such a thing; at least they did not confuse mass murder with service to the Almighty. And after all, Filimonov, as a high-ranking church figure, undoubtedly participated in liturgies with due regularity, prayed, confessed and received Holy Communion. Just like those churchmen, archbishops and priests who bless nuclear weapons of indiscriminate action and mass destruction—waving censers at them and sprinkling them with holy water—and thus bless the killing of civilians, including children.

In general, the idea of killing children for the sake of their spiritual salvation has great potential. Isn't that why the authorities are preparing a nuclear war—to rid mankind of sins at once and provide eternal bliss to all? People say about them: bandits, organized crime groups, but in their own eyes and in the eyes of the hierarchs who bless them, they are pious people, we can say, saviors of the human race, leaders before the Almighty. Will the ROC keep them from such a God-pleasing act? There is nothing more terrible than the connection of "churchiness" with cannibalism.

This theology of life denial was explored by Vladimir Sharov, author of nine historical fiction novels, who established a new genre in Russian literature: a mixture of politics and sectarianism, madness and pragmatics, utopia and apocalypse. His latest novel, *The Kingdom of Agamemnon*, was completed in the same year, 2018, that the mishap with the Orthodox justification of the death of children in Winter Cherry arose.

All of Sharov's novels confront the reader with an unthinkably difficult question: what is the central message of Judaism and Christianity? Usually a clear answer is given: salvation. Salvation from death, from sin, from slavery, from hell: to be forgiven by God and enter his kingdom. Hence, the intense expectation of the Savior, the Messiah. In Christianity, the most direct way of salvation is to accept the greatest suffering without any guilt, i.e., to repeat the mystery of Christ, to give oneself as a sinless lamb to the slaughter.

And then, in the logic of Sharov's heroes, who act as if compelled by the Holy Scriptures, a surprising theological reversal takes place. He who tortures and kills innocent people does them the highest good, because he immediately sends them to paradise. The most formidable rulers and torturers, like Ivan the Terrible and Stalin, are the greatest benefactors of humanity, because they grant thousands of their victims an exodus to a blissful life. Of course, all people are sinful to a greater or lesser degree, but they are killed for things that are not sins: for their class origin, for reading idealist philosophers, for imperfect crimes like cooperating with Swedish-Japanese intelligence or digging a tunnel to India. Or just for the sake of statistics. By doing so, all the sins they have committed in life are absolved from them, and, as innocent martyrs, they go straight to heaven.

In the words of one of the characters in *The Kingdom of Agamemnon*—the theologian and historian Smetonin's work *The Oprichnoe Pravo*—the author explains this strange theology of redemption:

> The Terrible explains to Kurbsky that life is a garden of suffering, therefore those who are killed without guilt by him, the anointed of God, the king of the Holy Land, that is, those whose blood he is constantly reproached with, not only are not at a loss, but at a considerable profit. As the innocently killed, they, having suffered here on earth, will be taken immediately to the throne of the Lord after their death, and for eternity will escape the far more terrible torments of God's judgment.
>
> (Sharov, 2018, 227)

And here is the epiphany of the writer and convict, monk and theologian Nikolai Zhestovsky, the protagonist of *The Kingdom of Agamemnon* and, in fact, the author of this novel within a novel:

> Here he, Stalin, has built a huge altar and, purifying us, he is offering sacrifice after sacrifice, hecatombs of purifying sacrifices are necessary to atone for our sins. … He is doing everything to save us. The innocents, who are perishing, will become our intercessors and prayers before the Lord, that is why it is necessary for us, before the world falls behind the Antichrist, to help them to be saved from sin, that is, there is no place for them on earth. The main thing is that they, having accepted suffering here, will be spared from the torments of the Last Judgment.
>
> (Sharov, 2018, 155)

It turns out that Stalin is a savior of sorts. This theological twist is not a fantasy; it reflects not only the desperate search for apocalyptic meanings among the intellectuals of the Stalinist years, but also the mindset of the modern Orthodox milieu. Olga Dunayevskaya, the wife of Sharov, recalls that the impetus for the last novel were the words of a good friend of the family, a priest. When it came to talk about Stalin's repressions, he said: "Yes, everything is terrible, but at least now the Russian land has many prayers before the Lord. Russia has not yet known as many saint-passion-bearers as Stalin's time gave" (Dunayevskaya, 2020, 32). According to this mournfully enlightened logic, "heaven is thirsty" for the shedding of the blood of the innocent, so that from there they can pray for those who had the misfortune to remain on earth. "Thousands of thousands of thousands of new saints and martyrs are needed. The State that compels us to testify for the future innocents, and we who give them, together make this atoning sacrifice. Undoubtedly," he finished then, "the Higher Power is pleased with it" (Sharov, 2018, 258–9).

Of course, according to the logic of Sharov's heroes, Ivan the Terrible and Joseph the Steel are the spawn of hell, through them Satan rules the world. But it is not without reason that God allows Satan himself to take possession of the earth before his second and final coming in order to save as many souls as possible and take them to the kingdom of heaven. Such is the Creator's amicable cooperation with the Hater. Satan may not know what he is doing, just giving the outcome of his evil and lust for power, but Christ walks beside him and almost blesses him, allowing the greatest evil to happen as the greatest good.

> By killing the righteous with our own hands, by breeding and producing new martyrs, we are not merely preparing the end of Satan, we are saving ourselves. This is certain. ... The people, as if it were a cup, drop by drop collects their holiness, and soon, very soon, without spilling anything, will fill itself to the brim.
>
> (Sharov, 2018, 265)

This is Sharov's circularity: the mutual salvation of the murderers and the murdered. By exterminating the innocent, I save them for eternal life, and thus I am saved myself. Where there is hell, there is heaven. Where there is fall, there is ascension. There is no need to invent any special means to gain paradise—they are given in the instruments of torture, in torture skill, in the feats of executioners. All the components of Russian history, from extreme atheism to extreme fanaticism, from the Bolsheviks building an earthly paradise (but turning it into hell) to the sectarians cursing everything earthly and longing for martyrdom, converge in this newfound formula of salvation: innocent suffering up to death is the means of gaining a higher life. The religious meaning of Russian history: an eternal engine of mutual salvation of murderers and murdered, sinners and saints, the living and the dead, an engine that runs on its own.

This theology of terror bears a resemblance to Islam, to the politics of jihad and shahidism. The simultaneous destruction of oneself and the enemies of Allah also leads directly to paradise, where virgin gurus await the shahid. But there is a huge difference. Islam encourages the killing of infidels, but not for their salvation: they go straight to hell. This is not the case in the theology of Russian terror. It is necessary to kill our own, Orthodox Christians, and together with them, embraced in a brotherly way, ascend to heaven. If in Islam there is a unidirectional action of the sword, here it is the rotation of the millstones: by killing you, I am saving you, which means that even though I am a murderer, I myself will be saved.

This miracle-working is possible only on Christian soil, but at the total trampling of it. It is a turn even more radical than that from the Old Testament to the New. It is no longer hatred in response to hatred, nor love in response to hatred, but hatred as the highest manifestation of love. Enemies are to be loved and blessed, and thus do mercy by destroying them. The murderer ascends to blessed life in the arms of the slain. Cruelty is mercy. Did the Bolsheviks want to destroy the world? No, to save it from its own sins. "The world's fire in blood—God bless." This is the eschatology of Blok in "The Twelve," as well as of A. White in his poem "Christ is Risen." This is not the logic of a straight line, the division of good and evil, as in Islam, but of the "red wheel," which turns in such a way as to embrace both victims and executioners simultaneously in a fraternal embrace.

Sharov's heroes have this theo-logic: Russia is a holy land, the third Rome, or the second Jerusalem, which was marked by the construction of the New Jerusalem near Moscow according to the plan and will of Patriarch Nikon. On the other hand, his opponents, the schismatics, believe that the Antichrist has already come to earth and that the Russian state and even the Orthodox (Nikonian) Church are already in the power of Satan. It remains to unite these two theologemes, which is what happens in Sharov's novels, in the images of his Bolsheviks–Old Believers and priests–secret informers. Yes, Satan already rules on this earth, but Christ follows him on his heels and immediately sends the soul of each innocent victim to the realm of the blessed. The polarity of Christ and Antichrist is kind of erased, or rather, they are two meanings of the same deeds.

Here the binarity of the Russian cultural code, about which Yuri Lotman and Boris Uspensky wrote, reaches its ultimate density and condensation (Lotman and Uspensky, 1977). Plus and minus, the sacred and the sacrilegious are not simply reversed in time, as in periods of revolutions, but are directly identified. "And I burned everything I worshipped, worshipped everything I burned." According to the logic of Sharov's torturers-martyrs, to burn is to worship. One thing is another. The poles are no longer interchanging, but sticking together. Antichrist does not precede Christ, but fulfills Christ's will. Theodicy merges with Satanodicy.

Sharov died when the Russian world began to move rapidly toward disaster according to the scenario of his novels: "more hell!" According to this logic, the world will become quite "Russian" not when it will give up a few more territories of the near abroad, but when it (the world) will not exist at all. The void or nuclear ashes will open up—and then all Sharov's sectarians and passion-bearers will find their place in the end of history, to which they so persistently aspired. Vladimir Sharov, to a greater extent than even Andrei Platonov, is the writer of the apocalypse that is coming upon the planet from those well-armed "magicians of the Great Tradition" who see it as their destiny.

"We will go to paradise as martyrs, and they will just die—because they will not even have time to repent" (*Kommersant*, 2018). This famous phrase of Vladimir Putin about a possible nuclear war caused at first laughter in the audience, and then general bewilderment even among his associates. What is this—an ominous joke, a cruel warning, a gesture of sacrifice or vindictiveness?

The easiest way to understand the meaning of this phrase is for someone familiar with Sharov's work. His heroes are seekers of the end of the world, martyrs and hedonists of the coming apocalypse, who, at odds with the whole world, have made the death of mankind their trade.

Sharov is best able to explain to readers all over the world what cannot be explained—this stubborn, absurd, but theologically justified will of a "separate country" to destroy everything. For the sake of this, beginning with Peter the Great, technology, science, and the whole civilization were mastered, and great literature and music turned out to be by-products—and essentially unwanted—because the main line was to be the increasing energy of "antimatter," "anti-civilization," capable of destroying the world. Those dissenters who regarded Peter as an enemy of Holy Russia were mistaken: having turned to the West for the fruits of civilization, he was looking for a way to make Russia stronger than the West.

Sharov allows us to trace the religious roots of this will to apocalypse, which is especially alarming today, when Satanodicea finds a worthy technical embodiment. As stated earlier, the R-36M Satan-class missiles are the most powerful of all nuclear-powered intercontinental ballistic missiles, each of which could wreak the destruction of a thousand Hiroshimas. Sharov's books, tracing the origins of domestic Satanodicea, can serve as an ironic and grotesque commentary on "Satan": this is our gift to you, and from the texts you will learn why we love you so much and why we wish you a speedy end.

Yes, to love as our blood loves,
None of you have been in love for a long time!
You've forgotten that there is love in the world,
Which both burns and destroys.
We love flesh—both the taste of it and the color of it,

And the stifling, mortal flesh odor ....
Are we to blame if your skeleton crunches?
In our heavy, tender paws?

This "Scythian" message of love, addressed by Alexander Blok to the world in 1918, was completed by Sharov exactly one hundred years later in his *The Kingdom of Agamemnon*: "Antichrist—here he is already ... and, therefore, the Promised Land itself, our land with all that was and is in it, having given itself over to Satan, has become an unclean realm" (2018). Out of love for our brothers, for all mankind, we are obliged to save it from itself.

We can advise everyone, and above all politicians, to read Vladimir Sharov's books to be convinced: this force cannot be negotiated with, cannot be compromised; it is rooted in the nature of the Yoke, the Third Rome, in the very nature of the Schism, which burns and destroys in the name of salvation.

Sanctimony. "Brotherly People" and Cain's Sin

In 2012, the members of the art group Pussy Riot were sentenced to two years in prison after a "punk prayer" to the Virgin Mary in Christ the Savior Cathedral for "insulting the feelings of believers." At that time, the propensity of believers, or rather, the hierarchs speaking on their behalf, to be "insulted" was clearly indicated—and Russia's entry into the era of sanctimony, *saint-obsession*, i.e., a truly demonic possession of one's own "sainthood." Boris Grebenshchikov best defined this windfall in his song "I Came to Drink Water" (2014):

When you're in Moscow, beware of talking about the holy.
When you're in Moscow, beware of talking about the holy.
Or the meek as doves will catch you,
The saints will ride you,
The ministers of love will drive you into the ground with a cross.
(Grebenshchikov, 2014)

Sanctimony, *sviatobesie*—obsession with one's holiness or the sanctity of one's principles and beliefs. This is how V. Trediakovsky proposed to translate the French word "fanaticism" back in the eighteenth century. At that time "*sviatobesie*" did not take root, but now it has a new chance. There are too many saints and sanctimonists around—people who know firmly what the salvation of everyone and everything is, who are ready to shepherd the nations and feel a sense of vengeful resentment for everything that violates their view of the world. That said, it is obvious that sanctimony and fanaticism are different things. A fanatic believes in God and is willing to sacrifice and die; sanctimony is an outpouring of hatred and pride under the guise of defending sacred things. It is aggression against dissenters on religious grounds. The most convincing way to defuse aggression is when a person gets into rage and fury not for himself, not for his small pains and offenses, but for something absolutely great and holy. Then one can flog, burn, execute, all in good conscience. Sanctimoniousness looks for heresies and heretics everywhere, uses any excuse to demonstrate "offended religious feelings," and incites the spirit of malice and intolerance in society. If a fanatic is willing to sacrifice himself for the sake of his beliefs, the "holier-than-thou" only sacrifices others. It is a mixture of fanaticism with pharisaism, narcissism and sadism.

Someone said of such holy men: "they believe in God according to Stanislavsky's system." That is, not just by showing off, but by living and experiencing. Stanislavsky himself described his system as follows: "It is magical 'if only'—the proposed circumstances, fictions, decoys make someone else's own. 'The system' knows how to make you believe in the nonexistent" (Stanislavsky, 1938). That's how sanctimony is—it believes the nonexistent, or rather, it makes itself believe it, winds itself up to hysteria, like an actor on stage.

Holiness is also the desire to please God more than others are able to do, the belief that my faith is more true than that of others, that I serve Him better, and that for this I deserve a reward from Him. It is not just pride, but the pride of faith, its arrogance over another's faith; in the Bible, the worst sin since the fall of Adam and Eve. How are original sin, Adam's, and that of his son Cain's, related? Plucking the forbidden fruit of the knowledge of good and evil leads to violence in the name of good, and therefore to evil. A faith that prides itself on its superiority over other faiths and is jealous of God over them is the Cain sin.

One of the main motives declared for Russia's war against Ukraine is the "brotherhood" of the two nations. "Ukraine is a brotherly country for us. And in a difficult situation, we are always ready to support a brotherly nation. ... And if we really say that it is a brotherly nation and a brotherly country, then we should act as close relatives and support the Ukrainian people in this difficult situation," the Russian president said just two months before the seizure of Crimea (Interfax, 2013). And even in 2022, already killing tens of thousands of peaceful Ukrainian citizens including children, depriving them of heat and light, destroying homes, schools, hospitals, and museums, the Russian authorities persist in calling them a "brotherly nation."

What kind of fraternization is this? The "sin of Cain" usually refers to fratricide. Is it a coincidence that the first murderer raised his hand specifically against his brother? It is a reminder that when we kill anyone, we kill our brother, for we are all children of one father. But the story of Cain also reminds us that the first murder was religiously motivated: "And the Lord looked upon Abel and his gift, but He did not look upon Cain and his gift. And Cain was greatly grieved, and his face was bowed down ... And while they were in the field, Cain rose up against Abel his brother and killed him" (Genesis 4:3-5, 8). It is religious zeal that turns out to be the worst sin. This crime is not motivated by greed, nor by the struggle for property, power, or women, i.e., for the most simple and "low" motives. Cain is tormented by an unquenched spiritual thirst, seeking blessing from above. He is jealous of his brother for his heavenly Father. It is the temptation to holiness, *holiness* is the source of Cain's sin.

Cain is the progenitor of many characters both in the Bible and beyond ... A similar collision is reproduced in Pushkin's "Mozart and Salieri." Why are Salieri's sacrifices to labor and vocation not claimed by God, why does no fire descend upon the altar? It remains to cry, "There is no truth on earth, but there is no truth above." This is the cry of Cain. Salieri poisoned Mozart, his "brother" and his muse, in music, following the same logic: God did not look upon his gift.

Adam and Eve were tempted by the hope of full knowledge: "you will be like gods, knowing good and evil." Cain's sin is derived from Adam's, as Cain himself is from Adam: if we are like gods, then we also have the right to another's life. Cain was the first who decided to "correct" God by violence. Hence *theocracy*, "godhood"—to take on the role of God, to rule in his name, to determine the fate of others. Cainism is the beginning of theocracy, which takes on the fate of humanity, believing that God is failing on his own. Cain, like Job, is outraged at God's injustice; like Salieri, jealous of God's gifts; and finally, like the Grand Inquisitor, takes God's work into his own hands. Thou hast not brought us happiness, thou hast not wished to exercise omnipotence, we will do it for thee. This is said to Christ, but even earlier Cain in his heart says it to God. The Devil is holier than God, the Inquisitor is holier than Christ. Jealousy of his holiness, self-blessing, *self-belief*, exalting his faith.

Where is the Center of Hell?

When I learned about the Russian army's atrocities in Bucha, I was understandably horrified—but not surprised. Why should I be surprised?

After all, I have long been familiar with the views of Alexander Dugin. The same one who, in 2014, in connection with the Russian army's invasion of Crimea and Donbass, uttered, addressing students: "Kill, kill and kill. There should be no more talk. As a professor, I think so" (Lyulka, 2014).

Dugin came to my attention much earlier, in the early 1990s, when I was writing a book on the newest currents of Russian thought.[7] Among the dozens of thinkers of the late Soviet era, Dugin was the youngest—and the most bloodthirsty. To realize his metaphysical plans, he needed to pour blood on half of the globe—the Western half. And if the West did not comply, he wanted to blow up the entire globe, because non-existence is ultimately better than existence. Existence divides people, and nothingness unites them.

The peculiarity of Dugin as a thinker is his outright hatred of everything that is not just human, but living and existent. And this is combined with a kind of religiosity. His writings are full of such concepts as "divine subject," "sons of light," "mighty spirits," "sweet angel," etc., etc., etc. This combination of "high-spiritedness" and world-hatred goes back to the ancient Gnostic heresy (first century AD), condemned by Christianity. Gnosticism preached that the existing world lies in evil and must be completely destroyed in order to take the path of higher spirituality, to enter the world of angels.

Dugin is sometimes referred to in the Western press as "Putin's brain," and he has been teaching geopolitics at the Military Academy of the General Staff of the Armed Forces for many years. He has an impressive array of titles: leader of the International Eurasian Movement, honorary professor at the Lev N. Gumilev Eurasian National University and Tehran University ... Dugin's books *The Foundations of Eurasianism* and *The Foundations of Geopolitics* are used by the highest ranks of the General Staff, who translate his slogans into strategems.

Dugin calls his worldview variously: "Eurasianism," "National-Bolshevism," "Integral Tradition," "Great Tradition," "Right Revolution," "Fourth Political Theory ... ." He finds the clearest embodiment of his theories in Andrei Platonov, whose anti-utopias *Kotlovan* and *Chevengur* he treats as utopias to be fulfilled. He regards Platonov as "the embodiment of National Bolshevism in all its dimensions" (Dugin, 1999).

What revelation, according to Dugin, does Platonov bring? A nagging sense of inescapable, agonizing, yearning emptiness. This is revolutionary Russia's message to the world: the mystery of self-disclosing nothingness. To quote Dugin:

> Longing is the bottom content of the Revolution, pressing from within, an unbearable weight. ... Emptiness in the body, emptiness in the mind, emptiness in the heart ... If man came from a worm, from a gut filled only with sticky darkness, then should not his spiritual mediastinum also be

like this? Exactly: the soul, revealing its true flavor of availability closest to the empty innards of a hollow earthy draughty and meaningless tube.

(Dugin, 1999)

For Dugin, the soul itself is nothing, a hollow tube, and the defilement of matter, the exhaustion of the flesh, hell on earth, the equality of existence and non-existence is the main national idea. Surprisingly enough, this is the last revelation of the Eurasian truth revealed to Dugin. The supreme goal is the transformation of being into nothingness. "A real encounter with the soul is like coughing up grave clay, suffocation, the intolerable odors of decaying herbs, merging with the empty consciousness of a worm."

Hence we come to the sexual and psychological motives behind the mass atrocities and violence committed in Bucha. Psychoanalysis, as we know, distinguishes two basic human drives: Eros, the drive to life and its generation, and Thanatos, the embodiment of death in Greek mythology, the desire to restore the primary (inanimate, inorganic) state. In Freud, Eros is opposed to Thanatos. In Dugin, who is concerned with the Russian national specificity of these categories, Thanatos is Eros: the dispersion of Eros in the world void. And here the traces of the bloody voluptuousness left behind by the Russian army in Ukraine are already quite recognizable. Dugin is a prophet of Bucha:

> The peculiarity of the Great Russian sex is that it is directed neither at itself nor at the other, there is no libido or narcissism in it. The Russian sex is agitatedly incorporeal, it is the fire-breathing excitement of the dead or the spirits of reeds, waters, burning skerries and ovines. The Russian sex winds through, picking up on its confused way everything in a row—tailcoats, men, comrades, cockroaches, a bloated, ready to burst lying corpse, laundered maidens that have fallen under the hand, shot limbs, ossified horses, swirling weeds, gray soil that has exposed its cracks, slanted or whitewashed cozy buildings, pale and dead Rosa Luxemburg ... and the unscrupulous heart's emptiness, pulling into the moldy well of the heart a huge, upset in its root knots, stolen existence.
>
> (Dugin, 1999)

What *eloquence*—in the direct and sinister sense of the word! For, in the words of Dugin, "only Red Death makes the subject of the human object." This is the global mission of National Bolshevism, or Eurasianism. Not just to pit one class against another, as happened in Soviet history on the basis of Marxist doctrines—this, according to Dugin, is necessary, but not enough. It is necessary to act more broadly, in the popular, Platonic way, i.e., together with the hostile classes and their fake culture, to destroy everything that lives and breathes separately from non-existence, for only through non-existence can one find the highest unity with everything. Everything else is an obstacle. This is how Dugin sees Platonov and honors him as a mentor:

> For us, Platonov is a doctrine. We take it upon ourselves and intellectually justify everything up to and including the *direct genocide of alienating classes and rational structures*. We accept as dogma the Chevengur madness. ... The dead huddle over us, they are crowded and stuffy. History is squeezing itself with the last nasty noose.
>
> (Dugin, 1999)

This is the metaphysical conclusion of Eurasianism—the suicide, the self-hanging of history on the "throat" of Russia. In the radicalism of his life-denial Dugin goes further than the Grand Inquisitor, who does not believe in future life, in a heavenly kingdom, but wants to create a paradise of universal satiety on earth. Dugin goes further than Andrei Platonov himself, who believes in building a communist paradise on earth and longingly observes its gradual transformation into hell, feeling compassion for its victims. Dugin goes further than the heroes of Vladimir Sharov, who are ready to accept hell on earth, rejoice in it, and even assist Satan in its creation, in order to break through the afterlife paradise, to achieve salvation through suffering. Dugin, on the other hand, simply affirms hell on earth, following his teacher Eugene Golovin, who in the 1980s led a Yuzhin circle of esoteric Nazi-Satanists called the "Black Order of the SS," where he was called "*Reichsführer*." "'Where we are, there is the center of hell.' Not 'We are in the center of hell' (that would still be okay), but 'Where we are, there is the center of hell,'" Dugin comments to Golovin (Guryanov, 2014).

This is the last word of the apocalyptic revolution: to spread hell—the dying Chevengur—to the entire globe. This mission is what the country is carrying out today in its metaphysical struggle not only with Ukraine or the West, but, to use Dugin's own language, with being as such, with the accursed habit of existence.

> Maturing ... the prelude of the New Chevengur, the Last Chevengur. The mysterious kiss of the Bolshevik dawn can be heard in the absolute silence, heralding nothing but midnight and an ocean of Blood. We will take everything from you again. Not to have, to be, to leave nothing as it

is, to abolish everything separate and to bring to the totality of Victory everything common, united, Whole ...

(Dugin, 1999)

What an elaborate necro-eschatology, truly ready to embrace the entire world as it turns into nothingness! And this is not just metaphysics, it is a call to action—it is clear what method of destroying all life Dugin has in mind when he proclaims the imminent end of the world. Why prevent the apocalypse? On the contrary, it is necessary to accelerate it by setting the world on fire:

We need to think not about whether or not the world will end, we need to think about how to bring it about. That is our task. It will not come by itself ... It is up to us to make that decision. We, moreover, must find a way to close this story ... There are not even theses, defended correctly, on why humanity needs to survive.

(Dugin, 2022b)

What a highly scientific approach! However, the value of life is proved not by dissertations, but by the experience of any living being. Does Dugin himself agree to easily part with life in accordance with his theoretical calculations? Is he ready to prove this favorite thought by purifying his children by burning them?[8] If you demand the end of the world, start with yourself and your loved ones! Otherwise, all this "fourth political theory" serves only to "quarter" mankind to satisfy the metaphysical taste for self-immolation.

Eurasians regularly rehearse the man-made end of the world. One of the programs of the training camp of the Eurasian Youth Union: "The eschatological mobilization of Eurasians is announced! Everything is nearing completion and resolution. *FINIS MUNDI*. The End of the World." Following Dugin's logic, it is now, with the outbreak of war, that the hour comes for Russia to fulfill its global destiny, because among all known civilizations it stands out for its conscious will for the end of history, for the death of everything. *Russia entered history not for the sake of finding its place in it, but for the sake of "victorious" termination of it, as the adherents of this world suicide believe.* This voluptuousness of total destruction is the metaphysics of contempt for existence, once again rehearsed in Bucha, in Irpen, in Mariupol, in Izyum—already on the stage of the theater of history.

It is "about Empire and the End of the World," according to Dugin himself, that he is now completing his new, "thousand-page" work, trying to keep up with the event he proclaims. Will he succeed? Will he find even one reader alive? The author confesses: "The picture comes out ominous" (Dugin, 2022a). Who would doubt it—no one expects anything good from Mr. Dugin. Actually, the pages of this work are already charred letters on the land of Ukraine. "There are still three chapters left." What Dugin has in his dreams, Putin has in his hands stroking the nuclear button.

Will the "Dead Hand" Drag the Living into the Realm of the Dead?

As is known, the USSR had developed a complex of automatic control of a massive nuclear strike, which is called "Dead Hand." Even after a country is defeated, this system is capable of striking back at the enemy and guaranteeing its nuclear annihilation. Current politicians and propagandists boast of this ability to strike the enemy to death after their own destruction much more frankly and convincingly than in Soviet times, and in this case it is hard not to believe them.

The Russian regime has not the slightest chance of winning a world war if it wants to wage one. There are no ideas, no prospects, no economic resources. There is no future but the past, and so remote, so medieval, that it cannot survive in the twenty-first century. He can't win, but he can destroy the world.

For what? For the thrill? The triumph of the living all-conquering doctrine—*pontocracy*? Pontocracy has replaced ideocracy as a strategy for conquering the country and the world. In Soviet times, ideas were paramount: communism, socialism, Marxism, Leninism, materialism—but who needs these "isms"? Ideas are not important, but *ponts* (*ponty*) are. Each pont is another demonstration of superiority, a victory in a game of chance. To disgrace the enemy, spit in a neighbor's soup, steal someone else's secret. A pont is a unit of criminal will. Another nastiness inflicted on "partners," another mockery of the honest, an insult to the proud, a threat to the weak, a humiliation of the worthy. Such ponts—the distinctive signs of criminal pride and audacity—build the hierarchy. Pontocrator—one who rules through ponts (not to be confused with "pantocrator"— "king of heaven" in Christian theology). The word "pont" (from the French Ponte—"bluffer," "gambler," "cardsharper") in criminal jargon has a broad meaning: to blind, to outplay through deception, to display signs of power and social prestige. The pontocrator demonstrates miracles of dexterity, accumulating ponts, i.e., the regalia of criminal honor, putting down all rivals. The pontocrator has no positive means of self-affirmation—no grand goals, ideas, talents, other than putting others down.

But it is not right to reduce everything to ponts—more precisely, in these ponts, there is something deeper, going into such an abyss that it can make one's head spin. In Fedor Bondarchuk's film *Stalingrad*, glamorous-official and untalented, there is one piercing phrase, as if emerging from another level of depth. A German captain, played by Thomas Kretschmann, remarks: It's impossible to fight normally with you Russians, because you don't fight for victory, but for revenge.

Let us reflect on the meaning of what's happening. If there is no chance of victory, then revenge remains the main goal. The moral distinction is that the will to victory is dictated by faith, hope, love, while revenge is dictated only by hatred. During the era of World War II, it was clear for what it was worth dying for, even though hatred for the enemies still prevailed over love for the socialist fatherland. But then there was still faith in the future and hope for victory, relying on the all-conquering communist doctrine and the support of progressive humanity. What can we say about our time! In the name of what love should we fight? Or is the only goal revenge against those who are more free, enterprising, fortunate, those who have history, rights, science, technology, breakthroughs into the future? Russian *bratki*'s revenge on Ukrainian "brothers" who want to become part of this history? Those who fight for victory, like Stalin's USSR or even Hitler's Germany, are still concerned about the fate of being and don't want to burn everything to the ground—they need to preserve fertile land, cities, villages, farms, museums, universities, where the future Reich will flourish. Those who fight for revenge do not see a future for the world or themselves, so they rely most of all on the power of nuclear weapons. If winning is not an option, and they are losing by all other means, there remains only one, but the biggest pont of all possible, a way to put down the Creator Himself—destroy the world He created.

They say that the dead grab the living; and the closer they are to the grave, the stronger the grip. "Dead Hand" is not just a system of automatic nuclear strike, it is a force that drags the living into the realm of the dead. *A dying empire, departing, is ready to slam the lid of the coffin loudly.*

Postscript

On May 7, 2024, following Vladimir Putin's inauguration for his fifth presidential term and blessing him in the Cathedral of the Annunciation in the Kremlin, Patriarch Kirill uttered an enigmatic phrase: "And I will say with boldness (*s derznoveniem*): God grant that the end of the age also signifies the end of your time in power. You have everything necessary to fulfill this great service to the homeland for a long time and successfully."[9]

What does the Patriarch mean by "the end of the age," and why does he himself acknowledge the audacity of his wish? Certainly, he doesn't imply the arrival of the twenty-second century, when the president would be 148 years old. "Age" in church language is a translation of the Greek "aeon." In the New Testament, "aeon" refers to the entire existing world, as opposed to the "future age" (aeon), which will come after the end of this world. This is the specific language of Church, theology and clergy, as further emphasized by the patriarch: "May God's blessing and the Protection of the Queen of Heaven abide with you in your life, until the end of the age, as we say." So what is implied here is *the end of the world*. Obviously, the patriarch is quite deliberately addressing this topic, since he notes the boldness of his judgment about the supernatural mystery. [10] The wish for the end of the aeon to coincide with the end of Putin's time in power testifies to the fact that eschatological obsession has moved from sectarian and neofascist fantasies, like those of Dugin, into the theological narrative of the Russian Orthodox Church. Moreover, the mission to complete the aeon is now entrusted not only to a certain country and "God-bearing" people but also—by the pointing finger of the patriarch—to its leader. Let him rule until the end of this world, which will be the successful completion of his "great service."[11]

Significantly, right before the inauguration, the Russian military unexpectedly declared exercises on the use of tactical nuclear weapons. In response, the Russian Orthodox Church, this time voiced by Archpriest Maxim Kozlov, the Head of its Educational Committee, welcomed the announcement with enthusiasm. He encouraged believers not to dread a thermonuclear disaster, reminding them that, after all, "Christians used to joyfully await the end of the world, which would bring the Kingdom of God closer" (Dzen.ru 2024).

Thus, the most characteristic feature of the latest Russian apocalypticism is that, unlike all previous such movements, it is technically armed. To embody its yearnings for a universal end, it possesses nuclear weapons, the substance of death and hell, which can indeed bring completion to all life on Earth. This objectification of planetary doom gives apocalypticism the power and "argument" that previous Gnostic sects, including Old Believers, lacked. They dreamed of a purifying fire that would burn the world mired in sin but were powerless to bring it to Earth. Now such power exists, and there is a vast country that necro-sectarians want to turn into the apocalyptic vanguard of humanity in order to carry out the mission of its self-immolation. There is a leader paving the way to this goal, and there is a clergy blessing him.

Notes

1 Patriarch Bartholomew's speech in Abu Dhabi has been compared to W. Churchill's speech in Fulton as a call for Western politicians to confront not only "Putin's Russia" but also the Russian Orthodox Church as the foundation of the Russian world.
2 The kinship between Russian Orthodoxy and fascism was pointed out before the war by Ivan Okhlobystin, a famous actor, director, and former Orthodox priest: "The closest to me is Julius Evola [one of the main ideologues of Italian fascism]. Yes, I gravitate towards fascism. I'm Orthodox, so it's basically normal" (Okhlobystin and Roschin, 2020). See also Barabash (2023).
3 "In some half a century, no more, the Russian people from the people of 'God-bearer' will become little by little and without noticing it, 'the people of the God-fighter,' and even more likely than any other people, perhaps. For, indeed, he is capable of going to extremes in everything… and we, unexpectedly, in about 100 years, out of our state bowels, at first unchurched, and then churchless or already weak-church, will give birth to the very Antichrist, about whom Bishop Theophan together with other spiritual writers speak" (Leontiev, 1996 [1891], 684).
4 There is also a more prosaic explanation: on December 17, 1959, the Strategic Missile Forces were formed, and according to the Orthodox calendar it is St. Barbara's Memorial Day. But the very crossing of the two calendars as a sign of the church-state union is significant. Now in any Russian missile division, an icon of the Great Martyr hangs at the command post.
5 Russian Deputy Defense Minister Timur Ivanov proudly said: "there are real relics there. There are unique things, up to Hitler's suit, which has been preserved to this day, there is Hitler's cap. To this we can add that the steps leading to the temple are cast from Wehrmacht trophy weapons" (Lenta.ru, 2020).
6 According to historian, religious scholar and publicist Andrei Zubov, Putin "is present at a Christian sacrament that is being performed illegally in an empty church… This is a complete mockery of the Christian sacredness and the principle of *sobornost*. … On the surface it looks like Christianity, but in essence it is anti-Christianity… What we saw on the night of January 6-7 is actually the most terrible and, I would say, mystical evidence… Many superstitious Russian people will soon say that Putin is the Russian Antichrist" (Zubov, 2023).
7 Published in English in two volumes Epstein 2020 and Epstein 2021.

8 This was written in April 2022, a few months before his daughter Daria Dugina, who ideologically continued her father's work, was burned alive after a car explosion on August 21 while returning from a "patriotic festival" organized by Dugin himself. In this sense, we can agree that Dugin presented a terrible proof of his imperative of the universal end. There are even reports circulating, based on the SVR General's Telegram channel (https://t.me/s/generalsvr), that Daria's murder was arranged by the FSB on the direct initiative of Dugin himself, who offered his daughter as a sacred sacrifice, as a way of inciting a holy war. https://alex-197.livejournal.com/72057.html

9 *Komsomol'skaia Pravda* (www.kp.ru). May 7, 2024. https://www.kp.ru/daily/27603.3/4928513.

10 Alexander Soldatov comes to the same conclusion in his article "Blessing into the Apocalypse," even suggesting that "striving to ingratiate himself with Putin even more, the Patriarch seems to have insulted him by urging him to emulate a sinister character from the last book of the Bible <i.e. Satan>... Revelation also mentions a religious organization that will lead the worship of the Antichrist – it is given the image of 'the harlot sitting on a scarlet beast' (Rev. 17:3). Many ancient saints interpreted this image as the appearance of a false church, preserving external Christian attributes, but inclining the people to worship the Antichrist and accept his 'values' and goals – in particular, those aimed at world domination." *Novaya Gazeta*. May 8, 2024. https://novayagazeta.ru/articles/2024/05/08/naputstvie-v-apokalipsis.

11 I am approaching this theme in more detail in my essay "New apocalypticism: Mikhail Epstein about the man-made end of the world" (Epstein, 2024). See also Epstein 2023.

References

Barabash, Ekaterina. 2023. "A Russian demon. How Ivan Okhlobystin turned from a petty freak into an ideologist of fascism." *Republic*, January 11, 2023. https://republic.ru/posts/106795?utm_source=republic.ru

Berdyaev, Nikolai. 2008. *Russkaia Ideiia [The Russian Idea.]* Saint Petersburg: Azbuka-Klassika Publishing House.

Blok, Alexander. 1918. "The Scythians." Trans. Kurt Dowson. *International Socialism* (1st series), No. 6, Autumn 1961, 24–5.

Dostoevsky, Fyodor. 2011. *The Brothers Karamazov*. Moscow: The Russian Messenger Ed. by S. M. Oddo. Transl. by C. Garnett. Revised by R. E. Matlaw and S. M. Oddo. A Norton Critical Edition. 2nd edition. New York, London: W.W.Norton & Company.

Dugin, Alexander. 1999. *Andrei Platonov's Magical Bolshevism*. http://viperson.ru/articles/aleksandr-dugin-magicheskiy-bolshevizm-andreya-platonova

Dugin, Alexander. 2022a. Video Interview. April, 2022. https://vk.com/video-45113453_456239127?list=4c200be84be467396e
Dugin, Alexander. 2022b. Blog post. April 28, 2022. https://vk.com/duginag
Dunayevskaya, Olga. 2020. "When the Clock Stopped." In *Vladimir Sharov: On the Other Side of History*, edited by Mark Lipovetsky and Anastasia De La Fortel, 10–35. Moscow: New Literary Review Publishing House.
Dzen.ru. 2024. "The Russian Orthodox Church urged not to fear the Apocalypse." May 7, 2024. https://dzen.ru/a/ZjnO-gNX-SOnqfZo
Epstein, Mikhail. 2019. *The Phoenix of Philosophy. Russian Thought of the Late Soviet Period (1953–1991)*. London/New York: Bloomsbury Publishing.
Epstein, Mikhail. 2021. *Ideas against Ideocracy. Non-Marxist Thought of the Late Soviet Period (1953–1991)*. London/New York: Bloomsbury Publishing.
Epstein, Mikhail. 2023. *Russkii Antimir: Politika na Grani Apokalipsisa*. [The Russian Anti-world: Politics on the Verge of Apocalypse]. New York: FrancTireurUSA.
Epstein, Mikhail. 2024. "New apocalypticism: Mikhail Epstein about the Manmade End of the World." *Radio Liberty*. May 19, 2024. https://www.svoboda.org/a/novaya-apokaliptika-mihail-epshteyn-o-rukotvornom-kontse-sveta/32948465.html
Filimonov, Valery Pavlovich. 2018. Interview on children killed in Kemerovo fire. https://inforesist.org/valeriy-filimonov-o-pogibshih-v-kemerovo-detyah-pogibli-vovremya-ubereglis-ot-greha
Grebenshchikov, Boris. 2014. Song "I Came to Drink Water." https://genius.com/Boris-grebenshchikov-came-to-drink-water-lyrics
Guryanov, Pavel. 2014. "Doesn't Dugin Want to Organize the Apocalypse?" *The Essence of Time Newspaper* No. 93. September 3, 2014. https://rossaprimavera.ru/article/ne-hochet-li-dugin-organizovat-apocalipsis?fbclid
Interfax. 2013. "Vladimir Putin held a big news conference in Moscow." Article on Interfax.ru. December 19, 2013. https://www.interfax.ru/russia/347727
Kommersant. 2018. https://www.kommersant.ru/doc/3773521
Lenta. ru. 2020. "The Deputy Minister of Defense of Russia called Hitler's suit a unique item." Lenta.ru. June 12, 2020. https://lenta.ru/news/2020/06/12/hitler
Leontiev, Konstantin. 1996 [1891]. "Nad Mogiloi Pazhukhina" [Above the Grave of Pazhukhin]. In Leontiev Konstantin N., *Vostok, Rossiia i Slavianstvo* [*The East, Russia and the Slavs*], 678–85. Moscow: Respublika.
Lotman, Yuri, and Boris Uspensky. 1977. "The Role of Dual Models in the Dynamics of Russian Culture (Up to the End of the 18th Century)." In *Works on Russian and Slavic Philology*, Vol. XXVIII: Literary Studies, to the 50th Anniversary of Professor Boris Fyodorovich Yegorov, 3-36. Tartu: Uchenye zapiski TGU.
Lyulka, Alexander. 2014. "Dugin: Kill, kill, kill!" June 18, 2014. Video clip, 0:23. https://www.youtube.com/watch?v=DgHiqVy79Zs

NN.ru. 2019. "Icons for VIPs: it became known why the nuclear center in Sarov needs images with rhinestones." https://www.nn.ru/text/economics/2019/05/24/66101368

Okhlobystin, Ivan, and Dmitry Roschin. 2020. "Okhlobystin: Constitution, Apocalypse, Warcraft." June 29, 2020. Video discussion, 43:49. https://www.youtube.com/watch?v=nSHNUZZdXVc&t=1870s

Patriarchia, 2007. "Celebrations have begun at the Cathedral of Christ the Savior to mark the 60th anniversary of the founding of Russia's nuclear weapons complex." http://www.patriarchia.ru/db/text/290617.html

Patriarch Bartholomew. 2022. Speech at international conference in Abu Dhabi. December 11, 2022. https://fosfanariou.gr/index.php/2022/12/11/omilia-ecum-patr-se-abu-dhabi-english-and-greek

Ponomareva, Alya. 2023. "A Criminal Between Two Christs." Bloggers on Putin at the World Council. Radio Liberty. November 29, 2023. https://www.svoboda.org/a/prestupnik-mezhdu-dvumya-hristami-blogery-o-putine-na-vsemirnom-sobore-/32706633.html

Putin, Vladimir. 2018. "Putin on the consequences of a nuclear strike on Russia: 'We will go to heaven like martyrs, and they will just die.'" *Novaya Gazeta*, October 18, 2018. https://www.novayagazeta.ru/news/2018/10/18/146054-putin-posle-inostrannogo-yadernogo-udara-my-kak-mucheniki-popadem-v-ray-a-oni-prosto-sdohnut-dazhe-ne-uspev-raskayatsya

Sharov, Vladimir. 2018. *The Kingdom of Agamemnon*, edited by Elena Shubina. Moscow: AST Publishing House.

Stanislavsky, Konstantin. 1938. *An Actor's Work on Himself*. Saint Petersburg: Khudozh. Lit. 8. https://alterozoom.com/ru/documents/28156.html

The World's Nuclear Stockpile. 2016. https://zloygames.com/threads/jadernyj-zapas-mira.10619

Zubov, Andrei. 2023. Interview on Radio Liberty "Christmas Amid Catastrophe." January 9, 2023. https://www.svoboda.org/a/rozhdestvo-na-fone-katastrofy/32215397.html

Part One

Unlearned Lessons from Russia's Bloody History

1

The War on Progress and the Missed Opportunities of Russian Enlightenment

Marina F. Bykova

In his recent book, the historian and cultural theorist Alexander Etkind has argued for "Russia's '*stop*modernism,'" claiming that "the war exposed the incompetence and anti-modern predilections of Russia's rulers better than the public sphere ever could" (Etkind, 2023, 1, 80). While it is hard to ignore the rise of anti-modern sentiments in contemporary Russia, and while the aggressive promotion of "traditional values" is just the tip of the iceberg of anti-modern propaganda, I believe that what we observe in Russia today is not just an attempt to "stop modernism" or to discard modernity as a distinct condition of the contemporary world. Rather, these and other apparent phenomena are symptoms. It seems that there is a more fundamental problem than is readily apparent, namely Russia's resistance to progress, deeply ingrained in its historical trajectory, political structures, and cultural values.

Many today wonder about the current resurgence of totalitarianism in Russia. While it can be attributed to a combination of historical legacies, political maneuvering, economic challenges, and the manipulation of nationalistic sentiments, Russia's obstinacy in the face of progress appears to be one of the primary contributors to this dramatic relapse. The echoes of resistance to progress reverberate throughout many events in the country's past and present. The hostile assault on Ukraine as it embarks on its path to modernity starkly manifests Russian anti-progressivism in its most ominous form. Indeed, this war is no mere result of imperial or colonial ambitions, nor is it driven solely by resentment and revenge stemming from the trauma of the Soviet collapse. What underlies all of these immediate causes is the conflict between the old and the new, the archaic and the progressive, which this war epitomizes.

Thus, the question worth examining is what may be responsible for Russia's persistent adherence to archaism and apparent anti-progressivism? Certainly, many factors have contributed to this development, most of which can be found in Russia's history, characteristically marked by periods of turmoil and decline. I would venture to suggest that a key cause is associated with Russia's largely elusive and unfulfilled Enlightenment.

While its European counterpart became synonymous with radical changes in culture, intellectual discourse, and crucially: in social, political, and economic spheres of public life—exerting profound formative influence upon them all and shaping the ideals and values of society—the Russian Enlightenment remained limited in its impact and moderate in its intensity. Committed to measured transformation, Russian monarchs, in their alliance with the Orthodox Church, carefully avoided radical changes in fundamental areas such as politics, social life, morality, and the legal system. In contrast to revolutionary European Enlightenment thinkers, especially those in France, who were driven by the spirit of human emancipation from political and social oppression and the realization of ideals such as secular morality, individual liberty, equality, and rights, the Russian Enlightenment served to preserve autocracy and the Orthodox Church's domination and to affirm their leading role in the cultural development of Russia. While we can point to several instances of radical Enlightenment thought on Russian soil in the eighteenth and early nineteenth centuries, they were scarce and promptly suppressed. Russia largely missed its opportunity for true enlightenment, and I believe the repercussions of this have shaped the development of Russian society over the past two centuries. These effects are still evident today.

This chapter explores the phenomenon of the Russian Enlightenment in an attempt to understand how the absence of a radical and comprehensive Enlightenment in Russia has influenced its subsequent history, fostering illiberal and anti-progressive tendencies. I begin with a brief overview of the history of the Russian Enlightenment, primarily focusing on its peculiarities that, in my opinion, led to Russia's resistance to the core principles of the European Enlightenment. I identify one key source of this resistance as Russian traditionalism, a cultural and societal orientation that emphasizes the preservation and continuity of values said to be deeply rooted in Russia's history and heritage, thus shaping its national identity. I then explore how these traditionalist concerns have manifested throughout Russia's subsequent history, focusing mainly on two periods—the nineteenth century, marked by a profound search for Russian identity, and the present day, with its renewed emphasis on tradition and traditional values. Finally, I comment on counter-Enlightenment tendencies evident in contemporary Russia and show their connection to the traditionalism that Putin's regime instrumentalizes to promote its anti-progressivist agenda. My account is not comprehensive; it aims to draw attention to the impact that the Enlightenment—both as a specific period in history represented by the seventeenth to eighteenth centuries' intellectual movement and as a formative process—has had on the nation's development and to what extent the absence of a thorough Enlightenment in Russia hinders progress and promotes the archaic.

The Phenomenon of the Russian Enlightenment in the Context of its European Counterpart

The Age of Enlightenment in Europe is usually dated from 1680 to 1789,[1] with the French Revolution of 1789 marking the culmination of its vision: the overthrow of old authorities and the reshaping of society according to rational principles. This period, often referred to as the "long eighteenth century," witnessed profound cultural transformation in Europe, driven by rigorous exploration of reason and its application to all aspects of human agency. Fueled by an "entirely new philosophical spirit," the most radical proponents of the Enlightenment—French *lumières* (widely known as *philosophes*) and the Central European *Aufklärer*—saw their goal in "bringing light to a benighted intellectual landscape" (Hamburg, 2021, 25). Advocates for transformative human progress, they placed learning and cognition at the core of their pursuit of enlightenment, firmly believing that knowledge held the key to social improvement. Championing the ideas of social liberty, individual human rights, and the equality of all people before the law, they aspired to establish a just society that would ensure the flourishing of humanity. The main achievement of the European Enlightenment is the normative idea of liberalism manifested in the declaration of the intrinsic value of each individual and respect for human dignity. When the Enlightenment descended into bloody terror in the aftermath of the French Revolution, it also revealed the limits of its own ideas. Nonetheless, liberalism and enlightened rationality, characterized by a spirit of self-criticism, creativity, social and political transformation, as well as the enhancement of humanity, gave rise to Modernity. This new era embraced the Enlightenment's liberal ideals, enshrining them in widely adopted principles of morality and human rights and actively applying them to social and political affairs, including representative constitutional law.

Highlighting the revolutionary spirit of the European Enlightenment, historian Jonathan Israel articulates its primary objective as emancipation of human beings "from the collective force of autocracy, intolerance, and prejudiced thinking," while also advocating for "establishing a secular morality" grounded in "ideals of equality (sexual and racial), democracy, individual liberty and a comprehensive toleration" (Israel, 2006, 524). This emphasis is reinforced by the call for the self-criticism of reason, a concept paradigmatically exemplified by Kant, who championed the idea of freedom of thought and stressed the critical role of the public sphere in self-reflection and self-assessment.

Despite the wide diversity of views and positions presented by Enlightenment thinkers in various national and cultural contexts within Europe, unifying them was their optimistic confidence in human reason as a self-legislative power—the sole authority that shapes our relationship with the world and empowers us as capable political and social agents. They did not encourage only the theoretical use of reason, they actively endeavored to improve society through rational inquiry and the practical application of knowledge. By upholding the principles of liberty, equality, and individual rights, they advocated transforming society and politics. The Enlightenment introduced secular thought to Europe and reshaped people's perception of morality and their moral obligations. It is worth noting that the Enlightenment wasn't entirely atheistic. Its secularism promoted the idea that reason alone is sufficient to identify and justify legitimate principles and their just implementation, independent of specific religious beliefs and confessions.

The extent to which this brief account of the Enlightenment project directly applies to the history of Russia is a contentious issue in its own right. However, even from a historiographical perspective, the question of the Enlightenment in Russia remains subject to debate (see Barran, 2002; Hildermeier, 2004). Furthermore, even those who are willing to acknowledge that, like its European neighbors, Russia was significantly influenced by the Enlightenment, cannot reach a consensus regarding the chronology of this period (Walicki, 2005, 37-45; Grechanaia, 2010; Schippan, 2012, 9-41; Berelowitch, 2015; Hamburg, 2021, 26). Here I will rely on the prevalent historiography concerning this matter, aligning myself with scholars who recognize the presence of a distinct Enlightenment era in Russian history, dating it to a century-long and mostly continuous period from 1689 to 1796. This era is marked by the reigns of Peter I (the Great) (r. 1682-1725), Elizaveta (Elizabeth) Petrovna (r. 1741-1762), and Catherine II (the Great) (r. 1762-1796), wherein the period of Catherine's rule is viewed as the peak of the Russian Enlightenment (Walicki, 2005; Schippan, 2012; Hamburg, 2021).[2] Effectively beginning with Russia's emergence from its medieval period, which approximately coincided with Peter I's assumption of power in 1694, it was a time of rigorous modernization, which affected virtually all areas of domestic affairs and many aspects of everyday life for the population.

However, the Russian Enlightenment demonstrated a great degree of moderation compared to its European counterpart, particularly in its radical French form. This moderation resulted from several important features of the Russian version of the Enlightenment that determined outcomes of this period and its impact on subsequent development of the country. Unlike France and Central Europe, where the Enlightenment was a project led by *lumières* and *Aufklärer*, initiated and carried out by intellectuals themselves, in Russia, the task of enlightenment was taken up by the state (or monarchy) and the Orthodox Church. As the historian Gary Hamburg points out, debates about the roots of knowledge, both religious and secular, found their origins within the Orthodox Church as early as the sixteenth and seventeenth centuries. These debates later extended to the community of believers who, guided by Church figures, began pondering questions about how to establish a just order on earth (Hamburg, 2021, 26). However, their primary focus remained the assessment of recent and historical events. Furthermore, from the reign of Alexei Mikhailovich (1645–1676) through the reign of Catherine the Great, Russian monarchs openly aligned themselves with the cause of enlightenment, generally understood as the pursuit of knowledge. In addition to promoting education, they decreed the importation of European books on theology, philosophy, history, and the sciences. This practice continued from the mid-seventeenth century until the very beginning of the nineteenth century. These developments resulted in a peculiar and, I would say—from the perspective of Russia's future development—highly detrimental situation, where the process of enlightenment was initiated from the top. In this "top-down" setting, a radical Enlightenment movement was unfeasible. The state and official Church collaborated to achieve their primary objectives of preserving autocracy and further strengthening their power. They introduced reforms which neither posed a challenge to this power, nor permitted any actions that could jeopardize it.

This first restrictive feature of the Russian Enlightenment determined another peculiarity—an almost entire lack of a free public space. Until at least the second half of the eighteenth century, the public sphere in Russia was effectively monopolized by the Church and the state, with their influence extending to press control (including ownership of the publishing houses, publication of newspapers, etc.) and domination of intellectual and cultural discourse, initially in the Tsardom and later in the Empire. Even as the public sphere expanded later and other actors entered the scene (e.g., the appearance of the first private journals as well as the increase of intellectual activity stimulated by Elizabeth's reforms), it continued to be closely monitored and strongly censored. During the reign of Catherine II, often regarded as the most "enlightened" Russian monarch, a close eye was kept on the public sphere, and any perceived threat to autocracy and the Empress' power was swiftly quashed. Notable examples include Catherine the Great's campaign against Freemasonry, which she launched after 1785, and the arrests of publicist Nikolai Novikov in 1792 and writer Alexander Radishchev in 1790, both of which she readily authorized (de Madariaga, 1981, esp. 521–31).

Russian Enlightenment: Its Major Attributes, Results, and Implications

It is not my intention here to provide a comprehensive account of innovations introduced during the Russian Age of Enlightenment. There is a vast body of literature devoted to this period in Russian history and its impact on the country's subsequent development. For the arguments central to this chapter, I would like to emphasize some selected relevant points, with a primary focus on the constraints that European Enlightenment thinking faced in Russia and the impact it had on Russian intellectual and social discourse.

1. Undoubtedly, Peter I's lengthy reign marked a significant period of reform in Russia, one of the few such transformative eras in the country's tumultuous history. His political, military and social reforms aimed at Westernizing Russia brought about profound changes in nearly every aspect of Russian life. However, while Peter may be rightly seen as an emblematic figure, introducing Western ideas into Russian social and political discourse, and while several of his reforms did reflect certain Enlightenment ideals (e.g., establishing a social structure where advancement was based on personal ability and performance rather than birth and genealogy, creating a new class of serfs known as state peasants, etc.), the interpretation of those ideals and their appropriation within Russia itself was very narrow and restrained.

Despite the spirit of innovation in Peter's social and political reforms, which set him apart from the Russian monarchs that preceded him, Peter created a state that further legitimized and strengthened authoritarian rule in Russia. The Enlightenment instigated by Peter I as an absolute ruler exemplifies "Enlightened Absolutism": he used his total power to encourage change and innovation, but always within the limits determined by the absolutist political system. Like previous monarchs and those who succeeded him, Peter did not tolerate any dissent. A "strongman for the state," he brutally put down the Streltsy uprising of 1682 and then publicly executed more than 1,000 rebels in 1698. In general, Peter's reforms were driven by a desire for a stronger and more centralized state, rather than a commitment to Enlightenment ideals. His heavy-handed approach openly stifled dissent, preventing any appearance of individual rights and liberty, even amongst the royal court and aristocracy.

Similarly, Catherine II, who was captivated by and well-versed in European Enlightenment ideas and who, by continuing the Westernization initiated by Peter the Great, exhibited her commitment to gradual enlightenment, nevertheless fell short of consistently realizing Enlightenment ideals. Her distinct interpretation of enlightenment is exemplified in the *Nakaz* (1767).[3] Published eight times during her rule and regularly recited in government institutions, *Nakaz* is a significant document of the era. For a comprehensive commentary on this document and Catherine's personal grasp of enlightenment, one can turn to Diderot's *Observations* (Diderot, 1992), which he composed after returning to The Hague following his five-month stay in Russia in 1773–1774, during which he engaged in numerous conversations with the Empress encompassing topics of philosophy, politics, religion, and culture (Bil'basov and Lentin, 1972; Hamburg, 2021, 36).

In his insightful commentary, Diderot characterizes the Empress of Russia as "certainly, a despot," driven to uphold and reinforce absolute control over the population (Diderot, 1992, 82). Confronting the absolutism propagated by Catherine's *Nakaz*, he argues that absolute governments "[put] all liberty and property in absolute dependence on a single person" (Diderot, 1992, 88). The central issue Diderot brings to light, closely related to our discussion, is that absolutism, even when labeled "enlightened," inevitably impedes progress and obstructs the innovative development associated with the Enlightenment. Diderot argues that the involvement of citizens in politics, their participation in legislating laws, and their engagement in open discussions about vital state matters are indispensable in order that the civilizing mission of such a vast nation as Russia may succeed. In response to Catherine's somewhat vague assertion in her *Nakaz* that good citizens seek their country's "prosperity, glory, and tranquility," which only pure monarchy can guarantee, Diderot, who fully endorses the ideals of the European Enlightenment, advocates for equality before the law and the natural liberty of the individual. He insists that in any country aspiring to attain happiness and good laws, "the sovereign authority should ... be limited, and limited in a lasting way" (Diderot, 1992, 89, see also 97–9). For him, "pure monarchy" is merely another term for despotism and tyranny (Diderot, 1992, 90).

Of particular interest is Catherine's reaction upon reading Diderot's critique of her *Nakaz* subsequent to his death. She responded angrily, writing in one of her letters: "If my *Instruction* had been drafted according to Diderot's taste, it would have been applicable to an entirely different state of affairs [than those in Russia]" (Tourneux, 1899, 519–20 (trans. modified); cited in Hamburg, 2021, 42). This response by itself already gives a good idea about the true incentives guiding the reforms of Russian monarchs.

Indeed, while Catherine II did consider implementing some reforms influenced by Enlightenment *philosophes*, her commitment to these ideas remained ambivalent; she never fully embraced them. Despite showing signs of cultural progress, her reign failed to bring about significant Enlightenment-driven reforms. Towards the end of her rule, she concluded that "the *philosophes* and others of their kind, who have participated in the revolution and embraced the *Encyclopédie*, ... have only two objectives: first, the abolition of the Christian religion; and second, [the eradication of] royalty" (Catherine II, 1878, 622). She found neither of these goals acceptable either for herself or for the Russian Empire.

2. Russian monarchs such as Peter I and Catherine II, as well as those who ruled during and after their reigns, viewed the Russian Orthodox Church as the guardian of moral values and justice. In her *Nakaz*, Catherine explicitly cited the Church's commitment to Christian values. Even Peter I, despite his extensive domestic reforms, hesitated to challenge the Church's authority. His Church reforms were primarily focused on curtailing Church autonomy. Abolishing the Patriarchate and replacing it with the collegiate Body of the Synod through the "Ecclesiastical Regulations" of 1721 served to exert state control over the Church, with the primary objective of preventing his opponents from rallying under its banner (Cracraft, 1971). While Peter I aimed to initiate a process of Westernization within the clergy, he did not forsake the canons and authority of the Orthodox Church. Orthodoxy remained the fundamental ideological core of the Empire, a principle upheld by all Russian monarchs until the abolition of the monarchy in 1917.[4]

To be sure, Orthodoxy played a leading role in spreading some ideas advocated by the Enlightenment. In the seventeenth and eighteenth centuries, several important efforts to promote education and the dissemination of Western knowledge originated in the Church, through the activities of learned Churchmen knowledgeable in a variety of disciplines. Among the prominent figures within the Russian Church who became instrumental in advancing Enlightenment values in the country, notable examples include the erudite Simeon Polotsky along with his student Silvester Medvedev, who opened a monastery school and started teaching Latin. Another important intellectual figure was Feofan Prokopovich (1681–1736), Abbot of the Kiev monastery and Rector of its celebrated ecclesiastical academy, where he taught theology, literature, and rhetoric. He emerged as the most influential figure during the reign of Peter I, serving (from 1716) as a counselor to the Tsar on church and educational affairs. It is also worth mentioning Platon (Petr) Levshin (1737–1812), a favorite Orthodox Christian clergyman of Catherine

II, who served as Archbishop and the Metropolitan of Moscow (Hamburg, 2021, 27–9; see also Hamburg, 2016, 191–230). In 1765, Platon published *The Orthodox Doctrine of the Apostolic Eastern Church; Or, a Compendium of Christian Theology*, in which he favorably discussed Western thought, including rationalism (Levshin, 2012).[5] These figures represented the erudite trend of Russian Orthodoxy, bringing knowledge of Western philosophy and theology, founding monastic and church schools, and contributing to the advancement of learning in royal court circles. Their efforts laid the foundations for new educational and science-oriented institutions in Russia, including primary and secondary schools and academies that substantially influenced the spread of knowledge.

However, the Orthodox Church exercised significant control over the process of advancing secular knowledge by resorting to restrictions and censorship of publications and other means of communication within the public sphere. Despite the Russian Orthodox Church's conflicting influence and impact during the Enlightenment, the Church as an institution was traditionally conservative and resisted many Enlightenment ideas, considering them to be challenges to its authority and dogma. It regarded secular knowledge and Enlightenment values with suspicion, as they often clashed with religious dogmas. Furthermore, as a political arm of the state, it was mobilized to maintain control over the population and stifle intellectual and political dissent. Promoting religious Orthodoxy, discouraging the critical examination of religious beliefs and practices, and restricting free thought, the Church effectively opposed the Enlightenment ideals of rationalism, critical thinking, and questioning authority. Consequently, it assumed an essential role in resisting the adoption of true Enlightenment values in Russia.

3. The Russian Enlightenment is usually viewed as a significant period illuminated by the ideas of knowledge and learning, and its achievements are primarily associated with educational initiatives and advancements in the basic sciences. Indeed, the Enlightenment emphasis on education and the dissemination of knowledge found great resonance in Russia, making reforms in education and the growth of scientific knowledge perhaps one of the most significant developments for the country.[6] In the eighteenth century, Russian monarchs introduced many important measures aiming to restructure archaic schooling practices into modern educational institutions. In addition to launching a national network of primary and secondary schools accessible to all social classes, they established the first universities (in St. Petersburg and Moscow) and other institutions of higher education, founded the Academy of Sciences and the Academy of Arts, and financially supported academic research (de Madariaga, 1981, 493–7; Hamburg, 2021, 31). Stimulating the advance of knowledge and science, the royal court

adopted policies that favored scientific discoveries, study abroad for young nobles, cultural exchange with Western Europe, and the importation and translation of Western works and scientific publications.

However, while from the very beginning the Enlightenment project in Russia was widely perceived as an endeavor to illuminate minds and encourage the formation of an educated population, education was rarely conceived as an end in itself. The ruling elites rather saw it as a means for inculcating obedience to monarchy and Christian piety. Thus, in Russia, the Enlightenment educational program consisted of two connected elements: first, establishing public education, and second, cultivating in Russians native virtues that encourage loyalty to the court and Church. The first was primarily associated with instituting a system of formal schooling for the broader general population, which could gain access to knowledge and learn useful skills. Focused primarily on the institutional framework of education and science, this first component addressed the question of form, or more precise structuring of the educational system. In contrast, the second component raised questions about the content of education. The realization of the goal of instilling obedience was seen as the development of a people deeply rooted in traditional values, practices, and religious beliefs, fostering a sense of "belonging" (to borrow Gadamer's terminology) to the distinctly Russian cultural heritage.

The multifaceted character of the Russian Enlightenment program on education is captured to some degree in the connotations associated with the Russian term for "enlightenment" (*prosveshchenie*). The word descended from Old Russian and Church Slavonic. It denoted the acquisition of spiritual life at baptism, dedication to Christian virtues, and to the goal of *theosis*. By 1750 or so, the word had acquired new connotations, such as possession of specialized knowledge and the practice of secular virtues. Based on these insights, Gary Hamburg concludes that

> eighteenth-century Russian speakers invoking *prosveshchenie* might have referred either to the moral or secular sense of the term or to both simultaneously. ... The persistence of the term's moral connotation disencumbered Russian thinkers from regarding themselves as *lumières* after the French fashion, even when the Russians in question were Francophones.
> (Hamburg, 2021, 27; see also Hamburger, 2016, 16–19)

This claim deserves attention, because it hints at a very important point often missed by historical and cultural studies of the Russian Enlightenment. Indeed, until the 1830s, the term "culture" (*kul'tura*) did not exist in the

Russian language, and all this time, the term *prosveshchenie* was used in the connotation of "culture," interpreted in a normative, value-laden way (Yanovsky, 1804, 454; Sugai, 2007; Asoyan, 2009, 11). However, the normativity in question did not arrive from some general theory of values, norms, or moral beliefs. It was rather produced by the values espoused internally by reference to "Russian spirituality," which emphasized the special and expressly distinct character of Russian culture and heritage with its utmost manifestation in Orthodoxy. This did not merely attribute (or reintroduce) a sacred content to the practice of what was called *prosveshchenie;* it effectively promoted a specific ideal of Russia's cultural uniqueness, which received its final form within the framework of Slavophilism and was openly exploited by most Russian thinkers of the nineteenth century.

Typically, scholars of Russian culture and intellectual history locate the source of the Russian idea of cultural distinctness and exceptionality in the nineteenth century, most specifically in the ideology of the Slavophiles. However, the original roots of this development can be traced back to the traditionalism evident in the earlier periods of Russia's history. The Orthodox Church had habitually cultivated the idea of Russian "chosenness" revealed in *starets* Filofei's (Philotheus of Pskov's) alleged proclamation of Moscow as the Third Rome, the insistence on the supremacy of the Orthodox faith, and Russia's messianic vocation. Given the role that the Russian Orthodox Church played in the country's governing ideology during the Enlightenment age, it would be more surprising if these values had not dominated Russia's intellectual and cultural discourse.

Seventeenth- and eighteenth-century thinkers, both Churchmen and those outside of the Church, including two scholars who are traditionally viewed as intellectual pinnacles of Russia's Enlightenment movement, Vasily Tatishchev and Mikhail Lomonosov, promoted the "integral spirit" of Orthodox faith, shielding it from the "intellectual fashion" and excessive rationalism of the West, even if their efforts appeared less extensive than those that emerged in the nineteenth century.[7]

Numerous decrees of Catherine II, as well as her literary works, expressed not only her politics and ideology, but also her approach to education. Her pedagogical beliefs, based on her studies of educational theories produced by European thinkers such as John Locke, François Fénelon, and Jean-Jacques Rousseau, significantly influenced the reorganization of schools and curriculum reforms in the later years of her rule (de Madariaga, 1981, 488–92). As reflected in her educational policies, her objectives extended beyond imparting fundamental knowledge, such as grammar, mathematics, and the sciences. To a greater extent, Catherine II's aim was to instill reverence for the absolutist law and the monarchy (de Madariaga, 1981, 490–92). In essence, she sought to cultivate habits of discipline and obedience among her subjects, and she willingly deployed archaic native virtues and religious Orthodoxy as powerful tools to achieve her goals. Relying in the conduct of education upon conservative traditional virtues and highly mythicized religious spirituality proved helpful in fostering public compliance with autocratic rule and court authority.

Strict obedience-oriented education was not Catherine II's innovation. It was a common feature of the educational legislation of most (if not all) Russian monarchs before and after her. Overstressing the submissive attitude and conformity in thought and conduct, this approach to education discouraged students from challenging dominant ideas and norms. The Church was instilled as the moral and cultural foundation whose authority could not be questioned. This is where the cultural discourse of Russian traditionalism with its strong emphasis on preserving and upholding traditional values, customs, and cultural norms came in handy.

There is no need to delve into the extent to which this education to obedience, rooted in traditional and often archaic values, deviated from the core principles of the European Enlightenment. The Russian version of educational reforms stood in stark contrast to the central ideas of the Enlightenment with its focus on rational agency and the critical ability of doubt.

***

Unquestionably, if comprehended on the plain of the entire history of Russia, the Enlightenment reforms initiated by Peter the Great, and continued by subsequent Russian monarchs, played a vital role in the modernization of the country. They transformed Russia from a vast yet stagnant agrarian settlement, economically and socially backward, into a major world empire, propelling it onto the global stage. However, despite Russian rulers' strong commitment to developing Russia in those regards, they never fully embraced the ideals of the European Enlightenment, especially those central to social and political discourse, such as freedom of an individual, equality, and rule of law. Their primary focus remained the preservation of imperial absolutism and the dominance of political and religious authority. Introduced "top-down," their reforms produced a heavily truncated, "castrated" form of the Enlightenment in Russia. By design, the country missed its opportunity for the genuine Enlightenment experienced by Europe.

Crucial tenets of the European Enlightenment, including concepts like social and political equality, respect for individual dignity, societal progress driven by rational principles, and practical applications of science and knowledge, as well as self-criticism in thinking and freedom of expression, faced significant opposition and were largely suppressed in the Russian context. In addition, the inevitable scarcity of domestic radicals created a situation in which the Enlightenment's core principles of advancing society and championing individual human rights and liberty were extinguished.

Despite the Russian Enlightenment's connection to its European counterpart, the Russian version not only had different goals and objectives, rooted in a desire to maintain the existing social and political status quo, it promoted established (traditional) norms and practices, including religious beliefs and customs, those perceived the most stable and effective for preserving autocracy. This development had two main implications. First, Russia failed to seize the moment to embark on a path of progressive advancement towards genuine national enlightenment, and instead continued faltering in its economic, socio-political, and cultural development. Russia's tradition of absolutism and the institution of serfdom proved inimical to the European Enlightenment, especially to the liberal ideas and principles it exhibited. Second, hostile to liberalism and resistant to significant social or political changes as disruptive to the established order and values, the Russian Enlightenment championed traditionalism, promoting it as the dominant state ideology.

Autocratic absolutism, the unquestionable authority of the Orthodox Church, and ambivalence among rulers, erected significant barriers to Russia's productive adoption of Enlightenment ideals; these factors also represented key sources and elements influencing Russian traditionalism. While the origins of this socio-political and socio-cultural ideology can be traced back to the medieval period, it began gaining prominence in the eighteenth century and became a dominant force in Russia's intellectual discourse and political landscape in the nineteenth century, when it gave rise to Russian ethno-nationalism, anti-Western sentiment, and messianic exceptionalism.

Embracing the commitment to preserve and safeguard Russia's historical, religious, and cultural heritage, this evolving ideology emerged as a primary obstacle to advancing the Enlightenment in Russia. It nurtured resistance to radical change, upheld conservative values, and stifled extensive social, cultural, and political innovations.

The Russian Question

It is somewhat ironic that today, more than two centuries later, the current Russian ruler is invoking traditionalism, making it instrumental to his war against Western liberal values and civilizational progress—precisely the ideals and values that the European Enlightenment affirmed and advanced. Noticeably, Putin's current outlook on Ukraine exhibits key tenets of this traditionalist attitude. The "special military operation" launched on February 24, 2022, is said to aim at "liberating" the hapless Ukrainians from their "Nazi" government and freeing them from the constraints of the liberal international order. Putin's regime conceives of the people of Ukraine as having been "brainwashed" by a hostile West—the enemy of choice in a long-standing narrative and the primary source of Russia's current sense of victimhood after the disintegration of the Soviet Union.

Contrary to what is widely suggested, this narrative did not first emerge from under the ruins of the USSR. Its roots can be traced back to what is often referred to as the "Russian Question," which is associated with debates and discussions about the national identity and "historical mission" of Russia.

One of the first and most powerful voices was Pyotr Chaadayev's, whose experience in the West made him aware of Russia's backwardness in political, economic, and cultural affairs. In his first "Philosophical Letter" (1829), he presented a devastating critique of Russia and its history (Chaadayev, 1969, 27, 30–2). Many debates about Russia's position in Western modernity can be traced back to Chaadayev. His great significance lies not only in shaping Russian intellectual discourse but also in bringing attention to the critical need of self-examination. He placed the Russian question at the center of intellectual debates in Russia, where this question received its specific shape as part of the search for Russian identity. It has since echoed consistently throughout Russian intellectual discussions, taking various forms and directions, with the pursuit of a national idea and "tradition" in all its combinations and derivatives emerging as the central theme in this endeavor. The nineteenth century provides plenty of examples of this development. Contrary to the previous century, which was inspired by the European Enlightenment and influenced by the West, nineteenth-century Russia broke away from its Western leaning. This signified Russia's fundamental shift toward the most dogmatic form of cultural and historical traditionalism, which was elevated to an official creed of the Russian state in its attempt to resist Western influence and became accepted within society as a dominant worldview.

In the early nineteenth century, Nikolai Karamzin insisted in his memoir *Of Old and New Russia* (1811) that the Russians should not attempt to imitate the West but rather should maintain the beliefs of their ancestors. According to him, "an Orthodox Russian was the most perfect citizen and Holy Rus' the foremost state in the world" (Karamzin, 1969, 123). Expressing anti-Western sentiments, he praised the era when Russians successfully resisted the influence of the "savage horde" of Europe and showed courage "to call ... Europeans *infidels*" (Karamzin, 1969).

Continuing the trend, about two decades later, in 1833, Count Sergey Uvarov, serving as the minister of education for Tsar Nicholas I (1825–1855), declared:

> Our common obligation consists in this: that the education of the people be conducted in the joint spirit of Orthodoxy, Autocracy and Nationality ... [I]t is necessary to establish our fatherland on firm foundations upon which is based the wellbeing, strength, and life of a people. It is necessary to find the principles which form the distinctive character of Russia and which belong only to Russia; it is necessary to gather into one whole the sacred remnants of Russian nationality and to fasten to them the anchor of our salvation.
>
> (Leatherbarrow and Offord, 1987, 62–3)

Inspired by the Christian Trinity, whose strength lies in unity, Uvarov's three principles—orthodoxy, autocracy, and nationality[8]—initially introduced to infuse a "national spirit" into educational reforms, soon extended beyond educational affairs to become a fundamental creed of Nicholas I's Russia as a whole. In his effort to counter Western European liberalism and emphasize Russia's distinctiveness, Nicholas I exploited the emerging sense of romantic nationalism—largely influenced by German Romanticism, which had captured the interest of Russian intellectuals. This exploitation served to promote the most reactionary chauvinism and bolster his oppressive regime. The triad that essentially summarized the ideological outcomes of the Russian Enlightenment has enthroned traditionalism as a national ideology of Russia, propagating a doctrine of "Official Nationality." Initially intended merely as a basis for the moral education of Russia's youth, this combination of the three principles grew into the central concepts that built and unified the national vision at that time. In addition to fostering a form of imperial patriotism bordering on nationalism, these concepts also laid the framework for approaching Russian history—its past, present, and future.[9] For decades, Nicholas I's formula of "Official Nationality" worked effectively, justifying and strengthening the Russian monarchy and furthering its obsession with power and status. It also left its mark on Russian intellectual discourse and influenced the development and choice of topics in nineteenth-century Russian philosophy.

Discussions regarding Russia's identity became dominant, reaching their peak in the contentious debate between two conceptually opposed intellectual streams: Slavophiles and Westernizers. In this dispute, Russian traditionalism emerged as one of the most powerful arguments used by Slavophiles. A significant practical motivation among Slavophiles was the desire to comprehend and define what is often referred to as the "Russian spirit," as well as to foster the spread of a Russian national identity in the multinational Tsarist Empire. The philosophy of Slavophilism, as a well-established theory, surfaced in the 1830s. However, as a distinctive worldview, it existed in the national and social consciousness long before it was crystallized in public doctrines. Peter the Great unconsciously awakened these latent, unexpressed Slavophilic feelings and values when he attracted leaders of Western European industry to follow his path to Muscovy and develop their enterprises on Russian soil.

The Slavophiles emerged as the champions of Russian traditionalism, embracing everything typically associated with it. They declared that Russia possessed true freedom, faith, and brotherhood, qualities lacking in its Western neighbors. Russia, according to the Slavophiles, boasted an ancient and splendid heritage of communal life and a land system where the inherent justice of the Russian peasant's heart was exemplified through the voluntary and brotherly division of land among fellow countrymen. While the Westernizers believed in an "integral worldview" and a unified vision of historical progress as the essential framework to theorize Russia's legacy and destiny, the Slavophiles aimed to promote *sobornost'*, Russian traditional spirituality. They regarded it as the unique Russian identity and the only means of escaping Western decadence. In Russian, the term *sobornost'* means "togetherness" or "spirit of communality," it has theological origins and connotations, representing the spiritual experience of religious faith in its purest form, namely Russian Orthodoxy. The Slavophiles insisted that this Orthodox spirit of organic "togetherness," uncontaminated by Western rationalism and immorality, is the only model for Russian society and should also become an ideal for all of humanity. In their ideas and theoretical doctrines, the Slavophiles not only invoked the spirit of traditionalism but also made it the ideological foundation of their aggressive Russophilism. Thus, the Slavophiles laid the philosophical foundations for a distinctively Russian tradition of cultural and religious messianism, encompassing figures like Dostoevsky (especially his political writings), the Pan-Slavic and Eurasian movements, and the apocalyptic visions of Nikolai Berdyaev. The messianic character of this Russian intellectual tradition is now widely accepted, but many overlook its most fundamental feature—its inherent counter-Enlightenment and traditionalistic nature.

There is no consensus among scholars of Russian intellectual history regarding whether Slavophilism as an intellectual and philosophical movement, was inherently messianic, chauvinistic, and deeply traditionalist in its main motifs and concepts, or if it gradually developed and fostered these ideas within its own depths. Despite the complexities of this debate, it is clear that at least some Slavophile thinkers, such as Yuri Samarin and Ivan Aksakov, expressed sentiments in their writings that leaned toward advocating the use of state power to implement a program of "Russification." This program aimed to marginalize the influence of non-Russian minorities within the Russian Empire, such as the Poles and the Baltic Germans. These thinkers argued that Russian "traditional values" should serve as a "standard" for Russification, asserting that the intended national unity could be achieved only on the basis of these values (see Aksakov, 1886, 30–1, 88–92; Samarin, 1889, 16–18). Furthermore, certain Slavophiles, particularly those addressing political issues related to the Russian state and its role in preserving social order in a multi-ethnic polity, urged the Tsarist state to use its power to eliminate any challenges to the supremacy of Russian culture within the Empire's boundaries. They also advocated for the imposition of a Russian identity (and tradition) on Russia's borderlands.[10]

While the Slavophiles made substantial contributions to the development of an aggressive "Russophile" mentality bordering on messianic exceptionalism and Russian ethno-nationalism, their ideas gained even more significance and prominence decades later through the efforts of various thinkers sympathetic to the messianic Russian idea. Although prophetic themes were characteristic of many writings by the Moscow Slavophiles, they took on a more pronounced form in the works of later non-Slavophile philosophers such as Vladimir Solovyov, Semyon Frank, Sergei Bulgakov, Nikolai Berdyaev, and various Russian literati. A detailed analysis of their ideas and the extent to which these ideas influenced Russia's intellectual discourse by emphasizing uniqueness and exceptionality is a topic for a special discussion. Here, I would like to underscore that despite differences in their initial intentions and the diversity of claims they presented, they all appealed to the Russian tradition as a repository of true Christian spirituality and ideal moral values. They juxtaposed to it the "decadent" West and Western morality, which they deemed "corrupted" by reason, heretical disbelief, and the lack of religious spirituality. They used traditionalism, specifically Russian archaic tradition, to assert the primacy of generalization and unification as tools for the religious and historical transformation of reality. Despite being introduced and developed under various names such as *sobornost'*, *tselostnost'* (wholeness, integrity), *vseedinstvo* (all-Unity), "universal Christianity," "national unity," "national identity," etc., the fundamentally traditionalist idea—albeit in different ways—promoted the old ideals established during the Russian Enlightenment and preserved in Nicholas I's triadic formula of the "Official Nationality." These ideals proved to be extremely durable in Russian history, eventually leading to ideocracy and totalitarianism in the first half of the twentieth century.

No matter how paradoxical it may appear, the ideas of Bolshevik and Soviet Russia were inherited from the Russian Empire. The cunning communist ideologues took Nicholas I's slogan and simply modified it. Orthodoxy gave way to Marxism (later Marxism-Leninism), autocracy was supplanted by the iron rule of communist leaders (in earlier and later versions, slightly modified as the rule of the Communist Party), while the concept of nationality (*narodnost'*) persisted. Throughout more than seven decades of Soviet rule, strong and persistent leaders wielded significant control, shaping life in this multinational empire. The ambitious social project of communism aimed to unify the people and foster national pride and self-respect. Yet, it failed, leaving the population disillusioned and dismayed. Furthermore, while the Soviet regime prided itself on developing a "unique Russian culture," established behind the iron curtain it persisted as a "prison culture," contributing to widespread apathy and civic disengagement among people. Thus, it is not surprising that in the aftermath of the twentieth century the Russian populace became even more averse to progress, unwilling to push for change, favoring instead traditionalism and conformity.

Putin and Russian Counter-Enlightenment

The Contemporary Faces of Russian Traditionalism

One does not need to be a Russia expert to recognize how the emerging order under Putin's regime echoes the darkest periods of Russia's tumultuous history. This is not only reflected in a grim new era of repressions and heightened punishment for opposition figures but is also evident in Putin's dictatorial control, the close collaboration between the state and the Russian Orthodox Church (so close that at times they seem inseparable), the ongoing "true patriots" campaign, and a significant emphasis on extreme ethno-nationalism and Russia's perceived exceptionalism. While today's regime may use a slightly different vocabulary, the core ideas it endorses and the principles it invokes in its propaganda remain unchanged.

The Russian question has resurfaced in the public agenda, but now in a more aggressive manner. Its ugly manifestations are apparent both inside and outside the country: internally, in the rise of radical-right conservatism and ultra-nationalism, and externally, in the brutal war in Ukraine with an attempt to dismantle an independent state and reshape the world order. Putin and his regime frame the war and the current confrontation with the West as "an existential battle for the survival" of Russia and the Russian people (see Faulconbridge, 2023). The endeavor to elevate the Russian question into a significant "ontological" issue is not a new concept and did not originate with Putin. In recent history, it was Alexander Solzhenitsyn who, following the dissolution of the Soviet Union, declared that what it is now at stake for Russia is the survival of the Russian nation.

In his short 1994 book titled *"The Russian Question" at the End of the Twentieth Century*, he poses a direct query: "Shall our people [Russians] be or not be?" (Solzhenitsyn 1995, 106). Three decades ago, he astutely identified threats emanating from various sources, including moral decay, economic degradation, the growing influence of Western values and institutions, and the reshaping of Russia through newly established state borders. In his endeavor to address this pivotal question, he turns to history, recounting Russia's narrative over the past four centuries. He does not hide his preferences, revealing his fondness for the final decades of imperial rule and portraying it as a paradise lost for the Russian Empire and the Russian nation. Though he is not an imperialist thinker, the message conveyed in this book and other writings from the same period is more dangerous than it may initially appear.

Solzhenitsyn diagnoses Russia's profound political, economic, and cultural crisis, attributing this calamity to the most fundamental crisis—the crisis of national identity. His primary concern is the Russian nation and its enduring existence, which he considers the fundamental constituent of the state. As a fervent opponent of communism, he attributes most, if not all, of the troubles afflicting the Russian nation to Soviet ideology and practice. In his view, progress means a return, not merely to pre-Soviet times, but rather to the deeper roots he associates with the vast Russian nation of imperial times, encompassing Ukrainians, Belarusians, and Russians alike. Rebuilding the Russian nation is thus seen as the top-priority task that, according to Solzhenitsyn, can only be achieved by reviving the traditions of our forefathers.

Some commentators treat the "conservative utopia of Russian nation-building that Solzhenitsyn proposed to the new Russian state and society" as "a time bomb that went off with the outbreak of the Russo-Ukrainian conflict" back in 2014. This perspective implies that the Russian president may have seized the opportunity to further his imperial agenda, presenting it as a response to the imperative of Russian national rebirth (Plokhy, 2021, 283, 284ff).

Solzhenitsyn's influence on Putin's decision regarding the annexation of Crimea remains a subject of speculation, and I do not intend to delve into this discussion here. However, it is worth considering the thinker's advocacy for traditionalism in the task of Russian nation-building, which appears to resonate effectively with the current regime and ruling authorities.

In his 1994 book, Solzhenitsyn calls on the Russian people to return to their spiritual heritage as the most steadfast foundation for the revival and unity of the nation. This argument, even in a slightly modified form, persists today. There is nothing inherently problematic with appeals to spirituality and traditions; they can indeed promote national unity, especially in times of change or uncertainty. However, the ideological instrumentalization and political manipulation of traditions have led to dangerous results throughout Russian history, resurfacing today in a no less troubling form. Although Solzhenitsyn's book is primarily written for Russians, it also serves as a call to the West. Drawing on historical details, such as those related to the Crimean War (1853–1856), the author asserts that the West is treacherous and should never be trusted. Criticizing the West for its double standards and immorality, he sees in the Russian spirit an unshakable underpinning that can resist the moral corruption pervasive in European cultures.

I am not suggesting that Putin and his regime use Solzhenitsyn's ideas as a tactical script for their current actions. On the contrary, the social and political deeds witnessed in Russia today, both internally and externally, suggest that neither Putin nor his close circle has a carefully conceived strategy or well-developed long-term plan of action. Even the goals of the "special military operation" are murky and not clearly stated, undergoing constant revision to meet the daily needs of political elites and legitimize the largely irrational actions on the Ukrainian front. Nevertheless, an appeal to Russian traditions and the system of values "passed down from our forefathers" remains a dominant argument in the country's contemporary political and social discourse. In this sense, Solzhenitsyn's advocacy of Russia's "spiritual heritage" as a solid foundation for national revival becomes highly instrumental for the current Russian regime, which has made traditionalism its official political and ideological agenda.

Indeed, if today the Kremlin promotes anything resembling an official ideology, it is the Russians' proclaimed capacity to uphold the traditions passed down by their ancestors and to embrace Orthodox spirituality. Putin's regime presents this as a "new" strategy, invoking it as Russia's geopolitical weapon in its fight against Western "outright Satanism," supposedly manifested in "a radical denial of moral norms, religion, and family" (Putin, 2022a).[11] However, what is portrayed as "new" is not at all new.

It is a centuries-long Russian traditionalist agenda with its archaic assertion of religious and traditional values that Putin glorifies as the embodiment of "great historical Russia" (Putin, 2022a). There is, however, a significant novelty evident in the present-day utilization of this well-known agenda. Its present uses extend beyond local boundaries, transcending the realm of confrontation between individual nations, states, or cultural regions. At stake is a global ideological clash between liberalism and traditionalism. In this assertive encounter, Russia is portrayed as a stronghold of traditionalism, engaging in a "sacred battle" against the morally corrupt, "Satanist," "decadent" West. All of this is done under the banner of "Russian tradition," which the Kremlin, in close alliance with the Russian Orthodox Church, seeks to protect and advance as uniquely sacred and supreme.

Traditional Values and Their Instrumentalization in Today's Russia

Some scholars equate the "traditional values" rigorously promoted by the current Russian regime with a Christian conservative idea of "family values" (Stoeckl and Uzlaner, 2022). While the recent decades coinciding with Putin's rule are indeed marked by Russia's powerful shift toward conservatism (lately in its reactionary forms), I do not believe that the recent fetishization and instrumentalization of "traditional values" can be plausibly explained solely by Russia's embrace of Christian moral conservatism inspired by "transnational influences," as Stoeckl and Uzlaner seem to suggest (Stoeckl and Uzlaner, 2022). Russia's current obsession with "traditional values" appears to be a continuation of a long-standing Russian traditionalism and, as such, is a homegrown phenomenon. Although the concept may have some religious roots, its use in contemporary Russia has effectively stripped it of any authentic religious meaning and significance, turning it into a blunt tool wielded by the Russian state.

The term "traditional values" has been adopted by the Kremlin from the Russian Orthodox Church, mirroring its well-known concept of "spiritual and moral values." Patriarch Kirill began incorporating the notion of "traditional values" into his speeches and writings as early as 2006-2007 (see Kirill, 2011). Initially developed as a derivative of "tradition," it was subsequently adapted for public use by a think tank organized at the behest of *Vsemirnyj russkij narodnyj sobor* [World Russian People's Council], an international public organization and social forum founded in 1993 (Chapnin, 2021, see also VRNS, 2010). Alexander Agadjanian notes that "tradition" in all its combinations and variations became a central concept in the Russian Orthodox Church's written and oral statements in the 2000s, constantly reiterated and expanded since then (Agadjanian, 2017, 39-42). The Orthodox understanding combines tradition in its general connotation with ecclesiastical canonical *predanie* (traditional legend, passed from generation to generation), signifying "the inherited sum of texts, ideas, norms and customs." Given that, in the broader and more "secular" sense, "tradition" is primarily associated with morality, it is not surprising that this particular use "has become the focus of the church's presence in public debate" (Agadjanian, 2017, 41). While the Russian Orthodox Church had virtually no engagement in public discourse during communism and still very limited participation during the early post-Soviet period, it now appears to be more involved, and not only through the World Russian People's Council but also via media and direct contribution to public affairs. Some commentators even suggest that Patriarch Kirill "seems to have personal commitment to the elaboration of a theological concept of the nature of morality" (Stepanova, 2023, 100). I am somewhat doubtful that this judgement presents the situation correctly. The church's leading role in moral matters may be more appearance than reality. The peculiar nature of the current alignment between the state and the church lies in the fact that the Russian Orthodox Church, with its consent, is entirely subservient to the state's interests. Its autonomy is limited to formal matters related to the organization of church affairs, which have no significant impact on society, its public space, or the functioning of the state itself. In past decades, Putin has personally replaced the church as the primary symbol of Orthodox moral values, incorporating secular traditionalism into his domestic and foreign political agendas. It is merely that with this religious rhetoric, Putin evokes the long tradition of a "great historic Russia" he seeks to advance. In reality, however, the spiritual and moral values glorified by the regime are essentially detached from religion. In this regard, Cyril Hovorun rightly points out that the current invocation of "traditional values" in Russia is based on a completely secular view (Hovorun, 2023). The instrumentalization of religion, with the consent of the Russian Orthodox Church, is a crucial aspect of the contemporary Russian traditionalism that Putin's regime openly exploits to advance its aggressive Russophilic, anti-Western, anti-liberal agenda.

In January 2023, Putin issued a decree amending the "Basics of the State Culture Policy," a foundational document with the status of law (Putin, 2023). This decree builds upon an earlier decree from November 2022, which outlines the goals, tasks, and instruments for the state's protection of "traditional spiritual and moral values" (Putin, 2022b, clause 4). Both decrees characterize traditional values as "the foundation of Russian society" and assert the "cultural sovereignty" of Russia, grounding it in these values.[12] The defense of traditional values is deemed a crucial element of the state's National Security Strategy, necessitating "urgent measures" to counter "the imposition of an [imported] system of ideas and values alien to the Russian people and destructive for Russian society" (Putin, 2022b, clause 12, 13; see also Putin,

2023, clause 4). It is evident that this description targets the "destructive ideology" of the liberal West. The decrees explicitly identify the source of the threat to traditional values and those "engaged in activities aimed at undermining the cultural sovereignty of the Russian Federation," pointing to "the actions of the United States of America and other unfriendly foreign states" as primary offenders (Putin, 2022b, clause 13; Putin, 2023, clause 4). Therefore, it is unsurprising that Russian propaganda, aligning closely with these decrees, frames the war in Ukraine as a struggle to protect "traditional spiritual and moral values" from perceived infringements by the "decadent and liberal" West.

Some Western religious conservatives appear to sympathize with Russia's dedication to safeguard traditional (spiritual) values, aiming to preserve Orthodox civilization from the perceived negative impacts of Westernization and secularization. Even those who remain skeptical of Russian propaganda, invoking cultural-spiritual justifications for the war in Ukraine, argue that, overall, the war holds significant religious meaning. They contend that in championing Christian ideas and spirituality, "Russian culture is closer to the truth than is the West's all too rigorous political atheism" (Dal Santo 2023, 5). To be sure, not all religious conservatives in the West are quick to embrace this perspective. Hovorun, an advocate of religious conservative values, rightly criticizes this view as "naïve and superficial." He observes that while Russian culture is indeed "imbued with Christian ideas," it often "distorts these ideas by advocating various forms of exclusivism, including anti-Semitism and, most recently, anti-Ukrainism" (Hovorun, 2023). He also highlights the instrumentalization of religion and religious-based "traditional values" in Putin's Russia, emphasizing the severe consequences that this manipulation brings—ultimately leading to the erosion of the true spirituality associated with religion and the destruction of the values themselves. Hovorun's observation about Putin's weaponizing of "traditional values" is undoubtedly correct, but I have serious concerns with the conclusion he draws from his discussion, openly arguing against abandoning the values Russia cherishes as "traditional" and essentially supporting them as true ideals worth pursuing.[13] This conclusion signals a serious misunderstanding of the concept of "traditional values" and its function in the contemporary Russian context. Although unable to delve into this issue in depth, I will briefly discuss how the concept is framed in the current setting and highlight problems associated with its usage.

Putin and his allies actively promote traditional values as the core of Russian civic identity, portraying the latter as deeply historical. It is not simply rooted in history; rather, the millennia-long history of Russia serves as its defining characteristic. This explains Russia's current fixation on history and its forceful instrumentalization. The underlying concept, invented and exploited by Putin's regime, is that the formation of national identity is owed to the collective experiences gained by the people of Russia from their shared history traced back to archaic times. Their collective historical past is said to give them a sense of identity. Approached from this perspective, events in Russian history, ranging from the victory of the Russian forces over the Tatars of the Mongol Golden Horde at the Battle of Kulikovo (1380) to the foundation of the newly independent Russian state following the disintegration of the Soviet Union (1991), are critical components shaping a specific Russian identity defined by common historical heritage. This identity is not variable from person to person; it is a single, homogeneous identity that allegedly defines all the people of Russia, with "Russianness" as their unifying mark and most fundamental identification. Ideas such as Russians' own way of life, "sovereign culture," and a unique value system, viewed as key characteristics of "Russia as civilization" (or the notorious "Russian world"), are all grounded in this flawed understanding of national identity. It is worth recalling that "national identity" as a social phenomenon is a relatively recent manifestation. It emerges clearly only in the eighteenth–nineteenth centuries and placing it or even detecting its sources in much earlier periods is problematic from sociological and historical perspectives. Additionally, the interpretation of history that accompanies this conception of identity also faces serious objections. Seeing history as providing lessons (or in a more assertive form, normative guidance) suggests the presence of unchanging aspects of human nature or, at the very least, it implies that human nature has some "transhistorical elements" able to offer a basis for transferring past experiences along with their associated norms and judgments into the present. Both assumptions have proven to be unsubstantiated. Furthermore, the distant past subsists only through the work of historians; it inherently represents a reality that ceased to be and no longer exists. Searching for identity in history, endeavoring to find it in past historical events, is the attempt to construct a national mythology essentially out of thin air. Yet, despite its inadequacy, this conception of identity prevails and gives rise to the no less problematic idea of traditional values.

As early as in 2009-2010, Patriarch Kirill declared that the roots of Russian civilization can be traced back to the Baptism of Rus (c. 988), thus moving the question of outlining the most fundamental, "truly Russian" values to the forefront. In response to this challenge, in 2011 the World Russian People's Council presented an extensive list of seventeen traditional values, encompassing faith in God, justice, peace, freedom, unity, morality, dignity, patriotism, solidarity, family, and so on (ROC, 2011).[14] These values are said to be markers of Russian national identity, distinguishing the people of Russia from their counterparts elsewhere. Undoubtedly, this perspective is deeply essentialist. It not only regards core values as essential characteristics of national and cultural identity, but more importantly, it portrays these values as timeless and unalterable categories, firmly established and beyond criticism. Presented as a set of fixed traits, they lack dynamism and vital power. Certain values, particularly those linked to concepts like justice, truth, love, do have the capacity to endure across time and cultures, maintaining their significance regardless of when, where, or by whom they are considered. But even they evolve in terms of their content and scope. Likewise, social and moral values are never static and change with time. Similarly, the meaning of concepts introducing values constantly transforms, reflecting social changes (including development or degeneration, as the case may be). Moreover, any general discussion of "values" is futile and dangerous because it is hollow until these "values" are specified as *principles* by which to identify and distinguish (in)justice, responsible autonomy from egoism, "harm" from "benefit," responsible from reprehensible exercises of "freedom," etc. Russian "traditional values" are merely abstract ideas devoid of real substance and vital content and presented as frozen in time, "concept-mummies," to use Nietzsche's terminology.

Another problem arises from Russia's openly anti-liberal stance in promoting traditional values. The position fostered by the Putin regime aligns with one form of communitarianism, that which emphasizes the importance of community and shared values in shaping individual identity. This stands in direct contrast to liberalism, which, in addition to stressing the universality of values, places greater emphasis on individual rights, autonomy, and personal freedom. Communitarian values prioritize communality and emphasize a sense of belonging. Their core is a recognition of collective beliefs and ideals, the social importance of the family unit, as well as advocacy of *common* moral values. While communitarianism is often praised for civic life, its application to matters of ethics or questions of cultural identity, especially if employed in a fundamentalist way—an attitude widespread in Russia—can lead to dangerous consequences. A central theme in some forms of communitarianism, certainly in Alasdair MacIntyre's version, is that there simply are no moral standards or principles "higher" than those which happen to be shared within some community, for some period of history (MacIntyre, 1985, 246-52). This is why communitarianism allows for exploitation by those who argue that society is more significant or fundamental than its individual members, thus promoting fascist type holism, whether right- or left-wing. Radicalizing communitarian ideas, Russian promoters of traditional values view individual identity as shaped by the community within a shared culture, determining people's beliefs, ideals, and values. Core values and moral precepts are seen as being passed down from generation to generation, influencing their way of life and moral preferences. Thus, what is considered good and moral by a German or a Croat may not be so for a Russian. Russian values are deemed fundamentally different from others, impacting not only the Russian peoples' identity but also shaping how they feel, think, and behave. This impact extends beyond the cultural and social realms, affecting the political regime, as well as specific understandings of individual rights, freedoms, and dignity. An embodiment of communitarianism, translated into the context of Russia as the idea of the "Russian way," this approach is readily adopted and advanced by Putin and his regime, as it allows for an active and largely unrestricted role for the government in fostering social cohesion, promoting the common good, and maintaining order, even if at the expense of suppressing individual rights and freedoms. In the name of retaining common unity, this approach undermines individuality with its uniqueness, sense of self, and individual responsibility. Furthermore, in striving for uniformity and internal homogeneity, it devalues and suppresses cultural and personal diversity.

For decades, Putin has sought to present Russia as the champion of Christian values, showcasing the Russian tradition as a guardian of true values necessary for human survival and progress. However, the values now promoted in Russia are far from universal; instead, they are conceptually limited and culturally restricted. Unlike genuine values associated with modernity and future progress that embrace free enterprise, boundless initiative, and dynamic mobility in a variety of forms and appearances,[15] the values Putin's Russia so vigorously protects promote submissive self-restriction, preservation of traditional practices and social roles, glorification of the past, and opposition to the future—a good way to keep the populace passive and obedient, the goal the regime pursues within the country. Putin's ambitions for Russia do not include the creation of anything new, nor does he aim to remake it in any productive way. Instead, his only program is returning to the "strong and glorious" Russia which is "destined for historical greatness."

Russian rulers' aims regarding their people have undergone little modification since the Enlightenment period; paradoxically, the primary premise—the spiritual and moral exceptionality of the Russian tradition—has largely remained the same at its core. Changes mainly concerned the means and ways of population control, becoming more sophisticated and skillful. In this process, both the history of Russia itself and the question of the cultural and national identity of its people were subjected to instrumentalization.

Appeals to spirituality and traditionalism are manipulated to bolster authoritarian agendas, quelling dissent and curtailing individual freedoms.

A strong emphasis on traditionalism fosters a sense of Russian supremacy, marginalizing those diverging from dominant cultural norms and instrumentalized religious beliefs. It promotes ethno-nationalism, fueling xenophobia and anti-Western sentiments. The current Russian regime's fixation on tradition impedes social and political reforms, resisting necessary societal changes. This makes its agenda not just anti-modern and anti-progressive but fundamentally counter-Enlightenment and reactionary.[16]

In addition to adopting ethno-nationalist and anti-rationalist attitudes and displaying an aggressive anti-Western stance, the state under Putin's rule demonstrates hostility toward international cultural and educational institutions, animosity toward intellectuals who persist in exercising independence and critical thinking, and neglect for genuine knowledge, science, and the arts. By promoting Russian traditionalism and values associated with this orientation, the regime openly opposes a range of ideas and practices that have been associated with the European Enlightenment since the seventeenth and eighteenth centuries, substantially contributing to the making of the modern world. Resistance to those ideas and an openly antagonistic outlook characterize the contemporary Russian cultural, political, and social landscape, which is saturated with resentment and hostility toward any form of diversity.

Conclusion

The origin of a deficiency in the understanding and implementation of universal liberal concepts, which echoes through Russian history up to today, can be traced back to missed opportunities for genuine enlightenment and to Russian traditionalism. The latter was fully molded and reinforced as a protective measure against the spread of European Enlightenment ideals. As a set of cultural, social, and political values deeply rooted in Russia's history and heritage, it is archaic by its very nature. Emphasizing the supremacy of Russian Orthodox Christianity, a hierarchical social order, autocratic governance, and a strong sense of unique national identity, Russian traditionalism is characterized by a reverence for historical customs, old cultural practices, and a belief in the continuity of communitarian traditional values across generations. Remaining unchallenged, it is now manifest in the openly hostile counter-Enlightenment stance of the current regime, signaling its fundamental disposition against progressive development.

The Putin regime's rejection of civilizational progress and humanity's shared future leads to social regression. This includes the disdain for "globalist" institutions, attempts to overthrow them, and the use of populist rhetoric such as "the will of the people" to undermine established laws and principles. These actions effectively legitimize lawlessness and aggression. The counter-Enlightenment attitude is more than merely a driving force behind current political decisions; it permeates virtually all aspects of daily life in contemporary Russia, influencing cultural, political, and social preferences and shaping other aspects of social reality.

By grounding its social and political policies in Russian traditionalism, Putin's regime throws the country back centuries, destroying established cultural and social ties with the world and erasing even the modest liberal and democratic accomplishments of the post-Soviet era. Russia is haunted by its past, which Putin's propaganda masterfully exploits, manipulating and distorting it to influence the collective consciousness of the people. Unfortunately, a significant number of Russians willingly adopt this narrative, holding onto a largely fictional and idealized rendition of their history as a retreat from present challenges. This tendency extends beyond the realm of consciousness, seeping into economics, social life, politics, international relations, and nearly every facet of society. Rather than prioritizing industrial development, social progress, and investments into its future, Russia remains fixated on its historical grandeur, celebrating its past achievements. This trend is not a recent phenomenon triggered solely by Putin's attempts to reverse the course of history. It has been gradually building for centuries, and we are only now coming to the full realization of its damaging and dangerous impact.

It is challenging to predict how the future will unfold. Nevertheless, it seems evident that for Russia to carve out a meaningful future, it must recognize the damaging effects of traditionalism on its history and destructive consequences for its culture. This entails a commitment to profound criticism and the dismantling of traditionalism as an ideological orientation once and for all. Russia stands in need of a new Enlightenment that recovers the value of universalism, reintroducing it into political, social, and intellectual discourses, and broadens the horizons of progress beyond the confines limited in scope by "cultural specificity," exceptionalism, and supremacy. Achieving this transformative vision demands a dedicated effort in cultivating a renewed Enlightenment ethos—a task attainable only through critical self-reflection and a radical shift in values from the narrowly understood "traditional" to the universal, toward openness, respect for rights, freedom, and the dignity of every individual.

Notes

1 Some commentators trace the beginning of the Enlightenment back to Descartes's *The Meditations* (1641 in Latin/1647 in French), pointing to the historical significance of the work and its crucial role in the "overthrowing" of authorities.

2 Some Russian scholars propose the existence of a "late Enlightenment" period in Russia's history, arguing that it distinguishes itself significantly from Europe. They contend that, unlike Europe, where the Enlightenment era paved the way for a new century and, along with it, a new intellectual direction—the Romanticism of the nineteenth century—in Russia, the Enlightenment era persisted, with some interruptions by periods of conservatism and reaction, beyond the eighteenth century. They suggest that the first three-quarters of the subsequent nineteenth century can be considered as its continuation. While well-intentioned as a representation of the "learned nineteenth century" in Russia, this position appears to lack strong substantiation.

3 The full title of the document is *Instruction of Her Imperial Majesty Catherine the Second for the Commission Charged with Preparing a Project of a New Code of Laws* (Catherine II, 1907).

4 Only the October Revolution of 1917 put an end to the unchallenged authority of the Orthodox Church, and the new Soviet government promptly declared the separation of church and state. It also nationalized all church-held lands. While the move toward separation aligned with Enlightenment ideals, it was enacted in the most barbaric way, leading to devastating consequences. The discussion of these consequences, however, is beyond the scope of this chapter.

5 For details on Platon (Levshin) consult https://dbpedia.org/page/Platon_Levshin.

6 Emphasizing the cultural significance of Petrine reforms, the historian James Cracraft argues that Peter I enacted a "cultural revolution" in Russia that transformed art, architecture, literature, and had the most significant impact on education and science (Cracraft, 2004, 193–254).

7 While Tatishchev actively promoted the value of education and learning and strongly argued against the belief that extensive learning leads to a rejection of religious faith, his advocacy of the enlightenment was rather moderate. Embracing the popular ideas of natural right, natural morals, and natural religion, he emphasized the primacy of religious spirituality over other virtues and defended the balance of spiritual forces. In his political views, he leaned toward a conservative position, asserting that autocracy had been proven to be the perfect form of government for Russia (Hamburg, 2021, 32). This confidence in the importance of autocracy in the development of the Russian state was also shared by Lomonosov, who reached this conclusion through his study of early Russian history, including the early Slavic tribes

and the foundation of the Kievan Rus' (see Lomonosov, 1766). As the Russian literature scholar Marcus Levitt demonstrates, in his poetry, Lomonosov also aimed to reconcile science and religious belief (Levitt, 2009).

8   The term "nationality" is used here in the meaning of "*narodnost*".
9   About the emergence of the concept of "national idea" and its use in eighteenth-century Russia, see Volodina, 2001.
10 Yuri Samarin, for instance, defending Russia's acquisition of the Baltic provinces at the beginning of the eighteenth century as a "historically necessary event," argued that the region should be fully integrated into the administrative structures of the Russian Empire. Although he rejected the complete Russification of these provinces as a general policy, he believed that its weaker model, namely an administrative and legal uniformity, was necessary.
11 See also Alexander Dugin's most recent interview (Stawiarski, 2024). It is noteworthy in this context that Dugin stands as perhaps the most representative proponent of traditionalism in contemporary Russia, with highly radical views. On his Telegram channel, he recently presented his "project" of the "ideal Russia of the future," advocating for the reestablishment of an old (autocratic) order and "traditional" family values. Notably, he strangely associates the latter with a rejection of urbanization, insisting on resettlement in villages: "Cities will be immediately resettled, on the land, strong Orthodox families with many children will form... For adultery—the stake. For theft—hanging. For blasphemy against the Tsar— eternal hard labor" (December 16, 2023; for more details see Glukhovsky, 2023).
12 "The Russian Federation considers traditional values as the foundation of Russian society, enabling the protection and strengthening of Russia's sovereignty" (Putin, 2022b, clause 7).
13 "It is not that the values that he pretends to stand for should be abandoned because Putin has weaponized them. However, everyone who cherishes these values should disassociate him or herself from Putinism" (Hovorun, 2023).
14 Interestingly, the state decree signed in November 2022, also provides a list of seventeen traditional values that purportedly define Russian culture. The values on the state list substantially overlap with those introduced by the Church. The differences are largely terminological, and "faith in God" is removed from the state list (see Putin, 2022b, clause 5). The full list of seventeen traditional values is available at https://www.youtube.com/watch?v=JAbQFSC7UP0
15 Far from holding an idealistic view of modernity and the values it fosters, I do realize that in the contemporary world many forms of this dynamic versatility become criminal, exploitative, or environmentally irresponsible. This makes their critical assessment within an open public discourse crucial.
16 While the question of the reactionary nature of the current Russian political regime deserves special discussion, which is beyond the scope of

this chapter, it is probably worth mentioning specific instances of Putin's reactionary government. These can be traced back to his first term in office, marked by the reversal of certain democratic reforms and the increasing etatization of industries and businesses, quickly moving them under state control—a process that opened the path toward even stronger financial and economic corruption (Shlapentokh, 2001; Hashim, 2005). However, perhaps some of the most indicative cases of Putin's openly anti-democratic actions are his prompt restructuring of the government to reinforce centralization that he undertook in the beginning of the 2010s. He instituted a new level of regional government authorities to constrain political activities at local and sub-regional levels. This included replacing elections of political officials with their appointment by Putin personally or via his own channels. For further discussion of these and other reactionary measures of Putin's regime, see, e.g., Rutland, 2008; Pastukhov, 2021; Snegovaya, 2023. I am grateful to Kenneth Westphal, who directed me to these examples and recommended further literature on the subject.

References

Agadjanian, Alexander. 2017. "Tradition, Morality and Community: Elaborating Orthodox Identity in Putin's Russia." *Religion, State & Society* 45 (1): 39–60.

Aksakov, Ivan. 1886. *Sochineniia* [*Works*]. Vol. 3. Moscow: Tipografiia M. G. Volcaninova.

Asoyan, Yulii A. 2009. "'Sumerki Prosveshcheniia': Kak v Rossii Prosveshchenie bylo pereimenovano v kul'turu." [Twilight of the Enlightenment: How Enlightenment Was Renamed Culture in Russia] *Vestnik RGGU. Seriia Filosofiia. Sotsiologiia. Iskusstvovedenie.* No. 15, 11-24.

Barran, Thomas Paul. 2002. *Russia Reads Rousseau, 1762–1825.* Evanston, IL: Northwestern University Press.

Berelowitch, Wladimir. 2015. "Francophonie in Russia under Catherine II: General Reflections and Individual Cases." *Russian Review* 74 (1): 41–56.

Bil'basov, Vasily A., and Antony Lentin. 1972. *A Philosopher at the Court of Catherine the Great: Didro v Peterburge.* Cambridge, UK: Oriental Research Partners.

Catherine II. 1878. "Pis'ma Imperatritsy Ekateriny II baronu Mel'khioru Grimmu (gody s 1774 po 1796)." Edited by Yakov Grot. In *Sbornik Imperatorskago Russkago Istoricheskago Obshchestva.* XXIII (2): 1–695. St. Petersburg.

Catherine II. 1907. *Nakaz Imperatritsy Ekateriny II, dannyi kommissii o sochinenii proekta novago ulozheniia.* St. Petersburg: Imperatorskaia Akademiia Nauk. (An English translation appears in W.F. Reddaway, *Documents of Catherine the Great.* Cambridge: Cambridge University Press, 1933.)

Chaadayev, Peter. 1969. "The Philosophical Letters Addressed to a Lady. Letter I." In *The Major Works of Peter Chaadyaev*. Translation and Commentary by Raymond T. McNally, 23–51. Notre Dame: University of Notre Dame Press.

Chapnin, Sergey. 2021. "K bol'shinstvu tserkovnyh ierarhov otnosiatsia uzhe kak k inoplanetianam." [Most Church Hierarchs are Now Regarded as Aliens.] *Znak*. https://www.znak.com/2021-09-07/zadavlennye_prihody_i_svyachenniki_oligarhi_intervyu_o_degradacii_rpc?fbclid=iwar2exnuq3f0g4nmey6yy9pzvnzd2vbg8_thdojjpv4rg3s76wl2upm-7u_a

Cracraft, James. 1971. *The Church Reform of Peter the Great*. Stanford: Stanford University Press.

Cracraft, James. 2004. *The Petrine Revolution in Russian Culture*. Cambridge, MA: Harvard University Press.

Dal Santo, Matthew. 2023. "Theopolitics of Ukraine." *First Things*, Issue 335: August/September 2023, 1-5. https://www.firstthings.com/article/2023/08/theopolitics-of-ukraine

de Madariaga, Isabel. 1981. *Russia in the Age of Catherine the Great*. New Haven, CT: Yale University Press.

Diderot, Denis. 1992. *Observations sur le Nakaz*. In *Diderot: Political Writings*, edited by J.H. Mason and R. Wokler, 77-164. Cambridge: Cambridge University Press.

Etkind, Alexander. 2023. *Russia Against Modernity*. Cambridge: Polity Press.

Faulconbridge, Guy. 2023. "Putin Casts War as a Battle for Russia's Survival." *Reuters*, February 26, 2023. https://www.reuters.com/world/europe/putin-russia-must-take-into-account-nato-nuclear-capability-state-tv-2023-02-26

Glukhovsky, Igor'. 2023. "Filosof Aleksandr Dugin imeet svoi retsept 'spaseniya Rossii'" [Philosopher Alexander Dugin has His Own Recipe for "Saving Russia."] *Argumenty Nedeli* [Mnenie], 31 October 2023. https://argumenti.ru/opinion/2023/10/864410

Grechanaia, Elena P. 2010. *Kogda Rossiia govorila po-frantsuzski: Russkaia literatura na frantsuzskom iazuke (18 – pervaia polovina 19 veka)*. [*When Russia Spoke French: Russian Literature in the French Language (18th – First Half of the 19th Century)*] Moscow: IMLI RAN.

Hamburg, Gary M. 2016. *Russia's Path toward Enlightenment. Faith, Politics, and Reason, 1500–1801*. New Haven, CT: Yale University Press.

Hamburg, Gary M. 2021. "Politics and Enlightenment in Russia." In *The Palgrave Handbook of Russian Thought*, edited by Marina F. Bykova, Michael N. Forster, and Lina Steiner, 25–50. Cham: Palgrave Macmillan.

Hashim, Salehhudin M. 2005. "Putin's Etatization Project and Limits to Democratic Reforms in Russia." *Communist and Post-Communist Studies* 38 (1): 25–48.

Hildermeier, Manfred. 2004. "Traditionen der Aufklärung in der russischen Geschichte." In *Interdisziplinarität und Internationalität. Wege und Formen der Rezeption der französischen und der britischen Aufklärung in Deutschland und Russland in 18. Jahrhundert*, edited by Heinz Duchhardt and Claus Scharf, 1–15. Mainz: von Zabern.

Hovorun, Cyril. 2023. "'Traditional Values' Are Russia's Geopolitical Weapons." *Public Discourse. The Journal of the Witherspoon Institute*. July 26, 2023. https://www.thepublicdiscourse.com/2023/07/90088

Israel, Jonathan. 2006. "Enlightenment: Which Enlightenment?" *Journal of the History of Ideas* 67 (3): 523–45.

Karamzin, Nikolai M. 1969. *Karamzin's Memoir on Ancient and Modern Russia. A Translation and Analysis*, ed. Richard Pipes. New York: Atheneum.

Kirill. 2011. His Holiness Kirill, Patriarch of Moscow and All Russia. *Freedom and Responsibility: A Search for Harmony—Human Rights and Personal Dignity*. London: Darton, Longman & Todd; Moscow: Publishing House of the Moscow Patriarchate.

Leatherbarrow William J., and Derek C. Offord (eds). 1987. *A Documentary History of Russian Thought: From the Enlightenment to Marxism*. Ann Arbor, MI: Ardis.

Levitt, Marcus C. 2009. "The Theological Context of Lomonosov's 'Evening' and 'Morning' Meditations on God's Majesty." In *Early Modern Russian Letters: Texts and Contexts Selected Essays*, edited by Marcus C. Levitt, 305–19. Boston, MA: Academic Studies Press.

Levshin Petr G. [Platon, Metropolitan of Moscow]. 2012. *The Orthodox Doctrine of the Apostolic Eastern Church; Or, a Compendium of Christian Theology*. Trans. G. Potessaro. Ulan-Ude: Ulan Press.

Lomonosov, Mikhail V. 1766. *Drevniaia rossiiskaia istoriia*. [*The Ancient Russian History*] St. Petersburg: Akademiia Nauk.

MacIntyre, Alasdair. 1985. *After Virtue: A Study in Moral Theory*. 2nd ed. London: Duckworth.

Pastukhov, Vladimir. 2021. "Deep Mind State. Bor'ba s Inakomysliem kak Uvertiura k Massovomu Terroru." MBX Media, June 9. https://mbk-news.appspot.com/sences/deep-mind-state-borba

Plokhy, Serhii. 2021. *The Frontline. Essays on Ukraine's Past and Present*. Cambridge, MA: Harvard Ukrainian Research Institute. The President and Fellows of Harvard College. https://books.huri.harvard.edu/books/chapters/122

Putin, Vladimir. 2022a. Speech at a Ceremony at the Kremlin on the Occasion of Annexation of Four Ukrainian Regions Partly Occupied by Russian Forces, September 30, 2022. Extracts from Putin's speech, trans. Reuters. https://www.reuters.com/world/extracts-putins-speech-annexation-ceremony-2022-09-30

Putin, Vladimir. 2022b. Ukaz Presidenta RF ot 9.11.2022 g. № 809: "Ob utverzhdenii osnov gosudarstvennoi politiki po sokhraneniiu i ukrepleniiu traditsionnykh rossiiskikh dukhovno-nravstvennykh tsennostey." https://base.garant.ru/405679061

Putin, Vladimir. 2023. Ukaz Presidenta RF ot 25.01.2023 g. № 35: "O vnesenii izmenenii v osnovy gosudarstvennoy kul'turnoy politiki, utverzhdennye Ukazom Prezidenta Rossiiskoy Federatsii ot 24 dekabria 2014 g." № 808. In *Prezident Rossii [Site of the President of Russia]* – pravo.gov.ru. http://www.kremlin.ru/acts/bank/48855

ROC. 2011. "Bazisnye tsennosti – osnova obshchenatsional'noy identichnosti." In *Russkaia Pravoslavnaia Tserkov'. Ofitsial'ny sait Moscovskogo Patriarkhata.* http://www.patriarchia.ru/db/text/1496038.html

Rutland, Peter. 2008. "Democracy in Russia, a Tocquevillian Perspective." In *Conversations with Tocqueville. The Global Democratic Revolution in the 21st Century*, 199–225, edited by Aurelian Craiutu and Sheldon Gellar. New York: Rowman & Littlefield.

Samarin, Yuri F. 1889. *Sochineniia*. [*Works*]. Vol. 7. Moscow: Mamontov.

Schippan, Michael. 2012. *Die Aufklärung in Russland im 18. Jahrhundert.* Wiesbaden: Harrassowitz Verlag.

Shlapentokh, Vladimir. 2001. "Putin's First Year in Office: The New Regime's Uniqueness in Russian History." *Communist and Post-Communist Studies* 34 (4): 371–99.

Snegovaya, Maria. 2023. "Why Russia's Democracy Never Began." *Journal of Democracy* 34 (3): 105–118.

Solzhenitsyn, Aleksandr. 1995. *"The Russian Question" at the End of the Twentieth Century*, translated and annotated by Yermolai Solzhenitsyn. New York: Farrar, Straus and Giroux, Inc. [First published in Russia in *Novy Mir*, 1994 (7).]

Stawiarski, Edward. 2024. "Alexander Dugin: 'I see no reason why we should not use nuclear weapons.'" *The Spectator*, January 6, 2024. https://www.spectator.co.uk/article/i-see-no-reason-why-we-should-not-use-nuclear-weapons-an-interview-with-russian-philosopher-aleksandr-dugin

Stepanova, Elena A. 2023. "'Everything Good Against Everything Bad': Traditional Values in the Search for New Russian National Idea." *Zeitschrift für Religion, Gesellschaft und Politik* 7: 97–118.

Stoeckl, Kristina, and Dmitry Uzlaner. 2022. *The Moralist International: Russia in the Global Culture Wars*. New York: Fordham University Press.

Sugai, Larisa. 2007. "Terminy 'Kul'tura,' 'tsivilizatsiia,' i 'prosvezhchenie' v Rossii 19 – nachala 20 vv." ["The Terms 'Culture,' 'Civilization,' and 'Enlightenment' in Russia in the 19th – Early 20th Centuries"]. In *Trudy GASKH. Vypusk II: Mir Kul'tury*, 39–53. Moscow: GASKH.

Tourneux, Maurice. 1899. *Diderot et Catherine II*. Paris: Calmann Lévy University Press.

Volodina, Tatyana. 2001. "At the Sources of the 'National Idea' in Russian Historiography." *Social Sciences* 32 (3). https://ciaotest.cc.columbia.edu/olj/socsci/socsci_01vot01.html

VRNS 2010 – Vsemirnyj russkij narodnyj sobor (VRNS). Spravka. In *RIA Novosti*, May 25, 2010. https://ria.ru/20100525/238031233.html

Walicki, Andrzej. 2005. *Zarys mysli rosyjskiej od oswiecenia do renesansu religijno-filozoficznego*. Kraków: Wydawnictwo Uniwersytetu Jagiellonskiego.

Yanovsky Nikolai M. 1804. *Novy slovotolkovatel', raspolozhenny po alfavity*. Part II: From K to N. St. Petersburg: Tipografiia Akademii Nauk.

2

Between Nationalism and Universalism: The Imperial Imagination from Vladimir Solovyov to Alexandre Kojève

Boris Groys

Today, when one speaks of Russian imperialism, one often has in mind the Soviet period of Russian history. At first glance, this connection seems misleading. Indeed, the Civil War between Whites and Reds was understood by its protagonists as a war between Russian patriots and anti-patriotic communist internationalists, a war in which the Russian patriots had lost and the internationalists won. One finds this diagnosis of the Civil War and its results in the memoirs of Russian emigrants from the Right (Piotr Krasnov, Vladimir Purishkevich) and the Left (Boris Savinkov). These authors describe the Bolsheviks as an anti-national, anti-Russian force and the White armies as defenders of Russia and its traditions. However, the inscription of Bolshevism into the imperial Russian political tradition seems to be quite legitimate in historical context. This legitimacy becomes especially obvious today as post-Socialist Russia turns back to its pre-revolutionary intellectual and political traditions.

Russian nationalism is one of these traditions, though it was never dominant in the times of the Russian Empire. The imperial bureaucracy did not embrace Russian nationalism because it ruled non-Russian as well as Russian territories. The legitimacy of Russian imperial rule was based on its sovereign control of the Empire's territory. The Tsar was considered as the God-given sovereign of the country. Thus, the Russian empire did not manifest any specific national interest or spirit, even that of the Russians. It required loyalty from its population but understood itself as loyal only to God. The state was defined by its territory, not the will of its population.

The modern age begins, as we know, by substituting the God-given sovereignty of the King with the sovereignty of the people—as the American and French revolutions proclaimed. But how do we define the sovereign people? How do we differentiate between members of the sovereign people and all other men and women? This problem was originally solved through the notion of "nation." The nation is defined by "nativity," by the genealogy of its new-born members. One belongs to a nation when one's parents (or at least one parent) belonged to it; or, in some cases, when one was born on the territory of a certain national state. Thus, the notion of nation inscribed humanity into the order of nature. The rights of a particular individual were understood as "natural rights" given to him or her by birth. Ideally, every nation would have its own state in which it could act as a sovereign. The right of all nations to self-determination became a logical consequence of this new mode of division of humanity into nations.

The right of national self-determination came into conflict with the political map of the late nineteenth century, which was defined by military conquests and colonization. Transnational, imperial states based their power on military control and not necessarily the will of the nations. In the nineteenth century, the traditional imperial states were Austria, Russia, and Turkey. However, European nation-states such as England and France created their own empires by means of overseas military occupation of non-European territories. The contradiction between imperial and national sovereignty produced numerous wars, revolutions, and revolts throughout the nineteenth and twentieth centuries. One can safely say that progressive public opinion sided with movements inspired by the ideal of national self-determination, whereas the conservative, even reactionary, sectors of society insisted on the sovereignty of the state.

In the twentieth century, this conservative position was eloquently presented by Carl Schmitt in his famous treatise *Political Theology* (1922). Schmitt compares the lawgiver with God and the moments of exception in the application of the law with miracles (Schmitt, 2005, 36). Miracles are needed when the regular, lawful movement of social and political life becomes interrupted. As Creator of the world, God subjugated the primordial Chaos and installed cosmic order. Analogously, the state subjugates the eruptions of public chaos and imposes political order. This is why, for Schmitt, the theory of the state is political theology: the state politicizes the relationship between God and chaos; or, what is the same, between God and nature. Schmitt accepts the fragmentation of the old imperial territories and their distribution among the individual nations as a historical fact that he has no reason to deny. However, according to Schmitt, the nation-state still acts as a sovereign vis-à-vis the nation living on its territory. All the wars between individual national states concern their territories. They end with new peace treaties that either confirm or change their borders. No war should be defined in moral terms as the war between Good and Evil:

> Such a war is necessarily unusually intense and inhuman because, by transcending the limits of the political framework, it simultaneously degrades the enemy into moral and other categories and is forced to make of him [the enemy] a monster that must not only be defeated but also utterly destroyed. In other words, he is an enemy who no longer must be compelled to retreat into his borders only.
>
> (Schmitt, 1996, 36)

Schmitt's political theology offers a good starting point to analyze the specific form that Russian political theology took at the end of the nineteenth and beginning of the twentieth century.

For Schmitt, the state manifests its sovereign character only in the "state of exception," when the normal functioning of a society becomes interrupted by economic turmoil, revolution, or civil war. In "normal" situations nations follow their regular way of life—their traditions, culture, social conventions, and established patterns of behavior. In other words, under normal conditions a nation does not need the sovereign control of the state: its unity is guaranteed by a shared national identity. From this perspective, the Russian nation presents itself as an exceptional nation or, rather, a nation in a permanent state of exception. Indeed, at least since the reforms of the Peter the Great, the Russian population was deeply divided into the Europeanized or, rather, Westernized upper class and the common population living according to the traditions of the Russian Orthodox Church. In this sense the Russian nation was—and still is—not a "normal" nation because it lacks a common ground, traditions, and way of life. Thus, national self-determination did not appear to be an appropriate means to solve the "Russian question" because such self-determination required the closing of the gap that divided the Russian nation in two incompatible parts.

But who could initiate the unification of the Russian nation? Obviously, only a sovereign state could unite a population that finds itself in a permanent state of deep cultural division. This is why Russian political theories are traditionally concentrated on the structure and role of the state. It is not, however, a "normal" national state of the European type that presupposes pre-existing national cultural homogeneity. Two radically divided and even opposed parts of the population of the Russian Empire could be united only in the name of "universal cultural values" that would be able to transcend all cultural divides and thus potentially unite the whole of mankind. If the

Russian state wants to fulfill its national goal and unite the Russian nation it must be conceived as the Universal State. Of course, the unification of the whole of mankind is necessarily a slow process—but it has to begin somewhere. Such a place must be an empire of a new type, a transitional empire—an empire that gives to every nation its place and, thus, ends the history of conflicts and wars among nations. Such a transitional empire should be able to envelop the whole world and become the Universal State. Unlike traditional empires, the transitional empire bases its legitimacy and sovereignty not on the past but on the future—as the model and core of the future Universal State. But how to define and find the territory that is best suited to be the core of the Universal State?

It cannot be a surprise that for Russian theoreticians of the Universal State this chosen territory was the territory of the Russian Empire. This is the typical trajectory that Russian political imagination followed in the nineteenth and twentieth centuries—the centuries of nationalisms, from the project of the Universal State as a means of overcoming the inner divide of the Russian nation to the restoration of the Russian Empire as a temporary territory of the future World State. Thus, under the specific conditions of the divided Russian nation, the ideological impact of European nationalism has led not to the fragmentation of the territory of the Russian Empire but to its re-interpretation as a transitional empire of a new type that was supposed to become the ultimate Universal State.

At least since the 1820s-1830s, political theology emerges as an important mode of thinking among Russian intellectuals and writers. At that time, it seemed that there existed only two possibilities to unite these two parts of the internally divided Russian nation: through an attempt to educate the masses in the Western way or to convert the upper class to Orthodox Christianity. Accordingly, two camps were formed within the Russian cultural context: Westernizers and Slavophiles. The Westernizers tried to re-educate the Russian masses in the spirit of the Western Enlightenment. Theirs was a progressive, emancipatory movement. But what about the Slavophiles? Their strategy also cannot be called conservative or reactionary because they took the side of the Russian peasantry, which was suppressed by the Western-oriented Russian imperial government and the whole Western educated upper class. And the Slavophiles could not be called nationalists either, because the notion of nation was a Western one. The Slavophiles have, rather, opposed the God-loving Russian people to the atheist nations of the West and the Western educated Russian elites.

In other words, the Slavophiles' ideology confirmed the split dividing the Russian nation: it denied to its Western educated class the right to be called "true Russians." Of course, the same can be said about the

Westernizers: they saw the Russian Orthodox peasantry as a backward, eastern, Asiatic population that had to be re-educated to become a nation in the European sense of the word. At the end of the nineteenth century the conflict between Westernizers and Slavophiles became repetitive and sterile. The total re-education of the Russian population seemed to be as impossible as the conversion of the Russian upper class and intelligentsia to Orthodox Christianity. Thus, the only possibility to unite the Russian nation lay in the cultural and political reconciliation of the East and West. The first project of such unification was the re-unification of the Russian Orthodox Church and Roman Catholic Church, as proposed by Vladimir Solovyov. True sovereignty would belong to the Universal Church that would emerge as a result of this unification. Then, the Russian Empire would function merely as a political tool of the Universal Church. Indeed, in this way the conflict between the Westernizers and the Slavophiles could be resolved, and the unity of the Russian nation achieved. That is the reason why Solovyov had such a powerful influence on Russian culture at the end of the nineteenth and beginning of the twentieth century.

After the October Revolution, the universalist Communist Party supplanted the Universal Christian Church. Russia became the motherland of all the oppressed and exploited people of the world. Here again, the local Russian state was subjected to a universalist institution—the Communist Party—which considered the whole world its territory. The goal of this institution was to create a Universal State of social justice in which the exploited classes of all the nations of the world would unite. Here the politics of emancipation are directed against existing imperial powers—but not for the sake of the self-determination of nations as they emerged in the historical past. The source of sovereignty is sought neither in the past or the traditional rights of the state nor in the self-determination of nations. The source of the sovereignty is, rather, seen in the future: history is understood as a history of the realization of a project—Christian or Communist—that uses the past and the present as means to achieve its goal.

This analogy between the Solovyovian Universal Church and the Communist movement went unrecognized during the Civil War. However, it became apparent to some philosophers, scientists, and intellectuals from the circles of Russian emigration almost immediately after the end of the Civil War. That is especially true for the Eurasian movement that played an important role in cultural life of Russian emigration between two World Wars. This movement was not homogeneous and included authors with very different political attitudes, but for all of them the Eurasian ideology meant a certain re-evaluation of the previous Russian political Utopias. Solovyov wanted to turn the Russian Empire into an instrument for establishing the Universal

Christian empire. The Bolsheviks wanted to use Russia as an instrument to create a universal classless society. The Eurasians, however, reversed the relationship between the goals and the means. For them the goal was the reconstruction of the Russian Empire that was devastated during the Civil War—and they were ready to say "yes" to any ideology that would promise to restore Russian imperial might. This pragmatic, "realistic," or, let's say, "imperialistic" interpretation of Russian universalist Utopianism as a mere tool to reassert imperial glory was inherited by contemporary Russian Neo-Eurasian ideologues. And it is this trajectory from universalist Utopianism to contemporary neo-imperialism that this chapter attempts to reconstruct.

1

In the most explicit and simultaneously eloquent manner, the Russian version of political theology was formulated by Vladimir Solovyov in his *Russia and Universal Church* (1889), which was written in French and published in France to escape Russian censorship. Solovyov opens his text with the following words:

> A hundred years ago France, the vanguard of humanity, set out to inaugurate a new era with the proclamation of the Rights of Man. Christianity had indeed many centuries earlier conferred upon men not only the right but the power to become the sons of God—εδωκεν αυτοις εξουσιαν τεκνα Θεου γενεσθαι (John, 1:12). But the new proclamation made by France was far from superfluous, for this supreme power of mankind was almost entirely ignored in the social life of Christendom.
>
> (Solovyov, 1998, 7)

Thus, from the beginning, Solovyov situates his text in the progressive, emancipatory tradition that was inaugurated by the French Revolution. However, immediately after that he inserts the French Revolution itself into the Christian tradition as a tradition of empowerment for the common man. The French Revolution becomes not an atheistic revolution against Christianity but a revolution against a false conception of Christianity in the name of its true interpretation. And what is this true interpretation? It is a political interpretation: Christ should be recognized as a King. This requires a revolution against all the other kings. For Solovyov the French Revolution was right in its rejection of the false, secular king but stopped half-way in the proclamation of the Kingdom of Christ.

According to Solovyov, the Christian message was interpreted by institutional Christianity as a promise of the other world beyond the grave—not as a requirement to transform the real world:

> The saying "My Kingdom is not of this world" is always being used to justify and confirm the paganism of our social and political life, as though Christian society were destined to belong to this world and not to the Kingdom of Christ. On the other hand, the saying "All power is given Me in Heaven and Earth" is never quoted. Men are ready to accept Christ as sacrificing Priest and atoning Victim; but they do not want Christ the King.
>
> (Solovyov, 1998, 8)

In other words, the process of Christianizing of the political and social life of the people that call themselves Christian is a thing not of the past but of the future. To become truly Christian, the people must build the universal Christian state that they would be able to freely accept. As Solovyov writes, the empire of ROMA must become the empire of AMOR.

As far as the political Christianizing of humanity remains a distant ideal, men live in Chaos. Like Schmitt, Solovyov associates nature with chaos:

> We know that the principle of chaotic existence ... is manifested in the life of natural humanity by the indeterminate succession of generations, in which the present hastens to supplant the past, only to be itself continually supplanted by an illusory and transient future. The parricidal children, becoming fathers, cannot but beget a new generation of parricides, and so on to infinity. Such is the evil law of mortal life.
>
> (Solovyov, 1998, 189)

However, according to Solovyov, God does not merely dominate Chaos through His will but, rather, attracts through His love: "But God loves Chaos in its nothingness and wills that it should exist, for He is able to draw rebellious existence back to unity and fill the infinite void with His superabundant life" (Solovyov, 1998, 152). To answer God's love, humanity should learn "universal love"—but this is a difficult task. It is natural to love one's own family and nation, but a universal love for all humans is unnatural. The population of a Christian, transnational state should, as Solovyov writes, "surrender" to this unnatural, universal love (Solovyov, 1998, 98). And here one begins again to see ROMA behind AMOR. One should surrender to an empire in order to be able to later transform it into a state of universal love. The traditional imperial state should not be dissolved into the constituent nation-states but, on the contrary, become the core for building a universal state of "all-unity" in which everybody will find their recognition and right. The sovereign of this state will no longer be a nation or a territorial administration, but the Church uniting humanity through universal, "unnatural" love.

For Solovyov the model of such a spiritual transformation is the Christianizing of the Roman Empire. Initially, the Roman Empire was based exclusively on military power and control over territories. In this sense, the Roman Empire was an heir of Babylonian and Persian Empires or the Empire of Alexander. Solovyov clearly sees the injustice and abuse of power on which these empires were based. However, he also recognizes them as necessary steps to create the Universal State of Justice and Love. He writes:

> In other words, we have here, on the one hand, the formation of natural universal monarchy and, on the other, the formation and development of spiritual monarchy or the Universal Church on the basis and in the framework of the corresponding natural organism. The first part of this great work constitutes the essence of ancient or pagan history; the second part mainly determines modern or Christian history.
>
> (Solovyov, 1998, 103)

But why proclaim the Universal Christian Church and not Reason as the sovereign of the universal state? After all, that was the proposition made by the French Revolution—Hegel also saw the universal state as governed by Reason. Indeed, Solovyov recognizes that the project of the universal state as the state of reason had emerged already during Greek antiquity, but he insists that it remained a merely philosophical idea that was not accepted and shared by the Greek population. Solovyov writes:

> The Athenian government, for all its democratic character, could do nothing but banish Anaxagoras and poison Socrates in the name of the Fatherland, that is, of the absolute State. While Socrates and Plato despised the Athenian democracy, Aristotle despised all the republican constitutions of the Greek cities and preferred the semi-barbarous monarchy of the Macedonians, until at last the Cynic and Stoic philosophers repudiated all idea of Fatherland or State and declared themselves indifferent to all public concerns. The independence and political organization of Hellas were destroyed by a philosophy and a philosophical religion which raised nothing upon the ruins of the Fatherland. This antagonism between the present existence of the nation, as represented by the Greek republics, and the higher thought, the future

of the nation, as represented by the idealism of the Greeks, this struggle between Philosophy and the State was fatal to both.

(Solovyov, 1998, 189)

This passage was formulated as a critique of the Westernized Russian intelligentsia who appealed to the universality of reason and tried to spread the universalist ideas of the Enlightenment among the Russian population. Indeed, Solovyov did not believe that one could persuade the masses by the means of reason alone. The educated strata of society are responsive to rational argumentation, but the people in their entirety is not. To lead the population to the new Universal State one needs not merely a change of mind but a change of heart. Christianity was able to produce such a change of heart and that is why it became the religion of the masses. It transcended the borders between nations and created a new, Christian world that became truly universal because it was open for everybody. However, according to Solovyov, the Christianizing of the masses did not go far enough because it did not change the economic, political, and social conditions under which these masses had to live. To change the social order, Christianity should take the next step—becoming a real political power. Here one sees the impact of Marx and Nietzsche on Solovyov's thinking. According to Marx, it is not enough to interpret the world—one should change it. And, according to Nietzsche, it is not enough to philosophize—one should live philosophically. Of course, both Marx and Nietzsche were atheist philosophers. But, as was the case with the French Revolution, Solovyov does not simply reject their philosophical activism. Instead, he tries to integrate it into the project of completely Christianizing social and political life.

Now, Solovyov was convinced that only the Roman Catholic Church, as the heir of the Roman Empire, was able to fulfill the project of universal Christianizing. Of course, Solovyov understood very well that the Catholic Church is a hierarchically organized bureaucratic institution that operates as a state inside the European state system. But it is precisely the politically independent status of the Vatican in which Solovyov saw the chance for his project to be realized:

> Since mankind on Earth is not, and was never meant to be, a world of pure spirits, it needs for the expression and development of the unity of its inner life an external social organism which must become more centralized as it grows in extent and diversity.

(Solovyov, 1998, 103)

The goal of Christianizing has a political dimension analogous to the political mission of early Roman Christianity: "Universal monarchy and international unity were to remain; the center of unity was to keep its place. But the central power itself, its character, its origin and its authority—all this was to be renewed"(Solovyov, 1998, 105). But what is the place of Russia in this historiosophic scheme? After all, the title of the book is *Russia and the Universal Church*.

In the part of the book that is directly dedicated to the role of Christianity in Russia, Solovyov argues the Russian Orthodox Church has completely surrendered its ecclesiastical freedom and became a part of the Russian imperial state and its apparatus of suppression. Solovyov quotes a leading Slavophile writer, Aksakov, who wrote that the Russian Church is so much under the total control of the state that "enrolled in the service of the State, the servants of the altar regard themselves as the employees and agents of the secular power" (Solovyov, 1998, 60). And further: "A Church which is a department of State, that is, of a 'kingdom of this world,' has renounced her mission and will inevitably share the fate of all the kingdoms of this world" (Solovyov, 1998, 64-5). Solovyov diagnoses this inability to emancipate itself from state control as the fundamental failure of the Orthodox Church ever since its Byzantine period. Solovyov calls this condition "Caesaropapism": here the emperor, being merely a representative of the secular power, acquires the power of the spiritual guidance that in the West is practiced by the politically independent office of the Pope. The problem of the Russian Orthodox Church is that it is too Russian, too deeply integrated into the administrative structures of the Russian national state. The Church can play its guiding role only if it politically emancipates itself from the state.

Now it becomes clear in what respect the political theology of Solovyov is different from the political theology of Schmitt. Schmitt views the authority of the state as secularized divine authority. Solovyov, on the contrary, sees in the state—every state, including the formally Christian states—a purely secular, pre-Christian institution. What he wants is not the theologization of the state but, rather, the politization of the Church. With this goal in mind, Solovyov believes the Russian Church must unite with the Roman Catholic Church and thus win political independence from the Russian national state.

Solovyov took his project of re-unifying the Orthodox and Catholic Churches very seriously and invested much effort in the practical realization of this project. However, at the end of his life he understood that this project would remain unrealized. In his last major text, *Three Conversation on Antichrist* (1899) (Solovyov, 2018), Solovyov ironically describes his own plan of world unification by peacefully harmonizing all the contradictions and conflicts that divide individuals and nations from each other as a plan of the

Antichrist. The conflict between the faithful and unfaithful, or between good and evil, cannot be peacefully overcome. The unification of the Christian Churches can be achieved only by a Christian revolution that dethrones the Antichrist in the final, eschatological battle. In this battle, the three Christian denominations—Catholic, Orthodox and Protestant—will finally be united. The submission of men under universalist love is impossible without divine intervention at the end of times. But also, in this eschatological and revolutionary perspective, the establishment of the Universal empire—be it even the empire of the Antichrist—is a crucial precondition for the ultimate re-awakening of mankind.

Solovyov was primarily interested in the unification of Russia with the West. But what did he plan to do with the non-Christian population of the Russian Empire—and, for that matter, of the whole world? As far as sovereignty of an empire was based on its ability to control a certain territory, this problem did not emerge. But if the new Universal Christian State should be based on the universally Christianized mankind, the fate of non-Christians was not to be ignored. Solovyov believed that Christianity is the only true religion and that in the course of history all nations will become Christian. But here one finds the main problem of Solovyov's version of political theology. As Schmitt correctly writes, the possibility to make peace between sovereign nations is always given but there cannot be peace between Good and Evil. Accordingly, there cannot be peace between Christianity and other religions or Christianity and atheism. Such a peace would be a treacherous work of the Antichrist and inevitably lead to the last battle between Christian Universalism and its enemies.

Now, one can also find a vision of the last battle between Universalism and its enemies in Communist eschatology. The Soviet Union also saw itself as a transitional empire that drew its legitimacy and sovereignty from the perspective of establishing a future Universal communist state. This analogy was recognized by some Russian authors. Thus, for example, Nikolay Berdyaev reflected on the religious, eschatological dimension of Russian Communism in his well-known book *The Origin of Russian Communism* (Berdyaev, 1959). The famous Russian poets Alexander Blok and Andrei Bely, who both experienced the strong influence of Solovyov, were sympathetic to the radicalism of the Communist experiment, at least for a certain period of their lives. All of these authors saw the Russian Revolution as an act of self-sacrifice of the Russian nation in the name of the universal, eschatological future. However, there was also a different interpretation of the same revolutionary events proposed by the post-revolutionary Eurasian movement. The latter saw the October Revolution as an attempt by the Bolsheviks to restore the crumbling Russian Empire by means of a new universalist ideology. The construction of socialism in one country created a gap between the transitional, temporary Soviet empire and the outer world, which was supposed to join this empire at a later date. However, as history shows us, everything temporary tends to become permanent. Solovyov hated this tendency, but for the Eurasians it was a source of hope. Not accidentally, in his highly critical text on the Eurasians, Berdyaev refers to Solovyov when he tries to defend romanticism, faith in the future, and eschatological aspirations against the pragmatic approach that was characteristic of the Eurasian movement (Berdyaev, 1925).

2

The concept of an empire as a historical compromise between the Universal State and national self-determination builds the ideological basis of the Eurasian movement that emerged in the Russian emigration after the Bolshevik revolution. This concept was inherited from Solovyov, but the Eurasians did not consider historical Christianity as the primary context of the Russian cultural identity or the overcoming of the split between the Eastern and Western Churches as a prerequisite for the formation of the Russian nation. For them, the revolution erased the cultural split of the Russian population: the old upper class was destroyed not in the name of Orthodox Christianity, but rather in that of the Marxist theories of Socialism coming from the West. For the majority of Russian émigrés that meant the end of the historical Russia—its disappearance from the political and cultural map of the world. The Eurasians, however, reacted early on to a new and somewhat paradoxical repositioning of Russia vis-à-vis the West to which the October revolution had led. The ideology of the new Bolshevik Government was totally Western, but its politics were directed against the West, which was considered to be the class enemy. This paradoxical situation was, of course, also well understood by Bolshevik leaders such as Leon Trotsky. They hoped to solve the paradox through a world revolution that would reunite Russia and the West. However, the Eurasians did not believe in such a possibility. They considered the West as stable and immune to any proletarian revolution. And that meant for them that the Socialist, Bolshevik Russia would be the enemy of the West forever. The Westernization of Russia, thus, led not to the overcoming of the gap between Russia and the West but, on the contrary, made this gap deeper than ever before.

Now, the Eurasians did not complain about this fact—they celebrated it. The conflict between Russia and the West was a guarantee that Russia would retain its cultural identity and political autonomy. It is characteristic that the Eurasians were unhappy about the introduction of the New Economic

Politic in Soviet Russia. They feared that these politics would lead to Russia's growing dependence on the economically better developed West: and, thus, to the colonization of Russia by Western powers. In the collective declaration by Eurasians from 1932, they assert that "state economy and state planning are of the central importance" because they should guarantee the "economic independence of Russia-Eurasia" (Evraziystvo, 1932). Like the Slavophiles before them, the Eurasians saw the Russian Orthodox Church as the foundation of the Russian cultural identity and condemned the atheist Bolshevism as an enemy of the Russian spirituality. However, political and economic independence from the West was even more important for them than the spiritual independence. They saw the world as colonized by the imperialist Western powers, and saw Russia running the risk of becoming another Western colony. The Eurasians argued that Russia had always participated in symbiotic relationships with other Eurasian nations, such as the Mongols, and that this symbiotic relationship should be continued because it offered the only guarantee of Russian independence from the domination of Western powers.

The Eurasian movement included many talented philosophers, historians and writers, but one can safely say that Nikolai Trubetzkoy was the most interesting and relevant among them. His father was a renowned philosopher who was close to Vladimir Solovyov. In the scientific world Trubetzkoy is known primarily due to his work on phonology that influenced the development of Structuralism. But here we will concentrate on the political writings of Trubetzkoy because they formulate in the most laconic and clear manner the Eurasian philosophical and political position.

Trubetzkoy's most interesting text is the book *Europe and Mankind* (1920). The title betrays the program. It reminds the reader of Nikolai Danilevsky's famous book *Russia and Europe* (1871) (Danilevsky, 2014). However, Trubetzkoy's Europe is opposed not to Russia but to the whole of mankind. For Trubetzkoy, European nation states do not represent the "normal case" and Russia the exception. It is Europe and the European nationalisms that are exceptional. Every non-European nation is split into the Europeanized upper class and ordinary, common people that carry indigenous, non-European cultures. That means that every non-European nation is confronted with the same problems and choices as Russia. Russia is normal, Europe is exceptional.

Trubetzkoy decided to present ideas from earlier in his career to the public because of their newfound relevance after the war. He writes:

> The Great War and especially the subsequent "peace" (which even now must be written in quotation marks) shook our faith in "civilized mankind" and opened the eyes of many people. We Russians find

ourselves in a special situation: we were witnesses to the sudden collapse of what we used to call "Russian culture." Many of us were struck by the speed and ease with which it occurred, and many began to ponder the reasons for these events.

(Trubetzkoy, 1991a)

Trubetzkoy begins his analysis by discussing the traditional opposition between national Chauvinism and Cosmopolitism.

He states that in the European cultural tradition Chauvinism has a bad reputation because it privileges one nation over all the others. Cosmopolitism seems, on the other side, to be interested in the progress of the whole of mankind and is ready to sacrifice national particularity in the name of universal human culture. However, Trubetzkoy argues that such a universalist interpretation of European Cosmopolitanism is illusionary. The European Cosmopolite hopes to civilize the whole of mankind. But he or she understands civilization as the common characteristics of the European Romano-Germanic culture and wants everybody else to accept this culture as universal. Trubetzkoy writes:

> In evaluating European cosmopolitanism one must always remember that terms such as "humanity," "universal human civilization," and so forth are extremely imprecise and that they mask very definite ethnographic concepts. European culture is not a culture of all humanity; it is a product of the history of a specific ethnic group.
>
> (Trubetzkoy, 1991a, 6)

Thus, European cosmopolitanism is simply Pan-European chauvinism. But Trubetzkoy asks himself and the reader why so many non-European people, including Slavs, have accepted European culture as universal and are ready to reject their own cultures in the name of the European culture? For Trubetzkoy, "Those who have been taken in by the propaganda of Roman-Germanic chauvinists have been misled by the terms 'humanity', 'universally human', 'civilization', 'world progress' and so forth" (Trubetzkoy, 1991a, 13). The intellectuals of non-European countries should understand that European culture is merely one of many human cultures—and, thus, cease to impose this culture on the population of their countries as "universal." However, one can still ask: Why do so many people believe in the supremacy of European culture?

One reason, Trubetzkoy argues, is the military supremacy of the European powers:

> The simplest and most widespread proof of the alleged perfection of Romano-Germanic civilization is the fact that Europeans always conquer "savages" … The crudeness and naivete of this "proof" should

be apparent to any fair-minded person. This argument shows clearly how much the worship of brute force—a fundamental characteristic of the tribes that created European civilization—is still alive in the consciousness of every descendant of the ancient Gauls and Teutons.

(Trubetzkoy, 1991a, 19)

> The second argument is that the "savages" cannot be educated in the European manner. One would expect Trubetzkoy to expose this opinion's basis in racist prejudice and contend that "savages" can indeed be educated in the European way. Instead, he reverses the argument: European culture could be considered hierarchically higher than "savage" cultures only if it would be easier for Europeans to become a part of a "savage" culture than for "savages" to become a part of European culture. Trubetzkoy disproves this notion with the following example: It is sufficient to recall Gauguin, the talented French painter, who tried to become a Tahitian, and who discovered that the price of this undertaking was madness, and later alcoholism, and who died ignominiously in a drunken brawl ... It just as difficult for a European to become a "savage" as it is for a "savage" to become a European—one cannot reach any conclusions here about who is "higher" and who is "lower" in development.
>
> (Trubetzkoy, 1991a, 21)

Cultures are not higher or lower—they are simply different. Every culture is equally complicated for foreigners to grasp. That is why the representatives of a particular culture experience the foreigners as children. Thus, Trubetzkoy remarks:

> Such an evaluation of another human being's psychology is observable not only between two nations but between social groups within the same nation if social differences are very great and if the upper classes have adopted a foreign culture. Many Russian intellectuals, physicians, officers, and nurses, when dealing with the common people, say that they are like grown-up children. On the other hand, judging by their folk tales, the common people perceive certain eccentric, naïve, childlike psychological traits in the upper class.
>
> (Trubetzkoy, 1991a, 26)

At this point, the strategy of the text becomes clear. Trubetzkoy tries to solve the same problem that plagued the whole nineteenth-century Russian intellectual tradition: how to unite Russia's radically split Western educated upper class and traditionally educated common people. As the title of Trubetzkoy's treatise *Europe and Mankind* indicates, Trubetzkoy universalizes this Russian cultural divide. Russia becomes an exemplary case of the cultural predicament that characterizes non-European mankind—namely, the split between the Europeanized upper class and the rest of the population. Rather than European culture itself, the cultural conflict within all the non-European cultures becomes universal. Only by overcoming this universal cultural conflict will Russia be able to constitute itself as a nation. Here again the Russian national problem becomes a universal problem, and the "Russian question" requires a universal solution.

Trubetzkoy rejects complete Europeanization as such a solution because an attempt to Europeanize any non-European nation can never overcome the cultural distance that separates it from the authentically European nations—thus, the non-European nation is condemned to permanent backwardness. Trubetzkoy writes:

> In comparing itself with native Romano-Germans, a Europeanized nation comes to view them as superior; and this perception together with now habitual complaints about its own inertia and backwardness gradually lead to a loss of self-respect … Patriotism and national pride are only occasionally encountered, while national self-assertion boils down for the most part to the ambitions of the rulers and leading political circles.
>
> (Trubetzkoy, 1991a, 51)

As a result, the Europeanized nation permanently feels itself as weak and underdeveloped. The trajectory of the technological development that this nation follows is the same as in Europe, but the difference is in the lower intensity of the industrial activity, so that the Europeanized nation remains forever unable to catch up with the Western technological progress. The feelings of backwardness and low self-esteem become permanent:

> And the worst aspect of these feelings is precisely their sporadic quality: the elimination of the consequences of these sporadic feelings of backwardness is possible only through equally sporadic historical leaps …. The consequences of such "leaping" evolution are genuinely terrible. Every leap is inevitably followed by a period of apparent (from the European standpoint) stagnation, when it is necessary to bring order to the culture, to coordinate the result achieved by a leap in a particular area with the other elements of the culture. During this period of "stagnation," the nation again falls even further behind.
>
> (Trubetzkoy, 1991a, 53-4)

And Trubetzkoy concludes: "Thus, the consequences of Europeanization are so deleterious and appalling that it must be considered an evil, not a blessing" (Trubetzkoy, 1991a, 54). And by the way, for Trubetzkoy, socialism is merely a continuation and even radicalization of the same evil by other means because socialism presupposes Europeanization.

According to Trubetzkoy, this evil can be overcome only if the intelligentsia of every non-European country reject the strategy of Europeanization and unite with the intelligentsia of all other non-European countries in the struggle against European domination. While, throughout his whole book, Trubetzkoy requires unconditional respect for the specificity of every particular culture, at the end of the text he postulates only two types of cultures—European and Non-European—and implies that all of the differences among non-European cultures are secondary and basically irrelevant. What really defines these cultures is the internal conflict between the process of Europeanization and indigenous cultural traditions. Trubetzkoy ends his text with the following sentence: "There is only one true opposition: the Romano-Germans and all the other people of the world—*Europe and Mankind*" (Trubetzkoy, 1991a, 64). Once again, Russia's internal split between its westernized elite and the non-western "backward" population can and should be overcome only in the universalist perspective, this time through the abandonment of the strategy of Europeanization and the universal struggle of all non-Western nations against the West.

But what is *Mankind*? The term sounds universalist. However, the title *Europe and Mankind* already suggests that Europe is not considered a part of Mankind by Trubetzkoy. What, then, is Europe—the enemy of Mankind? Trubetzkoy does not go so far. Rather, he sees Mankind as an arena for the struggle between two ideas: the idea of Europeanization and the idea of Anti-Europeanization. Earlier in the text Trubetzkoy, using a term taken from the sociological theory of Gabriel Tarde, describes a struggle of this type as *duel logique* (Trubetzkoy, 1991a, 47). Tarde's *duel logique* has nothing to do with logical contradiction as it is treated in the framework of traditional logic. He refers to competing ideas that should be understood, as Trubetzkoy rightly affirms, as competing cultural value systems, or competing life-forms. In this sense one can speak, for example, about the Russian idea as being in competition with the Western idea and set of values. However, the Russian idea is not considered by Trubetzkoy as a specific Russian national idea. The Russian idea is the general, universalist idea of the anti-imperialist, anti-Western struggle that has the whole world as its arena and its goal.

With *Europe and Mankind*, Trubetzkoy enters the logical duel between Europeanization and Anti-Europeanization and hopes to become a winner. So Trubetzkoy writes: "It is one of the fundamental theses of Eurasians that modern democracy must give way to ideocracy" (Trubetzkoy, 1991b, 269). Ideocracy should prevent such "irresponsible factors" as private capital and the press from influencing society. Trubetzkoy holds that "for this reason the ideocratic state is partly socialist" (Trubetzkoy, 1991b, 271). The central ideal of ideocracy is the readiness to self-sacrifice for the common good. Trubetzkoy begins to sound like Solovyov when he clarifies that he does not mean a sacrifice to "my biological or social group" because that is "what animals do." National and class interests determining human behavior in a democracy replicates the natural, animal condition. True sacrifice is sacrifice for the "common good," i.e., the welfare of the whole. But what is the whole? For Trubetzkoy, mankind is a too general and abstract idea for one to sacrifice one's life to. One can sacrifice oneself to a nation or class because they are opposed to something. "But what is mankind opposed to? Not other mammals, one should suppose!" (Trubetzkoy, 1991b, 271). One cannot struggle for humanity as such; thus, one cannot sacrifice to it.

Trubetzkoy proposes "not a class, not a nation, not mankind" but "a multinational whole" that is connected historically rather than biologically (Trubetzkoy, 1991b, 272). He promises the future to the ideocratic states based on common culture and historical traditions rather than national origin. In other words, Trubetzkoy seeks the middle ground between Cosmopolitanism and Nationalism and discovers an Empire redefined in universal terms, such as common cultural values and historical traditions. For Trubetzkoy, the ideocratic empire should hold fast to the sole goal of defense of common cultural values, not to the interests of a particular nation (as in the classical empires) or a particular class (like in the USSR). Only then will an empire cease to be despotic and find the support of the population. Trubetzkoy believed that the nations populating the territory of the Russian Empire and, later, USSR achieved such a cultural and historical unity. Indeed, he writes that the USSR is closer to the ideal of ideocracy than the European liberal democracies. "The European ideocratic states have still farther to go," because they are fueled by zoological nationalism and fight the idea of common European culture through the Fascist movements (Trubetzkoy, 1991b, 274). And Trubetzkoy remarks: "Paradoxically enough, 'Pan-Europeanism' which alone could have become the governing idea of European ideocracy (for no single European country can lay claim to any autarky), is now the ideology of liberalism and democracy, i.e., of ideocracy's sworn enemies" (Trubetzkoy, 1991b, 276). According to Trubetzkoy, in the "true ideocratic state" common cultural values should substitute the common religion. But Trubetzkoy overlooks the fact that liberalism and democracy belong to the common European values he defends from "zoological nationalism." Indeed, he associates liberalism and democracy exclusively with the domination of private interests over the interests of the state, overlooking the possibility that private and state interests could coincide. However, the European cultural idea consisted precisely in the realization of this possibility and European political thought traditionally tried to find a balance between "natural" human rights and political necessities.

3

After the Second World War II, Alexandre Kojève wrote a short text that is usually referred to as *Latin Empire*. The text takes a very specific place in Kojève's work. Written in 1945, it proposes a strategy for French politics in the post-War world.[1] In this text, Kojève formulates a series of predictions concerning post-War economic and political realities. Some of these predictions proved to be surprisingly precise, the most important being that Europe would be divided between Anglo-American and Soviet empires. According to Kojève, France could keep its culture, traditions, and ways of life only if it built its own empire by creating an association with Italy and Spain. As a national state, France would be too weak to withstand both the Western and Eastern empires, but by uniting the traditionally Catholic European countries it would give a political home to the cultural tradition that would otherwise be dissolved in the middle of the struggle between the Protestant Anglo-American and Slavic Orthodox empires.

In our time this document is mostly discussed and interpreted due to the active role that Kojève played in the initial stages of the creation of the contemporary European Union (Wilson, 2021, 27–30). Thus, the contemporary commentaries and analyses are mostly related to the political realities of Kojève's and our own time. These analyses are, of course, important and relevant. However, one should also take into account the theoretical tradition underlying the *Latin Empire*. When approached through such a lens, Kojève's text reflects the double influence of Solovyov's Christian Utopianism and the Eurasian concept of the "ideocratic state."

After emigrating from Russia to Germany in 1919 Kojève wrote a dissertation on "Religious Philosophy of Vladimir Solovyov" (in 1926). Soon after Kojève received his PhD at the University of Heidelberg, he moved to Paris and became affiliated with the Parisian Eurasian circle around the Russian philosopher Lev Karsavin (Tokarev, 2017). Similar to the Eurasians, Kojève believed that modernity is politically defined by the opposition between nationalism and universalist cosmopolitanism and that one should overcome this opposition through a compromise—this compromise being the idea of the empire as an association of culturally similar nations. In his *Latin Empire*, Kojève writes in a typically Eurasian manner:

> Liberalism is wrong not to perceive any political entity beyond that of Nations. But internationalism's sin is the fact that it sees nothing politically viable short of Humanity. It likewise was unable to discover the intermediary political reality of Empires, which is to say unions, or even international amalgamations of affiliated nations, which is exactly the political reality today .... Before being embodied in Humanity, the Hegelian *Weltgeist*, which has abandoned the Nations, inhabits Empires.
>
> (Kojève, 2004)

The reference to Hegel does not surprise the reader: Kojève became famous in French intellectual circles due to his lectures dedicated to Hegel's *Phenomenology of Spirit* that he delivered in Paris between 1933 and 1939. However, if for Hegel particular national cultures are merely stages on the way towards the State of Reason that finalizes world history, for Kojève the main goal of an Empire is to create a political order that allows the historical stabilization of a particular life-form or cultural identity:

> Anybody who would like to safeguard the existence and the influence of the traditional Latino-Catholic civilization, which is also that of France (and to which France has, moreover, contributed much more than all other Latin Nations combined), must thus want to provide it with a political base adequate to the given historical conditions.
>
> (Kojève, 2004)

Such a political basis presupposes, in the first place, the political autonomy guaranteed by adequate military force. Kojève underscores that by speaking about the military he does not mean any kind of "militarism." What he has in mind is political sovereignty alone because any national culture needs autarky and sovereignty to defend and secure its cultural identity.

Besides the Slavo-Soviet Empire of the Orthodox tradition and the Protestant-inspired Anglo-Saxon, and perhaps the Germano-Anglo-Saxon Empire, a Latin Empire must be created. Only an empire such as this would be at the political level of the two already existing empires, for it alone could possibly sustain a war where its independence was at stake. And it is only by putting itself at the head of such an empire that France could retain its political, and thus also cultural, specificity (Kojève, 2004). It is highly characteristic that in this context Kojève speaks about the "Slavo-Soviet Empire" and its orthodox tradition, rather than, say, the Communist empire. For him the historical role of Stalin consisted precisely in the abandonment of the internationalist, universalist perspective that was inherent to the Communist project and its substitution by the imperial project. Kojève writes:

> Stalin's political genius consists precisely in having understood this. The political focus on humanity characterizes the "Trotskyist" utopia, of which Trotsky himself was the most notable – but certainly not sole – representative .... His [Stalin's] anti-Trotskyist slogan: "Socialism in one country" engendered this "Sovietism," or if one prefers, this "imperial socialism," which manifests itself in and through the present Soviet imperial State.
>
> (Kojève, 2004)

Kojève sees Stalin as a conservative leader who abandoned all the Communist universalist projects and restored the Russian Empire on its traditional Orthodox basis.

This interpretation of Stalinist Russia was central for Kojève's diagnosis of the inner political condition of post-War France, leading him to believe that the French middle class could not become a political base of the Latin Empire. He writes:

> Not only in fact, but also in his own consciousness, the modern Frenchman lives as a "bourgeois" and not as a "citizen." He acts and thinks as an "individualist" in that sense in which "private," "particular" interests are for him the supreme or only values. And he is "liberal" or "libertarian" and "pacifist" above all because he no longer wants to be subjected to the weight and the demands of the "universal" reality of the State and the means it uses to assert and preserve itself.
>
> (Kojève, 2004)

Here Kojève repeats Trubetzkoy's arguments against the dominance of private interests over state interests. He sees the possibility of restoring the sovereign position of the state in a return to the empire and rejection of "egoistic" nationalism, including French nationalism.

According to Kojève, the political basis of the empire should be built through collaboration between French political elites and the Communist party. Indeed, Kojève sees the pro-Stalinist French Communist Party as a deeply conservative force, and points out: "In fact, at least insofar as the broad outline of its policy is co-determined by Moscow, the Communist Party currently looks like a conservative party, whose motto is expressed by the Vichy regime's formula: 'Work—Family—Fatherland.'" The only condition for this collaboration is this: the Latin Empire will be acceptable for the Soviets. But, as Kojève remarks, most probably the Soviets will regard the Latin Empire as a means to diminish the influence of the Anglo-American empire.

As far as the project of the Latin Empire is formulated in purely political terms, it vaguely reminds the reader of the parodic description of three warring empires as found in Orwell's *1984*. However, for Kojève, the division of Europe into three empires is only a temporary stop on the journey of Hegelian *Weltgeist* towards the end of history—even if he understands this end not in Hegelian but Solovyovian terms. Indeed, Kojève does not follow Hegel, who expected the unity of mankind to come as a result of the process of Enlightenment that gradually erases the vestiges of the irrational past and secures the final victory of reason. Instead, Kojève follows Solovyov, who sees the promise of unity and universality in the political theology that translates the Christian message into the practical organization of society. In his *Latin Empire*, Kojève repeats this politico-theological gesture of Solovyov: the Universal State is understood by both of them not as a state of Reason but as a return to the unified Christian empire after a long history of attempts to satisfy all possible private human desires and ambitions. When, in his *Latin Empire*, Kojève persistently characterizes Soviet State as Orthodox, Latin Empire as Catholic and Anglo-American Empire as Protestant, the coincidence of this political tripartition of the European world with its religious partition is not accidental. Christianity is here not a vague cultural characteristic but a promise of unifying Europe through the restoration of the original unity of Christian Churches.

The final chapter of the text, in which Kojève discusses the role of the Catholic Church, serves as a reformulation of the main positions of Solovyov's politico-theological project. Kojève writes that

> the real division of humanity resulted in the division of universalizing Christianity into three great autonomous and rival Churches. It thus seems that the separate Churches need a political counterpart in the existence of intermediary formations between Humanity and Nations, which is to say imperial formations. And in fact, the Protestant Church attached itself from the beginning to an Anglo-Saxon world, which is currently in the process of absorbing the Germanic world. The Orthodox Church, which would seem to have lost the Russian Empire, in fact found a Slavo-Soviet Empire in the course of being formed.
>
> (Kojève, 2004)

As did Solovyov before him, Kojève sets his hope of the unification of mankind on the Catholic Church that should reintegrate the other two

Churches. Kojève ends his *Latin Empire* in the same ecstatic tone that was characteristic of some of Solovyov's writings:

> Be that as it may, it is certainly clear that the true union of the Churches presupposes a real unification of the human race and that this unification cannot come about without the historic evolution which leads there going through a period of imperial-type and "confessional" concentrations. It is only by going through this stage and by surpassing it that humanity will be able to reach the final state of unity which will permit the permanent elimination of political, economic, and social conflicts. And it is only thus that one will be able to respond to the question of knowing whether the indefinite future belongs to the humanist irreligion predicted and praised by some, or to this Christian Catholicism which is the final end and the only raison d'être of Catholic Christianity, which engendered – among other things – the Latin spiritual world.
>
> (Kojève, 2004)

Kojève, despite insisting on his atheism in many writings, does not consider himself as belonging to the "some" who predict and praise humanist irreligion. Thus, the identification between the mankind as such and the Christian mankind that Kojève inherited from Solovyov leaves open the problem of the Earth's non-Christian populations. In the framework of his *Latin Empire*, Kojève only mentions that the colonies of the three Latin countries should be united under the common imperial administration. However, later in his lecture "Colonialism from a European Perspective" (Kojève, 2001, 115–28), Kojève identifies colonialism as the most serious problem of the twentieth century. He says that the class conflict Marx addressed was partially overcome in the West because of the emergence of the Social State to redistribute "surplus value." Instead of being accumulated exclusively by the upper class, as Marx described it, a part of the surplus value was given back to the proletariat. Kojève prefers "Fordism" to the social state as a model of such a redistribution—but, in any case, he underlines the lack of an analogous mechanism in relationships between colonizers and colonized countries. Colonial countries accumulate the whole of the surplus value produced by the colonized countries. In this sense, colonialism is a continuation of capitalism as it was described by Marx: "What is meant seriously is that the real problem of our time and of our world is not political, but economic colonialism" (Kojève, 2001).

Kojève proposes "giving colonialism" as a remedy to this condition. He means a global social state, a mechanism to redistribute surplus value to underdeveloped countries. But who should manage this globalized social state? The task is distributed among the three empires from the *Latin Empire*; only this time, the Russian Empire is addressed by Kojève as the "Mongolian Empire." Speaking about the current empires, Kojève writes: "Let us, to begin with, take the regions, which lie outside the Western world, of the Mongolian Empire, first founded by Genghis Khan, and which recently became politically and economically reestablished" (Kojève, 2001). The mentioning of Genghis Khan is a reference to Nikolai Trubetzkoy's famous text, *The Legacy of Genghis Khan*. But the Eurasian tradition is used by Kojève not with the goal to re-awaken its anti-imperialist, anti-Western impetus, but merely to restate the fact that Russia—and its whole Socialist camp—lie outside Europe. In a more indirect way, Kojève suggest that the Anglo-American empire is also not quite European, leaving the Latin Empire alone truly European. And, indeed, Kojève writes:

> And now, last but not least, the European region. Like the Mongolian one, this region also has an old, very old, history. For this region was once called the Imperium Romanum and economically preserved itself astonishingly viably and robustly ... Thus one can certainly calmly and confidently say that the economic conditions of the Mediterranean region's economic unity have been restored. And here one must say that, from the perspective of giving colonialism, this economic region is a region which has been blessed by God.
>
> (Kojève, 2004)

The perspective of the ultimate unification of the world by uniting the three main Christian denominations under the "blessed" Catholic rule does not fully disappear. But what was Latin Empire now becomes simply Europe—as good and old as Mongolia.

In the context of Russian cultural and political thought, Kojève consistently manifests the trend towards the post-national state that has the goal to overcome all national egoisms and, thus, to end the history of wars and revolutions. The nations were considered to have been based on natural determinations reminiscent of extended families, whereas the post-national state had to be based on a religious promise or commonality of "cultural values." In this sense, the post-national empires promised sovereignty of the spirit as opposed to the low, natural, animal, egoistic drives and desires that remained present and active in human beings. But what was the material basis of this sovereignty? All discussed authors ultimately saw this basis in military power. They insisted on the autarky of the post-national empires, as far as they did not yet lead to the emergence of the unified Universal

State. And this insistence on autarky and military power re-connects the post-national empires to their pre-national predecessors.

Solovyov reminds us of the Roman Empire, Trubetzkoy of the Mongolian Empire, and Kojève of both of them. The sovereignty of these empires was based on the military control of certain territories, regardless of their ethnic make-up. Solovyov condemns these ancient empires as based on brute force. But that does not mean that Solovyov is anti-militaristic. On the contrary, his last book *Three Conversations on Antichrist* was directed primarily against Leo Tolstoy's pacifism. According to Solovyov, the military is necessary to defend the territory of the Christian Empire as long as non-Christian peoples remain. Kojève also condemns pacifism as anarchistic and underlines the fact that autarky and sovereignty require military power and politics based on this power. Where abstract cultural values rather than natural commonality keep the individual nation together, an army and centralized administration are necessary to supplement cultural values' insufficient power to defend themselves from enemies.

Of course, Solovyov, Trubetzkoy, and Kojève envision the empires of the new type: based not on coercion but on the free consent of the population. These empires should unite the nations without the domination of one nation over the other nations. However, the border between consent and coercion is always precarious—what to do, for example, with "nationalistic" movements that want to break away from the empire? Here the sovereignty of the empire over its territory is brought into question and seems to legitimize the use of military force. Thus, the military is needed for defense against both external forces and enemies from within if they do not share the "idea" on which an "ideocratic state" is based, preferring their private, egoistic interests or "animalistic" national solidarity. Both preferences, according to Trubetzkoy, dominate under the conditions of liberal democracy.

Here, the post-national empires appear as mere revivals of the archaic empires based on military control over their territories with or without the consent of the population. It is not accidental that Solovyov, Trubetzkoy and Kojève go back to pre-modern history when speaking of the cultural commonality among nations that lived on the territories of the ancient empires. However, as we know from history, geographically neighboring nations have the longest history of conflicts, wars and mutual distrust, particularly those nations once enveloped by old-style empires that accumulated memories of mistreatment and repression. To rely on territorial proximity and common history as the basis for cultural similarity and potential political unity is worse than illusionary, especially when it is the case that the search for this unity leads as far back as the Roman and Mongolian empires. Modern nation states are the products of the dissolution of these empires, of a historical process that cannot be turned back. The inner divisions inside the Russian nation cannot be solved by any revival of the imperial past but only by the process of nation building that until now was neglected theoretically and practically.

Note

1 The contemporary context of *Latin Empire*: Giorgio Agamben on *Latin Empire*: https://www.liberation.fr/planete/2013/03/24/que-l-empire-latin-contre-attaque_890916. See also Hager Weslati: http://obsoletecapitalism.blogspot.com/2013/10/hager-weslati-replies-to-giorgio.html.

References

Berdyaev, Nicolas. 1925. "Evraziytsy." *Evraziiskii vestnik*. Kniga 4. Berlin.
Berdyaev, Nicolas. 1959. *The Origin of Russian Communism*, Ann Arbor, MI: University of Michigan Press.
Danilevsky, Nikolai. 2014. *Rossiya i Evropa* [*Russia and Europe*]. Moscow: Algoritm.
Evraziystvo 1932. *Evraziystvo. Deklaratsiya, Formulirovka, Tezisy, Izdanie Evraziytsev, Politika*. Prague.
Kojève, Alexandre. 2001. "Colonialism from a European Perspective," *Interpretation, A Journal of Political Philosophy* 29 (1): 115-28.
Kojève, Alexandre. 2004. *Outline of a Doctrine of French Policy*: https://www.hoover.org/research/outline-doctrine-french-policy and https://www.marxists.org/reference/subject/philosophy/works/fr/kojeve2.htm
Schmitt, Carl. 1996. *The Concept of the Political*. Chicago: University of Chicago Press.
Schmitt, Carl. 2005. *Political Theology: Four Chapters on the Concept of Sovereignty*. Chicago: University of Chicago Press.
Solovyov, Vladimir. 1998. *Russia and the Universal Church*. London: The Centenary Press.
Solovyov, Vladimir. 2018. *War, Progress, and the End of History: Three Conversations Including a Short Story of the Anti-Christ*. Northumbria, UK: Lindisfarne Press.
Tokarev, Dimitri. 2017. "Les Auditeurs russes 'inaperçus' (Gordin, Tarr, Poplavskij) du seminaire hegelien d'Alexandre Kojève a l'Ecole pratique des hautes etudes, 1933-1939," *Revue des Études Slaves* 98 (3): 496-514, 500.
Trubetzkoy, Nikolai S. 1991a. *Europe and Mankind*. In *The Legacy of the Genghis Kahn*. Ann Arbor, MI: University of Michigan Press.

Trubetzkoy, Nikolai S. 1991b. *On the Idea Governing the Ideocratic State*, in his: *The Legacy of the Genghis Kahn*. Ann Arbor, MI: University of Michigan Press.

Wilson, Trevor. 2021. "Kojève out of Eurasia." *Radical Philosophy* 2 (11): 27-30.

3

The Defeated Judge the Victors, or Bolshevism in Post-October Russian Thought

Alexander L. Dobrokhotov

The history of attempts to comprehend the phenomenon of Bolshevism in the first few decades of its existence is in itself a fascinating story, not the least because it shows the haunting phenomenon of Bolshevism slipping conceptualization into political and proximate discourse forms. When Dmitry Merezhkovsky predicts that evil will soon come to Russia in a new form in his *The Coming Ham*[1] (1905), his imaginative constructs prove more annoying than appealing. According to Merezhkovsky, Ham in Russia has three faces: the past, the present, and the future. The past is the face of the Church that renders unto Caesar the things that are God's; the present is the monarchy that begets political slavery; the future has the most frightening face, the face of hooliganism, vagabondage, the Black Hundreds. "These three principles of spiritual philistinism have banded against three principles of spiritual nobility: against the land and the people, or the living flesh, against the Church, or the living soul, and against intelligentsia, or the living spirit of Russia" (Merezhkovsky, 1991, 43). Merezhkovsky exhorts his readers not to fear "the silly old devil of political reaction."

> Fear one thing only, the worst slavery of all possible slaveries, the coming Ham, and the worst of all possible philistinisms, churlishness, for a slave enthroned is a churl, while a churl enthroned is the devil, not the old one, but a new one, a real devil that is truly frightening, truly black, blacker than he is painted, the coming Prince of this world, the Coming Ham.
> (Merezhkovsky, 1991, 42–3)

Such religious and philosophical constructs repelled members of the philosophical mainstream. For instance, Nikolai Berdyaev accuses Merezhkovsky of having no feeling for "the reality of the revolution" and of "still remaining in politics an abstracted writer." He observes how

"Merezhkovsky appears to see the mystical foundations of historical empiricism, while he does not see the historical empiricism itself" (Berdyaev, 1998, 108). We know, however, that most sober-minded philosophers will soon join the search for the mystical foundations of Bolshevism. Remarkably, the central topic of *The Coming Ham* is the denunciation of philistinism and "dead positivism"; so far, Merezhkovsky did not see and could not yet see that political lens that would focus in itself the energy of "hooliganism." Yet he already beheld "the terrible face" of Ham.

In *Vekhi* (*Landmarks*), philosophers already take notice of the Bolsheviks, yet largely see them as a peripheral movement, a political cult for the intelligentsia, a cult noticeable for its offbeat features rather than for its dangers. Berdyaev finds Bolshevik attempts at philosophy and their fascination with the philosopher Richard Avenarius ridiculous (Berdyaev, 2009a, 466); Alexander Izgoyev thinks that Bolshevism appeals to the young generation because it is so "close to the gallows" (Izgoyev, 2009a, 545). Bogdan Kistyakovski mentions the Bolsheviks as an example of being unable to reach a compromise by virtue of legal immaturity (Kistyakovski, 2009, 569).

The situation changes drastically in early 1917: the revolutionary events of February-March demanded a response and, consequently, attention to the awakened political forces and to their cultural implications, which, in turn, produced a recognition of how unique the events of the time were. While immediate reflection on the revolution of 1905-1907 produced a philosophy of hope, the focus of thought eventually shifted from optimistic projects to tragic presentiments. Philosophers discovered that neither conservative nor liberal ideology had expected to encounter the forces that now entered Russian history. The changing tone of Semyon Frank's articles in *Russkaya svoboda [Russian Freedom]* is a telltale case. In March, his works are marked by virtuous didacticism:

> There is a socialism of humanity and fairness, and there is a socialism of class hatred and jealousy. The idea of socialism bringing the principles of fairness and humanity into social relations is a necessary element of the moral and democratic ideal. ... This socialism is that kind of principle that unites and reconciles, while socialism founded in class egoism and class hatred is nothing but a principle of civil war and mutual rancor.
>
> (Frank, 2001, 204-5)

Yet by late April, the picture is already different: Frank discovers both a fault line between the main forces of the revolution, and a certain misalignment of programmatic statements and the opaque reality behind them. Frank perspicaciously notes that "socialists Kerensky and Plekhanov in their real aspirations have nothing in common with the 'Bolshevik' socialists and Lenin, and the struggle between these socialist movements is currently the most important and deeply arresting political struggle." Frank connects Lenin's arrival with "moral poison of violence" permeating the spirit of the heretofore morally just revolution: "*Khlysty*'s rites have started ... The spirit of *baseness* is now looming over the land of Russia .... It is frightening to think so, but we appear to be uncontrollably plunging into an abyss" (Frank, 2001, 221).

Berdyaev's newspaper articles from March 1917 to January 1918, a critical period of Russian history, offer a broad range of thoughts and emotions. The religious and mystical underpinnings of events that Berdyaev had thought to be out-of-place eccentricity in Merezhkovsky's works now became a recurrent topic in his own assessments of Bolshevism. He consistently emphasizes the orgiastic element of the revolution and particularly of its Russian version: "Obsession with Bolshevism is a new form of Russia's ancestral cult of *Khlysty*" (Berdyaev, 2007, 597). Berdyaev points out the paradox that was also discovered by other thinkers in those terrible months: Bolshevism turns the meaning of the revolution inside out; individual will and responsibility are dissolved in impersonality; what has been progressive now becomes regressive.

> Russian land lives under the power of the pagan element of *Khlysty* cult. This element drowns everything personal, it is incompatible with personal dignity and personal responsibility. This devilish element can equally produce from its depths not faces, but masks of Rasputin and Lenin. Russian "Bolshevik" revolution is a terrible worldwide reactionary phenomenon that is as reactionary in its spirit as "Rasputinism," as the "Black-Hundred *Khlysty* cult."
>
> (Berdyaev, 2007, 750)

Berdyaev is quite radical in determining the degree of regress: Bolshevism is "experiencing the pre-human, primeval communism." It offers nothing for the cause of civil freedom besides "communist darkness," "the dark demon of social class" (Berdyaev, 2007, 731). Berdyaev distinguishes the temptations of the Catholic and Orthodox worlds and "claims" that the former specializes in Satanism, while the latter specializes in the Antichrist. Western religiosity has virtually no sense of the Antichrist. Russia is different in this regard: "You cannot tempt the Russian soul with the devil, but you can easily tempt it with the Antichrist. The devil entails distinguishing, while the Antichrist rests on confusion and substitution" (Berdyaev, 2007, 597). Hence a program for combating substitutions:

> The religion of revolutionary socialism, magical socialism, the religion of Bolshevism captivating in its equality, fairness, and global triumph of

social truth and social paradise is particularly powerful among Russians. Western socialism is legalistic; Russian socialism is lawless. Bolshevism is a national Russian phenomenon, it is our national disease that existed in the past Russian history in different form ... This Russian disease cannot be vanquished with only rational, governmental, political cures. It can only be vanquished religiously, only by contrasting a fake simulacrum of the Good with the true power of the Good of Christ. ... If the element of Antichrist triumphs, the blame will lie with the Christian world, with its spiritual bourgeoisness. Christians do not exhibit even a modicum of the energy exhibited by Bolsheviks. The latter's energy is spurious, ghostly, it is nothing but devilish possession.

(Berdyaev, 2007, 598)

Here we see virtually all descriptions of Bolshevism typical for those tragic years. Let us take special note of the most unusual one as applied to Bolsheviks: "spiritual bourgeoisness." However, if we recall that Merezhkovsky saw the principal danger to lie in godless positivist philistinism, then Berdyaev's logic becomes clear. Of course, the expression "the Bolshevik religion" applied to militant atheists also sounds odd, but it was not Berdyaev's unique insight. Even Bertrand Russell writes, after meeting Lenin in 1920, "Bolshevism is not merely a political doctrine; it is also a religion, with elaborate dogmas and inspired scriptures" (Russell, 1920, 6). Although he affectionately adds, "To understand Bolshevism it is not sufficient to know facts; it is necessary also to enter with sympathy or imagination into a new spirit" (Russell, 1920, 13).

We should add that Berdyaev's rhetorical arsenal features another interesting philosophical twist: "In some ways, 'Mensheviks' are worse than 'Bolsheviks' because they are ambivalent and fearful. It is immoral to wish for power and to shirk responsibility" (Berdyaev, 2007, 536). This far-from-harmless paradox (Berdyaev was not alone in stressing it) will produce the concepts of creative violence and the stable feelings of admiration for open barbarity; later, followers of Eurasianism and *Smenovekhovtsy* will ride the crest of this wave. Both liberals and socialists frequently perceived Bolshevism as a useful extremity, as an *enfant terrible* that could eventually be brought to heel once its destructive energy has been used; in any case, for both liberals and socialists, Bolsheviks were people of their own kind who simply had gone berserk; they were not as alien as the notional "Black Hundreds." This illusion will make it easier to understand the troubling implications of even that mild form of affinity for the enemy.

After the October plunge into an abyss, the revolution-related musings of philosophers (and writer-philosophers who cannot be discarded if we want to grasp the full picture) essentially narrow down to the question "What is Bolshevism?," which is now seen as all-important. Let us look at different takes on Bolsheviks manifested by certain Russian thinker-poets (apart from such figures as Nikolai Gumilyov and Valeriy Bryusov, who are transparent in their polarity).

Vyacheslav Ivanov's response to the revolutionary events is highly equivocal. In his article "The Revolution and the People's Self-Determination" (1917) published in the *Narodopravstvo [People's Rule]* weekly and included in the "Matters Native and Universal" collection, Ivanov states that the revolution has opted for a path outside religion and therefore it does not reflect the people's self-determination.

> Revolutionary action forced to confine itself to proclaiming abstract patterns of public thought and civil morals as the new foundations for the people's life is inactive. When it is impossible for the revolutionary state to manifest itself in creative action, it takes on the character of a morbid state, revealed by the grave symptoms of growing anarchy and overall devastation, by the development of centrifugal forces that establish themselves in division and discord, and by the collapse of the people's integral organism into dead parts. The revolution will either reduce Russia to "a pile of smoldering bones" or will be Russia's true rebirth and a new embodiment of the people's spirit, an embodiment that is full and conscious for the first time. In order to achieve its true accomplishment in this sense, it should manifest an integral and, therefore, primarily religious self-determination of the people.
>
> (Ivanov, 1979, 364)

Gennadiy Obatnin's analysis shows that Ivanov's newspaper articles demonstrate the same stance. Obatnin singles out the following invectives in Ivanov's newspaper articles: criticism of the Bolsheviks' pro-German leanings and their desire for a separate peace, "cultural masochism" of the Russian people and the intelligentsia open to the "vibrations of the German culture," and murders of priests that Red Army soldiers committed with impunity. Obatnin also quotes Ivanov's talk in the House of Free Art on May 19(6), 1918:

> Revolutionary ages are ages of the least creative activity and of the greatest becoming. When the metal is molten, is creation of forms possible? Is action possible during birth? We feel that life is creating us, and not that we create life. Hence the feeling of fate. ... The only gesture we can make of our own free will is to grasp the hand extended from the darkness. This is not creativity, this is sacrifice. What is left for the spirit

is the readings of the stars and suggestions of the Muse Urania. ... And also hope!

(Obatnin, 1997, 228)

Obatnin sees this talk as Ivanov's gesture of resignation to what has happened.

Alexander Blok's attitude towards Bolshevism becomes largely clear in his extensive essay "Catiline," written in April 1918. It is more sincere than his famous article "Intelligentsia and the Revolution," where he calls for "listening to the music of the revolution." The Roman "Bolshevik" Catiline, as Blok calls him, rebels against the old world and attempts to blow up from within "the depraved civilization" a few decades before Christ. Christ is in front of him, as he is in front of the twelve Red Army soldiers. In Catiline's time, before the birth of Jesus Christ, the herald of a new world, a wind rose which escalated into a storm that destroyed the pagan world. Catiline throws himself into that wind; he lives and acts as the wind blows him. And Blok also points out that, in surrendering to the element, the hero pays for it with a moral, psychic, and even physical rebirth. (Now we understand why the revolution must be listened to "with [one's] whole body.")

> The simplicity and horror of the state of the soul of the doomed revolutionary lies in the fact that a long chain of dialectic and perceptible premises was apparently discarded from it, and the conclusions drawn by the reason and heart appear wild, accidental, groundless. Such a person is insane, maniacal, possessed. As it transpires, life appears to be subjugated to different laws of causality, space and time; hence, the entire composition, both material and spiritual, turns out to be completely different from that of "gradualists"; it is applied to a different time and a different space.
>
> (Blok, 1982, 274)

Yet, even here, Blok hears the music of the revolution:

> Here, on this black background of the nighttime (the revolution, like all great events, always emphasizes blackness), imagine a gang, at the head of which walks a man who has lost his senses from rage and has forced them to carry the signs of the consul rank ahead of him. This is the same Catiline, the recent favorite of the luminaries of Roman society and the demi-monde, the criminal leader of a degenerate band; He walks at the same "lazy, then hurried" pace, but his rage and fury endow his gait with a musical rhythm; he appears to be no longer the self-interested

and depraved Catiline; this man's steps are mutiny, rebellion, furies of the people's wrath.

(Blok, 1982, 289)

Blok finds a place for himself here as well. The poet apparently identifies himself with Catullus and analyzes poem 63, "Attis," which describes the beautiful youth Attis flying into frenzy because of his hatred of Venus and castrating himself. Blok interprets this poem (none too convincingly) as Catullus' experience of the civil war, claiming that "in the time of storms and trouble, the most tender, the most intimate strivings of a poet's soul also become filled with storms and trouble" (Blok, 1982, 287). Alexander Etkind undertakes a detailed analysis of this strange comparison (Etkind, 1998, 363–70), but for our purposes, it is sufficient to record the poet's desire to project his "most tender, most intimate" problems and worries onto the historical screen of the revolution. This virtually unsublimated intoxication with destruction and the ambiguous and mysterious attitude to *das Ewig-Weibliche* Blok had celebrated, which is oddly linked with the revolution, sets Blok apart from other Symbolists.

For a comparatively long time, Maximilian Voloshin managed to keep his aesthetic distance from the revolution. Remarkably, Voloshin greets the First Russian Revolution (also known as the February Revolution) with rather calm and pragmatic notes devoid of any eschatological thrust. As far as the system instituted by the new regime is concerned, Voloshin is mostly worried about the place it will accord to art and poetry. Yet his texts exhibit another motif that was common to many intellectuals in 1917: "Russia should head for a religious revolution, not for a social one. Transfiguration of the personality" (Voloshin, 2008, 662). He does not see any historical prospects in the ideology that became the principal resource of the revolutionary rhetoric: "Socialism is a negative phenomenon, because it is insufficiently practical to guide the present, and its ideal is too petty to elucidate the future" (Voloshin, 2008, 349). Certain that the poet's mission is to bring the religious revolution closer and to protect its sprouts from being trampled into oblivion by partisan battles, Voloshin does not even wish to notice the evident "Bolshevism" of some of his fellow poets. Later, in 1919, in the article titled "Poetry and Revolution," he will join the debate about Blok's "The Twelve," a debate that few in the intelligentsia avoided. Voloshin does not believe that Blok has become a "programmatic Bolshevik," and he exclaims

> what does a poet such as Blok care for the rabid fight between the two human classes that are so far removed from him, the so-called bourgeoisie and proletariat. ... Only two orders of phenomena could

interest a poet in this struggle: the great world forces that enthrall people against their will, as in Verhaeren's case, or the tragedy of an individual human soul thrown into the dark maze of passions and errors, a soul that has lost its Christ therein, as happened to Blok in this case.

(Voloshin, 2008, 32–3)

The years of post-revolutionary experience changed the nature of Voloshin's "aloofness." He still strove to stand above the fray, not as a sage advisor, but as a man of prayer, who realizes the truth proclaimed by each side and the inevitability of the collision itself. Summary formulas of his ruminations may be found in "Russia Crucified" (with poems included); he had been working on this lecture from October 1918 to May 1920, frequently giving public readings. In this lecture, he claims that already in 1917 he understood that "the Russian Revolution will be long, frenzied, bloody, that we are on the threshold of a new Great Devastation of Russia, a new Time of Troubles" (Voloshin, 2008, 459). The idea of the inescapable revolutionary nature of Russia's history is a leitmotif of his entire post-revolutionary poetic and journalistic output. Not only the lower classes or the opposition rise to rebellion in Russia; the key feature of the monarchy itself was its revolutionary character: the monarchy was more radical than the society and was always inclined to a top-down revolution. Voloshin believes that Bolshevism is a profoundly Russian phenomenon: those "horrible wraiths of the sixteenth and seventeenth centuries" which rose from the depths of the Russian people, summoned by the Bolshevist propaganda, turned out, as he says in "On the Scales of Poetry," to be "an unexpected and profound truth about Russia" (Voloshin, 2008, 428). It might appear strange that the 1917 revolution nonetheless struck Voloshin as ludicrous: a social revolution occurred in a country where, he believes, there is no capitalism, no proletariat, no agrarian question, no bourgeoisie, yet the struggle between these imaginary values reaches the highest of peaks. "This absurdity," the poet exclaims, "indicates the providential nature of Russia's history" (Voloshin, 2008, 485). Voloshin believes that what Russia experienced was not a social revolution, but an inoculation: Russia is injected with the disease that threatens Europe. "Of all the European countries, Russia is the healthiest socially, and she is currently performing a sacrificial feat in taking on the disease of the social revolution, in order to develop an immunity to it and to prevent the deadly outbreak of the disease in Europe" (Voloshin, 2008, 486). Voloshin does not explain what Russia's "health" consists of, but he does not doubt either its global ministry, or the existence of a "protective force" that will save Russia despite her own strivings. Subsequently, he offers another metaphor: the revolutionary intelligentsia contemplated the future European revolution with such fullness of a religious sentiment that, without being crucified itself, it accepted the stigmata of the social revolution. The Russian Revolution, therefore, is a neurotic religious disease. The second gestalt clearly undermines the first: an inoculation is a real way of preventing a disease, while stigmata are self-suggestion. Given Voloshin's passionate denunciation of Bolshevism, his self-positioning "above the fray" is also contradictory.

> I cannot have political ideals because they always strive for the greatest possible earthly well-being and comfort. I could only wish for my people a path that is right and straight, that corresponds perfectly to their historical, universal mission. And I know in advance that this is a path of suffering and martyrdom. What do I care whether this path passes through monarchy, socialism, or capitalism?—these are but varieties of the flame that the human spirit passes through to be burned and purified. I equally welcome revolution, reaction, communism, and monarchy.
> (Voloshin, 2008, 503)

Yet if we consider that, according to Voloshin, Bolshevism is not what a person believes in, but "the means and the limits within which the person believes it possible to exercise their faith" (Voloshin, 2008, 435), this contradiction disappears, or, at the very least, is transferred into another realm: that of historiosophy. The sources of such "Bolshevism" should be sought in the nature of the "flame" that purifies the human spirit.

The collection of articles *Iz glubiny* (*Out of the Depths*) (1918) was an outstanding attempt at offering a philosophical interpretation of the disaster. Paradoxically, however, the analysis of Bolshevism therein is not exactly small in scope, but rather thematically narrow. It is mostly represented by the works of Sergei Bulgakov and Alexander Izgoyev. The authors uniformly praise Bolsheviks' certain "directness" and "frankness," as they dared implement what remained mere rhetoric with other parties. Of course, the thinkers were not justifying Bolsheviks' crimes; they were speaking of socialism having essentially exposed itself for what it truly was. Izgoyev systematically shows that Bolshevism's war on the bourgeoisie was essentially a war on the principal achievements of civilization. "Whatever there is creative in European socialism, it is essentially 'bourgeois,' it is based on ideas that run counter to socialism. The tremendous, universal importance of Russian Bolsheviks' activities lies in their having showed this truth to the whole world" (Izgoyev, 2009b, 771). Bolshevism itself could only offer "bourgeoisness" in its worst form, as an "antisocial solipsism of individuality torn out of culture" (Izgoyev, 2009b, 786).

Bulgakov's discourse is more complex. In six polyphonically structured dramatized dialogues, he offers a virtual encyclopedia of polemical topics and takes on the revolution. It would hardly be proper to unequivocally identify one of them as Bulgakov's own (although as a rule, the Refugee is seen as the author's "voice"). Through the Refugee, Bulgakov asks, "Could it be that Bolshevism does, indeed, have the kind of depth and mystery that we so far failed to perceive?" The question is raised in connection with criticisms of Blok's "dysfunctional" visions in his poem "The Twelve," without clearly identifying Bulgakov's own stance, but the focus here clearly is on the eschatological meaning of the revolution and on the possibility of salvation via overcoming temptations and trials. These apocalyptic elements and a close connection between the revolution and a world war evinced in the dialogs are far from new for Bulgakov. What is new here is that Bolshevism is now seen as Europe's inevitable future, which tinges Bulgakov's cherished idea of Russia's great missions with colors typical for Konstantin Leontiev's prophecies:

> Still, Europe will not avoid its own Bolshevism. It will still be wracked by convulsions of a global revolution, and the red horse of social riots will thunder across it. And that despite the fact that socialism is already dead: the principle that is outliving itself still has to experience its own powerlessness. The Russian intelligentsia, as the spiritual culprit behind Bolshevism, is, indeed, the vanguard of a global riot just as revolutionary Slavophiles from Bakunin to Lenin dreamed despite their programmatic internationalism.
>
> (Bulgakov, 2009, 743)

The subject of Bolshevism, however, is far from being one of the main subjects of the collection as a whole, apparently because the collapse of Russian statehood made the role played by its destroyers far too obvious. At that time, it was more important to find an anti-crisis formula, and this is the purpose of the concluding articles by Peter Struve and Semyon Frank with their key topics of "culture" and "people" seen in the light of "the ideal of spiritual unity and organic spiritual creative power of the people, the ideal of *religious meaningfulness and national and historical foundations of social and political culture*" (Frank, 2009, 889).

The interpretations of the Bolshevik revolution above manifest a certain ideological invariant: each sees the driving forces of history as certain impersonal elements that a human being can fight, argue with, agree, et cetera, all the while having to acknowledge the objective logic of supra-personal developments. Since most Russian philosophers coming to grips with the revolution had gone through the schools of Marxism or Western sociology, such a paradigm is quite natural. Consequently, it would be particularly interesting to look at Mark Aldanov's peculiar concept. Aldanov understands history as a "fight against chance," as defending the "Good-Beauty" principle, the defense of which is, in his opinion, the mission of a morally responsible person in an indeterminate, morally neutral world. If we allow that history does have entelechy, then, in Aldanov's opinion, it lies in a person's capability to realize themselves as an agent of moral dignity. For Aldanov, revolution brings this collision of will and chance to a head, as it shows the impossibility of substituting natural and historical determination for moral freedom. The second part of Aldanov's book *Armageddon* (1918; published "as a manuscript" and quickly confiscated), titled "The Chariot of Jagannath," analyzes revolution in Russian and European contexts. In *Armageddon*, Aldanov claims:

> There are two kinds of revolutions. Those of the first kind are immediately suppressed and entail a larger or smaller number of executions. They are usually given the lesser names of "riots," while they are essentially the most elevated, the most heroic revolutions. ... Revolutions of the second kind unfold at a quick and terrible pace, but their "denouement" suggests mournful thoughts. ... And still something always remains behind. The question of justifying a revolution hinges on the price paid for this "something." And on intangible values, on the continuing legend. ... At best, the legend of the Russian revolution will be the fact that the leaders of its first stage, while having full ability to keep their power and save Russia from chaos at the cost of betraying an alliance and sacrificing their honor still did not travel down that path. Some of them clearly sensed it and preferred to perish.
>
> (Aldanov, 2006, 110–11)

Despite the "absurd nightmare" of revolutions, Aldanov is looking for a system of sorts in their madness and, since his historically substantial comparative studies go on for many years, he does not see this as an idle pursuit. The Great French Revolution at all its stages, through all its metamorphoses, constitutes for him the revolutionary paradigm par excellence. Aldanov sees the greatest difference between the French Revolution and the Russian Revolution in the latter being inorganic and accidental, qualities manifested in the nature of its terror (imposed top down, and not being an impulse traveling in the opposite direction, as in France) and in the anti-national foreign policy that, unlike the French patriotic expansion, resulted in a conscious military surrender. Still, Aldanov tried to take the French logic of proceeding from stage to stage and to project it onto the Russian Revolution, as he believed that the Bolsheviks would inevitably arrive at "Thermidorizing" their regime. With time, Aldanov's optimism vanishes. Early Aldanov allows that the revolution itself may help eliminate Bolshevism:

> Every country in Europe, except Russia, has institutions that allow for a conflict of ideas without recourse to barricades and machine guns. This

is why we hope that the revolution that is ultimately destined to destroy the Bolshevik tyranny, too, will be the last one. And if this is nothing but daydreams, well, more is the pity!

(Aldanov 1919, 8)

Later, he would come to see Stalinism as a mutation of the Robespierrean model, a mutation that is quite capable of surviving without a positive transformation. In his 1920s essay published in the *Fire and Smoke* collection (1922), Aldanov goes back to a question that is paramount for him: revolution's place in history. He still believes revolution to be a madly exorbitant price to be paid for fomenting positive change. At the same time, he hopes still that the revolutionary experience will make it possible to glean some positive results from the Bolshevik chaos. In his essay "The Third Rome and the Third International," Aldanov posits the question of Bolshevism's theoretical foundations. Figures usually associated with the ideas of Bolshevism (Razin, Bakunin, Tkachyov, Nechayev) are, in Aldanov's opinion, mostly practitioners of Bolshevism. He proposes a certain ideological kinship between Bolsheviks and Slavophiles, a kinship that eluded the "public mind": "Behind the difference in accidents, we must not overlook the similarity in substances, the similarity that is in places striking: Bolsheviks proved to be a very biting satirical caricature of Slavophiles" (Aldanov, 1922, 105–6). Aldanov sees the ideology of the Third International as being substantially similar to Slavophilism with its amalgamation of uniqueness and universality:

In May 1919, Lenin presented a major report to the Moscow Socialist Congress that laid the foundations of the Third International. He used this historical document to expose, with his typical fury, the abominations of the contemporary Western European system and eloquently argued that true freedom existed only in Soviet Russia. As I read this document, I found it hard to banish the thought that some of its ideas had been plagiarized from Konstantin Aksakov. ... Lenin does not expose the West in general, the West "as such," he exposes the capitalist West. But this objection does not ruin the analogy. We have seen that Slavophiles, particularly later-generations Slavophiles, loved to talk about stock exchanges of Western European bourgeoisie. Exposing the ruling classes and lauding the oppressed classes would not come as a surprise to them either. ... Slavophiles were no less democratic than Bolsheviks.

(Aldanov, 1922, 108–10)

Yet the ideational kinship discovered by Aldanov between the two mindsets manifests at an ever-deeper level in their respective concepts of relations between authorities and society. Aldanov quotes Konstantin Aksakov's memorandum "On the domestic situation in Russia" and offers a sarcastic comment:

> We have reasons to claim that Lenin has never clapped eyes on Aksakov's memorandum. Yet he implemented its precepts to a rather significant degree. In complete compliance with the first two precepts, he assumed absolute power. He only partially complied with the fifth precept. In the All-Russian Federative Soviet Republic, people that do not carry a political element do not have a right "to an opinion that the government is free to accept or reject." Lenin did impose restrictions of unprecedented brazenness in cultural history, yet they apply only to external manifestations of moral freedom. Bolsheviks separated freedom of spirit from freedom of speech. Aksakov thought that words have no need to translate into action; Lenin admitted that spirit has no need for words.
>
> (Aldanov, 1922, 111–12)

Today, such a comparison may appear unexpected and paradoxical, yet the political thought of the 1920s was still dominated by a paradigm where Bolsheviks were solidly entrenched in the position of extremist Westernizers who had perverted Marxist ideas. Let us compare Aldanov's insight with reflections in *Iz glubiny* that are nothing if not representative. One of the characters in Sergei Bulgakov's dialogues dwells, almost like Aldanov, on "Slavophile-style internationalist fairy tales that Bolsheviks have now learned, too" (Bulgakov, 2009, 730). Another character promises that soon "the red horse of social riots will thunder across" Europe just like "revolutionary Slavophiles from Bakunin to Lenin dreamed despite their programmatic internationalism" (Bulgakov, 2009, 743). However, Bulgakov stresses internationalism turned inside out, while Aldanov is interested primarily in the idea of a powerless people transferring political functions to a certain absolutist government. Berdyaev's analysis of the character of Shatov appears to be close to what Aldanov says: "Vacillating and ambivalent Shatov mixes Slavophiles' mindset with the revolutionary mindset"; "Shatov, a typical *narodnik*, mixes revolutionary elements with reactionary, 'black hundred' elements. ... The Russian revolution is full of such Shatovs; with them, you can never tell where their extreme left-wing revolutionary sentiments end and extreme right-wing reactionary sentiments begin" (Berdyaev, 2009b, 688). Characteristically, however, these elements are so mixed up "you can never tell them apart," while Aldanov is talking about the selfsame element. Consequently, when Berdyaev writes that Dostoevsky, "as an adherent of the native soil movement and a Slavophile of sorts" (Berdyaev, 2009b, 687), saw the Russian people as an antidote to the revolution, this claim does not contradict what he has to say about Shatov. Otherwise, the collection manifests traditional features of Slavophilism that Frank expressed with particular emphasis when he spoke about the missing ideal that "can be understood as a revival of Slavophiles' dream about organic development of spiritual and public culture from the profound historical roots of the religious and public understanding of life inherent in the entire people" (Frank, 2009, 888). Against this backdrop, the fundamentally apolitical ideal of Slavophiles as Aldanov sees it in the light of Bolshevik theory and practice acquires an ominous, if not directly infernal, meaning. This critical motif, however, was not popular even in émigré thought.

Lev Karsavin's views appear to be directly opposite to those of Aldanov, yet this is a more complicated case. Karsavin stands out with his Slavophile mysticism, yet, like others, he too argues that historical determination cannot replace moral freedom. Against the backdrop of a long history of discourse about the meaning of revolution, Karsavin's version is distinguished by a paradoxical connection between faith in the effective nature of the spirit of history and a resolute rejection of all types of fatalism.

Karsavin first engages with the topic of the revolution in his then-unpublished essay (1920—?) "Joseph de Maistre" (Karsavin, 1989) where his own opinions of the Russian Revolution are hidden in the exposition of de Maistre's views but are easily identifiable in the sympathetic passages. De Maistre's thoughts on the nation as a unified subject of history that bears a collective responsibility for sins that do not spare the individual, and his understanding of the revolution as a redemptive and cleansing sacrifice, were close to Karsavin's own; Karsavin liked de Maistre's ability to feel that a "mysterious element of life" (Karsavin, 1989, 96) and the will of Providence that controls that element "are manifested in revolution." Without these motifs, we might interpret Karsavin's first engagement with the theme of the Russian Revolution in his major 1922 work *Philosophy of History* as an apologia for Bolshevism. In sections 21 and 61, Karsavin discusses both the February and October Revolutions as if to illustrate his overall understanding, with a quite radical discussion of the Bolsheviks.

> In essence, Bolshevik policy was, if not the best means of preserving Russian statehood and culture, then a sufficient means in any case, and perhaps the only suitable means in the given circumstances.
>
> (Karsavin, 1989, 308)

Bolshevism, which does not coincide with communism, is the individualization of certain elemental desires of the Russian people, often as deformed Western ideology. The Bolshevik Party expresses this most fully and vividly. It is not the people who impose their will on the Bolsheviks, nor the Bolsheviks who impose theirs on the people. But the people's will is individualized in the Bolsheviks; some of its most significant motifs are realized in them: the thirst for social reorganization and even social truth, the instincts of statehood and great-power status.

(Karsavin, 1989, 310)

The reader may not even notice the trivial formulation "people's will," but this is where the main feature of Karsavin's idea is encoded: the doctrine of "symphonic person." In light of the symphonic person's mission, the ruling stratum is an organic connection among individuals of that active sociocultural segment of society that has resonated with the spirit of history and the people. In this case, the stratum "rules" along with parties and institutions, eventually passing judgment on them. Therefore, the Bolshevik principle of the primacy of will loses its valence and, along with it, Bolshevism's entire voluntarism and its pathos of the leaders' absolute power.

The range of takes on Bolshevism would be incomplete without Lev Shestov's work "What Russian Bolshevism Is" (1920). This article is written in a very accessible manner, in a style reminiscent of Leo Tolstoy's later non-fiction works, with its appeals to stark facts and the author's personal experience, but this somewhat affected artlessness is underpinned by a carefully thought-out logical outline. Identifying the most typical feature of the Bolshevik essence, Shestov claims that Bolshevism is "reactionary; it is incapable of creating anything. It takes what is in hand, what others have done without it. In short: Bolsheviks are parasites in their essence" (Shestov, 2001, 102–3); "the spirit of serfdom that permeates their entire activity, and their entire simplified ideology kill any creative effort at embryonic stage" (Shestov, 2001, 102–3). Given Bolsheviks' announced mission of being a driving engine of progress and creative revival, their reactionary nature uncovered by Shestov touches upon the essence of the historical event: all the forces of Russian inertia rose against the real possibility of progress, and Bolsheviks with their cult of violence found themselves in the vanguard. Of help here was the intelligentsia's passive stargazing ("no matter where you went, talks about Russia's elevated mission were everywhere. Not about fixing Russia up, no one wanted to think about it, or knew how") and Romantic anti-bourgeois leanings ("all writers were most afraid of Russia accidentally getting to lead a materially comfortable existence") (Shestov, 2001, 108–9).

Parasitic inability to work and create results in a "dictatorship over proletariat," which, in turn, requires violence and putting red tape everywhere: "the stamp of churlishness lies on the entire activity of Bolshevik bureaucracy" (Shestov, 2001, 113). However, that destructive conclusion entails, in Shestov's opinion, the Bolsheviks' *ultima ratio*:

> We need to 'blow up' the West, destroy the philistinism of Europe and America. And we will keep up the conflagration in Russia until the blaze spreads to our neighbors and from thence throughout the world. This is our highest mission, our utmost, cherished dream. We will give Europe ideas, Europe will give us its 'technique,' its skill, its organizational gift, etc.
> (Shestov, 2001, 108–9)

The answer to the question of what's next manifests classical Shestov with his Biblical history of philosophy: the wrathful God "confounded their language," monarchs killed the monarchy, democracy killed democracy, socialists and revolutionaries are killing socialism and the revolution. Will people ever be rid of this confusion? It is easier for Shestov to believe that Bolshevism will spread throughout the world (Shestov, 2001, 120–1).

An overview of the most representative reflections on the essence of Bolshevism from the intellectual elite in the era of the three revolutions evidences the difficult paths these thinkers traveled to come to grips with this phenomenon. After 1905, Bolshevism is perceived as a significant and instructive, yet peripheral, element in political life. After February 1917, the framework of social and political discourse breaks down. Attempts are now made to conceptualize Bolshevism within greater discourses (both traditional for Russian thought and new ones) such as historiosophy, eschatology, Sophiology, syncretic religious mysticism, national and cultural messianism, the metaphysical meaning of world wars, etc. After October, Bolshevism is seen as some infernal substance deeply rooted in Russian history. This insight produced highly variegated reactions: despair, resignation, and repentance, yet also a desire to soberly analyze the mechanisms of this catastrophic plunge. Metaphysics gives way to ethics and sociology. The 1920s emigration and the overall cultural space see a reduced intensity and shallower philosophical depths of Bolshevism analysis: the topic is politicized and dissolved in the pragmatics of émigrés' immediate objectives. The conflict (subdued yet fundamental) between Struve and Frank who had been habitually like-minded thinkers is typical in this regard: decisive political struggle appeals to Struve, while Frank is attracted by attempts to avoid an unequivocal confrontation with Bolshevism and understand its "ties" with the people. Both paths, however, lead to dead ends. The topic of Bolshevism transitions to a new level in the 1930s, in the works published in the *Novy grad* (*New City*), but this is another era that requires a special approach and a different hermeneutics. Still, we can state that the problem of coming to grips with Bolshevism has not been solved and has not been intellectually shelved. On the contrary, with every new turn of the historical spiral, it manifests its terrible relevance and readiness to take revenge upon those who neglect its challenges.

Note

1 The original title features a pun: Ham is the second son of Noah punished for his irreverence, while the homonymous Russian word *ham* means churl, originally, a person of low social origins, and then a rude, ill-bred person. In the nineteenth century, the term "ham" (*kham*, or its derivative *khamstvo*) was used to describe anyone who showed disrespect towards others.

References

Aldanov (Landau-Aldanov), Mark A. 1919. *Lénine*. Paris: Édit. Jacques Povolozky.
Aldanov, Mark A. 1922. *Ogon i dym*. Paris: Franko-rus. pechat.
Aldanov, Mark A. 2006. *Armageddon*. Moscow: Intelvak.
Berdyaev, Nikolai A. 1998. *Duhovnyi krizis intelligentcii*. Moscow: Kanon+.
Berdyaev, Nikolai A. 2007. *Padenie sviashchennogo russkogo tcarstva: Publitcistika 1914–1922*. Moscow: Astrel.
Berdyaev, Nikolai A. 2009a. "Filosofskaia istina i intelligentskaia pravda." In *Manifesty russkogo idealizma. Problemy idealizma. Vehi. Iz glubiny*, 455–71. Moscow: Astrel.
Berdyaev, Nikolai A. 2009b. "Duhi russkoi revoliutcii." In *Manifesty russkogo idealizma. Problemy idealizma. Vehi. Iz glubiny*, 671–705. Moscow: Astrel.
Blok, Alexander A. 1982. *Sobranie sochinenii*. Vol. 4. Leningrad: Khudozhestvennaja literatura.
Bulgakov, Sergei N. 2009. "Na piru bogov." In *Manifesty russkogo idealizma. Problemy idealizma. Vehi. Iz glubiny*, 706–61. Moscow: Astrel.
Etkind, Alexander M. 1998. *Khlyst: Sekty, literatura i revoliutsiia*. Moscow: Novoe literaturnoe obozrenie.
Frank, Semyon L. 2001. *Neprochitannoe … Stat'i, pis'ma, vospominaniya* [*Unread … Articles, letters, memories*]. Moscow: MShPI Publ.
Frank, Semyon L. 2009. "De profundis." In *Manifesty russkogo idealizma. Problemy idealizma. Vehi. Iz glubiny*, 871–89. Moscow: Astrel.

Ivanov, Vyacheslav I. 1979. *Sobranie sochinenii*. Vol. 3. Brussels: Foyer Oriental Chrétien.
Izgoyev, Alexander S. 2009a. "Ob intelligentnoi molodezhi." In *Manifesty russkogo idealizma. Problemy idealizma. Vehi. Iz glubiny*, 530–51. Moscow: Astrel.
Izgoyev, Alexander S. 2009b. "Sotcializm, kultura i bolshevizm." In *Manifesty russkogo idealizma. Problemy idealizma. Vehi. Iz glubiny*, 768–91. Moscow: Astrel.
Karsavin, Lev P. 1989. "Joseph de Maistre." *Voprosy filosofii* 3: 79–92.
Karsavin, Lev P. 1993. *Filosofiia istorii*. St. Petersburg: Komplekt.
Kistyakovski, Bogdan A. 2009. In *Manifesty russkogo idealizma. Problemy idealizma. Vehi. Iz glubiny*, 552–76. Moscow: Astrel.
Merezhkovsky, Dmitry S. 1991. *Bolnaya Rossiya*. Leningrad: Izdatelstvo Leningradskogo universiteta.
Obatnin, Gennadiy V. 1997. "Shtrikhi k portretu Viach. Ivanova epokhi revoliutsii 1917 goda." *Russkaia literatura* 2: 224–30.
Russell, Bertrand. 1920. *The Practice and Theory of Bolshevism*. New York: Harcourt, Brace and Howe.
Shestov, Lev I. 2001. "Chto takoe russkii bolshevizm." In *Istoriia filosofii* 8, 97–121. Moscow: IFRAN.
Voloshin, Maximilian A. 2008. *Sobranie sochinenii*. Vol. 6. Bk. 2. Proza 1900–1927. Moscow: Ellis Lak.

4

War in Ukraine and the Ethics of Pragmatism

Dmitri N. Shalin

In the run up to his first presidential campaign, Putin sat down with journalists and, eager to dispel doubts about his KGB past, vigorously defended his democratic credentials. "I am not a dictator," he told the interviewers. "We are part of western European culture." Ours is "the path of democratic development." "We must preserve local government and a system of election for governors," "the confiscation and nationalization of property" would be "catastrophic" (Putin, 2000, 155-6; 163-74; cf. Shalin, 2007).

While hesitating to label his overall stance, Putin singled out for praise Ludwig Erhard, the German Chancellor, as "a very pragmatic man" whose savvy political stewardship helped navigate West Germany after World War II (Putin, 2000, 175). The adjective "pragmatic" pops up several times in this compilation of interviews and hagiographic testimonies, applied among others to Anatoly Chubais, who had pleasantly surprised Putin by endorsing his decision to subdue the rebellion in Chechnya. The compendium compiled during the 2000 election season also contains a quote from Sergei Raldugin, Putin's longtime friend, who noticed, not without trepidation, his companion's mutation into a veritable "pragmatist" (Putin, 2000, 91).

In 2013, the Russia leader gave an interview on the eve of the G20 summit where he embraced the moniker. "I am a conservative pragmatist," Putin (2013) assured foreign journalists who pondered his political sensibilities ever since the second Russian president assumed the reins of government. The expression "Putin's pragmatism" and its iterations turn up frequently in the news media, expert reports, and scholarly accounts (Caryl, 2001; Lozansky, 2013; Boykoff and Smith-Spark, 2017; Pertsev, 2017; Crosston, 2018; Baker, 2019; Rogov, 2022). Early comments were generally positive, as observers praised Putin's decision to close military bases in Cuba and Vietnam, tacit approval of US bases in Central Asia, and willingness to engage in talks about troop reduction in Europe. Commentators warned that "A pragmatic, cool-headed policy oriented toward Russia's interests (including Russia's interest in a robust market economy) will present a far greater challenge to the West than Yeltsin's emotional oscillations between friendship and confrontation" (Sokov, 2000). "Russia's stated adherence to the values of democracy has little to do with her liberal idealism of the early 1990s, but rather is a pragmatic approach in which accepting dominant Western norms has a long-term strategic value, a means of advancing the national interest" (Medvedev, 2004). Cautious optimism about the direction of Russian foreign policy was palpable: "Russia would pursue its 'national interest' wherever it sees fit—but without the interference of 'ideology,' which, as Putin argues, regrettably complicated Soviet foreign policy" (Caryl, 2001). "Putin's clear-eyed pragmatism and his visceral support of George W. Bush's war on terrorism," explained Lilia Shevtsova (2005), "have given Russia otherwise unattainable international significance."

Inside Russia, the foreign policy establishment echoed Putin's call for pragmatism. Sergey Lavrov (2007) defended his country's increasingly assertive foreign policy: "We hear complaints about the lack of ideology which our foreign policy supposedly demonstrates. Yet, pragmatism does not signify the lack of principles. What it means is that we proceed from the real needs of our country and its citizens. Russia has settled on the ideology of common sense." "It is high time for U.S. policy toward Russia to change drastically in the spirit of pragmatism," urged Edward Lozansky (2013), President of the American University in Moscow. "Not only have all the 'color revolutions' failed, but America is currently in retreat almost on every front." President Dmitry Medvedev weighed in on the issue. *The New York Times* (Levy, 2008) prominently featured the friendly advice he gave to Americans: "I am sure that any administration of the United States of America, if it wishes to succeed, among other things, in overcoming essentially a depression that exists in the American economic market, must conduct a pragmatic policy inside the country and abroad."

The speech that Vladimir Putin delivered on February 10, 2007 at the Munich Security Conference raised some eyebrows, but his warning against NATO expansion toward Russia's borders went unheeded until the next year when Russia launched "a peace enforcement operation" in Georgia, featuring a full-blown land and air assault on the neighboring country. Facing few repercussions, Putin moved in 2014 to annex Crimea and spearheaded the separatist movement in the Donetsk and Lugansk regions. That is when pundits began to raise questions about Putin's pragmatist credentials, observing that "the regime gradually shifted from pragmatism to spirituality," with the president establishing himself as "a moral or national leader" (Pertsev, 2017).

On February 24, 2022, Russia launched a "special military operation" in Ukraine, at which point the Putin-the-pragmatist meme was replaced with the Putin-the-ideologue mantra. Now commentators painted Putin as a leader determined to defend traditional values and carry out "an existential war between the Russian civilization and the West" (Kolesnikov, 2022). Critics slammed the Russian president's indifference to means and disregard for principles that the popular imagination has long associated with pragmatism. Some decried "President Vladimir Putin a ruthless but pragmatic autocrat" who wreaked havoc on the world order (Zubok, 2022). Others maintained that "The ongoing war in Ukraine, however, contradicts any notion of Russian 'pragmatism'" (Casula, 2022). Still others blamed the West for its "cynical pragmatism" that allows the carnage in Ukraine to go unabated: "What looks like pragmatism from the Western point of view seems like cynicism to Ukrainians [who are] bleeding to death for the sake of exhausting Putin" (Shenderovich, 2023).

Pragmatism has been getting bad press in Russia for a long time. Liberal thinkers are especially incensed with pragmatism, which rarely appears in their discourse without the adjectives "crass," "cynical," "naked," "cold," "wicked," or "devoid of principles." This is quite understandable given the official pronouncements on the subject, like the one put forward by Kirill, Patriarch of the Russian Orthodox Church:

> The politics of cooperation between the East and West was based on naked PRAGMATISM, on the hard bargain and balance of interests. Which is why nobody ever believed that the idea of human rights and freedoms would be realized ... Soviet diplomacy, when joining the U.N. Universal Declaration of Human Rights, never meant to extend the reach of this document to the Soviet Union. It was also a political ruse [*blef*] when in 1975 we signed the Final Act of the Conference on Security and Cooperation in Europe.
>
> (Kirill, 2006)

Applied to the Ukrainian crisis, this attitude translates into the proposition articulated by the RIAC fellow in a post titled "A pragmatic approach to peace in Ukraine"—"Thus, the only solution for peace in Ukraine is for Ukraine to take a humble look at the situation, to accept its position in world politics, and to stop provoking the country it perceives to be a threat, expecting the West to bail them out" (Fors, 2021).

For critics incensed with such noxious dicta, pragmatism was indeed "just a polite name for the lack of principles" (Bukovsky, 2006), "a cover for cynicism, hypocrisy, and corruption" (Navalnaya, 2021), "the abject form of slavery, all the more pernicious since choosing between shame and humiliation, man ends up with shame and humiliation at the same time" (Bykov, 2021). Something was missing in such wholesale rejection of pragmatism, however. This image had little to do with the intellectual current that sprang to life in the second half of the nineteenth century and evolved into an influential political and philosophical movement in the United States.

Note that Russian disdain for pragmatism is not unique—it was widespread in twentieth-century Europe, where academics and public intellectuals gave a cold shoulder to the philosophical pragmatism of William James, John Dewey, George Herbert Mead, and Jane Addams, who spread the gospel of collective inquiry deployed in the service of free society and democratic culture. For the intellectuals "bred in the veneration of theory and history, and contempt for empiricism and pragmatism" (Neumann et al., 1953, 19; cf. Shalin, 1992, 2010), the American project signified little more than crass materialism and utilitarian cunning. The reactions of Max Scheler and Martin Heidegger exemplified this attitude. In his "Letter on Humanism," Heidegger ([1946] 1961, 231, 200) condemned "the blindness and arbitrariness of what is ... known under the heading of 'pragmatism,'" a species of the intellectual malaise called "humanism" whose proponents equate thinking with the "*l'engagement dans l'action*" (Heidegger [1946] 1961, 194, 197). The pragmatist stance, Heidegger contended, breeds the "peculiar dictatorship of the public realm." Only a solitary thinker impartially contemplating the "Being of beings" can escape the impersonal domain of *Das Man* suffocating humanity.

Frankfurt School thinkers fit well with this tradition. Belittling its emancipatory rhetoric, Marcuse ([1939] 1940) and Horkheimer (1937, 1947) dismissed pragmatism as "the abasement of reason," "a genuine expression of the positivistic approach," the "reduction of reason to a mere instrument," a philosophical "counterpart of modern industrialism, for which the factory is the prototype of human existence, and which models all branches of culture after production on the conveyor belt, or after the rationalized front office" (Horkheimer, 1947, 45-54). Such contempt for pragmatism hardly abated after the authors of *Dialectics of Enlightenment* escaped Nazi Germany and settled in America.

It fell to the younger generation of Frankfurt theorists to rediscover American pragmatism and take its democratic ethos seriously. Following World War II, they undertook a systematic reexamination of the German tradition that privileged pure reason and flirted with authoritarianism. John Dewey's writings alerted Jürgen Habermas to the continuity between scientific inquiry and democratic politics, to the fact that "freedom of inquiry, toleration of diverse views, freedom of communication, the distribution of what is found out to every individual as the ultimate intellectual consumer, are involved in the democratic as in the scientific method" (Dewey, 1939, 102). Having pondered Dewey and Mead, German intellectuals came to appreciate the role of collective inquiry into communal affairs (Apel, 1981; Habermas, 1984; 1987; Joas, 1985). The problem, as Habermas (1986, 98) identified it, was that "the old Frankfurt School never took bourgeois democracy very seriously." It failed to acknowledge that the academic freedom which bourgeois democracy fosters is a major historical accomplishment. Habermas and his colleagues understood Dewey's reverence for democracy which "rests upon persuasion, upon ability to convince and be convinced," upon "the improvement of the methods and conditions of debate, discussion and persuasion. That is the problem of the public" (Dewey, 1916, 134; 1939, 102).

Few signs point to a pragmatist awakening in Russia, although several critics have taken a more sympathetic approach to pragmatist epistemology and its political agenda (Etkind, 2001; Zhirina, Nazarenko and Nigai, 2006; Shalin, 2017). Here is a statement by a Russian born historian who found his way to the West and urged his countrymen to take a closer look at this movement:

> Pragmatism is the only philosophy, American in its origin, that did not compromise itself by its collaboration with some of the worst political regimes of the twentieth century. Such collaborations had bitter consequences and marred quite a few careers of thinkers subscribing to Marxism, phenomenology, and deconstruction. These and similar intellectual currents do not acknowledge practical significance of thought, textual creations, even philosophy itself—in other words, they disclaim the responsibility for intellectual activity as such. Pragmatism, by contrast, focuses not on the truth value of a proposition but on the practical consequences of what is held to be true. That's to say, pragmatism considers the text and its author responsible for the consequences of reading.
>
> (Etkind, 2001)

I find the spectacle of the Russian establishment wrapping itself in the mantle of pragmatism nauseating. Equally disconcerting is the promiscuous use of concepts like "patriotism," "sovereignty," "humanitarian mission," "denazification campaign," "special military operation," and "the Russian World." Such staples of the official discourse clearly do not pass the pragmatic test. The regime opponents, in turn, struggle to achieve clarity when they deliberate on whether to leave the country or stay put, collaborate with the regime or defy the authorities, settle for a reasonable compromise or hide till the storm passes and it is safe to venture one's opinions again. The questions of personal responsibility, collective guilt, and national trauma haunt the regime's opponents.

I cannot do justice to such thorny matters in the few pages allotted to this chapter. What follows are sundry reflections of someone who studied pragmatism for a long time and sought to follow its ethical guidelines. No final answers or formulas are propounded below, just a few thoughts for the perplexed, including myself, in the spirit of philosophical pragmatism and with the hope to further the discussion.

Applying the Pragmatic Test

The pragmatist eschews concepts loosely connected to the mundane world. This is crucial when we deal with the arid abstractions and vapid generalities inundating politics where audiences are exposed to lofty words whose meaning and practical consequences are kept deliberately obscure. Take the "patriotism" that war mongers invoke to excuse the invasion of Ukraine. This term, endlessly bandied around, is wrought with contradictory connotations. The mob carrying out a pogrom and shouting nationalistic slogans sees itself as patriotic, and so does a couple offering safe harbor to their Jewish neighbors fleeing the hyperpatriotic crowd. A battlefield commander sending soldiers to clear the minefield with their bodies justifies his orders by the need to defend the homeland; the soldier volunteering to stay behind to ensure the safe retreat of his comrades shows love for his countrymen too. Patriotism as "the last refuge of scoundrel" (Dr. Samuel Johnson), the kind a corrupt official caught with his hands in the public trough likes to invoke (Saltykov-Shchedrin), has nothing in common with the patriotism of Aleksey Navalny unmasking corruption among Putin's cronies and receiving a twenty-year jail sentence for his public service. Take any other term exploited by the Moscow propaganda machine—traditional values, partial mobilization, denazification campaign—and you run into the same problem. Kept deliberately vague, such expressions leave ample room for the authorities to suffuse them with whatever sense the situation demands. What could be more traditional than the seventeenth-century Russian codex of family life advising parents "to flog the child mercilessly" to ensure its affection and admonishing wives "to live in fear and obey scrupulously their husbands" (Domostroi, 2007, 159, 237)—are these the traditional family values the authorities plan to enforce? Part belongs to a whole, as in "partial mobilization," but with twenty-four million eligible men, we are left to wonder how many might be drafted. So, when we hear Z-patriots defend "the Russian World," we must not let them get away with obfuscation and demand to know how far the borders of this world stretch and what objectives the "special military operation" strives to attain. The Russian World hinges on the propaganda of national superiority and the right to meddle into affairs of the countries where Russian language speakers are allegedly mistreated. Was not German Nazism based on a similar claim regarding German nationals? That is what Peirce's pragmatic test calls for when it directs attention to the consequences of our significations—"the ultimate meaning of any sign consists either of ... feeling or of acting or being acted upon" (Peirce, 1931–1935, vol. 5: 7).

Navigating the World-in-the-Making

Rendering meaning clear is not the sole purpose of pragmatist inquiry. The world we inhabit is in flux—it is a "blooming, buzzing confusion," as William James put it (James, 1890, 462). The logic commensurate with this world does not take for granted its foundational principles of identity, non-contradiction, and the excluded middle (*tertium non datur*). It emphasizes the ethical dimension of logical thinking insofar as it helps people entering a universe of discourse to get on the same page, live up to their definitional commitments, acknowledge the contradictions, and follow through on their claims to an identity. The uncertainty embedded in this world can never be completely expunged. Indeterminacy endemic to the human condition stems not from the paucity of terms but from their overabundance (Shalin, 1986). As a rule, we can terminate indeterminacy in more than one way by recourse to competing terminological devices. Whatever the choice, we must acknowledge alternative terminologies and accept the responsibility for elevating some accounting frames over others. Such frames do more than reflect the world out there—they bring it into existence as a meaningful whole. "For rationalism reality is ready-made and complete from all eternity while for pragmatism it is still in the making" (James, [1907] 1955, 167). This world-in-the-making is not a private conceit; it is a collective accomplishment subject to challenges and revisions, which grow violent at times. The question is who controls the terminological means of production which enable us to tame chaos, to transform the world of flux into objective and meaningful reality. In a democratic society, such control is widely dispersed; everybody can raise a truth claim; terminological practices are open to criticism in light of their consequences and in line with the majority's notion of public good. In an authoritarian polity, the authorities limit the range of terminological practices and the scope of legitimate criticism, presiding over a semi-ordered chaos they take to be eternal and natural. Bringing to light the obscene riches Putin's cronies acquired through their control over national oil resources could land the critic in jail, publicly expressing doubts about the legality of the military operation and annexation of foreign territories will earn you the label "foreign agent," and aiding the Ukrainians devastated by the war is to court the charge of high treason. Wrestling over control of the terms of public discourse and ensuring freedom of communication is a pragmatic imperative.

Aligning Knowledge and Experience

Viewed from this vantage point, democracy is a historically specific mode of managing uncertainty that spurns the monopoly over truth claims and leaves no area of life exempt from public scrutiny. We join "the community of inquirers" (Peirce) as participant observers demanding accountability for actions taken on its behalf. Such an inquiry does not discard truth as a public good, only its rationalistic version predicated on "comparing ready-made ideas with ready-made facts." The rationalist approach is supplanted with the pragmatist insight that "both idea and facts are flexible, and verification is the process of mutual adjustment, of organic interaction" (Dewey, [1890] 1969, 87). We mold things into objects to make them fit our hypothetical constructs and revise our theories to align them with practice. As citizens, we engage in social reconstruction aiming to build the world that stands to reason, acknowledging in the process the limits of our power and, when necessary, the failure of our efforts. Truth is understood here not as the sure grasp of things themselves, nor as the intellectual revelations transcending experience, but as a historically specific, practically accomplished, collectively sustained, and continuously revised alignment between knowledge and practice. Terminating practices play a crucial role in the historical process of worldly truth making. As we terminate indeterminacy, we come to grips with the fact that "to terminate" simultaneously means "to put an end to" and "to frame in specific terms," "to narrow the potentialities of being" and "to render things into meaningful objects." As we open some hermeneutical horizons, we obscure other ways of making the world into an objective and meaningful whole. If the thing-in-itself is an object wrenched from its historical reference frame and treated as fact that speaks for itself, then the object is a thing-in-itself framed in contingent terms and backed up by requisite practice. The world we constitute is informed by our ideals and transformed by our undertakings, yet this is not the postmodern world where anything goes, where truth is an adjunct to power. (There is a reason Putin is called "Russia's first postmodern president" [Caryl, 2001].) Ours is an obdurate world which compels us to take note and change course when the actions staked on the truth of our propositions fail to bring anticipated consequences.

Enlivening Reason with Emotions

Those who charge pragmatism with being Machiavellian miss the mark. The juxtaposition of cold reason and destructive emotions is inimical to the pragmatist imagination. Affect is present in all ideas, as Spinoza noted centuries ago, and when we try to suppress emotions and escape into the rarified domain of pure reason, we pay a heavy price. "Rationality, once more is not a force to evoke against impulse and habit. It is the attainment of a working harmony among diverse desires. 'Reason' as a noun signifies a happy cooperation of a multitude of dispositions, such as sympathy, curiosity, cooperation, exploration, experimentation, frankness, pursuit—to follow things through—circumspection, to look about at the context, etc., etc." (Dewey, [1922] 1950, 195–6; cf. Shalin, 1992). Pragmatists are not oblivious to the fact that private interests and crude emotions can distort reasoning. The question they raise is how intelligent our emotions are and what we can do to keep our intellect sane. To quote from Dewey again, "the conclusion is not that the emotional, passionate phase of action can be or should be eliminated in behalf of a bloodless reason. More 'passions,' not fewer, is the answer" (Dewey, [1922] 1950, 195). That is, if we are passionate about the right things and keep our eyes on the public good. Putin's oscillation between cold cunning and violently lashing out illustrates the point. It is hard to say whether Putin-the-calculator plotting to kill his opponents is better than Putin-the-macho rousing his nation on the eve of the Russian invasion. Both mark a man who is emotionally hobbled, and perhaps deranged. There are inspiring examples of emotional intelligence among Russian nationals—of moral fortitude in the face of unfolding catastrophe—but the emotional littering that has enveloped the nation is suffocating. It is not just the intelligentsia that is becoming extinct; it is emotional intelligence itself (*intelligentnost*) which Chekhov ([1882] 1912, 238) saw as binding for those who follow the intelligentsia creed, i.e., who "respect human personhood, are quick to forgive, show soft touch, are polite to everyone and ready to yield." Cruelty—intellectual, emotional, physical—is on a continuum. Scurrility pervading public discourse distorts our reasoning and breeds the violence that leads to Bucha and Irpin. All sides of the political divide should bear in mind that reason unenlivened by humane sentiments is a ticking bomb waiting to explode.

Balancing Ends and Means

Much ink has been spilled in defense of the proposition that pragmatism lacks principles, that its adherents cynically spurn values and resort to expedient means to achieve their self-serving goals. This is a spurious charge. Popular opinion confuses opportunism with pragmatism, the former common among politicians who resort to expedience and triangulation to stay afloat at all costs, the latter practiced by those who stay true to values, acknowledge a lesser good sacrificed to the larger one, and allow experience to test their assumptions and cherished theories. John Dewey, one of the movement's founders and indefatigable defenders, condemned Stalin's crimes and spearheaded the committee investigating Leon Trotsky's murder. George Herbert Mead marched with demonstrators supporting women's suffrage, mediated the garment workers' strike, and led the progressive education drive to aid Chicago immigrants. Jane Addams counted herself among "men and women longing to socialize their democracy" and displayed the "passion for the equalization of human joys and opportunities" which earned her the Nobel Peace Prize (Addams, 1902, 139; 1910, 116, cf. Shalin, 1986). There was nothing cynical about the public engagements of these intellectuals steeped in the Protestant spirit of dissent. Avowed goals, pragmatists insist, are encoded in our means rather than declarations about our noble intentions. So, it is not so much *zelepoploganie* as *sredstvoprimenenie* that should concern us if we follow Dostoevsky's tale of the Grand Inquisitor. Given that we commonly choose and adjust our objectives to fit available resources, it is incumbent on us to be upfront about the evolution of our rationales and their potentially self-serving implications. A glossary of suitable motives deployed at the right time will not fill the gap between words, deeds, and emotions working at cross-purpose. Recall how Putin moved the goalposts to explain the "special military operation" in Ukraine, which he identified at various points as the demilitarization and denazification of Ukraine, putting its leaders on trial, defending the Russian-speaking population, removing biolaboratories producing chemical weapons, securing the borders of the Donetsk and Luhansk breakaway regions, preempting the imminent invasion of Russia by Ukraine, fighting back the NATO attack designed to dismantle the Russian Federation. Never did Putin clarify the means he was ready to deploy to achieve these shifting goals—will he stop at sending regular troops into battle, recruiting volunteer contract soldiers, mobilizing the draft-age population, destroying Ukraine's infrastructure, dropping an A-bomb on the "fraternal people" of Ukraine? His angry displays only underscore the discontinuities in his self-production and mendacity of his declarations and promises. He sues for peace and is open to negotiations, the Russian president tells journalists. What he means is, "Lay down your arms, surrender to the victor's mercy, give up plans to join NATO, and accept the Russian protectorate—only then you may have peace." It is anybody's guess what devious means Putin still has up his sleeves, his somatic-affective indicia and depraved actions defying his peaceful declarations.

Repairing the Word-Body-Action Nexus

The principled pragmatism driving this historical project is based on the premise that we disclose our values discursively, affectively, and interactionally, that the word-body-action nexus is bound to get out of whack, and that constantly realigning our verbal-discursive, somatic-affective, and behavioral-performative practices is the mark of ethical agency. Whatever ethical stance we take, it falls short if we fail to align our verbal stance with practical deeds, if our emotions contradict our verbal posture, if our behavioral commitments stray from professed goals. Denouncing dominant values while acquiescing to the status quo is what distinguishes the cynical attitude. The ancient cynics adopted lifestyles inimical to the established norms and reveled in derisive discourse. Irony, parody, and travesty go a long way to expose the reigning hypocrisy, as Russian sots-artists demonstrated, yet deconstructive engagement takes you only so far. If your goal is "pragmatic reconstruction," as Dewey ([1920] 1950; cf. Shalin 2022) urged, cynicism will not suffice. You need to sign yourself in the flesh, to body forth your convictions, which forces you to take a public stance, to articulate what you take to be public good—market economy, limited government, free speech, personal autonomy, public education, universal healthcare, gender and marriage equality, and so on. People will clash about the centrality of this or that public good, but the democratic ethos demands a robust debate about such matters undistorted by the fear of reprisals and thoughts of personal gain. Such are the communication-specific conditions of possibility for an emotionally intelligent democracy—conditions that are missing in today's Russia, mired in the cycle of violence and soul-crushing fear and hopelessness (Shalin, 2018, 2019).

Practicing Civic Imagination

Among our many selves, we single out some that go to the core of our identity, which we embrace as "the real me." This is especially common among individuals and groups fighting a stigma imposed on them by society. Nothing is more important for the afflicted than to make others acknowledge their grievances and show deference. Pushed too far, such identity politics stifle civic imagination and breed political myopia (Shalin, 2021). The urge to band together morphs into a desire to keep aliens at bay, to gather all of us in and push foreigners out. No matter where we draw the line, however, some of "us" will be caught on the other side, and some of "them" will be found in our midst, and it is only a matter of time before we discover that our politically identical twins spawn selves we cannot embrace. Your comrades may dislike your gender politics, sexual orientation, position on reproductive rights, or resent the fact that you made more sound life choices. What drives Russian ultra-patriots mad is not just that Ukrainians speak a different language and refuse peaceful overtures to join the Russian world; it is also the suspicion that they may enjoy freedoms denied to their neighbors. And now that Ukrainians have put up stiff resistance, they are demonized, ridiculed, and subject to inhumane treatment. In the face of this assault on their dignity and livelihood, the Ukrainians are apt to treat all Russians as enemies and potential fascists (Russists) whose cultural signposts must be eradicated from the land of Taras Shevchenko and Lesia Ukrainka. The civic imagination that propels pragmatist ethics counteracts identity politics. It goads us to see that identity is not ingrained in our bodies, that it is the product of our ongoing effort to make sense of the world and our place in it. The search for the excluded middle, *tertium datur*, is an ongoing concern in this pragma centered universe. Our identities, along with the discursive values undergirding them, breed ambivalence—the hallmark of an emotionally intelligent person alive to the contradictions inherent in the human condition. Give the markets free reign, and they will spawn monopolies. Ignore the plight of the downtrodden, and liberty will breed inequality and make a mockery of the call to brotherhood. Allow populists to force their will on the polity, and you can say goodbye to liberty, representative democracy, and constitutional order. The relationship between such competing values is that of uncertainty—they cannot be maximized simultaneously with an arbitrary precision. "There is the conflict between the old and the new, between the radical and the conservative," wrote Mead in the spirit of mediation, but "we may not wish to be either radical or conservative. We may wish to comprehend and to do justice to the changing valuations" (Mead, 1938, 480). Letting some of our cherished convictions push aside other principles risks plunging our lives into mayhem. Recognizing the contingent nature of our values distinguishes the ethical life steeped in pragmatism and civic imagination.

Reaching a Reasonable Compromise

Edifying as such considerations might be, they are quite removed from the practical decisions confronting a person trying to figure out how to safeguard their dignity and survive oppression. Nor do they tell us much about the limits of reasonable compromise. We must start by acknowledging that our predicament is not unique, that other epochs confronted the question of how to lead a moral life in an immoral society. Our teachers and mentors faced tough choices in Soviet Russia. Yuri Levada, the founder of Levada Public Opinion Center, joined the Communist Party and presided over the party organization in the Institute of Sociology before he was forced out (Levada, 2008; Shalin, 2008). Igor Kon, a leading Soviet-era sociologist, was commissioned to do research by the Party Central Committee (for which he wrote, among other things, a brief on the scourge of antisemitism) and published in *Kommunist* and other party outlets essays on ethnic prejudice and intelligentsia (Kon, 2011, 2019a, 2019b, 2019c; Kon-Shalin, 2018). Vladimir Yadov, dean of Leningrad sociologists, let go of a few coworkers to save his research team from being disbanded (Yadov 2015; Yadov-Shalin, 2016). Some things these iconic figures said or did make us wince today (Starovoitova, 2007; Levada, 2008; cf. Shalin, 2008; Chudakova 2021). These academics chose to collaborate with the authorities, and in the process nurtured two generations of social scientists and public intellectuals without whom Russian sociology and the *perestroika* reforms would not have been the same.[1] The situation is different today when closeted liberals are increasingly forced to take a stand on the war in Ukraine as a condition of their continued employment and, in some cases, freedom. Will they do more good by compromising with the authorities, or should they attempt a moral-political coming out and publicly condemn the invasion? Chulpan Khamatova lent her name to Putin's election campaign in exchange for the state funding of children's cancer clinics; after Putin savaged Ukraine, she left the country to underscore her disagreement with the regime and salvage whatever was left of her dignity. For the time being, emigration remains an option for those fed up with Putin's policies and willing to vote with their feet, but the situation might change at any moment. "Germany under the Nazi regime was a prison," wrote Carl Jaspers. "The guilt of getting into it is political guilt. Once the gates were shut, however, a prison break from within was no longer possible ... To hold the inmates of a prison collectively responsible for outrages committed by the prison staff is clearly unjust" (Jaspers, [1946] 2001, 76). Whatever pathway the person charts in this moral minefield, one cannot escape compromises and must be aware of the stones left unturned, the moral cost incurred.

Owning Up to One's Responsibility

The extent to which one bears responsibility for the unfolding tragedy has been debated at length, with no consensus over the matter and much blame to go around. Those responsible for the bloodshed—the nation's leaders, professional propagandists, soldiers committing war crimes—may feel no guilt, but their role in triggering the war and legal liability for the atrocities is beyond doubt. Then, there are the foreign players who coddled the Russian Federation president in the past and continue aiding and abetting Putin's war efforts—all of whom share a measure of responsibility for allowing this tragedy to happen and doing less than they could in helping Ukrainian resistance. It is harder to ascertain the culpability of ordinary citizens, those who shielded themselves from the ugly realities and refused to fight or even acknowledge the evil their country inflicted on the world. Here is the perspective of a man from another era, a philosopher with a wounded conscience and vivid moral imagination:

> Are we Germans to be held liable for outrages which Germans inflicted on us, or from which we were saved as by a miracle? Yes—in as much as we let such a regime rise among us. No—insofar as many of us in our deepest hearts opposed all this evil and have no morally guilty acts or inner motivations to admit.
>
> (Jaspers, [1946] 2001, 55)

Karl Jaspers helped the postwar Germans to come to grips with crimes committed by them and in their name. With admirably pragmatic clarity, he distinguished between *political responsibility*—"We are politically responsible for our regime, for the acts of the regime, for the start of the war in this world-historical situation, and for the kind of leaders we allowed to rise among us"; *moral guilt*—"Blindness for the misfortune of others, lack of imagination of the heart, inner indifference toward the witnessed evil—that is moral guilt"; *collective guilt*—"'You are inferior as a nation, ignoble, criminal, the scum of the earth, different from all other nations [we are told].' This is the collectivist type of thought and appraisal, classifying every individual under these generalizations [which] is radically false and itself inhuman"; and *metaphysical guilt* known only to God.

> There exists a solidarity among men as human beings that makes each co-responsible for every wrong and every injustice in the world, especially for crimes committed in his presence or with his knowledge. If I fail to do whatever I can to prevent them, I too am guilty. If I was present at the murder of others without risking my life to prevent it, I feel guilty in a way not adequately conceivable either legally, politically, or morally.
> (Jaspers, [1946] 2001, 26; see also 44, 55, 63–4, 72)

These distinctions resonate with pragmatists, who struggled to articulate what John Dewey called a "common faith" responsive to the needs of humanity as a whole:

> Here are all the elements for a religious faith that shall not be confined to sect, class, or race. Such a faith has always been implicitly the common faith of mankind ... In that way the churches would indeed become catholic. The demand that churches show a more active interest in social affairs, that they take a definite stand upon such questions as war, economic injustice, political corruption, that they stimulate action for a divine kingdom on earth, is one of the signs of the times.
> (Dewey, [1934] 1986, 59, 56)

As imperative as it is to look back and take stock of one's inaction, it is even more important for pragmatists to ascertain what guilt and repentance mean in practical terms, and how they can shape the future. This is when one starts with oneself.

Choosing a Self in the Time of Crisis

Russian history is teaming with cataclysms that left deep scars on the nation's psyche. Surviving wars, revolutions, political and ethnic purges was no mean feat for the people of Russia, and it is understandable when they wish to insulate themselves from political headwinds. If you won't play politics, that does not mean politics will not play with you. Much as we try to live unnoticed and resist being dragged into the vortex of history, we are forced to take a stance, even if an unspoken one. Actions speak louder than words, somatic indexes point to existential quandaries, and conflicted emotions hint at the broken semiotic chains in the continuing self-production. Thus, Vladimir Putin's autocratic rule flies in the face of his early disavowal of being a dictator. Vladimir Soloviev's hatred toward Ukraine and its people makes mockery of his paeans to religious tolerance. Vladmir Posner's refusal to take a stance on the war crimes committed by Russian soldiers tarnishes his credentials as a liberal intellectual. If there is a man who talks the talk and walks the walk in today's Russia, it is Vladimir Kara-Murza, and as his friends attest, he also rocks the rock, i.e., embodies emotional intelligence uncommon in our toxic times. Staying true to oneself is a formidable challenge that tests ethical resolve of those refusing to be indifferent to evil. Aleksey Losev (1989) elucidated this predicament in his sixth thesis on the intelligentsia and its affective underpinnings: "[T]rue *intelligentnost'* is always a heroic feat, the ability to forgo one's egoistic needs and concerns; it is not always an actual battle, but the readiness to enter a battle at any point and to cultivate the spiritual, creative armament for it ... *Intelligentnost'* is a steady heroic feat, even when it is not fully realized" (Losev, 1989). Open defiance is not always feasible or wise. Passive resistance is a viable option, whether in the form of a refusal to partake in official lies, giving up an appointment in government structures, or offering help to the publicly disgraced dissenters. Living a moral life in the immoral universe starts with acknowledging where we fall short of our commitments, when we fail to redeem in the flesh our claims to selfhood. To reconcile our contradictory enselfments (selves) we may resort to creative accounting, but this is a poor substitute for the willingness to realign our words and deeds. That, in turn, means getting in touch with the emotional springs of our humanity and imparting a quantum of sanity to the affectively polluted environment. To change oneself is harder than to change the world, but if you succeed in embodying a more intelligent self, your decency will reverberate throughout the world and nudge it in the right direction. John Dewey had this in mind when he pressed the following point: "No social modification, slight or revolutionary, can endure except as it enters into the action of a people through their desires and purposes" (Dewey and Child, 1933, 138).

Taking Stock of One's Life

Those preaching to others need to start with themselves. Looking back at the nearly half century I have lived in America after emigrating from the

USSR, I see a common thread guiding my relationship with the homeland. To secure an exit visa, I paid for the honor of renouncing my Russian citizenship and signed the pledge that I would never claim it back. Emigration felt like an ultimate divorce, where you part not only with people you loved and the family you might never see again, but also with your language, culture, backyard, campgrounds you could not visit again, and so much more. I kept track of what was going on back home. My engagements were sporadic, and they probably helped me to feel connected more than they made a difference in the larger scheme of things, whether I sent proscribed books to Russia, organized support of the imprisoned Memorial Foundation's founder Arseny Roginsky, or arranged a petition by the American and British Sociological Associations to shield the Levada Center from government interference. Things grew more urgent in the wake of the current humanitarian catastrophe, which afforded me an opportunity to move beyond speaking to journalists and recording podcasts to donating money to the refugee programs, monitoring human rights violations, and furnishing expert testimony to the court reviewing applications for a refugee status in the US. With *perestroika* reform lifting the iron curtain, the opportunity arose to bring old colleagues to the United States for a series of conferences on Russia (Nevada Conference on Russian Art and Culture 1992-2018) under the aegis of the UNLV Center for Democratic Culture that "draws its philosophy from American pragmatism, which regards democracy as an ongoing experiment in collective living and institution building" (Center for Democratic Culture, 2002).[2] The last event in this series took place in 2018, with plans for the next gathering suspended after the war in Ukraine broke out. All along, I tried to keep in mind Chekhov's advice—start with yourself, reach out to your neighbors, communicate to others' goodwill, give credit to your enemies wherever it is due, have courage to admit when the problem has no ready solution, avoid grand-standing and take up small deeds (Shalin, 1993).

Raising Difficult Questions

There are questions of moral and legal responsibility, of circumstances triggering the war in Ukraine, which will remain with us for a long time. In the months preceding the war, experts agreed that invading Ukraine would be catastrophic—no rational man would want to take the plunge. The first part of this prediction proved accurate, the second one raised doubt about Putin's sanity. That his close aids and intelligence services fed him wrong information in no way excuses the action of a man who surrounds himself with people telling him what he wants to hear. Putin fancied himself a restorer of the Russian Empire, invincible and destined for greatness, and it would be no small historical irony if he causes its final demise. Now he is trapped in history, his reign contingent on the continuation of the military campaign and war in Ukraine, which is likely to persist as long as he stays in power. Putin will have to rebuild Ukraine if he wins, and his country will pay reparations if he loses, with Russian taxpayers left holding the bag in either case. And yet, Putin's hubris is not the only factor that set off and exacerbated the conflagration. Western powers, which failed to contain Putin's aggressive policies and opted for lucrative trade agreements, need to examine their own historical records. When America tells Russia it cannot stop the expansion of the North Atlantic Treaty Organization, it should recall the Monroe Doctrine, which warned European states to refrain from projecting power in the Americas or face reprisals from the US. When the charge is leveled against the Russian Federation that it violated the world order in acting unilaterally, we should own up to the fact that Western powers engaged in unilateral military action as well. Although no formal commitment was made at the time, Western leaders left the impression with their counterparts in the disintegrating Soviet Union that they would not rush to incorporate its constituent republics into NATO. There was a consensus inside Russia in the 1990s, spanning the political spectrum from Andrey Sakharov and Boris Yeltsin to Gennady Zyuganov and Vladimir Zhirinovsky, that bringing military bases and ballistic rockets to the Russian borders could undermine international peace and set back reforms in the fledgling Russian democracy (Shalin, 1997). Given recent experience, we may conclude that Putin's aggressive politics have validated the decision of Russia's former constituents and allies to seek NATO protection, and still wonder if the advancement of NATO military installations had spurred resentment toward the West and fed Putin's belligerence.

There are other difficult questions that must be addressed in the pragmatist key. Should the West have closed the skies above Ukraine to prevent the destruction of its cities by the Russian air force and risk directly entering the war with Russia? Did Western allies err in refusing to provide Ukraine with longer range missiles and aircraft? Is it moral to let Russia and Ukraine exhaust themselves in a fight which undermines the Russian Federation's capacity to wage war on several fronts while eschewing more forceful action? If actionable intelligence shows that Putin is ready to use nuclear missiles, should the West preempt the launch or wait until the atomic attack is underway, and what should its response be?

Let me be clear that nothing justifies the brutal assault on the Ukraine and the repressions Putin unleashed at home in the service of his messianic pretensions. What he did is more than a mistake—it is a crime for which he must answer, in person at the world tribunal and certainly in the court of history. I do not claim to have answers to the queries raised above. No formula, pragmatic or otherwise, can deliver final answers, which must be considered with an eye to the changing situation and the need to balance competing values. We should not shy away from raising such questions, however, and let pragmatist ethics inform our collective inquiry.

Notes

1 "For Gorbachev to emerge—and we wouldn't have been talking here without him—generations of people [had to] come around to do something, to change what was commonly said, and so on. Arbatov and Inozemtshev played a tremendous role in this matter. I am a small potato, nothing depended on me, and all the briefs that I wrote [for the Central Committee] are accidental things, facts of my biography with no relationship to the biography of the Soviet power and Communist party. Arbatov and Inozemtshev did something that really mattered. They dealt with the Politburo members and the General Secretary. They taught these folks to deal with the unpleasant missives and very unpleasant statistics. Information that streamed through different channels was filtered at every level. The authorities were accustomed to hearing only what they wanted to hear, even though everybody at the bottom knew this information to be bogus. Whatever the level of decrepitude, people on top did not have objective information. With the help of their institutes, Arbatov and Inozemtshev changed this practice … It is fashionable to damn Arabatov nowadays, accuse him of this and that. But he was the soviet version—well, maybe a little below that level given our conditions—of Dr. Kissinger. He was the man behind Brezhnev's détente on our end. Détente did happen, and even though in the end it was aborted, it was not Arbatov's fault" (Kon, 2011, 118).
2 "Democracy, according to John Dewey, begins at home, in a neighborly community, and is first and foremost a quality of experience shaped by free communication. We take this to mean that civic virtues are as central to democracy as political institutions, that civil society thrives in the culture which encourages trust, tolerance, prudence, compassion, humor, and withers away when overexposed to suspicion, hatred, vanity, cruelty, and sarcasm" (CDC, 2002).

References

Addams, Jane. 1902. *Democracy and Social Ethics*. New York: Macmillan.
Addams, Jane. 1910. *Twenty Years at Hull-House*. New York: Macmillan.

Apel, Karl-Otto. 1981. *Charles S. Peirce: From Pragmatism to Pragmaticism.* Amherst: University of Massachusetts Press.

Baker, Bryan T. 2019. "Placing Putin's Pragmatism in Perspective." Carnegie Endowment for International Peace. January 3. https://smallwarsjournal.com/jrnl/art/placing-putins-pragmatism-perspective

Boykoff, Pamela, and Laura Smith-Spark. 2017. "Russia's Putin urges 'pragmatic cooperation' with US in New Year greetings." *CNN.* December 30. https://www.cnn.com/2017/12/30/world/putin-trump-new-year-greetings-intl/index.html

Bukovsky, Vladimir. 2006. "Their dream is to get a million." *Index/Dosie na tsenzuru.* http://www.index.org.ru/journal/23/buk23.html

Bykov, Dmitry. 2021. "Odin." *Ekho Moskvy.* December 16.

Bykova, Marina F. 2022. "Russia and power: Unmasking the historical origins of the present crisis." *Studies in East European Thought* 74: 439–46. https://link.springer.com/article/10.1007/s11212-022-09532-8

Caryl, Christian. 2001. "Putin's Pragmatism." *Newsweek.* November 14. https://www.newsweek.com/putins-pragmatism-149883

Casula, Philipp. 2022. "On 'Pragmatism' in Soviet and Russian Foreign Policy in the Middle East and Ukraine." *NYU Jordan Center.* April 4. https://jordanrussiacenter.org/news/symbiosis-and-revolution-the-soviet-encounter-with-the-war-in-dhofar/#.Y9IRFXbML30

Center for Democratic Culture. 2002. "CDC Mission Statement." University of Nevada, Las Vegas. http://cdclv.unlv.edu/index.html

Chekhov, Anton. [1882] 1912. *Pisma.* Vol. 1. Moscow: Izdanie M. P. Chekhovoi.

Chudkova, Marietta O. 2021. "'I have seen my ideas in Yieltsyn's speeches.' Interview with Marietta Chudakova." *Vestnik obshchestvennogo mnenia* 3-4: 146-59. https://cdclv.unlv.edu/archives/articles/shalin_chudakova_interview_96.pdf

Crosston, Matthew. 2018. *Russia Reconsidered: Putin, Power, and Pragmatism.* Dallas: Brown Books Publishing Group.

Dewey, John. [1890] 1969. "The logic of verification." In *John Dewey, The Early Works.* Volume III, 83–92. Carbondale: Southern Illinois University Press.

Dewey, John. 1916. *Essays in Experimental Logic.* New York: Dover.

Dewey, John. 1939. *Freedom and Culture.* New York: Capricorn Books.

Dewey, John. [1920] 1950. *Reconstruction in Philosophy.* New York: Mentor Books.

Dewey, John. [1922] 1950. *Human Nature and Conduct.* New York: The Modern Library.

Dewey, John. [1934] 1986. "Common faith." In *The collected works of John Dewey, 1882-1953.* Carbondale: Southern Illinois University Press.

Dewey, John, and John Childs. 1933. "The underlying philosophy of education." In *The Educational Frontier*, edited by W. H. Kilpatrick, 287–319. New York: Appleton-Century.

Domostroi. 2007. *Literaturnye pamiatniki.* St. Peterburg: Nauka.

Etkind, Aleksandr. 2001. "New historicism, Russian version." *NLO* 47. https://magazines.gorky.media/nlo/2001/1/novyj-istorizm-russkaya-versiya.html

Fors, Kristian. 2021. "A pragmatic approach to peace in Ukraine." Russian International Affairs Council. https://russiancouncil.ru/en/blogs/kristian-fors/a-pragmatic-approach-to-peace-in-ukraine

Habermas, Jürgen. 1984. *The Theory of Communicative Action*. Volume I. Reason and the Rationalization of Society. Boston: Beacon Press.

Habermas, Jürgen. 1986. *Autonomy and Solidarity. Interviews*. Edited by Peter Dews. London: Verso: The Imprint of New Left Books.

Habermas, Jürgen. 1987. *The Theory of Communicative Action*. Volume II. *Life World and System: A Critique of Functionalist Reason*. Boston: Beacon Press.

Heidegger, Martin. [1946] 1961. "Letter on Humanism." In *Martin Heidegger. Basic Writings*. Edited by D. F. Krell, 190-241. New York: Harper & Row.

Horkheimer, Max. 1937. *Eclipse of Reason*. New York: Oxford University Press.

Horkheimer, Max. 1947. "Der Neusten Angriff auf die Metaphysik." *Zeitschriftfur Sozialforschung* 6: 4-53.

James, Williams. 1890. *The Principles of Psychology*. Vol. 1. New York: Henry Holt and Co.

James, Williams. [1907] 1955. *Pragmatism, and Four Essays from the Meaning of Truth*. New York: Meridian Books.

Jaspers, Karl. [1946] 2001. *The Question of German Guilt*. New York: Fordham University Press.

Joas, Hans. 1985. *G. H. Mead. A Contemporary Reexamination of His Thought*. Cambridge: Polity Press.

Khodorkovsky, Mikhail. 2016. "Deja vu." Radio Liberty. April 22. https://www.svoboda.org/a/27686937.html

Kirill, Metropolit. 2006. "Mitropolit Krill: U cheloveka est ne tolko prava, no i dusha." *Trud*, March 28. https://www.trud.ru/article/28-03-2006/102285_mitropolit_kirill_u_cheloveka_est_ne_tolko_prava_n/print

Kolesnikov, Andrei. 2022. "Scientific Putinism: Shaping Official Ideology in Russia." Carnegi Politika. https://carnegieendowment.org/politika/88451

Kon, Igor. S. 2011. "'I tried to change this system many times.' Interview with Igor Kon." *Sotsiologicheskii zhurnal* 2, 100-37. http://cdclv.unlv.edu/archives/articles/kon_96.pdf

Kon, Igor. S. 2018. Selected correspondence of Igor Kon and Dmitri Shalin. *Monitoring of Public Opinion* No. 6: 20-47. https://monitoringjournal.ru/index.php/monitoring/article/view/547/489

Kon, Igor. S. 2019a. "'If in the early 1980s I was permitted to travel abroad, I would have certainly not returned.' Interview with Igor Kon." *Monitoring of Public Opinion* No. 2: 120-57. https://monitoringjournal.ru/index.php/monitoring/article/view/631/541

Kon, Igor S. 2019b. "'You can publish this interview after my death.' Interview with Igor Kon." *Public Opinion Herald*, 2: 85-101. http://cdclv.unlv.edu/archives/articles/shalin_kon_interview_07-19.pdf

Kon, Igor S. 2019c. "'I could have written my autobiography where I figure as a regime's victim, a successful careerist, a talent not completely realized, and a mediocrity that fulfilled its potential to the max'. Interview with Igor Kon." *Sociological Research* 6: 157-75.

Kurnyshova, Yulia, and Andrey Makarychev. 2022. "Explaining Russia's war against Ukraine: How can foreign policy analysis and political theory be helpful?" *Studies in East European Thought* 74: 507-19. https://link.springer.com/article/10.1007/s11212-022-09494-x

Lavrov, Sergey. 2007. "Global politics in contemporary and future perspective: Moscow's point of view." *Russian in Global Politics* No. 2.

Levada, Yuri A. 2008. "'I thought it would be unnatural for me to behave otherwise … ' Interview with Yuri Levada." *Sotsiologicheksii zhurnal* 1, 155-77.

Levy, Clifford J. 2008. "U.S. is in no shape to give advice, Medvedev says." *The New York Times*, July 3. https://www.nytimes.com/2008/07/03/world/europe/03medvedev.html

Losev, Aleksei F. 1989. "Ob intelligentnosti," *Sovetskaia kultura*, January 1.

Lozansky, Edward. 2013 "Toward a new pragmatism on Russia." *The Washington Times*, December 1. https://www.washingtontimes.com/news/2013/dec/1/lozansky-toward-a-new-pragmatism-on-russia

Marcus, Herbert. 1939/1940. "Review of John Dewey's Logic. The Theory of Inquiry." *Zeitschrift fur Sozialforshcung* 9: 144-8.

Mead, George Herbert. 1938. *The Philosophy of the Act*. Chicago: University of Chicago Press.

Medvedev, Sergei. 2004. "Rethinking the National Interest: Putin's Turn in Russian Foreign Policy." The George C. Marshall European Center for Security Studies, August 2004. https://www.marshallcenter.org/en/publications/marshall-center-papers/rethinking-national-interest-putins-turn-russian-foreign-policy/rethinking-national-interest-putins-turn-russian

Navalnaya, Daria. 2021. "Address on the occasion of Andrey Sakharov's Award to Aleksey Navalny." Skat Media. December 15. https://www.youtube.com/watch?v=0QIkNJxfesc

Neumann, Franz L. et al. 1953. *The Cultural Migration: The European Scholar in America*. Crawford: University of Pennsylvania Press.

Nevada Conference on Russian Art and Culture. 1986-2018. Center for Democratic Culture. University of Nevada. Las Vegas. http://cdclv.unlv.edu/archives/conferences.html

Peirce, Charles. 1931-1935. *Collected Papers of Charles Sanders Peirce*, vols.1-6. Cambridge: Harvard University Press.

Pertsev, Andrey. 2017. "Russia's Choice of Moral Rhetoric Over Pragmatism Is a Ticking Time Bomb." Carnegie Endowment for International Peace. July 21. https://carnegiemoscow.org/commentary/71593

Putin, Vladimir. 1999. "Rossiia na rubezhe tysiacheletii." *Nezavisimaia Gazeta*, December 30. https://www.ng.ru/politics/1999-12-30/4_millenium.html

Putin, Vladimir. 2000. *Ot Pervogo Litsa. Razgovory s Vladimirom Putinym.* Moskva: Vagrius.

Putin, Vladimir. 2013. "Interview to the First TV Channel and Associated Press Agency." September 3. http://kremlin.ru/events/president/news/19143

Putin, Vladimir. 2022. "Meeting on Socioeconomic Support for Regions." March 16. http://en.kremlin.ru/events/president/transcripts/67996

Richardson, Paul B., Anand A. Yang, and Kieko Matteson B. 2018. "Putin and Pragmatic Patriotism." In *At the Edge of the Nation: The Southern Kurils and the Search for Russia's National Identity*, edited by Paul B. Richardson, 72-93. Honolulu: University of Hawai'i Press.

Roberts, Kari. 2017. "Understanding Putin: The politics of identity and geopolitics in Russian foreign policy discourse." *International Journal* 72: 28-55. https://www.jstor.org/stable/10.2307/26414074

Rogov, Kirill. 2022. "Putin's Blackmail Works Domestically as Well as Internationally." *Wilson Center*. December 1. https://www.wilsoncenter.org/blog-post/putins-blackmail-works-domestically-well-internationally

Rojek, Paweł. 2022. "Imperialism and nationalism: The Nature of Russian Aggression in Ukraine." *Studies in East European Thought* 74: 447–61. https://link.springer.com/article/10.1007/s11212-022-09501-1

Ryvkina, Rozalina. 2006. "Intelligentsiia v postovetskoi Rossii. Ischerpanie sotsialnoy roli." *Sotsiologicheskie issledovaniia*. 3: 134–46.

Shalin, Dmitri. 1986. "Pragmatism and social interactionism." *American Sociological Review* 51: 9-30. http://cdclv.unlv.edu/pragmatism/shalin_psi.pdf

Shalin, Dmitri. 1992. "Critical theory and the pragmatist challenge." *American Journal of Sociology* 98: 237-79. http://cdclv.unlv.edu/pragmatism/shalin_ct.pdf

Shalin, Dmitri. 1993. "Emotional barriers to democracy are daunting." *Los Angeles Times*, October 27. https://www.latimes.com/archives/la-xpm-1993-10-27-me-50060-story.html

Shalin, Dmitri. 1997. "NATO expansion could topple Yeltsin regime." *Las Vegas Review Journal*, April 13. http://cdclv.unlv.edu/pragmatism/ds_nato.pdf

Shalin, Dmitri. 2007. "Vladimir Putin: Instead of communism, he embraces KGB capitalism." *Las Vegas Review Journal*, October 24. http://cdclv.unlv.edu/pragmatism/shalin_putindemo.html

Shalin, Dmitri. 2008. "Phenomenological foundations of theoretical practice: Biocritical notes on Yuri Levada." *Vestnik obshchestvennogo mnenia* 96: 70-104.

Shalin, Dmitri. 2010. "Hermeneutics and Prejudice: Heidegger and Gadamer in their Historical Setting." *Russian Journal of Communication* 3: 7-24. http://cdclv.unlv.edu/pragmatism/shalin_heidegger_gadamer.pdf

Shalin, Dmitri. 2011. *Pragmatism and Democracy: Studies in History, Social Theory and Progressive Politics*. New York: Routledge.

Shalin, Dmitri. 2016. "On being human in an inhuman world: Remembering Vladimir Yadov." *Global Dialogues* 6: 20-22. https://globaldialogue.isa-sociology.org/articles/on-being-human-in-an-inhuman-world-remembering-vladimir-yadov

Shalin, Dmitri. 2017. *Pragmatism and Democracy: Studies in History, Social Theory and Progressive Politics*. London: Routledge.

Shalin, Dmitri. 2018. "Communication, democracy and intelligentsia." *Russian Journal of Communication* 10: 110-46. https://tandfonline.com/doi/full/10.1080/19409419.2018.1558495

Shalin, Dmitri (ed.) 2019. *Russian Intelligentsia in the Age of Counterperestroika: Political Agendas, Rhetorical Strategies, Personal Choices*. New York: Routledge.

Shalin, Dmitri. 2021. "Identity politics and civic imagination." *Tikkun Magazine*, April 5. https://www.tikkun.org/identity-politics-and-civic-imagination

Shalin, Dmitri. 2022. "Progressivism, old and new: The spiritual moorings of progressive reforms." *Society* 59: 648-59. https://link.springer.com/article/10.1007/s12115-022-00706-y

Shenderovich, Viktor. 2023. "Udar po Dnepru, Angarsky Man'iak, Ekspropriatsiia." January 20. https://www.youtube.com/watch?v=Cae3j4q1bho

Shevtsova, Lilia. 2005. *Putin's Russia*. Washington DC: Carnegie Endowment for International Peace.

Sokov, Nikolai. 2000. "Foreign Policy Under Putin: Pro-Western Pragmatism Might Be a Greater Challenge to the West." PONARS Policy Memo 101. bit.ly/4dZhy9R

Starovoitova, Galina. 2007. "'Na etot raz oni budut ubivat na meste … ' Interview with Galina Starovoitova conducted and introduced by Dmitri Shalin." *Teleskop: Zhurnal po sotsiologii i marketingovym islledovaniiam* 6: 2-12.

Troianovski, Anton. 2022. "Russians Now See a New Side to Putin: Dragging Them into War." February 24. https://www.nytimes.com/2022/02/24/world/europe/putin-russia-ukraine.html

Yadov, Vladimir, and Dmitri Shalin. 2015. "From Dialogues Between Vladimir Yadov and Dmitri Shalin." *Public Opinion Monitor* 19, 194-219. http://cdclv.unlv.edu/archives/articles/vy_ds_dialogues.pdf

Zhirina, Tatiana B., Galina A. Nazarenko, and Yuri G. Nigai. 2006. "Sistema stimuliov dlia uchashchikhsia. Kak povysit interes k ucheve?" http://festival.1september.ru/2005_2006/index.php?numb_artic=310763

Zubok, Vladislav. 2022. "After Putin – What?" *Bulletin of the Atomic Scientists*, November 9. https://thebulletin.org/premium/2022-11/after-putin-what

5

Against the West: The Weimar Republic and Post-Soviet Russia in the Yeltsin Era as Aggrieved Powers

Leonid Luks

All analogies are imperfect. This rule also applies to the comparison of post-Soviet Russia and Weimar Germany that Alexander Yanov put into circulation at the beginning of the 1990s. Nevertheless, striking similarities are apparent between the two state formations, and I would like to indicate these in the first part of the chapter. In the second part I shall proceed to the differences.

The Russian offensive against Ukraine that began on February 24, 2022 has added new dimensions to the discourse on the phenomenon of "Weimar Russia." It is therefore important to reexamine "Weimar Syndrome," both in its German "original" form and its Russian "replica."

Analogies Between the Weimar Republic and Post-Soviet Russia

The legend of the "internal enemy"

The political culture of the Weimar Republic was poisoned from the very start by the legend of the "stab in the back." It was invented by representatives of the ruling circles who had governed the country in dictatorial fashion during World War I and who, after the failure of the spring offensive of 1918, understood very well that the military might of Germany was completely

---

The present text is an expanded and revised version of Luks, 2008, originally translated from Russian by Stephen D. Shenfield. Reprinted by permission of Taylor & Francis Ltd. https://www.tandfonline.com.

exhausted and that catastrophe awaited the country unless hostilities were terminated immediately. But in order to evade responsibility for defeat, the ruling group transferred power to the previously impotent Reichstag. Thus, the country acquired a parliamentary form of government not by means of struggle from below but as a gift from above (Gurian, 1932; Nipperdey, 1992, 858-76; 361-77; Misukhin, 1998, 111-23).

And it was this unexpectedly empowered parliament that had to pay for the military collapse of the Reich, a responsibility that lay above all with the military command, which through its policy of total mobilization had brought the country to a condition of complete prostration.

General Erich Ludendorff—the undeclared dictator of the Reich during the last two years of the war—declared in his memoirs that Germany had lost the war not on the external but on the internal front. The pacifist and defeatist mood of the democratic opposition had supposedly undermined the army's combat morale (Ludendorff, 1919; Hanson and Kopstein, 1997, 256). In other words, it was not the all-powerful military command but the parties in the Reichstag, deprived of any political influence during the war, that were chiefly to blame for defeat. In this way the legend was born of the "stab in the back"—the belief that Germany's bid for world hegemony had failed not because this goal was an unrealizable dream but due to the treason of a small group of internal enemies.

This "theory" is strikingly reminiscent of the argumentation of imperially inclined Russian circles during the last years of *perestroika* and in post-Soviet Russia. The bard of the empire, Aleksandr Prokhanov, wrote in March 1990: "For the first time in the history not just of Russia but of the world, we see a state destroyed not by external blows ... or by natural disasters but by the deliberate actions of its leaders" (Prokhanov, 1990; Yanov, 1995; Hanson and Kopstein, 1997, 266).

The tone was set. Now everything was clear. The Soviet empire collapsed, so it turned out, not because the party distrusted the people and smothered its striving for autonomy, nor because the Soviet Union in the era of the third (electronic) industrial revolution had turned into a living anachronism, that is, into a paradise for bureaucrats, based on regimentation and suppression of the creative initiative of society. No, it was all the fault of the enemies of inertia and stagnation, who had tried to bring back into the world community a country that had been cut off from the rapidly developing "First World." However, modernization of the country was impossible without weakening the paternalistic *nomenklatura* structures that welded both the "external" and the "internal" Soviet empire (the socialist camp and the Soviet Union, respectively) into a single whole.

Nevertheless, the heart of the empire was not the managerial "new class" but the ideology inspiring it—the idea of proletarian internationalism. This idea—that is, the "superstructure"—was the "base" of the Soviet Union (an ironic reference to the Marxian distinction between the productive base of a society and its legal, intellectual, and cultural superstructure). After all, the Soviet Union's name did not even hint that this country was the successor to the empire of the Romanovs. A "Union of Soviet Socialist Republics" might have existed in any part of the world, on any continent. A very important prerequisite for the existence of this state was faith in the infallibility of the party and of its ideology. But by Brezhnev's time no one, except perhaps for Suslov and those like him, still believed in the "radiant communist future." There was only a play at faith, a masquerade in which the majority of the population—with the exception of the dissidents—took part together with the party. But with the advent of *perestroika* this camouflage collapsed under the impact of *glasnost'*. And Gorbachev had no choice but to abolish Article 6 of the Constitution, which had codified the party's leading role in the country. The Soviet empire was now in urgent need of a new ideological foundation to weld it into a coherent whole. But, as is well known, the feverish search for such a foundation failed. With extraordinary perspicacity, Prince Nikolai Trubetskoi, founder of the Eurasianist movement, foresaw this turn of events as early as 1927. He wrote that, due to the growing national awareness of the non-Russian peoples, the time of the exclusive domination of the Russians in Russia had passed, never to return. The Bolsheviks understood this well and found a new bearer of Russia's unity: instead of the Russian people, the proletariat. But, Trubetskoi continued, this was merely an apparent solution to the problem. The national feelings of the workers were much stronger than their class solidarity. If Russia wished to remain a single state, it would have to find a new bearer of its unity; in Trubetskoi's view, this could only be the Eurasian idea, emphasizing the commonalities of Russian-Eurasian peoples (Trubetskoi, 1927, 28-9).

Now, as in the past, the weakness of the Eurasian idea was that it had failed to achieve broad recognition, to "seize hold of the masses" and thereby prevent the collapse of the Soviet Union.

Nostalgically inclined circles in post-Soviet Russia attach no significance to these profound historical processes that have led to tectonic shifts throughout the space between the Elbe and Vladivostok. For them, the disintegration of the Soviet empire was merely the result of a plot by a clique of "internal enemies."

The Demonization of the West and of Western Values

Besides the legend of the "stab in the back," many national-patriotic circles in post-Soviet Russia share with the Weimar right a radical rejection of liberalism.

After the defeat in World War I of the nation that had allegedly never been "vanquished on the battlefield," the German nationalists persistently demonized the victors and their democratic values. The champions of national revanche considered the harshness of the Treaty of Versailles—in which respect, incidentally, it did not differ all that much from the victorious peace of Brest-Litovsk concluded by the Germans in March 1918—quite sufficient grounds for sweeping away the existing European order. Insulted national self-esteem became the dominant motif of their thinking and determined their tactics; considerations pertaining to the pan-European and Christian heritage no longer played any role. "We are an oppressed nation," Arthur Moeller van den Bruck, one of the heralds of the so-called Conservative Revolution, wrote in 1923. "The meager territory onto which we have been crowded conceals the enormous danger that comes from us. Should we not build our policy on the basis of this danger?" (Moeller van den Bruck, 1931, 71-2).

The liberalism borrowed from the West was declared by supporters of the Conservative Revolution and of other nationalist groups to be a mortal enemy of the Germans. For Moeller van den Bruck, liberalism was "the moral illness of a nation" bereft of any convictions passed off as a conviction (Moeller van den Bruck, 1931, 69-71).

The pseudo-ethical orientation that was characteristic of the conservative revolutionaries is manifested here with especial clarity. Those who were prepared to deride humanism and destroy the entire European order in revenge for the injustice of Versailles thoughtlessly reproached liberalism as indifference toward morality. It is not surprising that this moralizing immoralism, which absolved the sins of its supporters in advance but portrayed its opponents as incorrigible criminals, seemed very tempting to many.

The establishment of a liberal system in Germany was presented by German critics of the West as a consequence of the crafty intrigues of the Western democracies. The West possessed immunity against the liberal poison, Moeller van den Bruck asserted, because it did not take liberal principles seriously. In Germany, by contrast, liberalism was taken literally. Its corrupting principles might therefore lead the country to ruin. The Western states, unable to overcome the Germans on the battlefield, were trying to achieve the same result by means of liberal and pacifist propaganda, and the naïve Germans were drinking up the poison (Moeller van den Bruck, 1931, 69-71).

The self-pity of the supporters of the Conservative Revolution was as boundless as their megalomania. It turned out that the sole remedy capable of easing the suffering of the Germans was world domination. Moeller van den Bruck explained: "Power over the world is the only chance of survival for an overpopulated country. In defiance of all obstacles, the impulse of people in our overpopulated country strains in just this direction; its aim is the space that we need" (translated from Russian) (Moeller van den Bruck, 1931, 63; 71-2).

Parliamentary democracy was presented by its German ill-wishers as "devoid of chivalrous principles." The revolution of November 1918, Ernst Jünger writes, was unable to defend the country from the external enemy. That is why the soldiers turned away from it. This revolution, in Jünger's opinion, rejected such concepts as "manliness, courage, and honor" (Bastian, 1963, 66). Oswald Spengler, for his part, speaks of "the indescribable loathsomeness of the November days": "Not a single imperious glance, nothing inspiring, not a single significant face, recalled word, or audacious crime" (translated from Russian) (Spengler, 1920, 11).[1]

The demonization of Western values is also characteristic of many national-patriotic circles in post-Soviet Russia. For many years now, Alexander Dugin has been a sort of mouthpiece and ideologue of these forces. The journal *Elementy*, which Dugin put out in the 1990s, portrays liberalism as "the most consistent and radical form ... of European nihilism," as an embodiment of the spirit of antitradition, cynicism, and skepticism. Liberalism allegedly destroys any spiritual, historical, and cultural continuity; it is simply the enemy of mankind. According to *Elementy*, it is a fateful error that "liberalism" and "democracy" are often viewed as synonyms. In fact, liberalism has nothing in common with democracy in its true sense of people's power. The defenders of liberalism constitute a small power-hungry and unelected elite that uses democratic rhetoric only to give the people the illusion of involvement in the political decisions of the ruling group (*Elementy* 1994, no. 5, 5).[2]

The journal adamantly refuses to accept the final victory of its deadly enemies, the liberals, and calls for a counteroffensive, a cruel revenge to pay the Western enemy back for the shameful defeat. The journal boundlessly glorifies war and violence, as did the conservative revolutionaries in Weimar Germany. They relied on Carl Schmitt's "concept of the political," according to which the difference between a friend and an enemy was the obvious criterion in politics. This difference is also the alpha and the omega for *Elementy*. All adversaries of these "enemies" are placed by *Elementy* in the category of "friends." Conciliation of the two camps is impossible: "Between them there can be only enmity, hatred, the harshest struggle, ... to the point of annihilation, to the last drop of blood. ... Which of us will draw a line under history? ... They or us? ... War will decide—the 'father of things'" (Dugin, 1996, 2).

In the opinion of Alexander Dugin and of other publishers of the *Elementy*, Russia faces only one option: to become a province of an alien hegemon or to restore its own hegemony. But unlike those who feel nostalgia for the empire in today's Russia, the publishers of *Elementy* are not satisfied with simply returning to the past. Restoration of the former borders of the Russian empire is only the first stage of their strategic plan. For they see the chief purpose of restoring the empire as being the struggle against American global domination, against "world evil"—a fight not for life but to the death.

Just like the Weimar right, the Russian nationalist-patriots reject the universalism propagated by the West and are fervent defenders of cultural particularism and special national paths. Pro-Western circles are accused of a lack of patriotism. Accusations of this kind put both the German and the Russian "Westernizers" at a direct disadvantage. They tried in every way to prove that they were not indifferent to the fate of the fatherland. The first to speak of the "army that had never been vanquished on the battlefield" was Friedrich Ebert, head of the German social democrats, welcoming soldiers returned from the front in the name of the revolutionary government that had taken office in November 1918. But none of these assurances of their love for the fatherland helped either the social democrats or other democratic politicians rehabilitate themselves in the eyes of the right, for whom the democrats remained traitors, internal enemies who served the interests of the external enemy—that is, the West.

Here too we see a certain similarity with the fate of the democrats in Yeltsin's Russia.

When Yeltsin and his supporters abolished the communist dictatorship in August 1991, they appeared under not only democratic but also Russian national banners. The mood of exhilaration that reigned in Moscow immediately after the defeat of the communist putsch was very reminiscent of the atmosphere in 1848 in the Frankfurt *Paulskirche* (where the National Assembly was sitting): the idea of freedom and the national idea were joined in a single whole. We must not, however, forget the direction in which the German national movement developed, because the goal toward which it strove was not only freedom but also the might of a great power. A characteristic sign of this reorientation of the German national movement was the discussion in the *Paulskirche* in July 1848 of the Polish question. Up to that time, solidarity with oppressed Poland had been a sort of litmus test for liberal circles in Europe and in Germany. After the beginning of the revolution of 1848, however, this feeling of solidarity noticeably weakened (Kaehler, 1952, 418; Gollwitzer, 1964, 262; Nipperdey, 1983, 627-30; Wehler, 1987, 743-4).

A similar situation took shape in Russia after the removal of the Communist Party of the Soviet Union from power. The victorious democrats began to talk more and more about Russia's national interests and less and less about solidarity with small peoples. Many democrats who had spoken of "Russia's return to Europe" before August 1991 started to speak of "Russia's special path" after the August events. The supporters of a pro-Western orientation in Russian politics were portrayed by their critics as politicians without roots who had moved far away from the traditions of their country. Soon after the victory of the democrats, Evgeny Kozhokin, one of Yeltsin's advisers, declared: "When they come into power Westernizers must stop being Westernizers. You can be a Westernizer only in opposition" (Kozhokin, 1992).

Nationally inclined circles within the democratic camp reproached pro-Western groups in the government with excessive willingness to compromise in relations with the West, as well as with Russia's closest neighbors. Thus, Sergei Stankevich, a political adviser to the president of Russia, asserted: "Our neighbors often regard Russia not as a state but as a heap, a sort of relict from which one or another part can be cut off" (Stankevitch, 1992). Around the same time, Evgeny Ambartsumov, chairman of the Supreme Soviet Committee on Foreign Policy, suggested that the concepts of national pride, national affiliation, and national interest are quite natural in the West. Why should they not be extended to Russia?

This struggle of the Russian democrats in defense of national interests did not, however, rehabilitate them in the eyes of the "irreconcilable opposition." For the nationalist-patriots, the democrats are, above all, destroyers of a great empire and agents of the Western victors in the Cold War who have established an antinational regime on Russian territory. Despite their national rhetoric, the Russian democrats, like their counterparts in Weimar Germany, have not managed to bridge the chasm separating them from their radical opponents. But, on the other hand, the fact that in both cases the democrats to some degree adopted the arguments of their opponents led to them losing the initiative in political discourse.

The Transition from a Half-Closed to an Open Society

The Weimar Republic—that is, the "first German democracy"—was the freest state formation in the history of Germany apart from the Federal Republic of Germany. The Germans had long dreamt of this freedom, almost since the time of the war of liberation against Napoleon in 1813. The motto of the German revolution of 1848 was "Freedom and State Unity!" However, the revolution was unable to achieve either goal.

True, a quarter of a century later Bismarck succeeded in uniting Germany, but he did so in an authoritarian manner. The Germans achieved complete freedom only as a result of the revolution of November 1918. However, this unexpectedly won freedom evoked little euphoria, and this is not surprising. In Germany, the establishment of the democratic order was associated with defeat in the World War, the humiliating Treaty of Versailles, territorial losses, reparations, and the deep economic crisis that reached its apogee in 1923 with hyperinflation unprecedented in the country's history.

All these processes are reminiscent of what happened in Russia after the collapse of the Soviet regime and in the period of the birth of the "second Russian democracy." True, the second Russian democracy, unlike the Weimar Republic in Germany, was not the freest state formation in the country's preceding history. The order that emerged in Russia after the revolution of February 1917 was no less free.

In April 1917, Lenin called Russia "the freest country in the world of all the warring countries" (Lenin, 1962, 114-15). A few months later, he himself tried to rein in this freedom, and after the Bolshevik victory in the civil war, he finally managed to do so. The "freest country in the world" turned into the world's first totalitarian state. True, the character of the communist dictatorship changed substantially after Stalin's death. The totalitarian system turned into a semi-totalitarian or even paternalistically authoritarian order. However, the society itself remained a puppet in the hands of the ruling *nomenklatura* and only managed to make the transition from a "closed" to a "semi-open" condition during *perestroika*. Its final liberation took place in August 1991 on the barricades at the White House. But, just as in Weimar Germany, the euphoria that followed was short-lived. For after August came December (the disintegration of the Soviet Union) and January (shock therapy, which in the first years entailed hyperinflation, a fall in gross product of 23 percent in 1992, and an almost 50 percent reduction in the living standard of the population).

The Russian reformers very quickly lost their capital of trust. The democratic idea was also discredited by the confrontation between the executive and the legislative branch (the president and the Supreme Soviet), which culminated in the disbandment of parliament and the bombardment of the White House.

All these events inflicted a deep trauma on the public consciousness, and one of its consequences was the crushing defeat of the democrats in the Duma elections of December 1993. Russia found itself faced with the dilemma that once faced Weimar, Germany, when radical antidemocrats won an unexpected victory in the Reichstag elections of September 1930. Rudolf Hilferding, one of the leaders of the Social-Democratic Party of Germany, formulated this dilemma as follows: "To affirm democracy against the will of the majority, which rejects democracy, and moreover affirm it using the political means provided by the democratic constitution—this is almost like squaring the circle" (translated from Russian) (Hilferding, 1931).

Revenge of the Overturned Elites

The Revolution that began in Germany on November 9, 1918 differed qualitatively from the French revolution of 1789 or from the Russian revolution of 1917. Unlike the latter revolutions, it did not shift from a moderate to a more radical phase but developed in the opposite direction: it was radical at the start and grew increasingly moderate. Its main political force was the Social Democratic Party, which wished at any price to prevent the revolution from developing in accordance with the Russian model of 1917. The social democrats therefore constantly fought against their own radical left wing, bewitched by the example of the Bolshevik October. The influence of these extremist groups on Germany's traditionally moderate working class was marginal. Of the deputies elected to the Berlin Congress of Soviets that took place in mid-December 1918, 80 percent rejected the Soviet model and voted for the transformation of Germany into a parliamentary republic (Winkler, 2000, 385-6; Blasius, 2006, 17-18). But despite this, the social-democratic majority in the Council of People's Commissioners (CPC), which governed the country from November 10, 1918, saw the chief threat to German democracy coming not from the right but from the left.

The culmination of the chaotic attempts by left-wing extremists to bring about a revolution in Germany on the "Russian model" was the uprising in Berlin that began on January 5, 1919. The CPC suppressed this uprising without difficulty; in doing so, however, it made use not only of regular troops but also of corps of right-radical volunteers. As Arthur Rosenberg, chronicler of the Weimar Republic, was to note in the mid-1930s, the use of extremist opponents of democracy to defend the republic was an unforgivable error on the government's part (Rosenberg, 1961).[3]

In fact, the uprising in Berlin was suppressed in the space of a few days, by January 12. However, the social-democratic government lost control over the soldiery, which now began to institute mob law on its own account. Victims of the reprisals included Karl Liebknecht and Rosa Luxemburg, the leaders of the Communist Party of Germany that had been created on December 31, 1918, who were murdered on January 15.

The social-democratic government overreacted to the actions of the former left wing of its own party, not only due to an exaggerated fear of anarchy, but also because it wished to demonstrate its patriotism, the identity of its own interests with the domestic and foreign interests of the German state. The German social democrats, accused for years by the right of having no attachment to their fatherland, wanted to prove that the fate of Germany was not a matter of indifference to them.

Similarly, the November revolution, having overthrown the monarchy and initially sown panic in the ranks of the ruling conservative elites, confined itself to mere half-measures in the fight against the old regime. Its administrative, economic, and even military structures (despite the constraints imposed by the Treaty of Versailles) remained almost untouched. All the prerequisites for revenge on the part of the elites overthrown in November 1918 were in place. However, over time this striving for continuity, this desire to repair the break resulting from the revolution, spread to broad strata of the population. A symbol of this growth in nostalgic moods was the election as president of the Reich in 1925 of the aged Field Marshal Hindenburg, who had never reconciled himself to the republican order and remained a convinced monarchist. It is necessary to add that he was elected precisely at the moment when the Weimar Republic had managed to overcome the postwar crisis and stabilize the economy, during the period when the democratic parties of the so-called Weimar coalition were achieving their greatest successes in parliamentary elections.

This duality shows how fragile a state formation the Weimar Republic was: democratic rules of play had still not become "the only game in town"—to use the expression of contemporary political scientists Juan Linz and Alfred Stepan (Linz and Stepan, 1996, 5).

Because the president was supposed to act as a guarantor of the Weimar Constitution and in crisis situations could introduce a state of emergency in the country (Article 48 of the Constitution), Hindenburg's antidemocratic attitudes threatened the order that he was duty bound to defend. His predecessor Ebert, being a convinced democrat, had used his emergency powers, especially during the Ruhr crisis of 1923, but only to fight against the enemies of democracy both on the right and on the left (against both communist and Nazi attempted coups d'état). Such a consistent struggle on two fronts could not be expected from Hindenburg. The conservative circles that exerted influence on the aged president saw an important difference between communists and Nazis. The latter, they considered their potential allies. It was this orientation that eventually led to the transfer of power to Hitler and to the destruction of the Weimar democracy.

Is the revenge of overthrown elites also in store for post-Soviet Russia?

The revolution of August 1991 was, like the November revolution in Germany, a half-and-half affair. Many Russian democrats did not wish to regard the August events following the suppression of the putsch as a revolution, because they associated revolution with such concepts as mass terror and dictatorship. This is why they abstained from settling accounts with their vanquished enemies in the Bolshevik manner. According to G. Popov, one of the leading representatives of the democratic camp, this decision was of extraordinary significance not only for Russia but also for the whole world.

Later Yeltsin was to recall that in September and October of 1991 the country was literally poised on the edge of an abyss. But, nonetheless, Russia was saved from revolution and mankind from its catastrophic consequences. For a year, said the president, there were constant appeals for a decisive confrontation. But none of these appeals evoked a response in the hearts of Russian people. Yeltsin considered precisely this a common victory.

Arguments continue in Russia to this day over whether Yeltsin and his supporters made a mistake in August 1991 by taking the path of compromise rather than revolutionary struggle. It must not be forgotten, however, how modest an organizational base was at Yeltsin and his team's disposal at the moment of their victory. It should be added that after the defeat of the common foe the majority of democratic groups opposed the country's new leadership. In order to remain on the political scene, Yeltsin's government was compelled to seek a compromise with officials from the old structures who were prepared to accept reform. We see here a certain similarity with the behavior of the Bolsheviks after 1917. Although the Bolsheviks considered their revolution the most radical upheaval in history, within a few months of coming to power they had to seek support from the "bourgeois specialists"—that is, from representatives of the "old world" that the Bolsheviks wanted to completely destroy. Without such support, the regime would simply not have survived. However, the Bolsheviks had one extraordinarily effective means of forcing "class enemies" to work for them at their disposal—the "red terror." Such a means was not available to the victors in August 1991. In order to induce the cooperation of the most flexible people from the old structures, they had to appeal to their interests and at the same time convince them that the old regime could not be restored under any circumstances.

After recovering from the shocks of August 1991 and October 1993, managerial groups mounted a counteroffensive against the civil society that had emerged during *perestroika*, against the subjects of the federation that had broken free, and against the fabulous fortunes made by the oligarchs. While Yeltsin remained in power, this counteroffensive did not assume the character of a restoration of the order that had collapsed in 1991. Despite his rapprochement with the managerial structures of the old regime, Yeltsin, being a convinced reformer like Ebert in Germany in his time, was an obstacle to turning back the wheel of history. And here I would like to continue on to the differences between the Weimar Republic and post-Soviet Russia.

Differences Between the Weimar Republic and Post-Soviet Russia

Prehistory

Pluralistic structures in Weimar Germany were at a higher level of development than in post-Soviet Russia (see Hanson and Kopstein, 1997; Hanson, 2006, 343–72), and these differences are closely connected with the different prehistory of the two states. Weimar's predecessor—the Second German Reich created in 1871—was, notwithstanding its semi-feudal and patriarchal character, a law based state with a multiparty system, independent public organizations, and more or less free press. Although opposition parties, especially the social democrats, and some confessional and national minorities (Catholics, Poles) were persecuted from time to time, there were always legal loopholes that enabled them to survive periods of the most intense persecution and later return to the political or public scene as strong as ever.

Nothing of the kind existed under the Soviet regime that preceded the "second Russian democracy," with the exception of the Gorbachev period. The civil society built in Russia after the revolution of 1905, which in February 1917 broke completely free of state control, was destroyed by the Bolsheviks. Together with civil society (especially in the Stalin period) they destroyed the institution of private property, which guarantees society a certain degree of independence from the state. And so, the "second Russian democracy" came onto the political scene almost without experience of political competition or the organized defense of the rights and interests of specific social groups. The democrats managed to defeat the ruling apparatus in August 1991 with such ease by virtue of the weakness of their adversary rather than their own strength, an adversary that was undergoing an extraordinarily deep identity crisis due to the erosion of communist ideology and was therefore losing the capacity for resistance. But when the managerial apparatus recovered from the shock of defeat and embarked on the bureaucratic revanche that

I have already described, it turned out that civil society in Russia had not yet managed to emerge from its amorphous condition and did not have the strength to offer effective resistance to the well-organized managerial class. Not least of the factors underlying these defeats of the democrats was the fact that they too were going through an identity crisis. The discrediting of democratic ideas in the eyes of broad strata of the population due to the difficulties of the transition from a "closed" to an "open" society deprived the democrats of their characteristic self-confidence from the last years of the Soviet regime. Now they were swimming against the tide. And, indeed, the gradual dismantling of pluralistic structures by means of the methods of "guided democracy" has not evoked significant protest from the population. Besides the discrediting of the democratic idea, the lack of protest may also be attributed to the fact that this process has occurred in parallel with economic stabilization (mainly thanks to high world prices for oil and other energy goods). In addition, the striving of Putin's team to "statify" society has been in keeping with the traditional conceptions of many Russians concerning the role of the state as guarantor of social justice and national wellbeing. Uprisings and revolutions have broken out in Russia above all when the state has failed to cope with this role and not as a result of attempts by society to take over these functions.

The Threat from the Right and from the Left

The Weimar democracy fought constantly against two threats—the threat from the right and the threat from the left. Hitler rose to the surface on the wave of the ruling strata's fear of the Bolshevik danger. This fear was hardly justified. In Germany at the beginning of the 1930s, the conflict between the social democrats and the communists, provoked mainly by the Stalin leadership in Moscow, paralyzed the workers' movement, depriving it of practically any ability to act. Despite this, Germany's ruling circles were panic-stricken by fear of a "mass uprising"—that is, of an independent workers' movement. The Nazis took advantage of this fear. Speaking in January 1932 at a meeting with German industrialists in Düsseldorf, Hitler declared: "Were it not for us (the Nazis), the middle class in Germany would have already been destroyed. And the Bolsheviks would long since have resolved the question of power in their favor" (Domarus, 1962, 87).

And although the argumentation of the Nazi leader was of a wholly demagogic kind, he finally managed to convince the German conservatives that the weakened ruling order in Germany could be saved only by relying on the National Socialist Workers' Party (Luks, 1984, 158-61, 193-4; 1988, 100-3).

Unlike their German predecessors, the present-day Russian right-wing extremists say little about a danger from the left; what is more, in the struggle against the order established in August 1991, they have often found themselves on the same side of the barricades as the communists.[4] The "red-brown alliance," which in Weimar Germany arose only periodically, is a constant phenomenon in post-Soviet Russia (Laqueur, 1994; Allensworth, 1998; Shenfield, 2001; Luks, 2002, 256–6). This mishmash of "right" and "left" owes much to the amorphous and indistinct party-political landscape in postcommunist Russia, which is in turn explained by the amorphous condition of a society that lacks classes in the generally accepted sense of the word. But there are also other reasons why the differences between right and left are increasingly being erased in contemporary Russia. The point is that the Russian communists, perhaps for the first time since 1917, have lost faith in continuous social progress and are no longer sure that history and its laws are on their side.

Right-wing extremists, on the contrary, have always mocked the idea of progress. They do not want, and have never wanted, to swim with the tide of history; instead, they stop at nothing to stem it and turn it back. Everywhere they imagine symptoms of disintegration and decay, the intrigues of a mighty world conspiracy. They believe that the "decline and fall of Europe" can be prevented only by the violent annihilation of the bearers of this conspiracy—Jews, Masons, "plutocrats," Marxists. The golden age of fascism is the pagan, pre-Christian epoch. The pathos of communism, by contrast, is directed toward the future, when the leap will be made "from the realm of necessity to the realm of freedom."

This historical optimism, however, is now a thing of the past. Since the collapse of the Soviet Union, the communists have been bereft of faith in progress and a radiant future. The sudden disappearance of the second great power, which inspired the fear or at least the respect of the whole world, seems to them an inscrutable event; they refuse to see in it the action of historical laws. Their golden age has become, like the right-wing radicals, the past.

Besides the displacement of right-wing and left-wing positions, post-Soviet Russia also differs from Weimar Germany insofar as radical groups on both the left and the right (the Communist Party of the Russian Federation on one side, the Liberal Democratic Party of Russia on the other) are becoming increasingly "centrist" and finding a common language with at least part of the ruling groups. This process of interpenetration between the "irreconcilable" opposition and state structures accelerated after the coming to power of Putin, whom many national-patriots see as a new "ingatherer of the Russian land." According to a newly created myth, disseminated by a number of semi-official publicists, the Yeltsin period was a time of collapse and humiliation for Russia, while Putin has brought about a miraculous revival of Russian statehood.

Postscript: Dugin and Putin

For years, one of Putins's biggest admirers in the nationalist-patriotic camp was Alexander Dugin. Only after the establishment of Putin's "managed democracy" did Dugin's chances to strongly influence the internal Russian discourse with his extreme ideas increase. Nevertheless, Dugin initially failed to elevate his end-of-battle ideology, which was similar to that of the Weimar Right, to the status of an official government program. This was despite the fact that he had written countless praises of Putin. Only on the eve of Putin's offensive war against Ukraine did Putin's foreign policy begin to more closely resemble Dugin's postulates. One could speak of a kind of Dugin-Putin tandem. However, this tandem failed completely. As we know, Putin's planned "*Blitzkrieg*" against Ukraine did not happen. Not least because of this, Dugin publicly distanced himself from Putin in a spectacular way. Shortly after Ukrainian forces reentered the city of Kherson (November 11, 2022) Dugin emphasized in a letter that not the Russian generals, but the autocrat in Moscow was solely responsible for this defeat. Later, Dugin distanced himself from this letter and claimed it was not authentic. Regardless, the failure of Putin's original war plans shook the facade of Russia's alleged national unity.

Notes

1 On the theme of the "Conservative Revolution" in the Weimar Republic, see also: Rauschning, 1941; Mohler, 1950; Sontheimer, 1958, 1968; Kuhn, 1961; von Klemperer, 1962; Stern, 1993; Breuer, 1993; Luks, 1998.
2 On Dugin's ideology and the journal *Elementy*, see: Yanov, 2000; Luks, 2000, 2004; Mathyl, 2002; Umland, 2006.
3 Some contemporary authors make a similar assessment of the situation at that time. In 1990, the Berlin historian Heinrich August Winkler wrote: "[The social democrats] aimed above all at preventing economic and political chaos; they overestimated the danger from the left and underestimated the danger from the right" (Winkler, 1990, 307).

4 In speaking of a threat to post-Soviet democracy from both "right" and "left," some authors take insufficient account of this circumstance. See: Hanson and Kopstein, 1997, 267-8.

References

Allensworth, Wayne. 1998. *The Russian Question: Nationalism, Modernization and Post-Communist Russia*. Lanham: Rowman & Littlefield.
Bastian, Karl-Friedrich. 1963. *Das Politische bei Ernst Jünger*. Freiburg i.Br.: Krause.
Blasius, Dirk. 2006. *Weimars Ende: Bürgerkrieg und Politik 1930-1933*. Göttingen: Vandenhoeck & Ruprecht.
Breuer, Stefan. 1993. *Anatomie der Konservativen Revolution*. Darmstadt: Wissenschaftliche Buchgesellschaft.
Domarus, Max (ed.). 1962. *Hitler: Reden und Proklamationen 1932-1945*. Vol. I. Darmstadt: Verlagsdruckerei Schmidt, Neustadt a.d. Aisch.
Dugin, Alexander. 1996. "Subjekt bez Granits." *Elementy. Evrazijskoe Obozrenie* 7: 1-2.
Gollwitzer, Heinz. 1964. *Europabild und Europagedanke. Beiträge zur deutschen Geistesgeschichte des 18. und 19. Jahrhunderts*. München: Verlag C. H. Beck.
Gurian, Walter. 1932. *Um des Reiches Zukunft*. Freiburg: Herder.
Hanson, Stephen E. 2006. "Postimperial Democracies: Ideology and Party Formation in the Third Republic France, Weimar Germany and Post-Soviet Russia." *East European Politics and Societies* 20(2): 343-72.
Hanson, Stephen E., and Jeffrey S. Kopstein. 1997. "The Weimar/Russia Comparison." *Post-Soviet Affairs* 13(3): 252-83.
Hilferding, Rudolf. 1931. "In Krisennot." *Die Gesellschaft* 7: 1-8.
Kaehler, Siegfried A. 1952. "Realpolitik zur Zeit des Krimkrieges – eine Säkularbetrachtung." *Historische Zeitschrift* 174: 417-78.
Kozhokin, Evgeny. 1992. [Mnenie]. *Moskovskie novosti*, August 16. https://yeltsin.ru/archive/periodic/53448
Kuhn, Helmut. 1961. "Das geistige Gesicht der Weimarer Republik." *Zeitschrift für Politik* 8: 1-10.
Laqueur, Walter. 1994. *Chernaia sotnia. Proiskhozhdenie russkogo fashizma*. Moscow: Tekst.
Lenin, Vladimir I. 1962. *Polnoe sobranie sochnenii*, 55 vols. [1958-1965]. Vol. 31. Moscow: Gospolitizdat.
Linz, Juan J., and Alfred Stepan. 1996. *Problems of Democratic Transition and Consolidation: Southern Europe, South America, and Post-Communist Europe*. Baltimore: Johns Hopkins University Press.
Ludendorff, Erich. 1919. *Meine Kriegserinnerungen, 1914-1918*. Berlin: E. S. Mittler u. Sohn.

Luks, Leonid. 1984. *Entstehung der kommunistischen Faschismustheorie. Die Auseinandersetzung der Komintern mit Faschismus und Nationalsozialismus 1921-1935*. Stuttgart: Deutsche Verlags-Anstalt.

Luks, Leonid. 1988. "Bolschewismus, Faschismus, Nationalsozialismus – verwandte Gegner?" *Geschichte und Gesellschaft* 14: 96-115.

Luks, Leonid. 1998. "'Eurasier' und 'Konservative Revolution': Zur antiwestlichen Versuchung in Russland und in Deutschland." In *Deutschland und die Russische Revolution 1917-1924*, edited by Gerd Koenen and Lew Kopelew, 219-39. München: Wilhelm Fink Verlag.

Luks, Leonid. 2000. "'Tretii put'', ili nazad v Tretii Reich? O 'neoevraziiskoi' gruppe 'Elementy.'" *Voprosy filosofii* 5: 33-44.

Luks, Leonid. 2002. "Prizrak fashizma v postkommunisticheskoi Rossii." In Leonid Luks, *Tretii Rim? Tretii Reikh? Tretii put? Istoricheskie ocherki o Rossii, Germanii i Zapade*, 256-66. Moscow: Moskovskii filosofskii fond.

Luks, Leonid. 2004. "Eurasien aus neototalitärer Sicht – Zu Renaissance einer Ideologie im heutigen Russland." *Totalitarismus und Demokratie* 1: 63-76.

Luks, Leonid. 2008. "'Veimarskaia Rossia?' Zametki ob odnom spornom poniatii." *Voprosy filosfii* 2: 16-28.

Mathyl, Markus. 2002. "Der 'unaufhaltsame Aufstieg' des Aleksandr Dugin. Neo-Nationalbolschewismus und Neue Rechte in Russland." *Osteuropa* 52(7): 885-900.

Misukhin, Gleb. 1998. "Rossiia v Veimarskom zerkale, ili Soblazn legkogo uznavaniia," *Pro et Contra* 3: 111-23.

Moeller van den Bruck, Arthur. 1931. *Das dritte Reich*. Hamburg: Hanseat. Verg. Anst.

Mohler, Armin. 1950. *Die Konservative Revolution in Deutschland. Der Grundriss ihrer Weltanschauung*. Stuttgart: Vorwerk.

Nipperdey, Thomas. 1983. *Deutsche Geschichte 1800-1866. Bürgerwelt und starker Staat*. München: C. H. Beck.

Nipperdey, Thomas. 1992. *Deutsche Geschichte 1866-1918. Machtstaat vor der Demokratie*. München: C. H. Beck.

Prokhanov, Aleksandr. 1990. "Ideologiia vyzhivania." *Nash sovremennik* 9: 3-9.

Rauschning, Hermann. 1941. *The Conservative Revolution*. New York: Putnam.

Rosenberg, Arthur. 1961. *Geschichte der Weimarer Republik*. Frankfurt am Main: Europäische Verlagsanst.

Shenfield, Stephen D. 2001. *Russian Fascism: Traditions, Tendencies, Movements*. Armonk: Sharpe.

Sontheimer, Kurt. 1958. "Der Tatkreis." *Vierteljahrshefte für Zeitgeschichte* 6: 229-60.

Sontheimer, Kurt. 1968. *Antidemokratisches Denken in der Weimarer Republik*. München: Nymphenburger Verlagshandl.

Spengler, Oswald. 1920. *Preussentum und Sozialismus*. München: Verlag C. H. Beck.

Stankevitch, Sergei. 1992. "Rossiia 1992-I." *Komsomol'skaia Pravda*. May 26.

Stern, Fritz. 1993. *Kulturpessimismus als politische Gefahr*. Bern: Scherz.
Trubetskoi, Nikolaj. 1927. "Obscheevropeiskii natsionalizm." *Evraziiskaia khronika* 7: 24–30.
Umland, Andreas. 2006. "Postsowjetische Gegeneliten und ihr wachsender Einfluss auf Jugendkultur und Intellektuellendikurs in Russland: Der Fall Aleksandr Dugin." *Forum für osteuropäische Ideen- und Zeitgeschichte* 1: 115–47.
von Klemperer, Klemens. 1962. *Konservative Bewegungen: Zwischen Kaiserreich und Nationalsozialismus*. München: Oldenburg.
Wehler, Hans-Ulrich. 1987. *Deutsche Gesellschaftsgeschichte. Von der Reformära bis zur industriellen und politischen "Deutschen Doppelrevolution."* Vol. 2. München: C. H. Beck.
Winkler, Heinrich August. 1990. "Die Revolution von 1918/19 und das Problem der Kontinuität in der deutschen Geschichte." *Historische Zeitschrift* 250: 303–19.
Winkler, Heinrich August. 2000. *Der lange Weg nach Westen. Deutsche Geschichte vom Ende des Alten Reiches bis zum Untergang der Weimarer Republik*. Vol. 1. München: C. H. Beck.
Yanov, Alexander. 1995. *Posle Yeltsina: "Veimarskaia Rossiia."* Moscow: KRUK.
Yanov, Alexander. 2000. *Posle Yeltsina. Geopoliticheskoe Polozhenie Rossii. Predstavleniia i Real'nost'*. Moscow: KRUK.

Part Two

The War of Obsession

6

The "End of History" or the End of the Human Race? Rereading Fukuyama and Huntington During Russia's War Against Ukraine

Mikhail Sergeev

Introductory Observations

In 1992, after the collapse of the Soviet Union and its satellite states, American writer and political scientist Francis Fukuyama (b. 1952) published his famous volume, *The End of History, and the Last Man*. In this book, Fukuyama argues that liberal democracy represents the culmination of humanity's social and political development. Having no unresolvable internal problems after the defeat of the communist ideology, the liberal-democratic system faces no viable alternative and will eventually reign supreme worldwide.

Four years later, another American thinker, Samuel Huntington (1927–2008), offered his comprehensive rebuttal to Fukuyama's assertions by unveiling his classic *The Clash of Civilizations and the Remaking of World Order*. Contrary to his opponent, Huntington argues that liberal democracy is a unique cultural system that the West should not attempt to transplant to other parts of the world. Opposing both Fukuyama's universal claims and the national supporters of multiculturalism, Huntington emphatically remarks:

> Some Americans have promoted multiculturalism at home; some have promoted universalism abroad, and some have done both. Multiculturalism at home threatens the United States and the West; universalism abroad threatens the West and the world. Both deny the uniqueness of Western culture. The global monoculturalists want to make the world like America. The domestic multiculturalists want to make America like the world. A multicultural America is impossible because a non-Western America is not American. A multicultural world is unavoidable because global empire is impossible.
> (Huntington, 2011, 318)

The ensuing discussions between the adherents of Fukuyama and Huntington may have reminded those familiar with the history of Russian thought about the polarizing intellectual debates between the two opposing camps of nineteenth-century Russian intellectuals—the so-called Westernizers and Slavophiles. The first wanted their motherland to abandon the superstitions of its traditional culture and advance along the progressive path of the West. The second felt suspicious of the Western institutions and praised "The lore of ages long gone by, /In hoar antiquity compounded" (Pushkin, 1989, 131) in which they saw the uniqueness of Russian civilization (Edie et al. 1976, 1–16).

Similarly, the "Americanizer" Fukuyama believes in the global value and applicability of the Western type of civilization. At the same time, the "Americanophile" Huntington stresses its uniqueness to the West and the dangers of other nations and cultures adopting it. Both authors use the term "civilization" but employ it differently. Fukuyama analyzes humanity's progress from the state of barbarity to the pinnacle of liberal democratic civilization. Huntington, in turn, applies the terms "civilization" with "culture" interchangeably. He assumes that the institutions of American or Western civilization represent an inalienable part of its cultural identity. If we clarify this terminological discrepancy, we may discern that Fukuyama and Huntington's respective views are not opposite but complementary.

Civilization vs. Barbarism

Terminological Clarifications

The differentiation between "civilized" and "barbarous" people goes back to Ancient Greece. Herodotus, the first Western historian (fifth century BC), "famously made the distinction between 'civilized' Greeks and 'barbarous' non-Greeks in his *Histories*" (Mark, 2022). He stated at the beginning of the volume: "This is the Showing forth of the Inquiry of Herodotus of Halicarnassos, to the end that neither the deeds of men may be forgotten by lapse of time, nor the works great and marvelous, which have been produced some by Hellenes and some by Barbarians, may lose their renown" (Macaulay, 1890, 5).

It was also with Herodotus that "the 'West' first distinguishes itself from the 'East' (by chronicling) the Persian Wars fought in the first decades of the fifth century BC, in which a few Greek cities opposed that great empire" (King, 2000, 57). A contemporary American historian, Margaret King, notes that it "was not only a political struggle, but a war between competing visions of human society and aspiration." Most of the free cities in Greece abandoned monarchical rule and developed a communal government that was "hostile to kings and wary of tyrants" (King, 2000, 57).

By the time of Aristotle (384–322 BC), the conceptual boundary between civility and barbarity was already established, not on the ethnic or national grounds that separate "us" from "them," but on the firm foundation of political philosophy. In his treatise on politics, Aristotle made a fundamental claim distinguishing between the just and civil political regime on the one hand, and the unfair and barbaric rule on the other. He wrote that "governments which have a regard to the common interest are constituted in accordance with strict principles of justice and are therefore true forms; but those which regard only the interest of the rulers are all defective and perverted forms, for they are despotic, whereas a state is a community of freemen" (McKeon, 2001, 17–21). In other words, the good government should be "constitutional" in the sense that it "must have authority that those who are ruled acknowledge and accept ... based on laws, in which even those who govern are ruled by laws" (Adler, 1978, 123).

In modern times, the term "civilization" in the sense of "civilized condition," which is opposed to barbarity, appeared in French and English social and political thought since the age of the Enlightenment. In his *Essay on the History of Civil Society* (1767), English philosopher Adam Ferguson (1723–1816) described the characteristic features of cultures with prevailing barbarism and those advanced from rudeness to civility (Ferguson, 1767).

Spiritedness, Desire, and Unhappy Consciousness

Writing at the end of the twentieth century and observing an entirely different socio-economic and political landscape, Francis Fukuyama once more reexamined the Enlightenment idea of universal history and human progress. He argued that the evolution from barbarity to civilization has already found its consummation in the political institutions of liberal democracy. In this novel approach to the age-old problems, Fukuyama turned to the philosophical legacy of several critical Western thinkers, namely Plato (c. 428–c. 348 BC) and Hegel (1770–1831) as interpreted by a Russian-born French philosopher, Alexandre Kojève (1902–1968).

In *The Republic*, Plato advanced his well-known theory of the human psyche having three parts—reason (*logistikon*), passion or "spiritedness" (*thymoeides*), and desire or appetite (*epithymetikon*). For him, this tripartite composition of the soul corresponded to the three classes of people—the sovereign, the army, and the regular citizens. Plato argued that the role of "spiritedness" or *thymos* in the individual is to obey reason. This correlates to the social function of the military, which must submit to the rulers and defend the whole from external and internal disorders (Plato, 1997, Book IV: 435–45).

In the history of Western philosophy, the concept of *thymos* acquired various meanings. It designated passion, glory, prestige, or self-value characteristic of the aristocrats who pursued the honor of military victories. *Thymos* also referred to the spirit of moral freedom and dignity that distinguishes humans from animals. In the Hegelian sense, it meant a struggle for recognition by fellow humans.

According to Hegel, humans are social beings only partially driven by their biological needs for survival. What distinguishes us from the animal kingdom is our ability to overcome the fear of death by pursuing the "desire of desire," i.e., the acquisition of non-material values that other humans aspire for, which guarantees their acceptance and appreciation. As he wrote in the *Phenomenology of Spirit*: "Self-consciousness exists in and for itself when, and by the fact that it so exists for another; that is, it exists only in being recognized" (Hegel, 1977, 178; trans. modified).

In summarizing Hegel's views of universal history, American philosopher David Cooper writes that it "begins with man naively 'at home' in this world, 'sunk in nature,' like an animal." This "First Man" struggles to overcome nature, which leads to his sense of deep-seated alienation. He then asserts "one's freedom by enslaving other people," which brings about the relationship between mastery and slavery. The attained "goal of self-conscious freedom" bears the price of the millennia of "unhappy consciousness" resulting in the subservience of the enslaved person to his master and the consistent medieval efforts to entirely subordinate the material to the spiritual realm (Cooper, 2003, 331–2).

The history of alienation and splits calls for reconciliation and the restoration of unity. In Alexandre Kojève's interpretation of Hegel, the culmination of this process will mark the "end of history." As Kojève puts it,

> the historical "dialectic" is the "dialectic" of Master and Slave. But if the opposition of "thesis" and "antithesis" is meaningful only in their reconciliation by "synthesis," if history (in the full sense of the word) necessarily has a final term [and] if Desire must end in satisfaction ...— the interaction of Master and Slave must finally end in the "dialectical overcoming" of both of them.
>
> (Kojève, 1969, 9)

The engine that drives human activity—the desire to satisfy biological and, most importantly, social needs—will find its exhaustion (and fulfillment) in the capitalist economy and liberal political state, which affirms the worth and equality of all its citizens. In Kojève's words: "It is only by being 'recognized' by another, by many others, or—in the extreme—by all others, that a human being is really human, for himself as well as for others" (Kojève, 1969, 9).

The "Last Man" of Fukuyama

Like Kojève, Fukuyama believes that Universal History has exhausted itself in satisfying human biological needs in the capitalist economy and the social desire for equal recognition in the liberal democratic system. This does not imply that historical events will stop happening and that life, in general, will stand still. It only means "that there would be no further progress in the development of underlying principles and institutions because all of the really big questions had been settled" (Fukuyama, 2006, xii). From now on, the world will be divided into "historical" and "post-historical" societies. The fight between them will continue. However, authoritarian nation-states still driven by various religious or quasi-religious ideologies won't be able to offer a viable alternative to the global liberal-democratic order.

Let us suppose then that the external enemies and competitors are defeated and liberal democracies reign worldwide. Would there be any internal obstacles or contradictions in that planetary structure that would inevitably lead to its failure and ultimate destruction? Will it necessarily share the fate of past empires, including the totalitarian regimes of the twentieth century?

Fukuyama does not refer to empirical evidence of the many social ills and problems facing contemporary democratic societies: racial discrimination, economic inequality, partisan politics, skyrocketing education prices, drug addiction—the list goes on and on. Yet all those "clear and present dangers" could be successfully met and resolved within the democratic system. The more profound question is whether that system *per se* entirely satisfies the innermost human nature, namely, our desires and the yearning for recognition. Is it ever sustainable for people as such?

In his analysis, Fukuyama distinguishes between the criticism of liberal democracy from the Left and the Right. The leftists believe the capitalist system will remain deficient since it polarizes wealth and poverty. The impoverished will never achieve full equality and recognition from the prosperous because of the financial disparity, an inalienable feature of the free market economy. In turn, the critics from the Right question the very aspiration of shared human recognition. They contend, as Fukuyama writes, "that the problem with liberal society is not the inadequate universality of recognition, but the goal of equal recognition itself. The latter is problematic because human beings are inherently unequal; to treat them as equal is not to affirm but to deny their humanity" (Fukuyama, 2006, 289).

Here Fukuyama makes another very significant distinction based on the concept of *thymos*. He differentiates between "*isothymia*," or equal respect and appreciation, as contrasted with "*megalothymia*," which aims at superior recognition by others. As a reflection of the negative aspects of *thymos*, *megalothymia* in human history is responsible for wars, tyranny, imperialism, and countless other expressions of human desire for domination. Contemporary democracy is the *isothymic* society that suppresses *megalothymiacs* with insatiable ambition. However, the "Last Humans" in "post-historic" cultures have become too average and ordinary. They lose any criteria for distinguishing greatness from mediocrity:

> They want to go out and embrace everybody, telling them that no matter how wretched and degraded their lives, they still have self-worth, that they are *somebody*. They do not want to exclude any person or any act as unworthy … Self-respect must be related to some degree of accomplishments, no matter how humble … But in a democracy, we are fundamentally averse to saying that a certain person, or way of life, or activity, is better and more worthwhile than another.
>
> (Fukuyama, 2006, 303)

Still, Fukuyama believes that liberal democracy is the most suitable social system to satisfy Plato's three aspects of human nature—desire, spiritedness (*thymos*), and reason. Balancing desire and recognition, liberalism does not entirely abolish the latter but instead transforms it "into a more rational form." Even more so, as he continues, "no existing liberal society is based exclusively on *isothymia*; all must permit some degree of safe and domesticated *megalothymia*, even if this runs contrary to the principles they profess to believe in" (Fukuyama, 2006, 337).

In the contemporary American political arena, Francis Fukuyama was one of the leading voices for the neoconservative movement. However, in his later writings, Fukuyama distanced himself from its forceful agenda. In his book *America at the Crossroads* (2007), published after 9/11 and the beginning of the war in Iraq, he questioned "concepts like preemption, regime change, unilateralism, and benevolent hegemony" (Fukuyama, 2007, 7).

His overall philosophical position regarding the "end of history" did not change significantly but became more softened and balanced. Fukuyama strongly criticized the unwarranted militarism and armed interventionism of the Bush administration. He labeled the neocon approach to history as "Leninist," focusing on imposing one's will on the world by force. As an alternative, Fukuyama advocated ongoing, long-lasting, "Marxist-like" historical teleology (Fukuyama, 2007, 37–65).

Following the Russian invasion of Ukraine, Fukuyama wrote an article, "Preparing for Defeat," in which he predicted the collapse of the current Russian regime and the Ukrainian military victory. Considering this forecast, he made several important points:

> 8. The invasion has already done huge damage to populists all over the world, who prior to the attack uniformly expressed sympathy for Putin. That includes Matteo Salvini, Jair Bolsonaro, Éric Zemmour, Marine Le Pen, Viktor Orbán, and, of course, Donald Trump. The politics of the war has exposed their openly authoritarian leanings.
>
> 9. The war to this point has been a good lesson for China. Like Russia, China has built up seemingly high-tech military forces in the past decade, but they have no combat experience. The miserable performance of the Russian air force would likely be replicated by the People's Liberation Army Air Force, which similarly has no experience managing complex air operations. We may hope that the Chinese leadership will not delude itself as to its own capabilities the way the Russians did when contemplating a future move against Taiwan.
>
> 12. A Russian defeat will make possible a "new birth of freedom" and get us out of our funk about the declining state of global democracy. The spirit of 1989 will live on, thanks to a bunch of brave Ukrainians.
>
> (*American Purpose*, March 10, 2022)

Civilization vs. Culture

The Plurality of Cultural Worlds

In Western intellectual history, the term "civilization" was used not only in conjunction with "barbarism" but also as compared with or contrasted to the notion of "culture." The origin of the second meaning of "civilization" goes back to the European romanticism of the nineteenth century. Romantics viewed modern civilization not as an improvement upon savagery but as a superficial rational construct imposed upon the organic roots of folk culture. One of the precursors of romanticism, the Genevan philosopher and writer Jean-Jacques Rousseau (1712–1778), argued that social progress has led to the moral degradation of humanity. Later, romantics called upon their adherents to leave the cities and return to the rustic lifestyle of the villagers.

The idealization of the so-called "noble savages" evidently demonstrated the anti-modern and often counter-western drive and potential of European and non-European cultural philosophers who associated themselves with that line of thought. At the turn of the twentieth century, German historian Oswald Spengler (1880–1936) published his famous two-volume work *The Decline of the West* (1918), in which he openly opposed culture to civilization. In Spengler's view, cultures "appear suddenly, swell in splendid lines, flatten again and vanish, and the face of the waters is once more a sleeping waste." In other words, cultural organisms pass "through the age-phases of the individual man, [namely their] childhood, youth, manhood, and old age" (Spengler, 2006, 73–4). Spengler assigned the term "civilization" to the last cultural phase that marked its decline and inevitable deterioration. He saw European modernity as such a civilizational epoch, comparable to late antiquity when the exhausted forces of pagan civilization gave way to the young and nascent Christian culture.

Long before Spengler, a Russian sociologist and philosopher of culture, Nikolai Danilevsky (1822–1885) developed a similar theory of "cultural-historical types." In his book *Russia and Europe* (1871), Danilevsky distinguished a series of separate civilizations that evolved naturally without transmitting their specific characteristics to other civilizational organisms. The thrust of Danilevsky's theory referred to the rivalry between Europe and Russia, which belonged, in his estimation, to different, even opposing, civilizational forms. As a passionate ideologist of the panslavist union headed by the Russian state, he argued that "Europe recognizes Russia and Slavs as something foreign to itself, and not only alien but also hostile" (Danilevsky, 1991, 53).

Civilizational Approach to History

The civilizational view of the historical process in the twentieth century became well-established due to the *Annales* school of the French "new historians." The school co-founders, Lucien Febvre (1878–1956) and Marc Bloch (1886–1944), opposed the classical narrative method in historiography, which reduced history to political events and biographies of prominent politicians. Instead, they aspired to reconstruct the "total history" (*histoire totale*) that would incorporate a comprehensive study of geographic, economic, sociological, and psychological (collective mentality) components of the historical formations in question.

The second-generation leader of the *Annales* school, Fernand Braudel (1902–1985), in his last book, *A History of Civilizations* (1995), called them "the 'foundations,' the underlying *structures* of civilization: religious beliefs, for instance, or a timeless peasantry, or attitudes to death, work, pleasure and family life." He wrote:

> These realities, these structures, are generally ancient and long-lived, and always distinctive and original. They it is that give civilizations their essential outline and characteristic quality. And civilizations hardly exchange them: they regard them as irreplaceable values. For the majority of people, of course, these enduring traits, these inherited choices, these reasons for rejecting other civilizations, are generally unconscious. To see them clearly, one has to withdraw, mentally at least, from the civilization of which one is a part.
>
> (Braudel, 1994, 28)

In the Anglo-American intellectual tradition, the civilizational view of the world was represented by Arnold J. Toynbee (1889–1975), an English philosopher of history and culture and perhaps the greatest twentieth-century "civilizationist." In his monumental work, the multi-volume *A Study of History* published between 1934 and 1961, Toynbee rejected the Eurocentric view of history and sought to describe the entirety of human affairs by making a comparative study of civilizations from antiquity to the present day. He traced the growth and decline of twenty-six of them and argued that they flourished by effectively reacting to challenges under the leadership of their creative elite.

Toynbee believed that all those civilizations, each in its own way, reflected common aspirations and served as various manifestations of global human history. He thought that the Age of Civilizations, which began about five thousand years ago, aimed at the continuous spiritual progress of humanity. And he suitably defined civilization "as an endeavor to create a state of society in which the whole of Mankind will be able to live together in harmony, as members of a single all-inclusive family" (Toynbee, 1972, 44).

Cultural Capital and American Geopolitics

In his take on the civilizational approach to human affairs, American political scientist Samuel Huntington is interested not so much in human history but in contemporary geopolitical strategies. He agrees that "[h]uman history is the history of civilizations [and it] is impossible to think of the development of humanity in any other way" (Huntington, 2011, 40). As a typical American pragmatist, he applies this civilizational model to twenty-first-century international affairs.

Unlike his European predecessors, Huntington does not separate civilization from culture. For him, "both refer to the overall way of life of a people, and a civilization is a culture writ large" (Huntington, 2011, 41). Even more so, a civilization is "the highest cultural grouping of people and the broadest level of cultural identity ... It is defined both by common objective elements, such as language, history, religion, customs, institutions, and by the subjective self-identification of people" (Huntington, 2011, 43).

Students of history know that civilizations are dynamic and enduring. They rise and fall, "evolving through a time of troubles or conflict to a universal state to decay and disintegration" (Huntington, 2011, 44). Huntington counts seven such presently existing civilizational formations lasting more than a millennium. Those are Chinese, Japanese, Hindu, Islamic, Orthodox, Western, Latin American, and possibly, African cultures (Huntington, 2011, 45–7).

After victory in the Cold War and the dissolution of the Soviet Union, Western civilization became dominant in the international arena, which underwent considerable changes. "In the post-Cold War world," Huntington writes, "the most important distinctions among peoples are not ideological, political, or economic. They are cultural." "Nation states remain the principal actors in world affairs," he continues. But civilizations are cultural and not political entities. Therefore, the states' behavior will be shaped not only "as in the past, by the pursuit of power and wealth, but ... also ... by cultural preferences, commonalities, and differences" (Huntington, 2011, 21).

"In the post-Cold War world," Huntington contends, "for the first time in history, global politics has become multipolar and multicivilizational" (Huntington, 2011, 21). "In this new world," he adds, "local politics is the politics of ethnicity; global politics is the politics of civilizations. The rivalry of the superpowers is replaced by the clash of civilizations." And in those geopolitical circumstances, "the most pervasive, important, and dangerous conflicts," as he concludes, will occur "between peoples belonging to different cultural entities [while] the most dangerous cultural conflicts [may happen] along the fault lines between civilizations" (Huntington, 2011, 28).

What are the practical implications of Huntington's civilizational approach to global politics? First, the Western allies should realize the uniqueness of Western culture and that its "universalist pretensions increasingly bring it into conflict with other civilizations, most seriously with Islam and China" (Huntington, 2011, 20). Second, they should understand that modernization does not necessarily make non-Western cultures part of the West. In fact, "modernization is distinct from Westernization and is producing neither a universal civilization in any meaningful sense nor the Westernization of non-Western societies." Third, since, as Huntington and Harrison tell us, culture matters,[1] "societies sharing cultural affinities cooperate with each other [and the] efforts to shift societies from one civilization to another are unsuccessful." Finally, the continuous survival of Western civilization depends on "Americans reaffirming their Western identity" and all Westerners "uniting to renew it against challenges from non-Western societies" (Huntington, 2011, 20-1).

In that sense, the West is against the rest, and to preserve its accomplishments and progress further, it needs to consolidate and increase its "cultural capital." The concept of various forms of capital, including social, cultural, and symbolic, was introduced in the 1970s by the French sociologist Pierre Bourdieu (1930-2002). An American cultural theorist Lawrence Harrison (1932-2015), defines cultural capital today as a set of values, beliefs, and attitudes that drives societies toward the goals of the UN Universal Declaration of Human Rights:

- democratic governance, including the rule of law;
- social justice, including education, health care, and opportunity for all; and
- elimination of poverty.

(Harrison, 2013, 13)

Such an explicitly Western interpretation leads its adherents to proclaim the "end of multiculturalism," where the latter represents "the idea that all cultures are essentially equal, if different" (Harrison, 2013, 2).

The Russian Challenge and the Year 2022

Megalothymiac Nation in the "Post-Historical" World

Both Fukuyama and Huntington estimated that Islam, China, and Russia are the three primary opponents and long-term threats to the West in the international arena. However, the perspective from which each theorist made his predictions is different. For Fukuyama, humanity is now divided into historical and post-historical societies. Post-historical countries, in principle, completed their evolution and could only perfect their social systems. The situation is quite different in the historical sphere of influence. Here, as in the past, autocrats, tyrants, and dictators of all sorts usurp power, impoverish their nations, suppress human rights and freedom, and wage brutal and senseless wars. Post-Soviet Russia serves as an unfortunate example of this type of social behavior.

Russia was always a *megalothymiac* nation, which is evident from the enormous territory Russians have been able to conquer in the centuries of its violent history. A country the size of a continent, it has plenty of natural resources, inexhaustible human power, and enormous military might. During the Soviet era, Russia became a superpower, accumulating an arsenal of tactical and strategic nuclear weapons capable of causing irreparable damage to its primary rival, the United States.

After the demise of the Soviet Union, Russian leaders had a unique chance to join Western civilization. The required price to pay was to accept defeat and the leading role of the United States among the Western allies. Yet, as soon as Russia recovered economically from the devastating effects of the Soviet collapse, the nation made a different choice. Why?

Why would Russian citizens sacrifice the good life they enjoyed at the beginning of the twenty-first century? Why would they allow the demolition of the nascent democratic institutions in their country and the sliding back into lawless authoritarianism? Finally, why did the majority of Russians become so brainwashed by nationalist propaganda as to support the invasion of Ukraine?

The war against neighboring Ukraine would seem utterly irrational to any impartial observer. First, by unleashing the so-called "special military operation," Russia broke its pledge to ensure Ukraine's peace and security when it had signed the 1994 Budapest Memorandum, "by which Ukraine would turn over its nukes in exchange for those security assurances" (Blake, 2022). As a result, it must now endure international condemnation and isolation.

Second, by waging this war, Russia entered a confrontation with the West, which was the principal source of its recent economic stability and prosperity. Consequently, unprecedented Western sanctions in the technological and financial sectors destroyed the foundations of Russia's social progress. Third, by challenging the West on the battlefield and lacking the ideological and military strength of the Soviet Union, the Russian government doomed its armed forces to an inevitable and humiliating defeat. For all these reasons, by initiating the war against Ukraine, Russia practically committed national suicide.

A distinguished Russian-American émigré historian and scholar of Russian nationalism, Alexander Yanov (1930–2022), warned his former compatriots and Western intellectuals about such an outcome long before the collapse of the Soviet Union. In 1988 in New York, Yanov published his groundbreaking study *The Russian Challenge and the Year 2000*. In this volume, he traced the evolution of the "Russian New Right" or national-imperialist movements from the 1960s until the 1980s. Like their nineteenth-century predecessors, the champions of the "Russian idea" searched for the middle path between domestic "soul-destroying despotism" and the "decaying" secularized West. The final point of this ideological road spelled "a gigantic image of Satan planning to take over the world, which only Russia, which has a monopoly on political righteousness, can oppose" (Yanov, 1988, 322).

In his next book, *After Eltsyn: "Weimar" Russia*, published in 1995, already after the USSR disintegrated, Yanov came back to his alarming predictions with a vengeance. He compared post-Soviet Russia to pre-Nazi Germany. The nation was deeply humiliated by the downfall of the Soviet Union, and feelings of anger and frustration settled deep in its collective subconscious. The repentance turned out to be artificial and half-hearted. And as soon as the opportunity for payback presented itself, the Russians chose that path, forgetting their tragic historical experience.

From Fukuyama's point of view, that particular course of events may have happened for an apparent and predictable reason. The Russian hierarchy of national values dramatically differs from that of the West. For the current Russian leadership, greatness is not in economic abundance, human rights, or political freedom. They readily trade a life of contentment for imperial grandeur, which in their eyes, represents true dignity and honor. In this respect, the Kremlin is not ready to play second fiddle. And if they cannot lead, let the world go to hell. As Putin candidly pointed out: "Why do we need such a world if Russia is not there?" (Meduza, 2018).

He made this infamous statement in the context of a potential nuclear catastrophe on a global scale. And as Yanov prophetically wrote back at the end of the twentieth century: "The Weimar scenario condemned our fathers to a world war, a Holocaust. To imagine what its ending would look like in the nuclear age is beyond imagination" (Yanov, 1995, 11). The ninety-one-year-old Russian-American historian passed away just one week before Putin, in fulfillment of those dire warnings, crossed the Rubicon and invaded Ukraine.

Orthodox Russia as the Nemesis of Western Civilization

For Samuel Huntington and his civilizational approach to history, the political drama of the twenty-first century has a slightly different meaning. After the downfall of the Soviet Union, the United States remained the only superpower with worldwide dominance. Together with the European Union, Canada, Australia, and New Zealand, it embodies Western civilization, which is heading toward likely confrontations with countries and alliances belonging to opposite cultural formations.

The first bell rang when Muslim terrorists hijacked the airplanes on 9/11 and used them as flying rockets to destroy the World Trade Center in New York. Then President George W. Bush declared the "War on Terror" and unleashed military operations in Iraq and Afghanistan in retaliation. American military forces invaded Afghanistan in 2001 and overthrew the Muslim government of the Taliban. Twenty years later, in 2021, American troops left the country, and the Taliban quickly regained control over the territories.

The invasion of Iraq proved no less disastrous. Beginning in 2003, it soon turned into a prolonged fight against various terrorist organizations such as Al-Qaeda and the Islamic State (ISIS). The ISIS insurgency continues in Iraq, although at a low level, despite the counteroffensive operations by the Iraqi military backed by the United States and its allies. As Samuel Huntington accurately predicted, the imposition of Western "values to places that have been deeply inoculated against them by culture and custom is to invite the very confrontation that we seek to avoid" (Scruton, 2002, vii).

In this respect, Russia is the ultimate example of the difference between modernization and Westernization. Russians became the first non-Western nation to respond to the West's challenge by initiating long-term military, economic, sociocultural, and educational reforms. In the first quarter of the eighteenth century, Peter the Great (1672–1725) transformed his backward tsardom into a potent European Empire. In 1721, he assumed the title of the first Emperor of All Russia.

However, Peter's selective modernization of the country did not involve the most crucial aspect of Western civilization, namely, the limitation of the ruler's power. On the contrary, Peter consolidated his autocratic rule by making the Orthodox Church politically worthless. He could not allow the patriarchs to exert authority superior to the Tsar and replaced the Patriarchate with the Holy Synod, thus effectively keeping the Church hierarchy under his control.

Political modernization remained the stumbling block to Russia's "Westernization" in the following centuries, including the two decades of Putin's leadership. The general Americanization of life that Russians enjoyed in those years did not make them a genuinely Western nation. Popular music, fast food, and technological gadgets do not automatically translate into Western cultural identity, the essence of which is not pop-rock, McDonald's, or Apple, but the *Magna Carta*.

The resurgence of religion or, as Huntington put it, the "revenge of God" is another significant feature of post-Cold War international politics. The events of the preceding twentieth century fully justified Friedrich Nietzsche's projection about the "death of God." It went down in history under the politically correct title of the "Secular Age" (Taylor, 2007). The following period witnessed the resurrection of God and the revival of traditional religions, which once constituted the heart of national self-consciousness.

Like the return of Islam around the world, the revitalization of Christian Orthodoxy after decades of atheist education and propaganda in Russia played a crucial role in forming the post-Soviet cultural identity. In his book *Russian and American Cultures*, American historian Konstantin Kustanovich distinguishes three unique traits of the Russian national spirit. They include religious tradition that cultivates external appearances (beauty over dogma), a collectivist mentality, and legal nihilism. Echoing Huntington, Kustanovich maintains that Russia "will never become a Western-type liberal democracy no matter who rules it and what laws it has on paper. [Instead, it] will remain an authoritarian, corrupt, mendacious, nationalist, even xenophobic country" (Kustanovich, 2018, 197).

This rather dire prediction, most certainly, should be taken seriously, especially nowadays when Russia is waging a brutal war against neighboring Ukraine. Its military forces destroy vital Ukrainian infrastructure and massacre civilian populations, while Russian leadership blackmails the West with the potential use of tactical nuclear weapons. What strategy should the Western allies employ to emerge victorious from such a confrontation?

The West and the Rest: Democracy Against Authoritarianism

Fukuyama's and Huntington's differing philosophical positions come together in the more straightforward doctrine announced by American President Joe Biden. During his 2021 trip to Europe, the President "has repeatedly argued the world has reached an 'inflection point' that will determine whether this century marks another era of democratic dominance or an age of autocratic ascendancy" (Brands, 2021). In his *Foreign Affairs* article, Hal Brands explained Biden's approach to global competition in detail.

He noted that the "community of democratic nations confronts three interrelated challenges. First is the threat from authoritarian powers—Russia and particularly China [which] want to weaken, fragment, and replace the existing international system because its foundational liberal principles are antithetical to their illiberal domestic practices." Second, as Brands continued, the world faces "transnational problems that take on added gravity in a contest of systems." And finally, as he concluded, the "third threat is the decay of democracy from within." In liberal-democratic countries, "anti-democratic sentiments and dissatisfaction with representative institutions have reached heights not seen since World War II [which makes the] crisis of democratic governance at home [correlate] with the crisis of democratic influence abroad" (Brands, 2021).

The clash between autocratic empires and democratic republics is not new to history. As I mentioned at the beginning of this chapter, it started with the Greco-Persian Wars of the fifth century BC. Backed by the confederate association of Greek city-states, Athens successfully defended its independence against the Persians. But the Hellenic alliance was short-lived. In the following Peloponnesian War (431–404 BC) between democratic Athens and oligarchic Sparta, the latter destroyed its competitor city with the support of the Persians, effectively ending the golden age of classical Greek civilization.

The contest between authoritarian and republican forms of government continued, with varied success for both sides, throughout the next two millennia. Since the rise of the Italian free cities during the European Renaissance and especially after the American and French revolutions in the eighteenth century, the balance slowly shifted to the democratic camp. The twentieth century became crucial in this race between authoritarian and republican statehood.

World War I destroyed four great military empires—the German, Austro-Hungarian, Ottoman, and Russian. During World War II, totalitarian regimes in Germany and Italy ceased to exist. In the second half of the century, the European colonial system broke down, leading to the eclipse of the British and French colonial empires and the creation of newly independent states, mainly in Africa and Asia. In the 1990s, most countries on the American continent established multi-party democratic systems of governance. The collapse of the communist Soviet Union near the end of the millennium cemented the retreat of authoritarian regimes worldwide.

Yet, in the twenty-first century, three strongholds of authoritarianism have retained their vitality and appeal—certain Islamic states, Russia, and China. The threat they pose to the West is of different kinds. Religious fanaticism in Islam, nuclear blackmail by Russia, economic ascendancy of China. Russian military aggression in Ukraine represents a "clear and present" danger to the West, but, in my view, this short-term problem pales in the face of the long-term Chinese economic challenge. Not only is China the oldest bastion of autocracy, lasting for more than two thousand years, it has also become the first—and so far, the only—authoritarian regime to compete successfully with democratic America on the economic front.

Compared to China, Russia is a decaying kleptocratic state that entertains military ambitions well beyond its current capabilities. Although European in external appearance, it always remained authoritarian in its system of governance—at least since the autocratic revolution of Ivan the Terrible (1530–1584). As a Eurasian empire, Russia became a successor to the Golden Horde—a Mongol Empire that originated under the leadership of Genghis Khan (c. 1162–1227) and survived as a unified political entity for several centuries. The confrontation between Ukraine and Russia in this historical framework is the age-old dispute between the Western Charter of Liberties or *Magna Carta* and the Mongolian imperial code of law known as the *Yassa*. Ironically, both documents appeared in the same (thirteenth) century.

In this context, it would be appropriate to discuss the importance of Eurasia as the largest continental land on Earth and its significance for geopolitics in the twenty-first century. In his book, *The Grand Chessboard*, a Polish-American diplomat and expert on foreign affairs, Zbigniew Brzezinski (1928–2017), wrote:

> Ever since the continents started interacting politically, some five hundred years ago, Eurasia has been the center of world power. In different ways, at different times, the peoples inhabiting Eurasia—though mostly those from its Western European periphery—penetrated and dominated the world's other regions as individual Eurasian states attained the special status and enjoyed the privileges of being the world's premier powers.
>
> The last decade of the twentieth century has witnessed a tectonic shift in world affairs. For the first time ever, a non-Eurasian power has emerged not only as the key arbiter of Eurasian power relations but also as the world's paramount power. The defeat and collapse of the Soviet Union was the final step in the rapid ascendancy of a Western Hemisphere power, the United States, as the sole and, indeed, the first truly global power.

He continued:

> Eurasia, however, retains its geopolitical importance. Not only is its western periphery—Europe—still the location of much of the world's political and economic power, but its eastern region—Asia—has lately become a vital center of economic growth and rising political influence. Hence, the issue of how a globally engaged America copes with the complex Eurasian power relationships—and particularly whether it prevents the emergence of a dominant and antagonistic Eurasian power—remains central to America's capacity to exercise global primacy.
> (Brzezinski, 2016, xiii–xiv)

Concerning Russia and its imperial aspirations, this means the engagement with Ukraine and its transformation into a European country. As Brzezinski stressed, "Ukraine, a new and important space on the Eurasian chessboard, is a geopolitical pivot because its very existence as an independent country helps to transform Russia. Without Ukraine, Russia ceases to be a Eurasian empire" (Brzezinski, 2016, 46).

At the present moment, we are witnessing the practical realization of that geopolitical strategy. Post-Soviet Russia cannot win the war against Ukraine because of the continuous support of Ukrainians by Western allies. Thus, the ancient Kievan Rus', the seed of the Russian empire, will eventually become its gravedigger. The only remaining questions are those of time, and the price humanity will have to pay for Russia's imperial demise.

Concluding Remarks about *Thymos*

There remains one final issue to address. Let us assume that in some not-so-distant future, Western civilization would eliminate—or at least neutralize—all external threats to its existence and establish a global commonwealth of peaceful democratic nations. After all, as Steven Pinker convincingly demonstrated in his book *Enlightenment Now*, the "Enlightenment principle that we can apply reason and sympathy to enhance human flourishing" and the ideals of "science, humanism, and progress" (Pinker, 2018, 5) brought about tremendous and positive changes to humanity. They encompassed practically all spheres of life—from health, environment, and longevity issues to political, economic, and social reforms.

Pinker supports his research with a bulk of statistical data, and the "evidence-based take on the Enlightenment project reveals that it was not a naïve hope. The Enlightenment has *worked*" (Pinker, 2018, 6). It is reasonable to imagine then that those achievements could spread globally. And if—and when—that happens, could any internal obstacles arise that will prevent the global commonwealth from long-lasting success and prosperity? Are there inherent flaws and weaknesses in the liberal democratic system that will lead it, like all previous civilizations, to its inevitable collapse and extinction?

Here we come back to the central idea of Fukuyama's book—the concept of *thymos*. Fukuyama's foremost authorities, Plato and Hegel, were rationalist philosophers for whom human reason was self-sufficient in discovering the truth about reality. Both considered the notion of *thymos* in rational terms as passion, spiritedness, and moral nobility. In his interpretation of Hegel, Kojève also understood *thymos* as "desire of desire," i.e., the projection of the social dimension of human life.

However, one translation of *thymos*, namely "spiritedness," suggests a level of meaning that is different from and higher than biological or social spheres of existence. I refer here to spirituality or the realm of the spirit. We know from history that the search for enlightenment, salvation, or liberation is common to all humans. Spiritual traditions offer various solutions and find different answers for their adepts. That, however, does not diminish the universality and significance of the existential quest per se.

What is it that makes a human being genuinely human? We can hardly find complete satisfaction and meaningfulness without recourse to the supernatural or divine power. In this, the most vital aspect of our nature, we are not self-sufficient but dependent on help from above.

The first person who intuitively followed the messenger of God—be it a prophet, avatar, buddha, or however various religions name those extraordinary beings—also became the "First Man." What sets humans apart from animals is not freedom but obedience to the divine command resulting in self-restraint. And human history unfolded not as the Hegelian master–slave subjugation but as the human–divine relationship that brought about the distinction between good and evil and, consequently, true moral nobility.

To sum up, it seems to me that the most profound internal problem of liberal democracy is that it does not rely on divine authority and is purely human-based. It cannot provide humanity with divinely conceived moral commandments that global society could submit to and follow. Consequently—and with widespread frustration, I might add—we observe the current rise and continuing influence of the old-fashioned faiths, which exploit the human need for heavenly guidance. Also, as Huntington so aptly pointed out, when transmitted to foreign cultural soil, liberal democracy often undermines traditional moral values, thus exacerbating the moral deprivation of humankind.

Liberal democracy targets people's external problems but cannot address their deepest internal needs. Western societies do not offer a collective spiritual vision for their citizens while creating exceptional economic, social, and political conditions. In the long run, this is the most vulnerable feature of Western civilization, which, in my opinion, has the potential to undermine and eventually destroy it.

Note

1 For more on the importance of culture in economics, politics, and other aspects of social life see: Harrison and Huntington, 2000.

References

Adler, Mortimer J. 1978. *Aristotle for Everybody. Difficult Thought Made Easy.* New York: Macmillan.

Blake, Aaron. 2022. "What the Budapest Memorandum means for the U.S. on Ukraine." *The Washington Post*, February 1. https://www.washingtonpost.com/politics/2022/02/01/what-budapest-memorandum-means-us-ukraine

Brands, Hal. 2021. "The Emerging Biden Doctrine: Democracy, Autocracy, and the Defining Clash of Our Time." *Foreign Affairs*, June 29. https://www.foreignaffairs.com/articles/united-states/2021-06-29/emerging-biden-doctrine?check_logged_in=1

Braudel, Fernand. 1994. *A History of Civilizations.* Trans. Richard Mayne. New York: Penguin Books.

Brzezinski, Zbigniew. 2016. *The Grand Chessboard: American Primacy and Its Geostrategic Imperatives.* New York: Basic Books.

Cooper, David E. 2003. *World Philosophies. An Historical Introduction.* Oxford: Blackwell Publishing.

Copleston, Frederick C. 1988. *Russian Religious Philosophy. Selected Aspects.* Notre Dame, IN: University of Notre Dame Press.

Danilevsky, Nikolai. 1991. *Rossiya i Evropa* [*Russia and Europe*]. Moscow: Izdatelstvo "Kniga."

Edie, James M., James P. Scanlan, and Mary-Barbara Zeldin, eds., with the collaboration of George L. Kline. 1976. *Russian Philosophy, Volume 1: The Beginnings of Russian Philosophy. The Slavophiles. The Westernizers.* Knoxville: The University of Tennessee Press.

Ferguson, Adam. 1767. *An Essay on the History of Civil Society.* Paris.

Fukuyama, Francis. 2006. *The End of History and the Last Man.* New York: Free Press.

Fukuyama, Francis. 2007. *America at the Crossroads: Democracy, Power, and the Neoconservative Legacy.* New Haven, CT: Yale University Press.

Fukuyama, Francis. 2022. "Preparing for Defeat." *American Purpose*, March 10. https://www.americanpurpose.com/blog/fukuyama/preparing-for-defeat

Harrison, Lawrence. 2013. *Jews, Confucians, and Protestants. Cultural Capital and the End of Multiculturalism.* New York: Rowman & Littlefield.

Harrison, Lawrence E., and Samuel P. Huntington, eds. 2000. *Culture Matters. How Values Shape Human Progress.* New York: Basic Books.

Hegel, Georg Wilhelm Friedrich. 1977. *Phenomenology of Spirit.* Trans. A. V. Miller. Oxford: Oxford University Press.

Huntington, Samuel P. 2011. *The Clash of Civilizations and the Remaking of World Order.* New York: Simon & Schuster.

King, Margaret L. 2000. *Western Civilization. A Social and Cultural History*, combined edition. Upper Saddle River, NJ: Prentice Hall.

Kojève, Alexandre. 1969. *Introduction to the Reading of Hegel.* Ed. Allan Bloom. Trans. James H. Nichols, Jr. Ithaca: Cornell University Press.

Kustanovich, Konstantin. 2018. *Russian and American Cultures. Two Worlds a World Apart*. New York: Lexington Books.

Macaulay, G.C., trans. 1890. *Herodotus' History*. New York. https://archive.org/details/HerodotusHistory2019/Herodotus_History_2019

Mark, Joshua. 2022. "Civilization." *World History Encyclopedia*. https://www.worldhistory.org/civilization

McKeon, Richard. (ed.) 2001. *The Basic Works of Aristotle*. New York: The Modern Library.

Meduza. 2018. "'Why do we need such a world if Russia won't be there?' Putin – about the global catastrophe after a nuclear strike." https://meduza.io/news/2018/03/07/zachem-nam-takoy-mir-esli-tam-ne-budet-rossii-putin-o-globalnoy-katastrofe-posle-yadernogo-udara

Pinker, Steven. 2018. *Enlightenment Now: The Case for Reason, Science, Humanism, and Progress*. New York: Penguin Books.

Plato. 1997. *Plato: Complete Works*. Ed. John M. Cooper. Cambridge: Hackett Publishing.

Pushkin, Alexander. 1989. *Ruslan and Liudmila. Collected Narrative and Lyrical Poetry*. Edited and trans. Walter Arndt. Ann Arbor, MI: Ardis.

Scruton, Roger. 2002. *The West and the Rest: Globalization and the Terrorist Threat*. Wilmington, DE: ISI Books.

Spengler, Oswald. 2006. *Decline of the West*. An abridged edition by Helmut Werner from the translation of Charles Frances Atkinson. New York: Vintage Books.

Taylor, Charles. 2007. *A Secular Age*. Cambridge, MA: The Belknap Press of Harvard University Press.

Toynbee, Arnold. 1972. *A Study of History. The First Abridged One-Volume Edition*. Revised and abridged by the author and Jane Caplan. New York: Weathervane Books.

Yanov, Alexander. 1988. *Russkaya ideia i 2000 god* [*The Russian Challenge and the Year 2000*]. New York: Liberty Publishing House.

Yanov, Alexander. 1995. *Posle Eltsyna. "Weimarskaya" Rossiya* [*After Eltsyn. "Weimar" Russia*]. Moscow: KRUK.

7

Point of Madness and the Search for History's Meaning

Mikhail Blumenkranz

Analyzing the events of which one is a contemporary is an extremely risky and thankless task. Thankless, because one is bound to offend an omniscient reader and receive this reader's expert opinion on the author's blatant ignorance and impenetrable stupidity. Risky, because a sober assessment requires a certain distance in time, which implies an emotional non-involvement in what is happening and allows one to not lose sight of the whole.

Immanuel Kant noted that when evaluating events, the historical scale that we set is important. If the scale is small, then accidents come to the fore; if it is sufficiently large (the scale of centuries or millennia), then there is an opportunity to see some regularities (Kant, 1949, 460). And although these patterns often make it possible to trace a certain logic of events, Fyodor Dostoevsky is still right in believing that there is nothing more fantastic than reality (see Dostoevsky, 1973). Thus, if an ordinary "Soviet man"[1] (the older generation still remembers this popular phrase) had been told that some 40-45 years later, a full-scale war would break out between Russia and Ukraine, it would have been perceived either as a bad joke or as a sign of serious mental problems in the person making the statement. Even today this war seems to be pure madness from the point of view of common sense, and until the last moment few people could believe in its possibility. The losses from such a campaign have clearly exceeded all possible benefits.

What has happened brings us back to an old, but still relevant, question: Are the reasons behind the many bloody conflicts throughout humanity's history not only and not so much rational—that is, dictated by considerations of practical benefit—as destructive impulses, which are by nature deeply irrational?

Let us turn to the events of some thirty years ago, to the time of the collapse of the Soviet Union.

This event not only significantly changed the situation in the world, but in many ways continues to have an impact on what is happening today. The collapse of the bipolar world gave a powerful impetus to the process of globalization, and it subsequently became the main detonator of the current Russia-Ukraine war, a war that could call into question the future prospects of globalization and lead the world again to a harsh confrontation between military-political blocs.

Let us take a broader view. Since the times of Ancient Egypt and Mesopotamia, numerous empires have arisen and vanished. However, the very idea of empire itself seems to remain immortal. It is possible that in the future it will take new and more bizarre forms: for example, if the hope for a world government comes true, or if the long-awaited "Golden Age" under the guidance of artificial intelligence arrives. Personally, I am somewhat skeptical regarding these prospects.

Of course, there is an irrepressible longing for the ideal of universal fraternal unity and the ultimate triumph of the collective, which is usually cemented by the impossible-to-resist use of the guillotine. But at the same time, the will for individual isolation, for the assertion of a personal space independent of others, is no less strong. These dual impulses find their analogy in the alternation of the centrifugal and centripetal tendencies of the historical process: the constant pendulum-like movements from the building of Towers of Babel to the construction of Great Walls of China. In nature, this corresponds to the undulations of the tides of the world's oceans. Yet, when it comes to the contemporary scientific picture of the world, characterized by alternating cycles of galactic expansion and contraction, is it not true that History, Nature, and the Universe obey a single rhythm of cosmic pulsation? Is not the emergence of empires one of the moments of this global process? Does not man carry the idea of empire in himself, in his own soul?

After all, it is precisely in the idea of empire that the human desire for unrestrained expansion is realized. Non-sublimated aggression and the irrepressible desire for the endless expansion of the boundaries of one's own self find their natural expression in the empire.

The very notion of empire has long had a purely negative connotation. It is associated with forms of state power based on brutal violence, ruthlessly oppressed peoples, and the exertion of arbitrary force by the strong against the weak. As a rule, this is the case. However, all of these evil acts do not lead to a moral condemnation of empire itself: we continue to talk about the reasons for their emergence and the consequences of their collapse. The specific question is whether the current war is a form of revenge for the collapse of the Soviet Union, and whether, in principle, a peaceful disintegration of empires is possible? If one looks at the many examples of the last few centuries, from Napoleonic France to the rapid collapse of empires in the twentieth century, their downfalls do not seem to have happened bloodlessly. While for a time it seemed that the collapse of the Soviet empire was a happy exception, it turned out that the bloody confrontation was simply postponed, appearing as a sort of a ticking time bomb. The collapse of the Soviet Union led over time to the development of ethnic and national conflicts.

The Chechen and Georgian campaigns were a prelude to the "special operation" in Ukraine.[2] The national question, which played a key role in these conflicts, was fraught with great bloodshed.

The rapid collapse of the empire posed the task of searching for a new self-identity to the former Soviet republics. The notion of the "Soviet man," which included the idea of common citizenship of all citizens who lived on the territory of the USSR, ceased to exist. This gave a powerful impetus to the formation of self-identification by nationality, which determined the search for national roots with a certain bias towards national mythology as opposed to ethnography. Both in the former metropolis and in the newly independent outskirts, a phenomenon that Russian thinker and cultural study scholar Grigory S. Pomerantz (1918-2013) called "a sense of national concern" began to rapidly gain strength (Pomerantz, 1998).[3] Sumgait was the first visible manifestation of this feeling.[4] The search for lost soil or territory is often a painful process leading to unpleasant excesses.

A number of factors, both geopolitical and socio-psychological, have led to tragedy, that is, to the war being waged today.

In the 1990s, during the Yeltsin era, a part of the post-Soviet intelligentsia began to suspect that Russian society was steadily drifting toward either national-communism or national-fascism (Vatoropin, 2011; Antyukhov, 2015). And not only because of the appearance of certain types of youth organizations and movements that are inherently nationalist, fascist, and anti-West,[5] but because of the alarming, oppressive atmosphere which seemed to be in the air, and which gave the Soviet-American historian, political scientist, and publicist Alexander Yanov (1930-2022) grounds to warn of the possibility of the arrival of fascism in Russia (Yanov, 1995). Gorbachev's *perestroika*, which had given many people hope for European prospects and the country's future development, was quickly replaced by bitter disappointment and the collapse of expectations. The new road to Western civilization turned out to be "the old road to the Horde," akin the Golden Horde of Batyi Khan, which Russia was under the yoke of from 1237 to 1480. A "Weimar complex"[6] emerged and actively began to take shape. From a great power that determined the fate of the world, Russia turned into one of the "third world" countries in the eyes of its own citizens. Average citizens, accustomed to seeing themselves as "the crown of the world" and "the hope of all progressive mankind," took the trauma of national humiliation hard, searching for culprits of the betrayal that had occurred. A sense of grievance seized all sectors of society. In 1998, during the Twentieth World Congress of Philosophy in Boston, I was invited to participate in a session on Russian philosophy. I was struck by the acute sense of resentment that permeated the speeches of my Russian colleagues. There was an unconcealed resentment at the alleged "disdain" in their opinion, and the Russian colleagues who organized this session powerfully manifested this kind of attitude. In some ways these claims may have been justified, but the very tone in which they were expressed was surprising. It reminded me of the psychological reaction of the main character of Dostoevsky's *Notes from Underground,* who has a feeling of resentment—negativity, anger, dissatisfaction, indignation. To the remark I made that they have a "Weimar complex" (complex of painfully wounded ego), I received an unexpected response: "Yes, we have a 'Weimar complex,' but there is no reason to insult us."

In this connection, it is also worth remembering the noisy success of the rather mediocre film *Brat-2*, an iconic film of the late 1990s in Russia. The film tells the story of Danila Bagrov, a young man from Moscow's suburbs, who goes to the United States to avenge the death of his brother, a gangster killed by an American drug lord. The main character, a slightly vulgar Rambo, "acts vindictively" as a dashing people's avenger in response to the suffering and insults caused by various foreigners, restoring original truth and violated justice. The film became a litmus test for the state of mass consciousness. The image of the tough macho man who defies insidious enemies and impresses the people with his lexical closeness to the native slang turned out to be in demand. The one who has long endured humiliation has, by virtue of this fact alone, an indisputable right to humiliate others in turn. This is how the logic of resentment works.

One cannot help recalling Vladimir Putin's emphasized delays to diplomatic meetings with his counterparts from other countries. However paradoxical it may sound, the Russian people liked it. The leader becomes the representative and transmitter of mass consciousness, the embodiment of their innermost dreams of just retribution. Life, of course, is full of injustices, and often gives us enough reasons to take offense, but often it is the case that a person who is overcome by the feeling of resentment does not need any such reasons. He already feels offended from the outset, so this individual is constantly inclined to see an ulterior intention in the actions and words of others to attack and humiliate him.

The waves of resentment grew stronger and broader, rolling across the country, picked up and swollen by the mass media. As a result, the country where socialism failed to win turned into the country where resentment triumphed.

One of the most striking manifestations of this transformation is the grand scale and sacred nature that Victory Day celebrations, which commemorate the Soviet victory over Nazi Germany, have acquired. For a consciousness which experienced its own humiliation in an agonizing way, memories of a time of triumph and power acquire special value. The shadow of the past, cast on the present, suddenly began to grow rapidly, as in Evgeny Schwarz's play of the same name (Schwarz, 2001),[7] until it covered the whole country, becoming its sovereign mistress. The people, just like the authorities, quickly came to believe that "we can do it again." At a certain point, instead of Moscow's trolleybuses bearing the inscription "To Berlin!", tanks crawled to Kyiv. Barbarism and boorishness are a frequent reaction of resentment in response to inconvenient realities. Eventually, the country seized by this feeling, rising from its knees, will certainly step on someone's throat.

This phenomenon is as old as the story of Cain and Abel in the Old Testament, one of the first testimonies to a sentiment that eventually led to a metaphysical revolt against God's wholly subjectivist conceptions of justice.

The situation which has now come about is reminiscent of a protracted divorce process: the woman tries to leave for another man, and, with all his might, the husband tries to prevent this. Formally, the divorce has long since taken place, but one of the parties has not taken it seriously. And so, instead of their relationship having a civilized outcome, it deteriorates into violence. In the course of the conflict there is a total settling of scores. It has been said that hatred feeds on every detail, just as love does. It manifests itself especially clearly when it comes to the division of jointly acquired property, and above all, language and culture. Then in every word, in every literary image, hatred finds its nourishment, proving the presence of a natural viciousness and the genetically and culturally determined propensity for violence inherent in *the other*. And in the course of this enmity, it is precisely the ruins of *culture* which are the first to dot the landscape.

The Indian intellectual Jiddu Krishnamurti divided people into two categories: those who tend to admire the view of the ocean without noticing the container with cigarette butts floating in it; and those who see only that container and do not notice the ocean (see Krishnamurti, 2003). If you are determined to find an ashtray, well, every ocean has one. Hatred focuses our vision solely on it. Hatred leads to the inevitable simplification of the world, painting it completely black and white. Certainly, unleashing war and killing peaceful civilians is an unjustifiable evil, but killing that which makes a person human is no less of an evil. If you cannot retaliate against someone who has hurt you, you shouldn't just attack whoever you are able to reach in that immediate moment. After all, the Russian authorities were glad to smash the creators of Russian culture and, after their death, they often solemnly mummified them and added them to the ranks of venerable heroes, instrumentalizing Russian culture and its great representatives for their own political and ideological purposes.

Unfortunately for the iconic Russian poet Alexander Pushkin, Putin turned out to be a better shot than d'Anthès, a French officer who fatally wounded Pushkin in a duel in 1837. No need to assist Putin in organizing a public funeral for the Russian poet. Only dragon's teeth can grow on a soil richly fertilized with hatred. And then, in the fight against the *other*'s arsenal, you often do not notice how your own grows at the same time. This is another aspect of the tragedy playing out, a metaphysical one.

Not only in Ukraine and Russia, which are fighting today, but also in the "peace-loving" West, the degree of mutual hatred and aggression has been growing in recent decades, producing increased radical sentiments and societal polarization. The everyday battle for the values of democracy has become belligerent and unyielding, tolerance has become more intransigent by the day, and calls for universal repentance have acquired more threatening intonations. "Cancel culture" became the priority and often the only way for the masses to enjoy the cherished fruits of civilization. This movement was enthusiastically supported by many intellectuals who are keeping up with the times. Well, as Russian revolutionary anarchist Mikhail Bakunin put it, the passion for destruction is a creative passion. "Decorations must be barbaric," Amadeo Modigliani once advised Anna Akhmatova. It seems that today, all the other values we are accustomed to adorning ourselves with have also become barbaric. A paradoxical time has dawned when scientific thought and unprecedented technological breakthroughs have accelerated against the backdrop of the spiritual emaciation of the human personality. The age of artificial intelligence is in fact turning into an era of digital savagery. *Homo sapiens* is steadily evolving into *Homo virtualis*. Whether we are aware of it or not, we are living in a situation of profound systemic crisis: political, social, and cultural. Crisis itself is an inevitable aspect of culture, a natural outcome of growth. One can only imagine a crisis-free world in Levitan's painting *Over Eternal Peace*.[8]

Crises come in various forms. There are crises as stages in the development of culture, that is, crises that take place within a single cultural paradigm: for example, the transition from the Renaissance to the Baroque, from the Baroque to the Enlightenment, from classicism to romanticism, and so on. But there are also crises of the cultural paradigm itself, often leading to catastrophe. As a rule, they end with the death of some cultural worlds and the birth of new ones. All of this has already happened in the past. However, under the conditions of global post-industrial civilization, the situation is somewhat different. Threats and risks have emerged that humanity has not faced before, such as the nuclear potential accumulated by some states, obviously fraught with the possibility of collective suicide. Moreover, there is little hope for the emergence of new barbarians capable of picking up the baton. The barbarians are no longer external, only internal. They have mastered the practice of destruction, but they are hardly capable of creation (if, of course, by creation we mean the construction of Gothic cathedrals and not the detonation of a nuclear reactor).

From this perspective, the ongoing war is one of the overdue boils of a seriously diseased organism. The human being is a continuous effort, as believed the widely known Soviet-era philosopher Merab Mamardashvili (2000). The question of the fruitfulness of this effort is now more pressing than ever. The road to hell is said to be paved with good intentions, but the fomenting of hatred forms high-speed routes.

The death of God, diagnosed by Friedrich Nietzsche, shattered our previous hopes of ascending to paradise after a successful life on earth. Instead, hell and purgatory, passed on in the will, have now become our full property. As a result, a struggle has broken out for a transition from the polluting flames of hell to modern clean energy. Thus, with the demise of God, our political responsibility has become more pronounced.

If we leave irony aside and try to look at the problem seriously, it is not surprising that today's desperate rebels and professional fighters against the world's evil, belonging to different political and socio-cultural currents, are somewhat similar to the religious-sectarian movements that we know from the history of the Middle Ages. Whether we want it to or not, one question inevitably arises: where do ideological convictions end and where does blind fanatical faith begin? And moreover, what precedes what? From those struggling with colonial legacies to those obsessed with a national idea, for all their differences of purpose, there is a subtle commonality that unites the participants in either of these kinds of movement: namely, the latent religious impulse.

These movements attract to their ranks not only people who are mostly naïve and unsophisticated, but also individuals who are intellectually sophisticated and well-educated. I would venture to guess that neither our analytical skills nor our broad-mindedness will guarantee immunity from such pandemics. Most likely the virus of mass movements works on the level of our subconscious. Some ancient archetypes seem to exist in the depths of our psyche and activate not the areas of our rational cognition, but, rather, the irrational mechanisms that go back to our tribal origins. Our consciousness then forms the corresponding rational grounds from which the mind forms a chain of logical proofs and arguments. This is how our firm beliefs are born.

David Hume wrote that our values are experienced rather than thought (see Hume, 2003). Ideas and values create a symbolic reality. Ernst Cassirer defined human being as a symbolic animal (Cassirer, 1955). Be that as it may, symbolic reality has a hypnotic power over our consciousness. It can both lift us to the heights of the creative spirit and turn us into a herd of swine under the insidious spell of Circe.

Sometimes it is difficult to resist the temptation to find protection for our fragile, vulnerable "I" in the mighty collective "we," to merge with it in a single stream, to experience the ecstatic feeling of the fullness and intensity of our own existence. Such a fullness of super-personal sacred meanings finally dissolves the weight of personal freedom into the anonymity of collective responsibility.

So far hate, like red-hot lava, has erupted in the eastern part of Europe, but volcanic activity is everywhere, and it is difficult to say where it will erupt tomorrow.

In his philosophical essay-parable *The Screwtape Letters,* Clive Staples Lewis describes the inhabitants of hell greedily absorbing the waves of hostility and hatred emanating from humans (Lewis, 2000). This is the source of their power. They feed their perpetual hunger with the blood that people spill, torturing and killing each other. War is the state that they constantly try to initiate and maintain in the world so that, at least for a while, they can satiate themselves.

Today these demons are in greater danger of dying of gluttony than of starvation. The world is at a point of madness that could be the last point in its history. The madness of the political elites fuels the madness of the masses. We need not fear global warming, for it seems that we cannot stop it before the onset of nuclear winter.

I would like to believe that I am wrong.

Notes

1 The term "Soviet man" was a concept that originated in the Soviet Union during the early years of the communist regime. It referred to the ideal type of person that the Soviet government wanted to create and promote as a model citizen in a socialist society. According to Soviet ideology, the Soviet man was supposed to be selfless, hardworking, dedicated to the common good, and loyal to the socialist state. The concept of the Soviet man was meant to contrast with the bourgeois individualism and selfishness associated with capitalist societies.

2 The First Chechen War began in 1994 and ended in 1996, while the Second Chechen War began in 1999 and officially ended only in 2009, although

sporadic violence and unrest continued even after that. The Georgian campaign, also known as the Russo-Georgian War, took place in 2008 and lasted for five days, from August 7 to August 12, when a ceasefire was signed.
3   The expression "national preoccupation" is an ironic paraphrase of the common expression "sexual preoccupation" and refers to a certain fixation on national issues.
4   On February 27-29, 1988, mass pogroms against the Armenian population were organized in the city of Sumgait in the Azerbaijan SSR.
5   Among such movements are skinheads, Barkashovtsy, and Limonovtsy. The first appeared in Russia in the early 1990s. Unlike skinheads in Western Europe, Russian skinheads emerged as a nationalist organization with the idea of white supremacy and the task of cleansing the country of alien elements and ideologies. Barkashovtsy—All-Russian patriotic movement, "Russian National Unity." Russian fascist neo-Nazi paramilitary organization founded on October 16, 1990 by Alexander Barkashov. Limonovtsy—National Bolshevik Party (leader Eduard Limonov). A Russified version of early German National-Bolshevism. According to the 1994 program, the main goal of National Bolshevism is to create "an empire from Vladivostok to Gibraltar on the basis of Russian civilization." And the essence of National Bolshevism is the hatred of the "anti-human system of the trinity: liberalism, democracy, capitalism."
6   "Weimar complex" is a concept used to describe the collective feeling in German society that emerged from Germany's defeat in World War I, instability in the Weimar Republic, and economic crisis; this situation soon led to the Nazis coming to power.
7   Evgeny Schwarz (1896-1958) was a renowned Soviet prose writer, screenwriter, playwright, journalist, and poet. *The Shadow* is a play by Evgeni Schwarz, written between 1937 and 1940. It is based on the plot of the fairy tale of the same name by Hans Christian Andersen and, along with *The Dragon* and *The Naked King*, forms a trilogy of plays that serve as political satire. In the play *The Shadow*, the hero's shadow comes to life, separates from its master, and becomes the ruler not only of the hero, but of the entire kingdom.
8   Isaac Levitan (1860-1900) was a classical Russian landscape painter who advanced the genre of the "mood landscape." *Over Eternal Peace* is one of the artist's famous paintings, expressing the idea of the end of life's journey.

References

Antyukhov, Yuri V. 2015. "Novye Vyzovy Rossii s 90-ye gody 20-go veka: ot Fashisma k Extremizmu." *Uchenye Zapiski Orlovskogo Gosudarstvennogo Universiteta* 68(5): 11-15. https://cyberleninka.ru/article/n/novye-vyzovy-rossii-v-90-e-gody-xx-veka-ot-fashizma-k-ekstremizmu

Cassirer, Ernst. 1955. *The Philosophy of Symbolic Forms*. In 3 vols. Trans. by Ralph Manheim. New Haven and London: Yale University Press.

Dostoevsky, Fyodor. 1973. *Zapiski iz Podpol'ia*. [*Notes from Underground*]. In *Polnoe Sobranije Sochinenij v 30 tomakh*, vol. 5 [*Complete Collected Works in 30 vols*. Vol. 5]. Leningrad: Nauka. Leningradskoe otdelenie.

Hobsbawm, Eric. 1990. *Nations and Nationalism Since 1780*. Cambridge: Cambridge University Press.

Hume, David. 2003. *An Enquiry Concerning Human Understanding*. Oxford: Oxford University Press.

Kant, Immanuel. 1949. "Idee zur allgemeinen Geschichte in der weltbürgerlichen Absicht." In I. Kant, *Die drei Kritiken*. Stuttgart: Alfred Kröner Verlag.

Krishnamurti, Jiddu. 1975. *The First and Last Freedom*. San Francisco: HarperOne.

Krishnamurti, Jiddu. 2003. *Tradition and Revolution*. Chennai: Krishnamurti Foundation India.

Lewis, Clive Staples. 2000. *Sochineniia v 8 tomakh*, t. 8 [*Collected Works in 8 vols.*, vol. 8]. Moscow: Fond o. Aleksandra Menia.

Mamardashvili, Merab. 2000. *Estetika myshleniia* [*Aesthetics of Thought*]. Moscow: "Moskovskaia shkola politicheskikh issledovanii."

Pomerantz, Grigory. 1998. *Strastnaia odnostoronnost' i besstrastie dukha* [*Passionate One-Sidedness and the Impartiality of Spirit*]. Moscow-St. Petersburg: Tsentr gumanitarnykh initsiativ.

Schwarz, Evgeny. 2001. *Ten'* [*The Shadow*]. Moscow: Izdatel'stvo "Detskaia literature."

Vatoropin, Alexander S. 2011. Russky Fashism v Sovremennoy Rossii: Sotsiologichesky Analiz. *Sotsium and Vlast'* 29(1): 28–32. https://cyberleninka.ru/article/n/russkiy-fashizm-v-sovremennoy-rossii-sotsiologicheskiy-analiz

Yanov, Alexander. 1995. *Posle El'tsina. Veymarskaia Rossiia?* [*After Yeltsin. A Weimar Russia?*]. Moscow: KRUK.

8

Nostalgia, Trickster, and the War

Mark Lipovetsky

From Nostalgia to Retrotopia

Russia's war against Ukraine, barbaric and insane in its cruelty and senselessness, has overturned many hopes and cultural axioms not only in and for Ukraine, but also in Russia. For Russia, the war reversed thirty years of attempts to "reconstruct" society—or, rather, to get rid of the Soviet legacy, to separate the present and future from the crimes of the past, including but not limited to the *Holodomor* and GULAG, collectivization and exiled nations, the anti-cosmopolitanism campaign and persecution of dissidents, and the murder of poets, writers, actors, philosophers, and millions of innocent victims. Just as the Soviet tanks in Prague 1968 showed everyone that Soviet pseudo-socialism could not be reformed, so the missile strikes on Kiev and other Ukrainian cities on the morning of February 24, 2022, proved with maximum clarity that Russia remains chained to its imperial past, which means that all change is just a thin film to be erased.

Nostalgia for the Soviet Union, which began with innocent postmodernist banter (for example, the 1995 TV show *Old Songs About the Most Important Things* by Leonid Parfyonov), eventually turned into a huge commercial project, with high-rise buildings stylized as Stalin's "Seven Sisters," or networks of "legendary" canteens that imitate Soviet public cuisine. Nostalgic cultural goods also helped: the whole wave of "nostalgic" TV series that filled television screens during the pre-war decade, for example. Together with Tatyana Mikhailova, we analyzed these series in the article "More Than Nostalgia," published a few months before the war (Lipovetsky and Mikhailov, 2021). These serials did not idealize the Soviet past; on the contrary, they depicted the repressions, the KGB, the stupidity of the party leadership, corruption, and the black market. But at the same time, the colorful and aesthetically profound *image of the past* was extremely appealing. In the foreground of these TV series, such as *Thaw*, *Fartsa*, *The*

An earlier, Russian-language version of this essay was published as Lipovetsky, 2022.

Optimists, Our Happy Tomorrow, and others were transgressive and cheerful cynics, bursting for the sky but hindered by Soviet ideological rigidity and the limitations of quasi-socialist economics. These series demonstrated the continuity between modernity and the most transgressive and rebellious subcultures of late Soviet history: between the *shtatniks* [fans of everything American] and the *stilyagas* [Western fashion buffs] of the 1960s and today's representatives of the Ministry of Foreign Affairs of the Russian Federation and TV propagandists; between the underground businessmen and today's state oligarchs ... Paradoxically, the rebels of the past were recruited to support the traditionalist and conservative project of the present.

This is no coincidence, since the cultural and political status quo of the Russian establishment in the 2010s, especially after the annexation of Crimea in 2014, included transgressivity as a crucial component. As Ilya Kukulin noted back in 2018, "performances of transgression in Russia's public sphere could be seen as elements of a shared system of public expression, almost unconnected to any specific political ideology and/or social stratum. These performances constitute the horizon of expectations for the conformist majority" (Kukulin, 2018, 229).

But the illusion that these shows reproduced and which, contrary to the real state of affairs, its viewers readily accepted, was that contemporary Russian capitalism was *not* the result of a break with the Soviet past, but an heir to the most radical and "progressive" tendencies in the very lifeworld of late socialism. This ideological phantasm mentally reversed the anti-communist revolution of the late 1980s, turning contemporary capitalism and its corresponding political regime into a natural, "evolutionary," and "normal" development of the Soviet system.

The nostalgic TV series merely articulated the cultural and political mainstream that emerged after 2014. Its main modality was one of *retrotopia*, which completely supplanted all images of the future. Zygmunt Bauman, who introduced the concept of retrotopia in his last book of the same name, defines retrotopia through Walter Benjamin's famous description of Paul Klee's *Angelus Novus* as the Angel of History whose face is turned towards the past, in which he sees nothing but "a single catastrophe which keeps piling wreckage" and who is smashed by the storm blowing from Paradise: "The storm irresistibly propels him into the future to which his back is turned, while the pile of debris [from the past] before him grows skyward" (Benjamin, 1968, 257). In Bauman's words, this Angel of History is changing direction nowadays, caught

> in the midst of a U-turn, his face turning from the past to the future, his wings being pushed backwards by the storm blowing this time from the

imagined, anticipated and feared in advance Hell of the future towards the Paradise of the past ... The road to future looks uncannily as a trail of corruption and degeneration. Perhaps the road back, to the past, won't miss the chance of turning into a trail of cleansing from the damages committed by futures, whenever they turned into a present?

(Bauman, 2017, 2, 6)

Retrotopian imagination in Russia of the 2010s-2020s dreams about Brezhnev's state capitalism, without any socialist nonsense in the economy and without communist ideology in politics; all the rest may stay the same. The complete and final victory of this fantasy over reality, no matter how disappointing, is the basis of the catastrophe that began in March 2014 and reached its climax in February 2022. The task of "cleansing" the trail of history cannot lead to anything but a war with the present and the future.

The Legacy of Cynicism

In my understanding of the Soviet legacy, cynicism is a central category. I do not claim that cynicism excludes enthusiasm or fear or resistance. It coexists with them, as with other social reflexes and affects. But it sets a certain level of "normality" present in Soviet society at various periods. In fact, the most popular writers of the Soviet period—Mikhail Zoshchenko, Ilya Ilf and Evgeny Petrov, Vasily Shukshin, Fazil Iskander, Mikhail Zhvanetsky, and Sergei Dovlatov—wrote about the *normality* of cynicism. On the one hand, cynical practices became a means of survival for the common man (see the books by Sheila Fitzpatrick, 2005 and Oleg Kharkhordin, 2002); on the other, the systemic cynicism of the Soviet regime was a "staple" that linked repressive practices with emancipatory slogans.

It is against this background that the complex and rich figure of the Soviet trickster comes to the fore. I have written about it extensively and will therefore limit myself to the briefest possible formulations (see Lipovetsky 2011, 2020). As I see it, the Soviet trickster is the offspring of the culture of Soviet cynicism and, at the same time, its aesthetic justification. It turns survival into adventure and adaption to difficult circumstances into a performance of freedom. Moreover, the trickster represents alternatives to Soviet modernity—and herein lies its most important, not only cultural, but also political role. He delivers the Soviet man from the doom of predetermined social scenarios, promising loopholes and workarounds leading in more interesting directions than the shining peaks of the communist future. The protagonists of Ilf and Petrov's satirical novels *The Twelve Chairs* (1928) and *Little Golden Calf* (1931/1933), witty and elegant con artist Ostap Bender and his brethren, having become the idols of millions, undermined the state ideology no less convincingly but more effectively than famous dissidents.

What happens to this hero after the fall of the Soviet regime? In a nutshell, he triumphs in a pyrrhic victory.

From an outsider, from a countercultural rebel hiding under a mask of conformism, from a transgressor and sarcastic critic of the system, this character turns into a *normative* type. The millions of Soviet citizens who threw themselves into capitalist business in the 1990s were not inspired by the Protestant ethic, rather they imagined themselves as tricksters like Ostap Bender or, more often, Benia Krik, the protagonist of Isaac Babel's *Odessa Tales,* which depicts a Jewish gangster as a new revolutionary messiah. Trickster tropes frequently appear in the life stories of all the big protagonists of post-Soviet capitalism, from Boris Berezovsky to Mikhail Khodorkovsky. However, by becoming normative, the trickster gradually (not immediately!) loses the qualities that define them as a trickster: ambivalence, transgressivity, performativity, liminality. Consequently, the aesthetically attractive facade of the trickster begins to reveal their other side—cynicism, which has always been present but was overshadowed by more compelling traits. It is precisely cynicism that becomes the unifying position and even a kind of ideology for all the post-Soviet tricksters who have come to power. (I want to emphasize that this scenario is not necessary and inevitable, and let us say that the example of Mikhail Khodorkovsky, whose multi-million business had been destroyed by government officials and who was placed behind bars for ten years, refutes it—but turning him into a convict and an exile also deprives the former oligarch of normative and power status.)

Post-Soviet Transformation of Cynicism

Journalist Peter Pomerantsev, the son of Russian dissidents who grew up and studied in Britain, published a book in 2015 under the title *Nothing Is True, and Everything Is Possible: Adventures in Modern Russia*. It has become the most widely read book in the English-speaking world about Russia in perhaps the last ten years, if not more. Having worked on Russian television in the 2000s, Pomerantsev has artistically documented the various forms of cynicism in contemporary Russian political and media culture. In doing so, he has been the first to show that cynicism had become the main unifying "staple" of Russia's political system by the 2010s. Pomerantsev calls this ideological construct "authoritarian postmodernism." In his view, the same thing happened to postmodernism that happened to socialism in the early twentieth century—"In an echo of socialism's fate in the early twentieth century, Russia has adopted a fashionable, supposedly liberational Western intellectual movement and transformed it into an instrument of oppression" (Pomerantsev, 2011).

Elsewhere, I tried to argue that it is strange to place the responsibility for cynicism on such a relatively "young" (in comparison to cynicism) aesthetic system as postmodernism (see Lipovetsky, 2018). That would be like denouncing romanticism for crimes of passion and modernism for the opioid crisis. However, a kind of selective affinity can still be observed. The cynical "multi-positionality" only superficially resembles postmodern "shimmering" (a term used by the Russian conceptualist poet and artist Dmitry Prigov[1]), suggesting an oscillation of the author's position between different discourses and ideological platforms, without committing to any of them and making fun of each. This strategy serves as a condition for a non-violent strategy and aesthetics, securing the author's freedom from all ideological or discursive dependence.

Cynicism presupposes simultaneous dependence on multiple discourses and ideologies, despite the contradictions that arise between them; the main thing is that they bring the greatest benefit here and now. Unlike postmodernism, which satirically exacerbates and dramatizes conflicts between languages and discourses, cynicism smooths over or ignores such contradictions, not only justifying their combination by pragmatic, egoistic, political, etc., needs, but even giving no importance to their incompatibility. Functioning as an ideology, if we understand ideology according to Žižek (see Žižek, 1989), cynicism offers a phantom defense against questions of moral choice or moral responsibility, presenting them as hypocritical and irrelevant to reality ("everybody does it," etc.). It does not matter whether it is about domestic or foreign policy, economics or family relations, xenophobia or corruption. Such an approach proves to be equally beneficial not only to power but also society as a whole.

How does the cynicism of the post-Soviet regime differ from Soviet models and prototypes? Soviet cynicism towards authorities and public figures was a concealed one, and anyone whose life was connected to official institutions (press, education, industry, party, etc.) greatly feared to be accused of cynicism. As Lev Gudkov wrote in 2005: "One cannot say that the former Soviet society was more moral or humanistic, but its cynicism was covered by a system of obligatory declarations and self-characterizations that did not allow 'toxic' layers or components to enter the public scene" (Gudkov, 2015, 152). In essence, this was what Soviet "doublethink" consisted of.

On the contrary, post-Soviet cynicism always contains demonstrativeness, be it demonstrative amorality, cultivated transgression, or spectacles of amorality. In other words, this cynicism is performative. Its performativity certainly resonates with trickster performativity. "Cheekiness that has changed sides" is how Peter Sloterdijk, in his *Critique of Cynical Reason*, defined historical situations in which cynicism of power appropriates the methods and techniques of subversion which are characteristic of non-conformist culture. In our context, this means that the post-Soviet cynic in general, and the cynic in power in particular, behaves as a trickster and fully possesses the entire arsenal of trickster strategies. However, all of these techniques are no longer used to undermine and criticize power, but to shamelessly assert it.

Many analysts have written about cynicism as a genuine, "deep" ideology of Putin's political regime. According to Lev Gudkov, cynicism as a political vector and as the dominant social attitude in the 2000s–2010s expresses, on the one hand, "mass disappointment with reforms and the conversion of hopes (illusions) into aggression against those with whom previous possibilities for their realization were associated—democrats, liberals, and politicians, who set another, much higher ceiling for aspirations and ethical ideas about the individual and his rights compared with the Soviet period" (Gudkov, 2015, 140). On the other hand, cynicism is inherited from the Soviet system along with

> the very constitution or organization of the regime, which is built vertically from the top down, when the higher authorities select the convenient and loyal executives for themselves, but not competent and professionally qualified specialists. Such selection in authorities is based on the mechanisms of negative selection of cadres and co-optation of the most unscrupulous, 'elastic' and adaptive examples of a person into the structures of management.
>
> (Gudkov, 2015, 142)

For Gudkov, cynicism is not so much the coexistence of incompatible moral positions as demonstrative and defiant amorality: "Cynical should be understood as a denial of the meaning of things significant for other people, when it is made with the full understanding of how sensitive and significant these circumstances are for them" (Gudkov, 2015, 137).

Ilya Kalinin explains the defeat of the 2011-2012 protest movement by the fact that both the authorities and the "creakles" [derivate of "creative class"] used the same language of cynicism:

[cynicism] is stylistically much clearer and acceptable to many participants and leaders of the protest movement than the 'dumb lingo of the masses' who are not capable of advanced cynical mind games. ... Irony and banter, which became the basic rhetorical strategies of protest and pro-government discourses alike, made it possible to build a clear boundary between 'our own' and 'others', which ran not so much between political opponents as between both active parties to the conflict and those who were presumed (again, by both sides) to be its passive observers.

(Kalinin, 2017)[2]

Natalia Roudakova, exploring post-Soviet journalism, emphasizes that in post-Soviet society, cynicism is strengthened as a mass position expressing, first, "the passive-aggressive *ressentiment* of the people who for a brief moment believed in the redemptive power of a new political order and who were then bitterly disappointed ... The ideals and value orientations of state socialism receded, while the new positive meanings of liberalism, democracy, and the market failed to materialize" (Roudakova, 2017, 171). Cynicism manifests mistrust of people and institutions, readiness for deception and manipulation and, at its worst, becomes an adaptive mechanism for survival in circumstances of constant crisis: "Like in Weimar Germany, cynicism in post-Soviet Russia became the adaptive mechanism for coping with the meaninglessness of it all" (Roudakova, 2017, 171). The final function of cynicism, as analyzed by Roudakova, is associated with spectacles of distancing and disinhibition displayed by post-Soviet power. Such spectacles are often combined with demonstrative insults and ridicule, of which Putin is the consummate master. These spectacles reproduce the distancing characteristic of late-Soviet "living *vnye* [outside]" (see Yurchak, 2006, 126-57), but their meaning is reduced to releasing the political figure from responsibility for what is happening—political assassinations, prosecutions of political opponents, beatings of peaceful demonstrators, introduction of troops into a neighboring state, "nullification" of the Constitution, bombing of villages and towns and other atrocities, and, finally, the war.

Ilya Kukulin also defined the cynicism of contemporary Russian power as "messianic," referring to the revival of providential notions about Russia's role in world history, which at the same time serve as pragmatic justifications for cynical politics and propaganda: "discrediting of moral and idealistic motivations for political action is presented as a defense of Russia's unique historical mission to implement universalist moral values forgotten by the 'West.' Thus, it could be called messianic cynicism" (Kukulin, 2018, 231). Messianic cynicism in culture, propaganda and politics, as Kukulin notes, is firmly associated with an aestheticization and even a cult of transgression, reminiscent of avant-garde and modernist culture and vividly represented by such political characters as Foreign Ministry spokesperson Maria Zakharova or member of the patriotic Night Wolves bikers club Alexander Zaldostanov. Nowadays, the entire Russian political establishment regularly displays transgressions associated with their "messianic cynicism," from ex-president Dmitry Medvedev's hysterical rants of hatred to Putin's threats and lies.

A Cynical Consensus

In contemporary Russian culture, at least since the failed revolution of 2011-2012, a surprising resonance has emerged between the cynicism of the powerful and the cynicism of the powerless. A kind of cynical consensus has taken shape. Both the elites and their everyday victims were united by distrust of social and political institutions and their formal discourses (see Mazela, 2007, 6): the elites use institutions as a means of personal enrichment, minimizing their other functions, while the population, not without reason, perceives these same institutions exclusively as mechanisms of economic, political, and cultural deception. This resonance of oppositely directed cynicisms has revealed its unpredictable potential before, and especially during, the war.

It is this cynical consensus that the rock singer Sergei Shnurov captured in his super-popular music videos of the second half of the 2010s. "In Piter We Drink" glorified the anarchic freedom of the refusal to comply with any power. A brief but touching solidarity of the underdogs emerged on these grounds, the solidarity of those at odds with the system. In their drunken escapades, they do not forget about each other and find a warm unity, interrupted by a cold St. Petersburg morning. Other famous clips—"The Exhibit," "The Candidate," "Ecstasy"—told stories not just of losers (that characterization remained constant), but of failed tricksters. Each of Shnurov's protagonists tries very hard to become or at least look like a dashing trickster, preferably an impostor, because, as it turns out, tricksterism is equivalent to social success (the latter thesis is vividly illustrated by another video of Shnurov's, "Cabriolet"). However, although the characters occupying a high social position are no better than Shnurov's protagonists (the mayor arrested for corruption backstage in "Candidate"), and although their own mischief sometimes reaches heights of virtuosity and inventiveness (just think of the heroine in "Exhibit"), this does not change matters: they are too late with their tricksterism. The resentment of a trickster society in which there is no place for another trickster is what has replaced social protest in Shnurov's songs and musical videos. This explains his further evolution.

Today, after the outbreak of war, with the same intonation and style, Shnurov sings songs in which he justifies nationalism and political repressions. The transition from the subaltern position to the position of power required only a change of costume (literally) and a new soloist. It turned out that the positions of power and the powerless were not antagonistic, and that the bombing of Ukrainian cities can be translated in the language of domestic violence: "My wife wanted to join NATO, which is why she has a black eye now" ("geopolitical"). Only there is no trace of tricksterism left—only naked cynicism.

Let me bring forward another example of the war-time cynical consensus: a series of comedy shows called *Out Loud* [*Vslukh*]. It exists on the Russian segment of the internet (Runet) and its first season, which began in June 2022, consists of twenty-four professionally produced 15–20 minute episodes. The authors compare *Vslukh* to the Soviet *Fitil*, a satirical film magazine edited by Sergei Mikhalkov, the author of three revisions of the Soviet and then Russian anthem. *Fitil* exposed ideological enemies and petty social flaws. Each program of *Vslukh* consists of three video sketches on "socially significant" topics. This is one of the projects of the Internet Development Institute, a state organization that gives out "subsidies for the creation and promotion of socially significant internet content" (from the Institute's site: https://ири.рф/). In other words, this organization is similar to Yevgeny Prigozhin's internet troll farm but works predominantly in culture.

The objects of *Vslukh* satire are the "world's West" (*sic*), "liberal values," "attempts to revive Nazism," "nationalism" (not Russian, of course), drug addicts, LGBT and, of course, "eternal human vices." If we replace drug addicts with alcoholics and LGBT with *stilyagi*, we are faced with a range of objects typical for so-called Soviet satire. Evgeny Dobrenko and Natalia Jonsson-Skradol write about it in their book *State Laughter*: "the Soviet feuilleton was occupied with the incessant creation of a controlled image of the Other ... The authorities considered the control over the production of the Other and its interpretation no less important than the production of the People as the highest legitimizing authority" (Dobrenko and Jonsson-Skradol, 2022, 348). That is precisely what the new *Fitil* is doing—they are also molding images of the Other in order to produce the People from what is left after "weeding out."

This is why the creators of *Vslukh* need "people's plots, accessible for the majority of viewers," as they announce on the page in VKontakte. Despite the involvement of popular actors, *Vslukh* writers and performers typically fail in their attempts to be funny. To date, the channel has only 227 subscribers, suggesting failure. However, one of the skits, "Tolerant Flight" became viral, thanks to a promotion from TV propaganda star Vladimir Solovyov.

The skit depicts a family—husband, wife, and teenage son—emigrating from Russia to America. The story is set on an airplane, which is presented as a micro-America. The newly minted emigrants are subjected to "minorities' terror." First, a female neighbor who glorifies America introduces them to her "husband," who turns out to be another woman. Then the father of the family is robbed of his distributed lunch because the sight of meat irritates the vegetarian couple, and in America, as the stewardess says, it is customary to respect democracy. Then the dad and mom are forced to kneel in front of an African American man who wants to cut the line to the bathroom. Finally, the family is asked to move to another part of the plane to keep their child out of the sight of the child-free couple. As a result, the family jumps out of the plane with the father yelling, "Sorry, Mother Russia! The devil confused us! We're going back!"

There is nothing particularly new in this skit. The horrors of political correctness have long been a folkloric theme in Russian culture, and many, from the writer Tatiana Tolstaya to the theater director Konstantin Bogomolov, have contributed to its development. What is new is the theatricalization of these fears and their connection to the theme of emigration from Russia—which is triggered by the war, of course. Russians—even those fleeing Russia—are portrayed as carriers of the absolute and universal anthropological, social, and cultural "norm." On the contrary, the West, especially America, is imagined by the authors of this skit as a place where "normal people" are constantly persecuted and marginalized, while "minorities" are terrorized by the authorities. In this phantasm one can see, for example, an echo of Soviet anti-Semitism in its "popular" form manifesting itself as hatred toward the minority that has supposedly seized power over the majority. We can also see a substitution for democracy in this phantasm: the propaganda discourse expresses its solidarity with the "majority" and makes fun of the excessive ambitions and demands of minorities.

In contemporary Russia, this phantasm primarily reflects the notion that power and violence are inseparable. In the minds of the authors of the newsreel, this notion is automatically transferred to the power that protects the rights of minorities. In other words, viewers are convinced that the "normal" in the West are treated the same way as those who deviate from the "norm" in Russia. In this way, xenophobia is essentially presented as the only possible form of social relations: if LGBT people are not subjected to homophobia and African-Americans are not victims of racism, then they can only be a source of similar violence against those different from themselves. A different kind of relationship is simply unimaginable and seems a manifestation either of hypocrisy or deceit. So, in the final analysis, the "terror of minorities" depicted in the "Tolerant Flight" is an expression of cynicism as the ideology behind the war, as a justification for supporting the "normal" Russia's aggression against Ukraine, allegedly "disoriented" by the West.

Create Realities

In *Critique of Cynical Reason*, Peter Sloterdijk shows how German Nazism was born from overcoming a similar consensus, with the illusion of order and clarity also created by the trickster means:

> Hitler's recipe is therefore: First simplify, then repeat endlessly. This will be effective. However, one can only simplify what one has already grasped as something ambiguous, multifaceted, multivalent. So that politicians can make an impression on the masses, they must learn to hide that "more" that they know and outwardly identify themselves with their own simplifications. With the concept of playacting, this procedure is not yet fully grasped. Thomas Mann [in *Mario and the Magician*] hit the mark very clearly not only by describing the vaudeville character of political seduction but also and especially by emphasizing the suggestive and hypnotic aspects of these phenomena. The suggestion, however, begins in the politicians themselves, and their own consciousness is the first addressee of suggestive persuasion.
> (Sloterdijk, 1987, 489)

Is this model applicable to contemporary Russia? It seems to be only partly applicable. Neither Putin nor his propagandists, oozing irony and sarcasm, expect that their narratives will be accepted as truth. They are not hackneyed, but simply do not think it necessary to present any evidence for their fabrications. It is no coincidence that Alexander Dugin raises to the banner precisely the fictional image of the boy crucified in Slavyansk—to obscure the real victims of Russian violence in Bucha and other Ukrainian cities. They do not hide the tricksterism, but defiantly bring it to the fore: this is their realpolitik. When Sergey Lavrov says, without blinking an eye, on March 10, 2022: "We are not planning to attack other countries, we have not attacked Ukraine either" (Interfax, 2022), he behaves like a con-artist, like a trickster confident in his success who created a parallel reality of illusions completely subordinated to his directorial will. Peter Pomerantsev quotes Gleb Pavlovsky as saying: "The main difference between propaganda in the USSR and the new Russia ... is that in Soviet times the concept of truth was important. Even if they were lying, they took care to prove what they were doing was 'the truth.' Now no one even tries proving the 'truth.' You can just say anything. Create realities" (Pomerantsev and Weiss, 2015, 9). In this sense, post-Soviet tricksterism in power shapes the contemporary type of society of the spectacle, which completely frees power from any ethical, legal, political or social constraints, opening the door for violence that is limited by nothing but counter-violence.

It is striking how this principle of "creating realities" resembles the statement of US Republican strategist Karl Rove on the eve of the invasion of Iraq: "We are an empire now, and when we act, we create our own reality. And while you are studying that reality ... we act again, creating other new realities, which you can study too ... We are actors in history ... and you, all of you, have only to study what we do" (Suskind, 2004).

However, the case of Putin shows how reckless, if not suicidal, this strategy turns out to be—when the trickster believes so much in the illusions he has created, in the reality he has constructed, that he becomes a victim of his own swindle. It is not advisable to start a war in this state, otherwise one will inevitably have to have a very painful encounter with another, unreconstructed reality. It is this encounter of the trickster-in-power with an unmanipulated reality that the course of the war demonstrates.

A Trickster in Power?

These days, many people remember Eugene Shvarts's *The Dragon* (1943). Even *The Economist*, on February 23, 2022, the day before the war broke, cheerfully retold the plot of the play, emphasizing the futility of expectations concerning popular uprisings against dragons—the people love their dragons (Anon, 2002). I, on the other hand, have been preoccupied lately with another figure in *The Dragon*—the Burgomaster. Shvarts has created some brilliant images of tricksters—the First Minister in *The Naked King*, Caesar Borgia and Yulia Julie in *The Shadow*, the Stepmother in *Cinderella*, the Minister-Administrator and the King in *An Ordinary Miracle*. Unlike other Soviet tricksters, Shvartsian tricksters, despite their undeniable charm, are portrayed as complete scoundrels. All of them are hyper-conformists who "overplay" their conformism, making it so excessive that it turns not only into a self-parody, but into a parody of power in general. Art historians Inke Arns and Sylvia Sasse call this effect subversive affirmation:

> Subversive affirmation is an artistic/political tactic that allows artists/activists to take part in certain social, political, or economic discourses and to affirm, appropriate, or consume them while simultaneously undermining them. ... In subversive affirmation there is always a surplus which destabilizes affirmation and turns it into its opposite. Subversive affirmation and over-identification—as 'tactics of explicit consent'—are forms of critique that through techniques of affirmation, involvement and identification put the viewer/listener precisely in such a state or situation which she or he would or will criticize later.
>
> (Ans and Sasse, 2006, 445)

The Burgomaster is one of such tricksters who overidentifies with the Dragon's power and thus produces an effect of subversive affirmation. His cynical conformism turns into a performance with numerous roles, voices, theatrical mise-én-scenes, and divertissements. It is not without reason that Schwartz gives him the best pearls of his wit—the funniest jokes in this play are inscribed in the quasi-schizophrenic delirium of the Burgomaster.

The first social-artists, these Shvarts's tricksters, are usually at arm's length from the supreme power. However, there are exceptions. The Burgomaster is particularly revealing in this respect, for he vividly demonstrates the transformation of the mean but, let's face it, charming Burgomaster into the cold and frightening Dragon. A master of contrary assertion, a chatterbox, and jester becomes a cold dictator, and, ultimately, a sadist and murderer in full cynical consensus with "the people."

The Trickster, who has seized full power, is the modern dictator. Shvarts's conclusion is quite applicable to today's situation—modern dictatorship derives from the cynical consensus shaped by the omnipresent trickster. But could it have been like this yesterday, i.e., in the 1920s and 1930s? And could it be that the flowering of tricksterism is not only a resistance to the cynicism of power, but also, in the first place, a symptom of impending dictatorship?

It is necessary to add: a missed symptom.

The Dead-end of Tricksterism?

Looking from today's war-shaped perspective at Soviet trickster discourse, one cannot help but see its dangerous limits. First, the trickster's total transgressivity does not allow for any ethical principles. "The trickster is not immoral, he is a-moral," wrote American trickster scholar Lewis Hyde (Hyde, 1998, 10). This is fine in art, but it is impossible to live next to a trickster, much less under the power of a trickster. A society in which everyone wants to be a trickster becomes hell. Orientation toward trickster scenarios is highly effective as a form of critique, but post-Soviet history shows that it is the absence of ethical boundaries that gives the trickster a head start in the struggle for authoritarian and dictatorial power.

Beginning with mythological narratives in which the trickster acts as the double of the cultural hero, the trickster creates only inadvertently. Actually, his function is related to the stimulation of the forces of chaos, which, to a certain extent, are the prototype of freedom. It is good to create a counterculture on this basis, but it is suicidal to assign more serious creative tasks to the trickster. Soviet tricksters were free spirits of capitalism within a quasi-socialist state feudalism. But when these spirits were allowed to run wild, what did they get? A fusion of Soviet cynicism and economic neoliberalism emerged. The Soviet trickster turned out to be the ideal neoliberal subject—both as a subaltern and as a figure of power.

As Slavoj Žižek wrote: "this is the reality of global capitalism. Everyone breaks the rules ... You have certain rules, but you are not really expected to follow them. There are rules that you are expected to break" (Schulson, 2015). It is neoliberalism that defeats communist ideology during the years of *perestroika* and defines the new Russian configuration of power and subordination. However, precisely because of the dominant role of the trickster figure in the Soviet cultural imagination, post-Soviet neoliberalism does not so much oppose the Soviet legacy as reformat it, retaining much of the continuity and important cultural logics. Interestingly, Žižek's description of neoliberalism sounds essentially like a paraphrase of his own description of the communist system: in his book *Did Somebody Say Totalitarianism?*, he wrote that in the Soviet political system "a cynical attitude towards the official ideology was what the regime really wanted—the greatest catastrophe for the regime would have been for its own ideology to be taken seriously, and realized by its subjects" (Žižek, 2001, 92). (Which is why Marxists were persecuted with a special cruelty.)

The Soviet trickster has been pushing Russia's neoliberal economy and political system towards the war and, eventually, suicide, precisely because he imagines transgression, playing against all and sundry rules, as the only and main driving force of history. And Russian society agrees with the supreme trickster, because this logic is deeply internalized and rooted in both Soviet and post-Soviet experience. Moreover, even if we imagine that this system collapses, the most probable scenario seems to be a succession of more or less evil tricksters in the role of saviors of the motherland and fathers of the nation.

What can oppose this anti-ethics? Only uncompromisingly honest and open ethics. Thus, Alexei Navalny has a brilliant command of trickster methods when fighting the regime—just remember his live conversation with the FSB officer, in which Navlany made his counterpart report how he smeared poison on the underpants of the "object." But Navalny, who has returned to Russia to go to prison, ceases to be a trickster and becomes a distinctly ethical subject. In fact, paradoxically, he returns to cynicism in its original philosophical sense.

Michel Foucault, in his last series of lectures, published under the title *The Courage of the Truth*, speaks of the Cynic as the embodiment of "a life without concealment, which holds nothing back, a life which was capable of having nothing to be ashamed of" (Foucault, 2011, 243)—life without dividing into public and private, in consistent rejection of all values of comfort and well-being. It is in this way that the Cynic embodies his philosophy—not as an abstraction, but as a concrete and open strategy of living. According to Foucault, it is by following these conditions that the Cynic achieves the fullness of freedom and power—"[The] Cynic is the only true king. And at the same time, vis-à-vis kings of the world, crowned kings sitting on their thrones, he is the anti-king who shows how hollow, illusory, and precarious the monarchy of kings is" (Foucault, 2011, 275). Foucault sees in this position of the ancient Cynic a source of a special political activism:

> This would be the idea of a militancy in the open, as it were, that is to say, a militancy addressed to absolutely everyone, which precisely does not require an education (a *paideia*), but which resorts to harsh and drastic means, not so much in order to train people and teach them, as to shake them up and convert them, abruptly. It is a militancy in the open in the sense that it claims to attack not just this or that vice or fault or opinion that this or that individual may have, but also the conventions, laws, and institutions which rest on the vices, faults, weaknesses.
>
> (Foucault, 2011, 301)

In the history of the trickster, two lines have developed since ancient times: one is associated with trickery and, accordingly, self-interest (the picaro, the knave, the adventurer, the impostor, the con artist). The other, on the contrary, is fundamentally unselfish, which is why it is often associated with stupidity and absurdity (the fool, the clown, the holy fool). The philosopher-Cynic belongs to this second line. The revival of Cynicism as a strategy of radical rejection of well-being and conformism, as a new activism based on total, often heroic, disinterestedness, seems to be the new image of the trickster. This image could "recalculate the coinage" of Soviet resistance culture, making it relevant for the present day.

The anti-war actions of contemporary artists are a striking example of this kind of trickster activism. Sasha Skochilenko's project about the crimes of the Russian military, created under the guise of supermarket price tags, led to her arrests for spreading "fakes" about the war. There are already quite a few projects like this, and more to come. Yes, of course, they "won't change anything." Resistance may not bring quick results, but that does not render it useless.

From this point of view, the fight against corruption, in which many saw Navalny and his supporters' rejection of the political program, takes on the significance of a broad ethical-political movement, without which liberation from the dominant political regime and the culture it has created is impossible. Corruption does not only include bribes and kickbacks to highly placed officials, lawlessness and arbitrariness in the courts and the police, and slavery and exploitation in production. Corruption includes the normalization of imperial nationalism, racism, homophobia, and sexism, which must be met with radical intolerance, even to the extent of boycotting the promoters and supporters of these ideas in cultural and academic circles.

Finally, in our own field, in the humanities, the struggle against corruption is not limited to fidelity to facts and rejection of amateurish and propagandistic exercises in history. The criteria of intellectual corruption are set by the categorical apparatus developed in the postmodern era: essentialism, binary thinking, operating with metaphysical categories ("the people," the historical destiny/mission of Russia, Orthodox/Russian civilization, the Russian soul, etc.) as scholarly concepts—all of these are manifestations of corruption, which should be countered consistently and uncompromisingly. And no, I am not talking about censorship, but about solidarity and intellectual honesty as fundamental conditions, without which a slow, painful, but nevertheless possible exodus from the current state of catastrophe will never come to pass.

Notes

1 In more detail see: Leiderman, 2018.
2 See also: Brock, 2018; Troitsky, Pomerantsev, and Carroll, 2013.

References

Anon. 2022. "How to kill your dragon: To understand modern autocrats, read Soviet children's literature," *The Economist*, 23 February. https://www.economist.com/culture/2022/02/23/to-understand-modern-autocrats-read-soviet-childrens-literature

Arns, Inke, and Sylvia Sasse. 2006. "Subversive affirmation: On mimesis as a strategy of resistance." In *East Art Map: Contemporary Art and Eastern Europe*, 444–55. Boston: MIT Press.

Bauman, Zygmunt. 2017. *Retrotopia*. Cambridge: Polity.

Benjamin, Walter. 1968. *Illuminations*. Edited and with an introduction by Hannah Arendt. Translated by Harry Zohn. New York: Harcourt, Brace & World.

Brock, Maria. 2018. "Political satire and its disruptive potential: Irony and cynicism in Russia and the US," *Culture, Theory and Critique* 59(3): 281–98.

Dobrenko, Evgeny, and Natalia Jonsson-Scradol. 2022. *Gossmekh: Stalinizm i komicheskoe*. Moscow: Novoe Literaturnoe Obozrenie.

Fitzpatrick, Sheila. 2005. *Tear Off the Masks! Identity and Imposture in Twentieth-Century Russia*. Princeton: Princeton University Press.

Foucault, Michel. 2011. *The Courage of the Truth (The Government of Self and Others II). Lectures at the Collège de France, 1983–1984*. Edited by Frédéric Gros. General Editors: François Ewald and Alessandro Fontana. Translated by Graham Burchell. New York: Palgrave.

Gudkov, Lev. 2015. "Ot dvoemysliia k tsinizmu: Obshchestvennaia tsena strategii ponizhaiushchei adaptatsii (po materialam issledovanii Levada-Tsentra)." *Politicheskaia kontseptologiia* 2: 138–63.

Hyde, Lewis. 1998. *Trickster Makes the World: Mischief, Myth, and Art*. New York: North Point Press.

Interfax.ru. 2022. "Lavrov zaiavil, chto Rossia ne napadala na Ukrainu." March 10. https://www.interfax.ru/russia/827361

Kalinin, Ilya. 2017. "O tom, kak nekul'turnoe gosudarstvo obygralo kul'turnuiu oppozitsiiu na ee zhe pole, ili Pochemu 'dve Rossii' men'she, chem 'edinaia Rossiia'." *Neprikosnovennyi zapas* 6: 261–82. http://magazines.russ.ru/nz/2017/6/o-tom-kak-nekulturnoe-gosudarstvo-obygralo-kulturnuyu-oppoziciy.html

Kharkhordin, Oleg. 2002. *Oblichat' i litsemerit': Genealogiia rossiiskoi lichnosti*. St. Petersburg, Moscow: European University, Letnii Sad.

Kukulin, Ilya. 2018. "Cultural shifts in Russia since 2010: Messianic cynicism and paradigms of artistic resistance." *Russian Literature* 96-98: 221-54.
Leiderman, Daniil. 2018. "Moscow conceptualism and shimmering: Not conforming with nonconformism." *Russian Literature* 96-98: 51-76.
Lipovetsky, Mark. 2011. *Charms of Cynical Reason: The Trickster Trope in Soviet and Post-Soviet Culture*. Boston: Academic Studies Press.
Lipovetsky, Mark. 2018. "Psevdomorfoza: Reaktsionnyi postmodernism kak problema." *Novoe Literaturnoe Obozrenie* 3(151): 223-45.
Lipovetsky, Mark. 2020. "The Trickster and Soviet Subjectivity: Narratives and Counter-Narratives of Soviet Modernity." *Ab Imperio* 4: 62-87.
Lipovetsky, Mark. 2022. "Trikster i rashizm." *Ab Imperio* 1: 31-50.
Lipovetsky Mark and Tatiana Mikhailova. 2021. "More than Nostalgia: Late Socialism in TV Series of the 2010s." *Novoe Literaturnoe Obozrenie* 3: 127-47.
Mazella, David. 2007. *The Making of Modern Cynicism*. Charlottesville: University of Virginia Press.
Pomerantsev, Petr. 2011. "Putin's Rasputin." *London Review of Books* 30(20). http://www.lrb.co.uk/v33/n20/peter-pomerantsev/putins-rasputin
Pomerantsev Petr, and Michael Weiss. 2015. "The Menace of Unreality: How the Kremlin Weaponizes Information, Culture and Money." A Special Report presented by The Interpreter, a project of the Institute of Modern Russia. https://imrussia.org/media/pdf/Research/Michael_Weiss_and_Peter_Pomerantsev__The_Menace_of_Unreality.pdf
Roudakova, Natalia. 2017. *Losing Pravda: Ethics and the Press in Post-Truth Russia*. Cambridge: University of Cambridge Press.
Schulson, Michael. 2015. "Slavoj Žižek on Obama, Bernie, sex and democracy: 'That's the reality of global capitalism. Everyone is violating the rules.'" https://www.salon.com/test2/2015/10/11/slavoj_zizek_on_obama_bernie_sex_and_democracy_thats_the_reality_of_global_capitalism_everyone_is_violating_the_rules
Sloterdijk, Peter. 1987. *Critique of Cynical Reason*. Trans. Michael Eldred. Foreword Andreas Huyssen. Minneapolis: University of Minnesota Press.
Suskind, Ron. 2004. "Faith, Certainty and the Presidency of George W. Bush." *The New York Times Magazine*, October 17. https://www.nytimes.com/2004/10/17/magazine/faith-certainty-and-the-presidency-of-george-w-bush.html
Troitsky, Artemii, Peter Pomerantsev, and Oliver Carroll. 2013. "Talking Point: Is Culture the New Politics in Russia?" *Open Democracy*, March 27. https://www.opendemocracy.net/en/odr/talking-point-is-culture-new-politics-in-//
Yurchak, Alexei. 2006. *Everything Was Forever, Until It Was No More: The Last Soviet Generation*. Princeton: Princeton University Press.
Žižek, Slavoj. 1989. *The Sublime Object of Ideology*. London: Verso.
Žižek, Slavoj. 2001. *Did Somebody Say Totalitarianism? Five Interventions in the (Mis)Use of a Notion*. London: Verso.

The Return of the Grand Inquisitor

Maja Soboleva

Since February 24, 2022, many people have been in a state of perpetual shock. Trouble came from an unexpected side, and Russians were divided overnight into participants, accomplices, witnesses, or accusers of the assault on Ukraine. The reasons given by President Putin for the so-called "special military operation" are purely discursive; they can only satisfy the part of society that for decades has been under the influence of state propaganda that produced the myth of a new Russian Leviathan. These reasons are well known and need not be repeated here, especially because they are constantly changing. However, one need not be a (political) psychologist to assert that the actions of any subject are grounded in their corresponding mentality, and that the bearer of the collective mentality is both the government machinery and society as a whole. Russia's aggression against Ukraine is thus a symptom of the intellectual state of the *entire* society. A simple argument in favour of this assertion can be the formula (using the rather apt terms in which Lenin formulated his theory of revolution) "those at the top cannot do anything if those at the bottom do not will it done." The assumption here is that society, even if only to a certain extent, is an integral organism, and, therefore, its external manifestations reflect its internal dispositions. This chapter aims to look into the secrets of the contemporary "Russian soul" to understand why the seemingly impossible—aggression against an independent state— has become possible. The author does not maintain that this analysis is fully scientific; some assertions must be verified, for example, by means of sociological research. Rather, this chapter embraces reflections of a person deeply hurt by these tragic events.

Social Values

If we examine the state of the public mind in Russia over the past years, its concern with social values becomes immediately apparent. The issue of "traditional" values has been raised repeatedly in presidential speeches, statements of the vice president and speaker of the Duma, television shows expressing the official point of view, and other mass media. The existence of authentic values that ensure the spiritual sovereignty of Russia, as well as the need to defend them in the face of alternative orders of value, is constantly declaimed. What these "traditional" values are is usually not explicitly disclosed because every Russian presumably knows them by default. The rhetoric of public statements on this topic allows us to define these values only *negatively* at the beginning: they are *not* Western European values. The latter include some economic ideas, chiefly respect for private property; political ideals, above all the rule of law founded on the rights and freedoms of citizens; and some cultural codes, which, in general, were developed during the Enlightenment era by its cultivation of the self-determined individual. However, according to President Putin, "the model of total domination of the so-called golden billion is unfair. … It divides people into the first and second class, and therefore is racist and neo-colonial, and the underlying globalist, supposedly 'liberal' ideology has increasingly acquired features of totalitarianism, inhibiting creative search and free historical creation" (Putin, 2022).

The "traditional" Russian values presented as an alternative to those of the West are outlined in the State Decree No. 809. However, they can be fully understood by *reconstructing* the public discourse on this topic as initiated by state authorities. The core of the proposed value model includes, in my view, biologically determined gender roles; a heterosexual, patriarchal, ideally monogamous, family; the idea of man as warrior, woman as mother; and a pyramid of power with the state at the top and human life as being significant only in service to it. If a man is not ready to be a soldier, as one acquaintance of mine (incidentally, the mother of a soldier taking part in combat operations in Ukraine) put it, then he is "useless to society." Let us note that the government used these values to carry out the so-called "partial mobilization." The question addressed to potential recruits, namely "Are you a man or not?" implies that a man is a living being whose social purpose is to fight. It is called now "to do the job."

It is not difficult to see that these "traditional values" understood as ethical guidelines are based on the so-called "naturalistic fallacy" discovered by George Moore, which consists in drawing moral conclusions from non-moral assumptions. For example, biologically determined, natural qualities are assumed to be morally positive. The *naturalization of values* in contemporary Russian public discourse testifies to the *archaization* and *primitivization* of society. Russia is becoming, on the one hand, conservative and intolerant to all that is "different"—what Karl Popper called a "closed society." On the other hand, owing to this value-based totalitarianism of public consciousness, society is becoming numb to political totalitarianism, which appears—according to its naturalistic and strictly hierarchical logic of thinking—as a natural and perhaps even necessary form of social regulation.

The question of whether the regression in contemporary Russian society's value system is a spontaneous process caused by a crisis of the collective worldview and a loss of reference points or the result of conscious manipulation by the Kremlin's political technocrats to optimize control over the masses can hardly be resolved unequivocally. But this is not important from the point of view of evaluating the state of society. What is important is the diagnosis itself, as well as the fact that the behaviour of such a society easily lends itself to management according to the binary stimulus/response mechanism of the political behaviourists.

Contemporary Russian Patriotism

The construction of national identity appears to be one of the primary tasks of contemporary Russian domestic policy, judging by the engagement of the official mass media in political education as well as by government-led educational and political projects. The basis of national unity, as can be deduced from circulating texts, must be *patriotism*. In my opinion, modern patriotism has four features.

First, it demonstrates *militarist character*. The central event around which today's patriotic narrative is built is the victory of the Soviet Union in World War II. This event, like any historical fact, acquires new meanings over time. The semantic shift of "Victory Day," a celebration led "with tears in one's eyes," moved from the concept of "liberation" to the concept of "demonstration of military strength." "Victory" as liberation encompasses a range of meanings, from the literal—the release of the world from fascism—to the ideal—the hope of freeing the Soviet Union from internal terror and moving toward the humanization of society. The core meaning of "victory" today emphasizes the physical strength of the country, ready at any time to fight back against a potential enemy. A new semantic series has been recently formed: "victory," "strength," "the great nation," "confrontation," "political and military domination." These semantics feed modern patriotism and, in fact, exhaust it of its content. "Patriotism" is thus the unity of society with the goal of self-preservation in the face of an undefined external danger based on the consciousness of one's physical superiority.

One might think that this understanding of patriotism concerns the entire society and works as a means of its consolidation. However—and this is its second feature—it does not apply to the ruling elite and serves primarily as a *means of mobilizing the masses*. Whereas an ordinary person must remain within the boundaries of the so-called "Russian world," which they must defend from the enemy, the boundaries of this world are easily expanded and removed by representatives of the elite. Simple facts demonstrate how diffuse, if not illusory, the boundaries of the ruling class can really be: most members, including the president, his ministers, and even deputy ministers, such as Timur V. Ivanov (Deputy Minister of Defence of the Russian Federation since 2016) live in "two worlds"; their families have residence permits in countries that are supposed to be hostile to ordinary Russians. "Patriotism" thus turns out to be an ideologeme for the plebs, an element of the dual morality of the powerful.

The next feature of present-day patriotism is that its primary mechanism is *affective naturalism*. Patriotic rhetoric does not appeal to people's reason but to their basic emotions, such as fear, hatred, and aggression. Along with this, the enemy is actively "dehumanized": the Ukrainians, for example, are referred to as "fascists," "Nazis," "freaks," "perverts," "homosexuals," etc. (see, for example, the political shows on the first channel of Russian television). Value devaluation serves to "justify" a hatred and contempt for the enemy. Such devaluation has, for example, escalated into open calls to kill Ukrainian children, as can be seen in the statements of Anton Krasovsky, editorial director of the RT television channel. At the same time, patriots themselves gradually lose their humanity. Such naturalized patriotism not only easily transforms into nationalism but, in the end, loses its ethical meaning. It ceases to be a moral phenomenon and becomes a phenomenon of mass psychology and social ethology.

This form of patriotism is endowed with a specific idea of heroism in the form of the *heroization of death*. A modern hero is any soldier who has fallen on the battlefield. A hero, therefore, is not anyone who carries out heroic acts while still alive, such as the Russian epic heroes Ilya Muromets, Dobrynia Nikitich, and Alyosha Popovich, or modern super-men of all sorts, but someone who dies. It does not matter how this person lived; the principle "death justifies everything" is valid. For example, the Wagner Group has been recruiting large numbers of prisoners who became "heroes" after their death. Accordingly, contemporary patriotism is connected with the spread of the *cult of death*: the actions of the "Immortal Regiment" usurped by the state, the paving of countless Alleys of Heroes, and the widespread installation of memorial monuments like the School Desks of Heroes are just a few examples of this social "being to death." The meaning of the ritualization of death is clear: like any ritualized action that constitutes everyday life, death ceases to be a subject of reflection and, therefore, escapes criticism.

To conclude this topic, I would like to mention the Russian philosopher Ivan Ilyin (1883-1954), who developed a theory of patriotism in his work *The Way of Spiritual Renewal*, first published in Belgrade in 1937, where he distinguished between instinctive and spiritual patriotism. An analysis of this theory would be beyond the scope of this chapter; however, it cannot be omitted within this context because it sets an entirely different vector of reflection. Let us note, in my opinion, the principal point. *Instinctive patriotism* is related to survival and security. Ilyin writes: "Trouble, danger and fear teach a man to form solidarity with his neighbours; out of this solidarity the first glimmers of legal consciousness, 'loyalty' and 'patriotic sentiment' arise. And thus 'patriotism' appears to be inevitable, expedient and life-sustaining" (Ilyin, 2006, 161). He calls this instinct-based patriotism "heteronomous," using Kant's term, i.e., unfree and imposed from the outside. He contrasts it with the notion of a homeland that an individual forms freely. The source of this autonomous notion of homeland is not an instinct but love. Moreover, Ilyin understands love not as a "blind and unenlightened" affect; for patriotism based on such an affect is "a strange and dangerous mixture of militant chauvinism and dull national conceit, or blind predilection for everyday trifles and hypocritical 'great-powerful pathos,' behind which personal or class self-interest often hides" (Ilyin, 2006, 162). On the contrary, he understands love as a deeply spiritual feeling that goes back to Spinoza's mystical-religious *"amor Dei intellectualis,"* that is, love for the true, good, and beautiful achieved through knowledge and striving toward personal perfection. The patriotic love for a homeland, according to Ilyin, likewise falls under the notion of love for the perfect. Ilyin formulates the necessary condition for the *real, spiritual patriotism*: patriotism "is a matter of freedom, the inner freedom of human self-determination" (Ilyin, 2006, 167). In other words, the bearer of patriotism must be a *person*, "since finding a homeland is an act of spiritual (albeit vague-spiritual, or at least spiritual-instinctual) self-determination, assuming that human himself lives by the spirit and that the spiritual organ in him is not atrophied; and this act of self-determination shows him his own spiritual sources and thereby unleashes and fertilises his spiritual creativity" (Ilyin, 2006, 164). The essence of patriotism understood in this way consists in the fact that the term "homeland" is not a physical object (*terra*), but an element of the subjective narrative that constitutes one's personal identity. Moreover, the homeland, understood as the spiritual, imaginary homeland of the self-determined individual, guarantees the morality of the political human being (*zōon politikon*). It is precisely that what is usually overlooked by those who readily refer to Ilyin (including President Putin) while reducing his theory of patriotism, which is part of his phenomenology of the human spirit, to either a vulgar sociological, empirical-psychological, or geopolitical doctrine.

Contemporary Archetypes of Power

Observers have characterized Russia's current political system—the onset of which is most often dated to the change of the Russian Constitution in 2020—as authoritarian with a distinct tendency to totalitarianism. The long-term goals for a state set under Putin's government are unclear; it is also quite possible that his administration is not aware of the principles that underlie the long-term governance of the country. However, these principles are observable in Putin's activities and fit in well with the famous formula "absolutism," "orthodoxy," "nationality" (*narodnost'*) worked out by Sergei Uvarov during the reign of Nicholas I. Of course, the contents of the concepts included in this formula have changed, but, as a whole, their validity persists. "Absolutism" is represented now not by the tsar but by the head of state, with the parliament and the electorate preserved only nominally. Today, we can observe the formation of a new cult of the state and its transformation into a supreme symbol of power. Moreover, the current state is personified in the figure of the president, and this leads to a false identification of Russia with Putin's Russia by the population (with all of the practical consequences that follow from this). The authoritarian state apparatus has reinstalled "Orthodoxy" on the political scene, leaving it to serve government interests. The Russian Church, led by Patriarch Kirill, is not so much a spiritual authority as an institution for controlling the state of collective mind and strengthening state ideology. "Nationality" (*narodnost'*) manifests itself in the systematic destruction of civil society, which must serve as a mediator, a buffer, between the citizen and the state, in favor of introducing direct administration, turning a "citizen" into a mere "subject." For the naïve mind, such relations often have a paternalistic connotation such as "*Tsar-Batushka*" or "Father Stalin." However, this contemporary "peoplehood" (*narodnost'*) marks the deprivation of popular civil rights and freedoms, still proclaimed in the Russian constitution, and the transformation of the citizens into a voiceless, passive population. The authorities actively enforce laws on fake news, discrediting the army, foreign agents, etc., to protect the state from the citizens without giving them anything in return: the penalties for political crimes are almost as severe as those for criminal offenses. President Putin's meeting with the mothers of soldiers in November 2022 demonstrates that the individual in Russia has been reduced to a means for achieving state goals. Self-serving egoism, blatant cynicism, and contempt for one's own compatriots, along with the complete devaluation of their lives, have become the rules of contemporary political management. The situation is aggravated by the fact that many people are highly dependent on the government: most of them are either government employees (and not just the bureaucracy and security services but also physicians, teachers, university professors, and employees of all state institutions) or work for the system of state-monopolistic capitalism that has developed in recent decades (for firms in which the government holds a majority stake). The Russian legal basis for small and medium-sized businesses is arranged in such a way that this sector of economic activity is practically undercut at the root. It is not difficult to understand that the lack of economic freedom is an enormous resource of state violence.

Besides the traditional triad, the ideology of the nineteenth and early twentieth centuries returns to contemporary Russian politics. Accompanying it are ideas about the specific "Eurasian" course of Russia's development, its messianic role in history, the hostility of the West, a bipolar world with a struggle between good and evil, and the cultural colonialism of Western European countries and the United States. These ideas, combined with the lack of a long-term vision of the country's future, allows us to characterize the policy of the Putin government as *retro-politics*. The unattractiveness of this kind of government is self-evident: it makes no room for liberal democratic ideas concerning the economic and political independence of citizens, their well-being, and their legally guaranteed rights and freedoms. Its purpose seems to be to force people to serve some formidable and bloody order against their interests.

History Lessons

Retro-politics, revolving around the political mythology of Russia's national greatness, is essentially directed against Russians, the majority of whom nevertheless paradoxically support it. What is the problem here? We have already spoken above about the epidemic of so-called "traditional," *de facto* naturalized values, which form the totalitarian structure of a personality that is immune to political totalitarianism. We have briefly mentioned the phenomenon of a specific "false consciousness," i.e., the replacement of Russia's unique culture as the country's identification with the state "Russia" and, consequently, with the regime ruling at the current time. In addition to the system of values and markers of identity that, to a more or lesser extent, function on a rational, discursive level, some collective archetypes among the factors that create the structure of collective personality operate unconsciously, as we know due to Carl Jung.

In light of Russia's recent history, one can assume that the collective unconscious of a great part of the Russians is the archetype "GULAG." GULAG is nothing less than a system of state slavery: people were first deprived of their civil status, then turned into items and used in forced labor. The prisoners suffered under complete lawlessness and arbitrariness on the side of the authorities and camp bosses. GULAG is still *our second signal system*, developed through the school of life under the condition of the lack of freedom so that it unconsciously determines our feelings, thoughts, and actions. Its essential element is fear, which has an existential character, fear of fear, because one constantly assumes the possibility of groundless abuse, humiliation, and physical violence by the state.

The GULAG itself might be one of the consequences of the fatalistic disposition to hardship inherent in our national character. An old Russian proverb says that one should never believe one can avoid imprisonment and poverty (*ne zarekaisya ot sumy i ot tiur'my*). Alexander Blok heard "the ennui of the prisoner" (*ostrozhnaya toska*) in coachman's songs and Soviet political prisoners would swallow "ennui like quinine" (*kak khinu glotali tosku*) (Vladimir Lifshitz) after the GULAG system had been officially abolished. There is plenty of evidence that this archetype still governs us today. We have only to look inside ourselves. "Freedom is when I am less afraid of policemen than of those from whom they protect me," said one young Russian some months ago.

GULAG forms a *specific optic* common to the Soviet man and the contemporary Russian when the unreal is perceived as the real. For example, it is possible to sing in 1936 about the endless vastness of the motherland, convinced that there is no other country "where man breathes so freely." One can go through the labor camps and feel nostalgic for the Stalinist times when "there was good order." One can feel proud of one's country living in a house without basic conveniences, a town without roads and social infrastructure, a shortage of schools and hospitals, surviving from one wage to another in an antisocial society. One can arrogantly despise other cultures for their way of life while ignoring one's own problems.

Fear and longing, as reflections of profound despair, form into an attitude of resentment. Resentment inherent in the GULAG-archetype can be reduced to a simple psychoanalytic formula of the *unconscious projection*: we hate the whole world because we live badly (a kind of aggression out of powerlessness and frustration). This includes such mental movements and emotions as envy, offence, distrust, suspicion, indifference, fixation on oneself and one's own problems (and the problems of those close to you), egoism, escapism, hostility, cruelty, and readiness to violence. The consequences of the constant preoccupation of a person, driven by resentment, with their self-preservation are the grinding factors of life resulting from the systematic exclusion of universal interests from it, the reduction of its content to their own well-being, the wasting of spiritual energy, the narrowing of the mind, and the erasure of the personality.

The breakdown of personality leads to the replacement of cultural mechanisms by social-biological mechanisms such as herd and adaptive behaviour, recognition of the authority of alpha individuals, and dominance of force over law, among others. The dignity of people and the character of events are then assessed and evaluated not according to moral criteria but by the parameters of power. A culture of recognizing the "strong," be they "heroes" or "bandits," is disseminated; the order of the penal zone is transferred to all levels of social interaction, including the state. The source of knowledge about such a subject of resentment, whose collective portrait I try to give here, is the extensive literature of Alexander I. Solzhenitsyn, Varlam T. Shalamov, Yevgenia S. Ginzburg, Vasily S. Grossman, Lydia K. Chukovskaya, Lev Z. Kopelev, and others.

Max Scheler, in *Resentment in the Structure of Morals* (1912), described resentment as "the self-poisoning of the soul." However, there must be an antidote for it. One needs only to accept the diagnosis and choose the proper course of treatment.

Literary Lessons

Reading Russian literature, both fictional and philosophical, provides another observation. It concerns the understanding of personhood in Russian culture. Its distinctive feature is that the core of personality is not an individual but a collective "I." There are many examples of this claim. There is the "communitarian" (*obschinnaia*) identity of an individual Alexander Herzen wrote about, linking the future development of Russia with "communitarian socialism." There is also the famous "*sobornost'*," a concept that was developed within Russian religious philosophy. This type of personality, in the Christian-Orthodox understanding, is a consciousness of internal unity of the individual with other people in God, resulting in a collective "spiritual labour" (*dukhovnoe delanie*) consecrated by God. Alexei S. Khomyakov, who introduced the concept of *sobornost'*, saw it as the spiritual unity of people bonded with each other by their love for God. There is also the Eurasian concept of "symphonic personality," a modernized concept of the catholic (*sobornaya*) personality. In the systematic presentation of their doctrine, the Eurasians declare that "personality is the unity of the multitude and the multitude of the unity" (Karsavin, 1926). Lev Karsavin, for example, writes: "Every act and every reaction of a Catholic (*sobornaia*) personality is not individual as such but is the coordination of a multitude of individual acts, of which each is specific and singularly individual, but nevertheless united with the others into a whole" (Karsavin, 1993, 128). There is also Vasily Rozanov's "generic nature" (*rodovoe nachalo*), in which he saw a socio-biological mechanism of regulation of interactions between people in addition to state regulation. There is also the "swarming nature" (*roevoe nachalo*) of the Russian people in Leo Tolstoy, personified in the image of Platon Karataev in *War and Peace*.

These theories share the belief that the personality expresses not a unique, pure "I," but an integrated whole to which the person's "I" organically belongs. This structure of personality was conceived (and is still conceived) by its adherents in a thoroughly positive sense. They associated it with openness to the world and with its communitarian, intersubjective character. Dostoevsky was one who recognized the problematic nature of the intersubjective personality and pointed to the negative cultural, historical, and political implications of such understanding of a person. Probably no one put it as vividly as he did in *The Brothers Karamazov*. Two chapters of the novel, *Elders* and *The Grand Inquisitor*, deal with the topic of delegating one's self.

The first of these chapters depicts the institution of spiritual teachers. An elder is

> one who took your soul, your will, into his soul and his will. When you choose an elder, you renounce your own will and yield it to him in complete submission, complete self-abnegation. This novitiate, this terrible school of abnegation, is undertaken voluntarily, in the hope of self-conquest, of self-mastery, in order, after a life of obedience, to attain perfect freedom, that is, from self; to escape the lot of those who have lived their whole life without finding their true selves in themselves.
> (Dostoevsky, 1985, 19)

Discipleship, connected with the renunciation of one's self, even if one hopes to find it again at the end of the way, is "the terrible school" of life. This implies that "the elders are endowed in certain cases with unbounded and inexplicable authority. That is why in many of our monasteries the institution was at first resisted almost to persecution." Besides, "this instrument which had stood the test of a thousand years for the moral regeneration of a man from slavery to freedom and to moral perfectibility may be a two-edged weapon and it may lead some not to humility and complete self-control but to the most Satanic pride, that is, to bondage and not to freedom" (Dostoevsky, 1985, 19).

In the chapter on the elders, Dostoevsky only pinpointed the dangers of alienating one's self. Further development of the plot reveals his deep skepticism toward this kind of practice. It is not a coincidence that the elder Zosima, Alyosha Karamazov's spiritual teacher, "stank" after his death, thus freeing the young man from his spiritual patronage and giving him back his self. Before the coffin of the elder Alyosha felt joy—"joy was glowing in his mind and in his heart" (Dostoevsky, 1985, 233). He felt this joy because "his soul, overflowing with rapture, yearned for freedom, space, openness" (Dostoevsky, 1985, 235). Alyosha "stood, gazed, and suddenly threw himself down on the earth"; however, "he had fallen on the earth a weak boy, but he rose up a resolute champion, and he knew and felt it suddenly at the very moment of his ecstasy" (Dostoevsky, 1985, 235).

Zosima's antipode, at first glance, is the Grand Inquisitor, who is convinced that "man has no greater anxiety in life than to find someone to whom he can make over that gift of freedom with which the unfortunate creature is born" (Dostoevsky, 1985, 166). Having usurped the freedom of the "weak" and "vicious" and made them "obedient," the Grand Inquisitor expects them to be grateful to those "who have consented to lead the masses and bear their burden of freedom by ruling over them" (Dostoevsky, 1985, 166). He requires gratitude for having freed the people from an independent choice in the knowledge of good and evil and compensated this with a concern for their material well-being. He explains his right to power over the people by the fact that he refers to those who "have possessed themselves of man's conscience, and hold in their hand man's daily bread" (Dostoevsky, 1985, 168).

The images of Zosima and the Grand Inquisitor seem to oppose each other, but, in effect, they differ only in the degree and purpose of the other's possession of freedom. Both carry with them the danger of the deprivation of one's self. The Grand Inquisitor can be regarded as the culmination and, at the same time, perversion of the idea of an intersubjective, externally formed personality. By showing this, Dostoevsky advocates the inalienability of individual freedom and the unacceptability of abandoning personal identity in favor of collective identity.

The inevitable consequence of understanding the human personality as the collective self is the underestimation of the individual. This can lead to a willingness to suppress the individual in favor of the collective, to prioritize the collective over the individual to the extent of ignoring the latter. Georges Florovsky, criticizing the Eurasianists' theory of the "symphonic personality" in his article *The Eurasian Temptation*, pointed to the peculiar dialectic of alienation of the individual personality in favor of the state. In Florovsky's view, the Eurasianists believe that in the free, internally guided growth of the "symphonic national personality," over the course of natural and necessary social differentiation, a kind of "catholic (*sobornaya*) personality" of the second order, the "ruling layer," emerges and forms. Within it, as its core, as its living stem, a "state active" appears— this is the "only ruling party." The system of consistent and continuous organic links between all layers, levels, and clusters of social being provides a direct and immediate correspondence between them in thought and will. By expressing and realizing their thought and their will, the ruling layer thereby expresses the "unconscious, spontaneous" but firm all-national common will, which in themselves they carry, know, and recognize (Florovsky, 1928, 322–3).

Florovsky states that

> in a naïve and fearful insensibility, Eurasianists do not notice that the people's will is fluctuating and diverse, that the 'people's cosmos' has never a single face. Not only because a single face manifests itself in a plurality of faces. That is the tragedy of the folk spirit—and it is an ineradicable tragedy—that there is not one face behind the variety of empirical faces.
>
> (Florovsky, 1928, 327)

He also argues that by delegating part of oneself to a higher authority one surrenders one's own freedom. In turn, a state is always ready to organize people and become their guiding force.

Dostoevsky's concern with the self-determination of a person and Florovsky's critique of Eurasianists' collective personality can be transposed to all institutions that do not regard the individual as a value in and of itself. The dangerous issue they have discovered in such institutions is an internal law of subordination, which ontologically degrades an individual and can lead the personality to complete and irreversible destruction. Its consequence can be the moral degradation of the individual, if the norms and guidelines offered to him by the authorities (a collective personality of higher order) are immoral. Following this logic, one can metaphorically say that the Great Inquisitor once returned in the image of the Soviet Union. In the image of Putin's Russia, the Grand Inquisitor achieves his second coming.

Mythological Consciousness

One of the tendencies in contemporary Russian society seems to be the mythologization of public consciousness. The myth appears as a condensed formula of a kind of knowledge that refers to a normative, undisputed logic of reasoning. Let us explain what we mean here. The mythologem "Moscow is the third Rome," attributed to the monk Philotheus of the Spaso-Eleazarovsk monastery in Pskov (sixteenth century), states that Moscow is the successor of the Roman Empire and Byzantium. Its use obliges us to accept the fact about the transfer of the political and religious center of the Orthodox world to Russia. Mythologems about the "golden" and "silver" centuries of Russian culture offer a schema of the degrading development of Russian culture. The myth of the "rogue nineties" is firmly associated with "Yeltsin's lawlessness" (*vol'nitsa*), inflation, unemployment, a total shortage of consumer goods, rampant violence, and flourishing corruption. This series of examples could be continued *ad infinitum*—"Kyiv is the mother of Russian cities" (hence, it is the Russian city), "The Great Patriotic War" (hence, the liberating, fair war), urban myths such as Moscow's and St. Petersburg's (as the antithesis of "specific way of development" and "Europeanization"), and so forth.

Myths share another commonality: they act as pressed texts and as mechanisms or codes of generating (unfolding) new texts while they set the direction of their production. As a result, myth-oriented knowledge is determined by this particular mythological code. It is obvious that, in this case, knowledge is incomplete, truncated, uncritical, often indoctrinated or ideologized, and sometimes even false. At the same time, it continues to be spread and ultimately forms the tradition within which people perceive facts and events. To some extent, the widespread distribution of mythologized thinking can be explained by the principle of economy of thought—myth provides ready-made, society sanctioned interpretations of reality. However, reality is often completely hidden behind the myth.

Mythologized thinking is most likely inherent in human beings as such. It fulfills many positive functions, including the integration of society (there is a vast literature on this topic). But a person who draws his beliefs about the world from myth easily becomes an object of manipulation, as Ernst Cassirer, for example, convincingly demonstrated in his book *The Myth of the State*. Yet Plato contrasted myth, which he referred to as unjustified opinion (*doxa*), with reliable knowledge (*epistēmē*). The problem in the field of history (past and present), the knowledge of which, in many ways, shapes our self-understanding, is that we rarely acquire this knowledge as immediate eyewitnesses. It is mostly not first-person but third-person knowledge, already mediated by someone else's interpretation. How, if at all, can we overcome myth?

Myth can be destroyed by literature. "Literature," as Lev Oshanin wrote, "is a confession. Under the guise of confession, it is preaching. For those we love it is a commandment. For those we hate it is a rebuke." Literature is a human attempt to understand life. Of course, there is *literature* and *Literature*, just as there are dishonest and honest people. And we are not talking about realism at all—not naturalist, socialist, fantastic, expressive, and its other literary forms. It is about truth, first-hand knowledge, an independent effort of the human being to understand what is happening. Viktor Astafyev's *Cursed and Killed* and Vladimir Voinovich's *The Life and Extraordinary Adventures of Private Ivan Chonkin*, despite the incompatibility of their respective genres, equally debunk the one-sided, superficially heroic myths of World War II.

Russian literature, the object of our national pride, which combines our philosophy, historiography, and psychoanalysis, has done a tremendous job of searching for historical truth, reworking the social traumas of the past, and revealing our true collective face. It is the most important source of our self-knowledge. The revolution, the two world wars, the Civil War, the foundation and the collapse of the Soviet Union, *perestroika*, the decade of failed democracy, Putin's time—all these events have received a lively echo in our literature. If we knew this literature, we would be different today. But unfortunately, we do not know it and, moreover, we are not ready for this type of self-critical reading and pursuit of the true meaning of what is being said and done. In fact, it is easier for us to bring a writer to trial than to accept our own faults (for example, the case of Svetlana Alexievich for her book *Boys in Zinc*). After all, the spread of mythology occurs not only through the narrowing of cultural space but also through the deformation of the real meaning of things on the part of the ideology of the dominant myths. Our literature, our national pride, now becomes increasingly subject to state censorship.

Some Parallels

Considering the revolution of 1917, which imposed party dictatorship on the country, Archpriest Georges Florovsky wrote that "one must understand and recognize that Russian turmoil has a deep spiritual root, it is the result and finale of an old and long-standing spiritual crisis, a painful inner collapse." He believed that "only in the feat of repentance, in the rigorous temptation of spiritual sobering, the true exit from the maelstrom of gleeful evil may be revealed and opened. Spiritual disruption should be answered by the feat of purification, internal work and gathering," even if "it is a difficult and harsh path" on which "the terrible abyss of Russian apostasy and infidelity will be exposed." He was convinced that "one should not to be afraid and be ashamed of such confessions, to indulge in cowardly dreams of past prosperity and shift everything to someone else's guilt. There is no apostasy or curse in repentance. And only in it is the fullness of patriotic boldness, courage, and strength" (Florovsky, 1928, 314).

Reflecting on today's historical situation—the war in Ukraine—and trying to understand its deeper causes, one suddenly notices that the distance separating these events reveals a strange closeness between them. In both cases, society's lingering illness has come to the historical surface, and in both cases, the settlement of the problems implies a change in people's worldviews and mentality. An effective way to do this is self-knowledge, which is accessible through an uneasy, honest, and sometimes unflattering study of our history and literature.

References

Dostoevsky, Fyodor M. 1985. *Bratya Karamasovy* [*The Brothers Karamazov*]. Moscow: Khudozhestvennaya literatura.

Florovsky, Georges. 1928. "Evraziyskiy soblazn*"* [The Eurasian Temptation]. *Sovremennye zapiski*, 34, 312–46. https://pravbeseda.ru/library/index.php?page=book&id=323

Ilyin, Ivan A. 2006. *Put' dukhovnogo obnovleniya* [*The Way of Spiritual Renewal*]. Moscow: ACT.

Karsavin, Lev P. 1926. *Evraziystvo. Opyt sistematicheskogo izlozhenija* [*Eurasianism. An Attempt of Systematic Exposition*]. Paris: Evraziyskoe knogoizdatel'stvo. https://predanie.ru/book/220959-evraziystvo-opyt-sistematicheskogo-izlozheniya/#/toc1

Karsavin, Lev P. 1993. *Zerkov', lichnost' i gosudarstvo* [*Church, Person and State*]. *Sochineniya* [*Writings*]. Moscow: Raritet.

Putin, Vladimir V. 2022. Obrashchenie k uchastnikam i gostyam X Moskovskoy konferencii po mezhdunarodnoy bezopasnosti [Address to the Participants and Guests of the 10th Moscow International Security Conference on August 16, 2022]. http://www.kremlin.ru/events/president/transcripts/69166

10

The Viscosity of Russian Space: An Essay in Structural Analysis

Helen Petrovsky

In his prewar novel *Doctor Garin*, Vladimir Sorokin, who is known to readers worldwide, describes the trials and tribulations of his main character, an unorthodox psychiatrist, who is driven out of his comfortable Altai clinic by a regular outburst of war (Sorokin, 2021, 9ff.). He is forced to embark on a long eastbound journey for the city of Khabarovsk, which, in this new world shattered by repeated wars, enjoys the status of an independent republic. The journey itself is long and fraught with danger. This voluminous book is indeed a travel novel, if one wants to define it in traditional terms. However, Sorokin is famous for his experiments with form as well as his sharply cinematic vision. Without going into details, let us pay attention to two indicators that will be important for my further remarks related to the problematic of space and its topological coordinates. First, Garin is forced to cross Eurasia, which is split into autonomous and conflicting spaces due to a permanent state of war between a whole set of newly established republics. At one point he even rows a boat along the powerful Siberian river Ob. In short, he is traversing, almost blindly, a big expanse of land guided by a general sense of direction. Of course, one might think of this lack of orientation (Garin carries no belongings, fleeing Barnaul in a bathrobe after its sudden bombardment) in terms of how the novel is structured from a purely formal perspective. He *has* to be unaware of the exact itinerary in order to experience the various adventures that will accompany his journey and thus form the plot of the novel. However, on another level, this account is about the dangers of boundless and ill-defined space, which points not so much to a contested political map as to heterogeneity, so to speak, in action.

Second, one of Garin's most traumatic episodes is his capture by the so-called "filthies"[1] or "sooties" (*chernyshy*), a tribe of mutants firmly settled in cold Siberian swamps. As the story goes, they are survivors of a special breed of super soldiers "impervious to cold and unfavorable climatic conditions" (Sorokin, 2021, 397). In fact, their name derives from the thick black hair covering their bodies and faces. This clandestine population, which has created a whole city out of tree trunks and other wooden debris in the middle of a forest quagmire, emerged as a result of a genetic research project first overturned by the US Senate and later stolen by the KGB. However, as time went by, the secret research was canceled during *perestroika*, and adult mutants, both male and female, were expected to move to the far north to explore new oil and gas resources, while teenagers were destined for special children's homes. Instead, the sooties rebelled and ran off to the Barabinsky wetlands. Since they became involved in heavy looting, it was decided to get rid of the mutants with the help of a tactical nuke. The surviving sooties moved still farther to the north and their forays continued. As Garin later discovers, all captives (including himself) are engaged in the preparation of a magic ritual, namely, they keep carving wooden smartphones that will eventually combine into a huge cross-like stake in the form of an axe. The destruction of the axe signals the beginning of a local orgy meant to increase the mutants' repopulation rate. Of course, this chapter is likely to be seen as a parable and/or some sort of dystopia: the sooties are ruthless with their prisoners, whom they regularly punish by drowning in the swamp without any sign of remorse.

It is not my intention here to give a reading of these science fiction characters, comparing them with the zombies in Sorokin's saga (*Doctor Garin* is a sequel to *The Blizzard* (2010)), for example, who incidentally inhabit the underground world. Rather, I would like to emphasize their tenacious boggy existence as well as the complex image of the quagmire developed in this chapter. It is interesting how Sorokin mixes fact and fiction, since the Barabinsky wetlands are an actual site located in Western Siberia. In fact, the geographical aspect of his entire account seems to be thorough and truthful. Of course, the style in *Doctor Garin* is reminiscent of nineteenth-century writing, including choice of words (i.e., the lexicon in general), depictions of nature and a rather unusual lyrical tone. Still, Sorokin is a truly modern writer in that expectations produced by such literary devices stand in contrast to the imaginary and oftentimes ironic content of the narrative itself (the cargo—or perhaps anti-cargo—cult gulag hidden in a forest; Garin's escape through a poetically frozen swamp[2]; the doctor's sex with an albino sootie; his own initiation into magic, which leads to an airplane appearing out of nowhere, and so on). However fantastic, the sooties clearly display one obvious truth: it is impossible for humans to survive in such an environment, bitter cold in winter and full of swarming mosquitoes in summer. But most importantly, it is the swamp itself that denies any regular movement whatsoever. In order to inhabit or even cross it, one has to be a sootie, that is, a supernatural being. It is not accidental that Garin flees the camp with the secret help of a local guide and does so only when the impassible swamp begins to freeze over, in other words, when the wetland shows signs of transformation into something other than itself.

At this point we might switch from literature to physics, which has been my intention all along. Sorokin's metaphor of the bog, containing a whole array of cultural connotations (besides the ones already mentioned in passing), can be expressed in one single word—viscosity. Indeed, what *is* a wetland or a bog? A substance that sucks in, sucks down, engulfs, paralyzing any kind of movement or maneuver. It is helpful to be reminded of the physical definition of the term:

> resistance of a fluid (liquid or gas) to a change in shape, or movement of neighboring portions relative to one another. Viscosity denotes opposition to flow. The reciprocal of the viscosity is called the fluidity, a measure of the ease of flow. ... Because part of a fluid that is forced to move carries along to some extent adjacent parts, viscosity may be thought of as internal friction between the molecules; such friction opposes the development of velocity differences within a fluid.
> (Gregersen, 2023)

From this definition I would like to retain, first of all, the opposition between viscosity and fluidity, as well as the idea of internal resistance. In the following pages I will dramatically change the scale by observing my chosen object—i.e., space—from a bird's eye view. However, the space I am interested in is not a neutral entity. It is an abstraction with respect to the territory of a single country that has historically gone by different names—Muscovy, the Russian Empire, the USSR, and currently the Russian Federation. This transcontinental state, spanning both Europe and Asia and remaining the largest country in the world, has repeatedly demonstrated its aggressive nature. It is my hope that by giving a closer look at the problem of space we might acquire some understanding as to why this country has dramatically set itself against the rest of the world by invading Ukraine on February 24, 2022.

* * *

I will now turn to a concept that was formulated back in 1993 by Vadim Tsymbursky (1957–2009), a refined classicist turned political thinker. Whatever the interpretations of his geopolitical constructs may be (and indeed there are attempts to line him up with the most conservative figures, especially these days), his vision of "Island Russia" remains original and captivating (Tsymbursky, n.d.). It should be mentioned that, according to the author, the very question of Russia's geopolitical identity becomes particularly poignant after 1991, that is, after the dissolution of the Soviet Union. Tsymbursky sets himself the task of singling out a "basic pattern," underlying the Russian Empire, the USSR, and the post-1991 Russian Federation. Right from the beginning, he rejects both the "heartland" theory advocated by the pioneering British geographer Halford Mackinder and the concept of Eurasia, which has always had many enthusiastic proponents. In other words, it is not control over the steppes and the wasteland, bordering in the north on a colossal forest range, that defines Russia's geopolitical identity. Tsymbursky makes it clear that Russia's new—noticeably more modest—territorial composition allows one to discern "signs of some very early alternative to the great imperial development." The implied pattern, connecting different forms of Russian statehood, is rooted in Muscovy, or the Tsardom of Russia, in its seventeenth-century guise. Although attentive to political geography and geography in general, Tsymbursky opts for what he claims to be an antireductionist approach: he insists on defining geopolitical identity in terms of "ethnocivilizational platforms" and their spatial distribution. So, essentially, it all boils down to space.

After these preliminary remarks the scholar goes on to examine Russia's three basic features in its capacity as a geopolitical object. The first is defined precisely by the Russian ethnocivilizational platform, which, however, has nothing to do with the idea of "Russia for Russians." This specific "niche," which occupies a huge expanse of land between Europe and China, is a combination of several smaller "niches," forming a single state, namely, those that were historically inhabited by the peoples of the Volga region, the Urals and Siberia. Russia's second defining trait is the vastness of its eastern lands, which hampers their colonization and development. Despite antiquated fears, there is no threat coming from those parts. Indeed, Muscovy succeeded in the solution of the "Kazan question" (the suppression of its gravest enemy, the Tartars) and provided for a breakthrough into the "seeming boundlessness of eastern difficult spaces: the steppes, the taiga, the tundra, and the oceans." Still, the true enemies remained extremely far away, separated by the "difficult spaces," which left the eastern boundary open before the encounter with the Chinese and "for a long time indeterminate even after." Finally, the third defining feature is the fact that in the West Russia is separated from Romano-Germanic Europe, the hotbed of liberal civilization, by a belt made up of peoples and territories, adjoining "native" Europe without, however, being its part. The interspace between the "first center of modernization and the Russian platform" is what Tsymbursky chooses to call *strait-territories*.[3] This geographical region (Eastern Europe as opposed to Central Europe) has a dramatic history influenced by both of its neighbors: suffice it to recall the constant presence of the "Russian heel," on the one hand, as well as a "barbaric" refeudalization of the region in question, on the other.

I will not go into all the intricacies of this model. Tsymbursky declares Russia an insular state with its own geopolitical priorities. They include, first of all, western *strait-territories* successfully involved in early twentieth-century modernization, then southern *strait-territories*, pointing to lands regarded as "appendages of the West," and, finally, the difficult spaces that were already there before the beginning of the "great imperial phase" and that appear to be full of promise for the future of the Russian Federation. I would suggest that Tsymbursky's primary interest lies in the dynamic aspect of his model: depending on historical circumstances, Russia would either expand to embrace its *strait-territories* or, on the contrary, shrink to its initial seventeenth-century core. Moreover, there is a hidden dialectic at work in this process: whenever Russia would make a move to the East, it would do so, in one way or another, to counter Europe and its strategic interests in other parts of the world (this is described in terms of "a calculated western ricochet"). As for the desire itself to "absorb" the *strait-territories* separating Europe and Russia, it is motivated by the strongest geopolitical myth since the time of Peter the Great, namely, the "abduction of Europe." This age-long leaning toward the West potentially leads to a shift in the balance of power. Tsymbursky insightfully explains such "Euromania" from the perspective of space: "Our Westernizers never wanted to acknowledge that precisely as a European nation Russia, because of its vastness, even irrespective of the intentions of its leaders, is incompatible with European balance." His general conclusion is that Russian (pan)continentalism (the expansion of the heartland toward the seaboard) is itself but a derivative of the powerful abduction myth.

I am tempted to mention other intriguing remarks, such as the fate of European culture as it was disseminated in Russia throughout the eighteenth and nineteenth centuries. Tsymbursky does not content himself with simply stating that the European traits of Imperial Russian culture combined with a non-European type of sociality. He speaks instead of the endogenous rhythms of this reception, which resulted in a "fantastical heterochronic concentrate," generating a series of "non-western syntheses" (his examples of artistic styles, including the Russian Baroque, Renaissance, romanticism and realism, could be supplemented with others not necessarily connected with aesthetics). Still, my primary concern is space, so I will have to limit the scope of this doctrine by focusing on what Tsymbursky calls *difficult spaces*. We remember that they are situated in the east and that their boundary remains essentially fuzzy. Although the author's emphasis is Russia's insularity, by recalling grotesque accounts of early European travelers, he actually refers us to those spaces: a vast and impassable country, Russia is covered with shrubs and swamps; to cross them, log paths have to be built; the land is uninhabited for dozens of miles and yet is heavily guarded. To this we must add Tsymbursky's own poetically vague definition: "the steppes, the taiga, the tundra, the oceans." It should come as no surprise that these depictions fit very well into Vladimir Sorokin's *Doctor Garin*. "Difficult spaces," a way of implying the colonization of the east, its terminal points being Sakhalin and North Kazakhstan (Tsymbursky briefly compares it to the American frontier), are paradoxically neither a geographical location nor even direction. Rather, they serve as an indication of two interrelated things: first, the difficulty in rational thinking and, second, something other than representation itself. I would argue that "difficult spaces" are a necessary precondition for conceptualizing Russian space.

However, let us take a moment to ponder on what this word combination might actually stand for. Prompted by Tsymbursky's reference to travelers' accounts, I will briefly mention the connotations implied by the notion of Siberia or, prior to that, the lands situated in the east. Thus, in a text dating from 1689 and written by a French Jesuit in disguise, we already come across the following passage:

> Having conquered the kingdoms of Astrakhan and Kazan, he [Ivan the Terrible] at last discovered part of that vast land called Siberia, which means 'prison' in the Slavonic language, for this naturally cruel prince dispatched to these formerly nameless lands those whom he had disgraced. It is to the latter that we owe the Siberian marten and also a route to China. They found it by penetrating further and further into those vast deserts, full of chasms, impenetrable and unmapped forests which, by all appearances, stretch right to the polar sea.
>
> (De la Neuville, 1994, 65)

Here, despite the false etymology (*sibir* means simply "northern"), we get an immediate sense of two combined significations, namely, of a form of punishment—forced colonization prefiguring penal servitude (*katorga*) in Imperial Russia—and the "difficulty" of the land itself.[4] I will pick up on the mythological characteristics of this space later on. The other, much more famous account belongs to an earlier time and was written by the German scientist and traveler Adam Olearius. His meticulous and lively narrative of the Russian and Persian legation, being a big success, was translated into several languages during his lifetime. It contains descriptions of the Russian state in terms of its political, geographical and climatic features.

Although I focused on Olearius's remarks about the Russian land, it so happened that, working with two different translations, I came upon a telling omission in the English version of his text. As I hope to show, it is not accidental and has to do with the ramifications of the space in question.

Since Olearius writes about Russia in the beginning of the seventeenth century, he cannot but give a general sketch of its territory, mentioning either the "Moors and Fens, which take up a great part of the Country," or the "Fens and Forests, which *Muscovy* is well stor'd with," which, however, does not hinder agriculture whenever and wherever the land is cultivated by the locals (Olearius, 1669, 48). Naturally, this forested country is "very well furnish'd with all sorts of Venison and Fowl." Next comes a rather detailed passage about hares and the reason for their seasonal changing of color:

> The Hares are grey, but in some Provinces they turn white in Winter, as in *Livonia*; and yet in *Courland*, which is contiguous to that Province, and divided from it only by the river *Dune*, the Hares change not their colour. 'Tis no hard matter to find the reason of this change, which must proceed from external cold; since I have known, that, even in Summer, Hares have chang'd their colour, when they have been kept some time in a Cave.
>
> (Olearius, 1669, 49)

However, in the Russian translation the same passage is enhanced with a most striking supplement:

> The reason for this change of color is their temperament. ... The truth is that, because of the fenny and moist terrain, these animals are of a much more phlegmatic, that is, moist and cold nature, than our hares [sic!]. If external cold is added in winter ..., they become white, since the white color is produced by the cold ... in the same way as black is produced by the heat. Now, if in summer they are again exposed to hot and dry air, which, of course, occurs in those parts, both their temperament and color change.
>
> (Olearius, 1986, 332)

This is something that would not find its way into a "faithful rendering" into the English language performed around 1669, even if the translator's task was also to shorten the text.[5] Indeed, the passage is mythological and not scientific. Moreover, it defies scientific rationality, including the content and composition of Olearius's own carefully structured account.[6] But what it does bring to light is that aspect of space which remains irreducibly "difficult," in other words, which, in the most "fenny" and obstinate manner, resists any notion of form, be it solid ground, mainland Europe or even geopolitics. The swamp, therefore, far from simply representing some impossible terrain, points to space in terms of its structure.

* * *

Why is it so important to understand the structure of Russian space? If we use the word structure in the proper sense, then we will have to admit that what we are dealing with in "real life" are only so many of its actualizations. And they are not at all random, to be sure. The specificity of Russian culture is often accounted for by an exploration of its chthonic elements, the ancient Greek χθών, *khthōn* meaning "earth" or "soil" (to be more exact, the Greek adjective is used in reference to what is beneath the surface of the earth, i.e., the underworld). And indeed, there are attempts to analyze contemporary Russia in terms of waste, darkness, and death, especially after the beginning of the Russia–Ukraine war in 2022.[7] However, the chthonic itself is a well-established and even respectable term dealing first with ancient Greek mythology. Of course, whatever is chthonic in Russia can be seen as one of the infinite variations of some basic underlying matrix. And this brings us back precisely to the notion of structure. Here I am guided by both the work of Claude Lévi-Strauss on structural anthropology (Lévi-Strauss, 1963) and an early interpretation of structure proposed by Gilles Deleuze (Deleuze, 1967). Of the many ways of explaining myth offered by Lévi-Strauss in his study, Deleuze singles out a parallel that the anthropologist establishes between myth and psychoanalysis. Highlighting the unconscious in terms of its symbolic function, Lévi-Strauss describes it as that which is "always empty— or, more accurately … alien to mental images as is the stomach to the foods which pass through it. As the organ of a specific function, the unconscious merely imposes structural laws upon inarticulated elements which originate elsewhere—impulses, emotions, representations, and memories" (Lévi-Strauss, 1963, 203). This might serve as an accurate definition of structure. However, it would be legitimate to pose the following question: why cannot a mythology linked to the earth be the starting point for one's reflections on Russian culture and its repetitive traits? As I have indicated, it can and already has. Yet the distinguishing feature of any structure is that it is neither binding nor static. In addition to the symbolic, Deleuze speaks of it in terms of differential relations and singular points.[8] Therefore, the myth of the earth is only part of the story. Besides implying the underground, it also presupposes a vertical thrust, so to say, which in Russian history is famously embodied in the triad of tsarist autocracy, Christian Orthodoxy and serfdom, an effective way of "attaching" peasants to the soil. All this, however, is on the side of form and its permutations.

The structure I am implying is dual in the sense that it is an *oscillation between form and its constant denial*, and this is what I choose to call *viscosity*. In a word, it is the ever reappearing swamp—a dangerous imitation of earth or a real chasm (whatever it is) in the desert.[9] As a structure it does not even have to be named, but for the purposes of clarity a physical connotation might prove to be helpful. At this point it is necessary to bring together the various strands of thought presented in this chapter. I will start by reiterating that structure is opposed to the idea of the whole. In other words, it is a dynamic relationship between the whole and its parts.[10] This needs to be emphasized, because structure tends to be associated exactly with a finished whole, something that we can represent or imagine, whereas what is implied is a specific theoretical construct. In the language of philosophy, it would be the same as admitting that a change of attributes brings about a change in essence. However, structure has absolutely nothing to do with essence, it is a version of non-essentialist thinking that privileges transformation and its laws over the stability of concepts. Speaking of viscosity somewhat complicates the case, for we are seemingly dealing with structure per se. And yet it is my understanding that viscosity viewed as the structure of Russian space allows us to account for what Tsymbursky calls endogenous "non-western syntheses" or "non-European sociality." Something not unlike an ongoing tacit resistance to form permeates the Russian cultural and political landscapes. In other words, the expanded myth of the earth[11] must be treated in conjunction with its other, that is, viscous or "difficult" spaces. We may decide to associate them with wetlands or bogs, and that would be a rightful image pointing to the structure itself. I would suggest that this image is, perhaps, its most salient manifestation, since it appeals to our experience at different levels all at once (the swamp as a natural feature of the landscape, an element of folklore, a metaphor or literary theme and even, as we have discovered, an intriguing scientific myth). It is remarkable how Russian folklore already pinpoints the dangers of the bog: this charmed place is inhabited by supernatural creatures precisely because of its dual nature, that is, neither water nor earth. However, it should be understood that any structure generates series of alternating images, including outright substitutions and replacements, so my examples are just the very first step in this direction, if one decides to follow it.

Indeed, so far, we have been dealing with space in a more or less direct way. There is another aspect of the problem that I would like to briefly mention in conclusion. The territory of Russia has been a challenge already at the level of imagination: it is very hard, perhaps impossible, to grasp or imagine its scope. Tsymbursky mentions ancient and justifiable fears voiced at various times by Karl Marx, Astolfe de Custine, and Henry Adams of "an encroachment on Europe of some alien force." For him, it is the question of control over the *strait-territories* bordering Russia. I will leave aside this geopolitical interpretation and simply focus on the issue of scope. To get a better sense of what it may stand for in structural terms, let us recall Dostoevsky's famous idea of "universal responsiveness" demonstrated by the Russian people and best of all expressed by Alexander Pushkin in his works.[12] According to Oleg Aronson's fresh reading of the "Pushkin Speech," the hidden logic of this responsiveness is of a very special order. It is not about whether Russian culture is original or secondary (that is why, in fact, the speech was enthusiastically accepted by both the Westernizers and the Slavophiles). Being an "autochthonous entity," the culture we are analyzing displays a rare capacity "to accept foreign cultures as if they were *always already* part of Russian culture" in spite of their alterity and even hostility. Moreover, Pushkin himself as the embodiment of universal responsiveness is "a part" of both Russian and world culture, which is indistinguishable from "the whole." Therefore, what is at stake is not the "sovereignty or the unity of the 'Russian,' but universality [*vsemirnost'*] (the whole), which knows no boundaries and surpasses all the boundaries between peoples and cultures" (Aronson, 2017, 227-8). This logic may be equally applied to Russian space; I would even go so far as to suggest that its cultural manifestation derives precisely from the vastness of the land. In other words, universal responsiveness—i.e., a responsiveness congruent with the entire world, nothing less—corresponds to pure space, an entity that is boundless or formless. We are well aware of the political ramifications of this attitude, be it conscious or unconscious: it translates into expansion. Time will show under what circumstances this attitude will be ultimately overcome.

P.S. Commenting on a recent survey conducted by the Levada Center, an independent polling and sociological research organization, one of its leading members Alexei Levinson attempted to describe the current state of mass consciousness in Russia (Fishman, 2023). The figures are indeed stunning: three-fourths of the adult population of the country declare their support for the so-called "special military operation" (an official euphemism for the ongoing Russia-Ukraine war). This correlates with Putin's exceptionally high ratings, which remain almost unaltered since March 2022 at a little over 80 percent. Levinson insists that those ratings are not the assessment of Putin as a person, but instead have to do with a "symbolic object." Now the object in question is nothing less than the "grandeur" of Russia. And the only aspiration that Putin fulfills, which defines his actual function, is "to maintain the glory of Russia." This observation and especially the respondents' readiness to endure hardships produced by Western sanctions cannot but contradict common sense. Yet the cited figures uncover one simple truth: they do not stand for the approval of Putin's personality, but affirm "one's symbolic importance on the earth." Hence a general "numbness" or, I would add, a shocking indifference to what is actually happening in Ukraine. This is not a mere reversal of "universal responsiveness." (We should not underestimate the power of Russian propaganda; besides, the survey does not account for the entire population of the country.) There is something in this attitude that corresponds to the enormity of space itself—indifferent, totalizing, and empty.

Notes

1 This translation is proposed by Galina Dursthoff (Dursthoff, n.d.).
2 "He looked back too. The fallen timber was already far behind. There was no pursuit. Behind there lay the swamp in all its monstrous and chaotic grandeur" (Sorokin, 2021, 481).
3 The term is given this English equivalent by the author himself.
4 It is interesting that the Russian translation altogether omits the disturbing attribute "full of chasms" (cf.: " … ces vastes deserts, couverts de fonds, de forêts impraticables, & inconnus, qui s'étendent jusqu'à la mer glaciale" in the French original (De la Neuville [1699], 208)). In fact, this can be seen as an indirect reference to the *tundras*, if we take into account that they are "northern uninterrupted bogs, lowlands [des fonds? chasms?] with purely mossy vegetation, with reindeer and Iceland moss" (Dahl, 1955, 110).
5 The cave Olearius speaks of turns out to be his late father-in-law's, where he kept those hares in preparation for the wedding of one of his daughters.
6 In alluding to humoral theory, Olearius is bravely applying it well beyond the human realm.
7 In a most recent study the cultural critic Mikhail Epstein, for example, speaks of the chthonic as a "religion of the earth." For Epstein, the chthonic stands for penetration "into the bowels of the earth" as well as proliferation on its surface (Epstein, 2023, 162, 164).
8 "Symbolic elements are incarnated in the real beings and objects of the domain considered; the differential relations are actualized in real relations between these beings; the singularities are so many places in the structure, which distributes the imaginary attitudes or roles of the beings or objects that come to occupy them" (Deleuze, 1967, 177).
9 I am indebted to Oleg Aronson for his brilliantly insightful and helpful discussions.

10 "[S]tructure is not at all defined by an autonomy of the whole, by a preeminence [*pregnance*] of the whole over its parts, by a *Gestalt* which would operate in the real and in perception. Structure is defined, on the contrary, by the nature of certain atomic elements which claim to account both for the formation of wholes and for the variation of their parts" (Deleuze, 1967, 173).

11 I do not see how the chthonic, according to Epstein, stands for proliferation on the surface of the earth, although I would agree with his remark about the territory of Russia displaying its own expanding—"hustling"—gravitation (Epstein, 2023, 168). On the other hand, the so-called "vertical" (an allusion to Putin's political system) has been there all along, dating from the Russian Tsardom and the corresponding notion of a divine communal essence.

12 "There had been in the literatures of Europe men of colossal artistic genius—a Shakespeare, a Cervantes, a Schiller. But show me one of these great geniuses who possessed such a capacity for universal sympathy as our Pushkin. This capacity, the pre-eminent capacity of our nation, he shares with our nation, and by that above all he is our national poet. The greatest of European poets could never so powerfully embody in themselves the genius of a foreign, even a neighboring, people, its spirit in all its hidden depth, and all its yearning after its appointed end, as Pushkin could" (Dostoevsky, 1880).

References

Aronson, Oleg. 2017. *Sily lozhnogo. Opyty nepoliticheskoi demokratii* [*The Powers of the False. Essays in Non-Political Democracy*]. Moscow: Falanster Publ.

Dahl, Vladimir. 1955. *Tolkovyi slovar' zhivogo velikorusskogo iazyka. T. I* [*Explanatory Dictionary of the Living Great Russian Language. Vol. I*]. Moscow: Gosudarstvennoe izdatel'stvo inostrannykh i natsional'nykh slovarei Publ.

De la Neuville, Foy. M. DC. XCIX [1699]. *Relation curieuse et nouvelle de Moscovie. Contenant L'état present de cet Empire. Les Expeditions des Moscovites en Crimée, en 1689. Les causes des dernieres Revolutions. Leurs Mœurs, & leur Religion. Le Recit d'un Voyage de Spatarus, par terre, à la Chine.* La Haye: Chez Meyndert Uytwerf Marchand Libraire près de la Cour.

De la Neuville, Foy. 1994. *A Curious and New Account of Muscovy in the Year 1689*, edited and introduced by Lindsey Hughes. Translated by J.A. Cutshall. London: School of Slavonic and East European Studies, University of London.

Deleuze, Gilles. 1967. "How Do We Recognize Structuralism?" *PLACE (Psychoanalysis California Los Angeles Extension)*. https://www.topoi.net/wp-content/uploads/2012/12/How_Do_We_Recognize_Structuralism.pdf

Dostoevsky, Fyodor. 1880. "Pushkin Speech." *SAC*. © *Alan Kimball*. https://pages.uoregon.edu/kimball/DstF.Puw.lct.htm#DstF.Puw.lct

Dursthoff, Galina. n.d. "Vladimir Sorokin. Doctor Garin. Proposal." *Literary Agency Galina Dursthoff*. https://dursthoff.de/?page_id=640

Epstein, Mikhail. 2023. *Russkii antimir. Politika na grani apokalipsisa* [*The Russian Anti-World: Politics on the Verge of Apocalypse*]. USA: Franc-Tireur.

Fishman, Mikhail. 2023. "I tak dalee s Mikhailom Fishmanom [Etcetera with Mikhail Fishman]." *TV Rain*, May 26. https://www.youtube.com/watch?v=2fFguTht1nI

Gregersen, Erik. 2023. "Viscosity." *Britannica*. Last modified June 26, 2023. https://www.britannica.com/science/viscosity

Lévi-Strauss, Claude. 1963. *Structural Anthropology*. Translated by Claire Jacobson and Brooke Grundfest Schoepf. New York: Basic Books.

Olearius, Adam. 1669. *The Voyages and Travells of the Ambassadors Sent by Frederick Duke of* Holstein, *to the Great Duke of Muscovy, and the King of Persia, Begun in the year M. DC. XXXIII. and finish'd in M. DC. XXXIV. Containing a Compleat History of Muscovy, Tartary, Persia. And other adjacent countries. With several Publick Transactions reaching near the Present Times; In VII. Books*. Faithfully rendered into English, by John Davies. The Second Edition Corrected. London: John Starkey, and Thomas Basset.

Olearius, Adam. 1986. "Opisanie puteshestviia v Moskoviiu [An Account of the Travel to Muscovy]." In *Rossiia XV–XVII vv. glazami inostrantsev* [*15th–17th Centuries Russia as Viewed by Foreigners*]. Edited and introduced by Yu. A. Limonov, 287–470. Leningrad: Lenizdat Publ.

Sorokin, Vladimir. 2021. *Doktor Garin* [*Doctor Garin*]. Moscow: AST Publ.

Tsymbursky, Vadim. n.d. "Ostrov Rossiia [Island Russia]." *Intelros*. http://www.intelros.ru/subject/figures/1072-vadim_cymburskijj_ostrov_rossija.html

Part Three

Does Russia Have a Future?

Cyclical Progress: The Eternal Return of Modernity

Vladimir Marchenkov

Introduction

This collection of chapters transparently draws inspiration from the tradition established by the *Milestones* (sometimes translated as *Landmarks*), published in 1909, as a philosophical summing-up of Russia's historical experience in the preceding half-century or so, especially as far as the intelligentsia was concerned. The *Milestones* became an epochal event in Russia's intellectual life, but we know how hostile the intelligentsia's reaction to it was. This was not surprising, for it was this social group's outlook that the authors of the collection subjected to a devastating critique. Their criticisms had no effect on the immediate course of history. In the words of Peter Struve, publisher of the next instalment in this tradition, *De Profundis* (1919), "The [future] historian will note that the majority of the Russian educated society did not heed the warning addressed to it, failing to comprehend the great danger that threatened culture and the state" (Askol'dov, 1991, 5).[1] Russia's choice over the decade in between seemed to be a direct polemic against the *Milestones*, with a vengeance. The Revolution and change of political system took the country down a far more radical path than even the intelligentsia had wished and in the opposite direction of the one the *Milestones* stood for. Our "collective statement" (this volume) is likewise unlikely to affect the course of history—not in the foreseeable future at least. By saying this I do not presume to equal such thinkers as Nikolai Berdyaev or Sergei Bulgakov but simply acknowledge a sad fact. Politics is removed from the deeper life of the mind even farther today than a century ago. Contemporary politics is a dense blend of farce and *danse macabre*. It is a farce, in part, because, according to Hegel's famous observation, when history repeats itself, it turns from tragedy into that less earnest genre. The political process has become a burlesque, while the actions of various regimes bring death and destruction to the less developed regions of the world and frequently condemn to further suffering the poorest and most oppressed populations in their own homelands. Politicians are Macbeth's "poor players who strut and fret their hour upon the stage and then are heard no more" (Shakespeare, 1975, 1068, modified). But their third-rate acting is a threadbare veil over the bloody *danses macabres* unleashed upon nations that are the most defenseless against their power. The reader will be deeply in error if he or she decides that I have only the Husseins, the Gaddafis, and the Putins in mind. Far from it. I see these figures, whose reality is no longer discernible under thick layers of gory makeup applied by Western propaganda, in the same line-up as the Clintons, the Bushes, the Trumps, the Merkels, and the Johnsons of the world.

What, then, are we counting down *to*, what finale in this cruel performance act, in which, as Jean Baudrillard noted with apprehension, reality has become indistinguishable from fictions propagated by the media? As I write these lines, on the 25th of January 2023, the *Bulletin of the Atomic Scientists* has moved the Doomsday Clock to 90 seconds to midnight. Noam Chomsky has been tirelessly speaking, for decades, of two scenarios that the notion of countdown is applicable to: the impending ecological catastrophe and humanity's nuclear self-annihilation (Chomsky, 2020, 14-45). The same pair of fatal threats, we may recall, was raised by Andrei Sakharov in his 1968 *Progress, Coexistence, and Intellectual Freedom* (Sakharov, 1968, 33-7), and then raised again, polemically, by Alexander Solzhenitsyn in the 1974 collection *From Under the Rubble* (Solzhenitsyn, 1974, 3). Among numerous others, significantly for my argument, these thinkers are echoed by the philosopher Errol E. Harris, who sees precisely these two problems as the most urgent and pressing today (Harris, 2000, 79).

Both outcomes can be avoided, Chomsky believes, with the help of a common effort of all nations, guided by a rational political will. One could agree with him, if one put the emphasis on the notion of "rational will" and especially on the concept of *reason* that ought to direct history to the path of salvation. It is doubtful that the form of reason embraced by most contemporary scientists, including Chomsky, is fit for this task. The triumphalist liberalism of Francis Fukuyama is even less suited for the purpose: Hasn't "liberal hegemony," to use John Mearsheimer's phrase, been the banner under which neoliberalism conducted its policies over the past thirty-odd years, with devastating consequences (Mearsheimer, 2018, viii *et passim*)?[2] Poststructuralism dons the pseudo-revolutionary colors of the rainbow but, in fact, is least of all attuned to breaking the vicious cycle that history has become. It has tucked itself comfortably into the folds of the reigning ideology, whose cosmetic prettification is its main concern. Neither liberalism nor poststructuralism, nor Marxism, nor existentialism, nor any other doctrine remaining within the confines of the modern outlook is capable of changing contemporary social consciousness in a way that would fill our will to action with *rational* content. Their common denominator, which renders them unfit for stopping the countdown to modern civilization's nuclear-ecological suicide, is precisely their *modern* nature. Over a century ago the authors of the *Milestones* called for a breakthrough beyond this outlook but the Russian society, seized by the fury of progress, cast them aside as its sworn enemies.

The approach I propose is different from that of Berdyaev or Bulgakov in significant philosophical detail, but it shares their overall goal: replacement of the modern worldview with a new, holistic one. It would be naïve to think that such a project will meet universal acceptance, but the need for a transformation of today's dominant outlook is increasingly recognized, while the arguments for the holistic nature of its replacement continue to accumulate. The current condition of Russian society appears to run counter to this proposal, but Russian religious philosophy has been one of the key contributors to the worldwide tradition of the holistic comprehension of reality, human person, and truth.

The liberal-democratic intelligentsia in Russia and in the West have framed the Russian-Ukrainian war as a struggle of democracy against dictatorship, freedom against authoritarian oppression, national liberation against imperial domination, and humanitarian values against reckless genocide. Such a framing is tantamount to the proclamation that the historical path forward for Russia is to adopt a Western-style democratic political system, stop trying to invent a special path for itself among the nations of the world, and, generally, become a "normal" country, like the rest of Europe. The word "existential"—as in "existential threat," "existential moment," and "existential choice"—is often heard in the media describing this conflict and politicians' speeches on all sides. Over thirty years ago we witnessed a world-historical event, the collapse of the Soviet system within and around Russia. Today we are witnessing another, when Russia and its closest neighbor are again in the world-historical limelight. Such a moment requires a fitting lens through which to view it. Russian history is too narrow for it, so is Ukrainian history, and even European history is not broad enough to encompass the significance of what is happening. The fitting lens is the philosophy of world history. One can truly grasp the dimensions of the question of Russia's future only in the planetary context, across centuries.

None of this relates to Russia alone. Russia moved in the historical current along with a multitude of other nations, likewise in the grips of the dream of progress, that is to say, progressivist ideology. It is this general current that needs to be comprehended in order to weigh the alternatives facing Russia. Our future, in the meantime, has become at once near and ultimate.

Cyclical Progress

To describe the current moment in history as cyclical progress is merely to state the obvious. Modern progress has lost its moral and intellectual authority—in large measure under the blows of poststructuralist critique and postcolonial revaluation. I shall return to this critique presently. But even its harshest critics have failed to offer an alternative to it and thus the civilization that has been built on the ideology of progress continues to function according to its logic. The teleology of modern progress resembles nothing so much as the tsar from a Russian folk tale, when he commands the soldier Fedot to "go know not where" and "bring know not what" (Afanas'ev, 1979, 161-71). A version of this mission sounds today in the interviews of Hollywood stars even more frequently than the American politicians' obligatory ritual incantation, "God bless the USA!" "It is not about the destination," intone the stars of all sizes, genders, races, and sexual orientations, "but about the journey (stupid)!" These innocents repeat, unbeknownst to themselves, and by endless repetition affirm a fundamental dogma of the ideology of progress. The ubiquity of the dogma and the unthinking ease with which it is accepted are sure signs of its obsolescence.

Still, the ideology is neither omnipotent nor is its power eternal. It always had its critics and opponents and it always had to overcome the resistance of various rivals. In these contests it learned to disarm its opponents by declaring them "myths" which, from the modern point of view, were nothing but the products of fantasy at best, and ignorance, prejudice, and superstition at worst. But its rivals refused to be dispelled so easily. One finds among them the traditional pre-modern doctrines of history, driven to the periphery of culture but never entirely absent from the scene. In the twentieth century this trend culminated, for example, in Mircea Eliade's critique of modern conceptions of time and space on behalf of their pre-modern counterparts (Eliade, 1954, 1959). Ananda Coomaraswamy was another towering figure in the rise of unfavorable comparison of the modern outlook against non-Western alternatives (Coomaraswamy, 2004, especially 123-51). There were also new alternative teachings that kept harassing the modern doctrine whose domination spread more and more widely without gaining much in depth. The theories of Nikolai Danilevsky, Konstantin Leontiev, and Oswald Spengler challenged modern progress from positions that combined both modern and non-modern features. But the most lethal blow to this ideology came from within, from its own latest variant. Known under the dubious name of "post-history," this variant arose from the logic inherent in the modern view of history itself. The same logic that drove class exploitation, colonial imperialism, misogynist patriarchy, racist oppression, and heteromasculine intolerance led the adherents of "post-history" to denounce progress as an oppressive "metanarrative." To this one could add the growing disillusionment with one of the chief axes of progressive history: the tale of "the conquest of nature."

It seemed like the entire edifice of the progressivist outlook, from its unconscious mythological base to critical theory as its most self-reflexive phase, had to crumble and its influence on the course of history to dissipate in the dust of the crash. But, in fact, something different has happened. The ideology of progress lost its inner meaning but remained the dominant doctrine both for the global political elites and the vast majority of the masses. Despite the fact that faith in infinite progress grows more manifestly irrational with each passing day, the elites and the masses continue to act in accordance with its basic principles. The most ardent defenders of the planet against environmental degradation continue to believe in science and technology as the means of stopping it. Closely linked to this faith is the conviction that modern social praxis—mass political movements, for example—is necessary for changing the course of events. But both science and mass politics are products of the ideology of modern progress, "fruit of the poisoned tree," and can hardly bring any radical change for the better in our predicament. If progress is infinite, then *no* planetary resources will be enough, and *any* course that the masses can presumably compel the elites to follow will lead, again, "know not where." Rather than tweaking and minor adjustments, our view of the world needs a fundamental reorientation at its deepest level, and the transformation of our thinking that meets this need should aim towards a holistic, dialectical, and goal-oriented self-creating rational thought: in short, *reason*.

It is curious that what the soldier Fedot finally discovers in his quest and brings back to the tsar is the invisible Shmat-Reason (*Shmat-razum*), whose abilities recall the jinn of the *Arabian Nights*. There is no information about this magical creature either in Vladimir Dahl's dictionary or the literature on the Russian folklore. It does not seem to appear in any other fairy tales. Dahl has an entry for *shmat* as a "piece," "fragment," and similar meanings, and, actually, "Piece-Reason" would not be a bad way of translating this demon's name (Dahl, 1935, 660). Both the jinn of the *Arabian Nights* and the Shmat-Reason of the tale published by Aleksandr Afanas'ev are "reason" only in the most pragmatic and narrow sense. The hero of the tale learns nothing about himself from him or about the nature of the reality in which he lives and acts. Fedot gains only riches and power: Shmat-Reason is very much like the "science and technology" of modern progress. But Shmat-Reason's ubiquity—"know not where"—and resistance to reductive definition—"know not what"—have affinity to the philosophical conceptions of universal intelligence. Too bad Fedot never thought of asking him to explain the nature of universal existence, human soul, or the trajectory of Russian history.

The Modern Subject

The ideology of historical progress arose and evolved on the basis of the modern model of the human being. The model is unique, nothing like it had appeared in the history of human culture before, and those who condescendingly regard history as an endless repetition of eternal archetypes articulated in the Bible, the Vedas, or the Eddas are deeply in error. Archetypes do exist and repeat themselves and, having once arisen, never vanish entirely but continue to live and evolve in the history of culture. However, for the most part they are not the model for, but rivals of the modern subject. Cultural history is, among other things, the story of interaction among the most varied types of human personhood and unfolds as the evolution of the *human person* standing in its center: not "the forces of production," nor "the laws of history," nor "the climatic conditions," but the human person. In this sense the Russian—and not only Russian—personalist philosophers were right a thousand times when they made the human person the focal point of their concerns. The modern subject is, to repeat, a wholly unique type, not easy to comprehend. And yet comprehend it we must, for it needs to be surmounted and transcended before, like the Pied Piper, it plunges humanity into the abyss.

As it takes shape in history, the subject generates its own equally peculiar view of the world, with its own forms of time and space. The dogma of an infinite journey without a destination flows with necessity from the Newtonian-Cartesian picture of the universe as an endless, homogeneous, and most importantly, *dead* space and time, filled with inanimate material objects colliding and flying apart, where the only force that mindlessly reigns over these "celestial mechanics" is gravity that came no one knows whence. In the depth of this picture there writhes a two-headed monster, a coupling of infinitism and immanentism. The former is the faith in the infinity of the universe, while the latter, the faith in the exclusively immanent nature of all being, that is to say, the rejection of the existence of anything transcendent. Hegel was right to call this infinity "bad," for, unable to include its own limit, it is, in fact, something limited: its limit lies outside it, which renders the concept internally contradictory. A similar logic—or rather failure of logic—haunts modern immanentism. Its exclusion of the transcendent renders the concept of the immanent void of meaning; the immanent keeps sprawling and losing its outlines in modern thought. Immanentist infinitism is a conceptual monstrosity which, like the dragon Nidhögg gnawing at the root of Yggdrasil, the *arbor mundi* of Norse mythology, lurks in the depths of the modern worldview (Guriand, Aldington and Ames, 1960, 255). Modern history is its offspring to the same extent as the modern picture of the physical universe.

This "I-I" construct is supplemented by another irrational concoction in the modern subject's design: rationalistic voluntarism, that is to say, the will to power armed with instrumental intellect. The primacy of will over reason suffuses modern culture in all its manifestations, including philosophy. As Solzhenitsyn once remarked, drawing an unflattering contrast between traditional and modern ethical attitudes,

> One of the fundamental proverbs expressing the Russian view of the world was (before the revolution at least) "God is not in the might but in right." This belief ... was powerfully reinforced by the Orthodox faith, which was once sincerely embraced by the whole mass of the people. (*It is only nowadays that we are persuaded, almost to a man, that "might is right," and act accordingly*).
>
> (Solzhenitsyn, 1974, 115, emphasis added)

But this affliction of the mind is typical not of modern Russia only, but of the entire modern order, its most "advanced" and "developed" parts emphatically included. The primacy of the will to power defines the entire outlook and nature of the modern subject.

Ideology is the highest form of modern rationality; it reigns over science and morality—to say nothing of culture. From the modern point of view, art, for example, is a slave of ideology and its highest mission is to help move progress along. Slavoj Žižek struggles mightily to rid progressivist consciousness of ideology—which he confuses with *myth*, falling into the modern intellect's favorite bad habit. The modern intellect brands all forms of thinking that do not conform to the ideology of progress as "myth" in an effort to deny them any claim to reality. According to Žižek, the immanent human subject creates "the big Other" (God) by "the 'empty gesture' (Hegel's expression) by means of which the brute, senseless reality is *assumed*, accepted as our own work." The gesture is, further, "the most elementary *ideological operation*, the symbolization of the Real, its transformation into a meaningful totality," that is, precisely what mythical thinking accomplishes (Žižek, 1989, 230, emphasis added). Among innumerable examples I can point to the popular historian Aleksei Kuznetsov's discussion of the "myth of Stalin the good manager" on his show "*V gostiakh u liubimykh mifov*" (Visiting our favorite myths) (Kuznetsov, 2023). The "myth" is obviously an ideologeme rather than a myth in the proper sense, and the historian is following the modern custom of using the term to denounce a belief as a delusion rooted in ignorance. But there is a grain of truth in Žižek's invectives, too: the modern ideology of progress is indeed a spawn of modern mythology, and Žižek's strenuous effort to dethrone "ideology" is nothing other than the struggle of a mythical subject against itself. Without any hope of success, I would add. Žižek and the entire cohort of thinkers to which he belongs think precisely in a modern, that is to say, infinitist, immanentist, voluntaristic, and rationalistic way and are thus incapable of breaking beyond the modern outlook. They are among those who are not only caught in, but also affirm and impel a progress that is no longer going anywhere.

The predominant ideology of the so-called "developed societies" has reached its limit and can no longer offer any path forward that would not be suicidal. A breakthrough into modernity of *all* societies around the world, which is demanded by the egalitarian principle of this ideology (but has never been practised), means a total war of all against all. Permanent war is a prerequisite for the existence of the most powerful state in today's world, the United States, where the entire political system is designed for the maintenance of the war machine and its uninterrupted operation. Every society that wishes to join modern history is obliged to imitate this system, as Russia and Ukraine are both doing at the moment, but they are merely one example among a multitude of similar conflicts, down to the threat of a nuclear confrontation. The standing conundrums of India and Pakistan, India and China, Israel and Iran, China and Taiwan, North and South Koreas are identical in their underlying dynamic. The price of admission into the club of modern nations is war. Another, equally alarming aspect of such a breakthrough is the looming ecological catastrophe of planetary proportions. Clearly, to raise the level of consumption for the entire human race to that of the West would lead to an immediate destruction of all currently available natural resources and what Chomsky calls bringing "the human experiment of 200,000 years to an end" (Chomsky, 2020, 15).

In the modern world, ideology reigns over pure reason, aesthetic judgment, and religious faith. Under its pressure religion assumed the well-known "enlightened" form of deistic moralism where faith is viewed as a system of moral norms with a minimal, vanishing significance of mysticism, an indispensable element of traditional religious faith and practice. Far from being a tool for the repression of the unwashed masses, however, religion is the domain where human goals and principles of conduct reach for their ultimate horizons, thereby seeking a grounding in the basic principles of a worldview at large. In a quite substantive sense religion is, in fact, a worldview. Hegel and the Romantics had good cause to speak of religion as the quest for "the infinite," and by infinity they meant something quite different, of course, from the false infinity of modern cosmology and history. The Romantic and the Hegelian infinite was understood *holistically* and therefore *organically*, but the modern subject cannot tolerate a whole and living reality confronting it. This subject needs the entire universe to be fragmented, unliving, and therefore unable to resist its domination. *This* is why modern history ends with the destruction of all life on planet Earth—unless its course is fundamentally redirected, which amounts to saying that history must become something other than modern.

I already briefly mentioned art: no sooner had modern thought delved into the nature of the "aesthetic judgement" than the latter was harnessed into the cart of progress as a vehicle for the moral betterment of the human race. This is evident from Kant's *Third Critique*, where aesthetic judgement is meticulously scrutinized, only to become a wheel in the machinery of the modern project. Kant's discussion in the *Third Critique* culminates in proposing the moral human agent as the pinnacle of creation and in arguing that God's existence is best demonstrated on moral grounds, by means of what he calls "ethicotheology" (Kant, 2000, 308ff.). The furious casting about from one extreme to another, from Romanticism to Realism, from Victorian moralizing to Aestheticism, from Symbolism to the revolutionary Avant-Garde, were symptoms of the internal dynamics within the very concept of art. The more this concept was clarified by the modern intellect, the more violent reaction it provoked from the modern subject itself, an arch-moralist *par excellence*. It is fitting to recall, perhaps, at this juncture that in *De Profundis* Berdyaev chose to frame his response to the Russian Revolution as a comparison of Dostoevsky's novels with Tolstoy's moral teaching: Russian literature, for him, was the preferred lens through which to comprehend the significance of that fateful turn in history. Contrary to a common misapprehension, however, art does not question—let alone "interrogate"—reality: it simply foregoes this step and suspends *all* of reality in a state of frank illusion. This operation alone is a tremendous leap in the evolution of human intelligence, but art does not stop there. Having lifted reality into ludic being, art then manipulates it in a highly peculiar way. Dostoevsky's novels may present soul-rending pictures of Russian life torn asunder by multiple crisscrossing contradictions but, miraculously, the novels themselves are brilliant exempla of masterfully wrought totalities. Berdyaev may have been unfair to Tolstoy and his invectives too harsh, but there was a certain justice in his preference for Dostoevsky's novelistic (negative) prophecies over Tolstoy's moralizing. When the will to power, that pinnacle of the modern moral world, suppresses artistic creativity, one's vision of reality is impaired.

In today's discourse about art, a veritable witches' sabbath of ideological and political moralism is taking place, especially in the West and especially in the most advanced segment of society, the academy. As the culmination of several trends and doctrines leading up to it, poststructuralism stripped art of its last pretensions to independent significance and asserted, with maniacal single-mindedness, the attitude towards art as a weapon in ideological and political struggles. "All art is political" is the dogma of this aggressive moralism. It is quite distinct from the traditional philosophical attitude. Plato, for example, deeply understood the nature of art and knowingly rejected it as incompatible with his peculiar political project. This is equally evident from both the *Republic* and the *Laws*. The current wave of moralism, by contrast, is based on a thorough confusion and hopeless incomprehension of art's essence and role in culture, and even more so in society at large. The only alternative to ideology left for understanding art is a brainchild of the abstract intellect, formalism, now hiding in the catacombs of the academy. But it is being found out there as well.

Giorgio Agamben recalls the metaphor of a burning building to describe the current moment in the Western intellectual discourse on art: the basic flaw in the structure's design becomes evident when the building is on fire (Agamben, 1999, 114-15). This flaw, Agamben argues, is the hegemony of the aesthetic mindset in the modern story of art, its bearer is the "man without content," Nietzsche's "uncanny guest" at the feast of art. Along with Heidegger, Agamben is deeply disillusioned with the modern outlook and seeks to re-evaluate its foundations. Much like the Russian Symbolists before him, Agamben would wish to see the return of art to its mythical and ritual function, to serve as "the very space where [man] can take the original measure of his dwelling in the present and recover each time the meaning of his action" (Agamben, 1999, 114). My diagnosis is different: the edifice of contemporary art is on fire and art is losing its vital function precisely because it is under heavy pressure to *fuse* with life, to become a direct tool for improving the latter. The erasure of the boundary between art and life—the cherished dream of numerous twentieth-century artistic movements—leads to the death of art rather than improvement of the human condition. In fact, the latter gets worse when art vanishes as an independent domain in cultural life. The return of art to its mythical-ritual origins turns it once again into religion, another distinct and special sphere of culture. Philosophy has understood art as a *negation* of religion since Plato's time, a transformation of myth and ritual into poetry and theater, and this is a profound insight into art's essence. Poststructuralist thought, in turn, has assiduously sought to erase the boundary between art and life by two contrary but converging arguments. On the one hand, it claimed that at its core artistic creativity is nothing other than ideological struggles (the point of Jacques Derrida's famous *deconstruction*), while, on the other, it simultaneously declared that all reality is, in fact, play. The pan-moralism was thus married to pan-ludism in depicting politics as performance acts and performance acts as politics. But art *lives* by its difference from serious pursuits and, conversely, the latter receive their distinct outline by virtue of contrast with art's play. Those who want art to have a beneficial effect on life should uphold this distinction with all their might. Instead, the modern subject constantly attempts to "cancel" art's ludic autonomy and today, finally, it appears to be dangerously close to its goal.

Finally, even in scientific thought, where assurances of loyalty to the ideals of rational cognition and pursuit of truth were always especially vociferous, the dependence of science on practical application displaced the quest for truth and pure knowledge to the periphery of interests as quaint and irrelevant. One sooner learns about the extravagant antics of some Kurzman than about the fact that the theory of relativity has nothing to do with relativism and everything to do with the universal omnilateral relatedness of all parts of the cosmic whole. This aspect of Einstein's doctrine appears to have made little impression on modern consciousness which, instead, became terribly excited by the possibility of using the great thinker's discoveries to make the nuclear bomb. Einstein's name evokes sacred vibrations in modern consciousness precisely because of the part his theory played in the creation of the ultimate weapon, while his doctrine of the integrity of universal existence has remained virtually unnoticed. This is a vivid manifestation of the primacy of will over reason, the so-called "good" over truth, and practical over pure thought.

The New Worldview

The philosophical task of first priority is to redesign the concept of the human person—away from the modern subject that must be liberated from its own irrationalities. The hierarchy of will over reason is the first object of this rethinking and liberation; it must be overturned, and reason should be acknowledged as the faculty that imparts rational content to will (a classical, Aristotelian thought, in fact). But this also demands a transformation of reason itself—away from its predominant modern form, the instrumental intellect or abstract understanding, into an intrinsically self-creating ideational activity, *noesis noeseos*, whose self-externalization infuses human life and action with direction and meaning.

Overcoming Infinitism and Immanentism

The surmounting of the modern subject is already under way, and it did not begin yesterday. Furthermore, the new outlook has been forming in the very heart of modern rationality: scientific cognition. The new picture of the world that emanates from what Harris calls "the new science," to which I shall turn momentarily, can no longer be regarded as modern, for it has left behind the main parameters of the modern outlook.

There is a philosophical precedent to this development: in the early nineteenth century European philosophical thought likewise made a breakthrough beyond the limits of the modern worldview. This happened in Hegel's philosophy, which was the peak of Romantic Idealism but, having assimilated the Romantic critique of the Enlightenment, transcended the limits of Romanticism in turn. This breakthrough deeply affected the course of modern philosophy, but the latter was able to learn only isolated and partial lessons from it, remaining in the main modern, that is to say, an immanentist-infinitist form of thought. From Hegel's philosophy of history, for example, modernity assimilated only the idea of relentless development, which fitted the schemata of the ideology of progress, while Hegel's doctrine of absolute knowledge as the *goal* of history was discarded, and without it progress is so much nonsense. The classical criterion of *integrity* as proof of the rational nature of all things, fully shared by Hegel with the entire philosophical tradition, was likewise jettisoned, although its lingering influence continued for a long time, until poststructuralism publicly declared the concept of totality the object of its hatred. "We have paid a high enough price for the nostalgia of the whole and the one," wrote Jean-François Lyotard in his seminal *Postmodern Condition*, "Let us wage a war on totality ... " (Lyotard, 1993, 81-2).

Many regarded and continue to regard Friedrich Nietzsche as the thinker who accomplished a resolute turn in the history of modern thought and initiated a new course for it, but this is a profound misunderstanding. Nietzsche's great accomplishment consisted in finally revealing the true nature of the modern subject: the primacy of the will to power over reason in a world totally devoid of a transcendent dimension. For some reason he also decided that, having relinquished all that inhibits its own will, this subject would become the savior of mankind, leading it to a genuine self-transformation, in a purely immanentist key. One could say that he mistook a fatal sickness for the panacea.

To return to our theme, by far the most telling symptom of the impending demise of the modern subject is the turn that is occurring in the historical consciousness of our age. The shape of modern history is changing before our eyes; there is a tectonic shift in its meaning. Progress used to provide moral justification for the actions of those who posed as its guardians and chief agents. However, over the past half a century or so, this moral authority was consistently challenged and has now been largely eroded. The colonies that rose to independence in the middle of the last century are now emerging as significant actors on the global scene. Nor are they small by any measure: almost all of Asia, Africa, and South America—whole continents, in other words—enter as agents of modern history. They bring their historical experience to bear on the Western story of progress. Up until the late twentieth century the West could appeal to liberal democracy as the only viable and morally justifiable form of progressive political order. Open and closed societies, democracies and dictatorships, free markets and command economies were the frameworks for "the free world's" superiority over all existing alternatives. In the late twentieth and early twenty-first centuries poststructuralist critics gnawed at the epistemological foundations of these claims, while their postcolonial colleagues eagerly dismantled the political historiography that lent them credence. The picture of modern history that has emerged from this process—and the process is far from over—almost reverses the moral poles on which progressivist historiography was based. The grand march of Western values across the world has become a relentless, violent, and racist crusade of colonial oppression. Militaristic imperialism has now almost entirely replaced the West's civilizing mission in the name of humanity's progress as the lens through which modern history is viewed.

In a poem written in the ancient Lebanese city of Byblos half a century ago, the Kazakh poet Olzhas Suleimenov remarked how his local guide described the arrival of the English who had forced out the Turks: "Civilization advanced on Byblos." He pronounced "civilization" as "syphilization." "The Arab tongue is remarkably soft," commented the poet, "it strips the bark off every word" (Suleimenov, 1979, 145). The world's tongues are rubbing the deceptive varnish off the word "progress" and revealing its darker essence: the ravenous will to power. Endless wars have bared the true driving engine behind the "export of democracy," the military-industrial-government-media complex, and the regularly recurring economic crises have likewise laid bare the true driving force of globalization: the freedom of financial capital, the only thing—although it is precisely *not* a thing—that enjoys absolutely unencumbered planetary circulation, whose goal is infinite self-expansion. The governments of the self-described "free societies" exist mostly as laundromats transmuting public wealth into private capital through military expenditure and neoliberal economics, while ignoring, decade after decade, public opinion on the most critical issues that confront global humanity.

It is this dynamic that is being played out in the Russia-Ukraine conflict: there are three wars, intertwined into one, that are under way there. The civil war within Ukraine is the product of a reactionary ethnic nationalism, which is incapable of sustaining a multi-ethnic modern state. This is the kind of a war that the Kyiv government cannot win and, in fact, no other government can either. This civil war has been enfolded into the war of national liberation against the Russian invasion, a war that Russia cannot win, no matter the outcome of the current military hostilities. Ukraine is a classic case in the story of empires: constituent countries develop their own national consciousness that soon rises beyond the possibility of suppression. Ukraine will be independent, even if it takes three hundred years. The question is *what kind* of a nation it will be, not *whether* it will be one. And, finally, these two equally unwinnable wars have, in turn, been absorbed into the proxy war that the United States and its overeager allies have launched against Russia, a war for global dominance, which is slipping away from the West. This is a war where victory in the usual sense is impossible, the most dangerous push towards the terminal nuclear catastrophe. But it is not being fought for a military victory. Rather, like dozens of wars conducted by the West in the past half-century and more, it pursues other goals. The hasty, chaotic departures of the US military from Vietnam or Afghanistan amply demonstrate this. The warfare is a procedure by which the lead of public wealth is transmuted into the gold of private capital. The proxy war in Ukraine will end the moment the US and Western-European financial elites decide that its costs have come dangerously close to balancing its benefits. Still, one would be too hasty to rejoice when it happens: The war will simply migrate elsewhere, and the preparations for this move are already under way. The only way to stop this insanity is to break the link between money and politics, which, I confess, I find difficult to imagine under the current liberal-democratic political regime. And yet, this regime, too, like the ideology of progress of which it is part and parcel, must be transformed at the same basic level as the modern outlook in general. To suggest that Russia—or any other nation for that matter—should "join the West" is to invite it to become more democratic domestically, perhaps, but more imperialistic internationally. It is to invite Russia to regress into the militaristic aggression all the advanced liberal democracies have embraced in their past: the British, Dutch, Portuguese, French, German, Japanese, and, above all, the US. The pattern that one sees in their trajectories—establishment of democratic institutions of government at home invariably coincides with a drive to expand their colonial possessions around the globe—makes one wonder about the link between democracy and empire, an underlying dynamic that turns the one into the other.

The implications of the erosion of the progressive view of history have not been sufficiently grasped by philosophers, let alone political actors. Ecological thinkers, for example, do acknowledge that continued economic growth is antithetical to their goals but have not gone so far as recognizing that infinite "development" is unsustainable in principle. If they had, they would soon realize that such an acknowledgement compromises the deepest logic of progress at large. But this, in turn, would cast a shadow over such notions as progressive politics and progressive ideology, the very banners under which ecological thinking and environmentalist politics unfold. Progressivists uphold their faith in science as one of the cornerstones of their outlook, but it is a basic feature of modern scientific rationality that the progress of knowledge is infinite. The epistemological infinitism buttresses, and is in turn demanded by, the infinite progress of technology, and it is precisely the progress of technology that environmentalist thinking appeals to as the path towards "saving the planet." Hence, cyclical progress, for hasn't it been the progress of technology, fueled by an infinite expansion of consumption and assured by the progress of science, that has put our existence on the planet in peril in the first place? The advance towards a view of history that can serve as an alternative to the ideology of progress is halting and does not reach far enough. Postcolonial, environmentalist, and other discourses erode the modern outlook, exposing modern thinking as deeply flawed, but they rarely if ever reach into the metaphysical depth of this thinking and thus fail to address its deepest flaws.

The Concept of the Whole

Abstract understanding is fundamentally incomplete. It is for this reason that it subordinates itself to other faculties of the mind: will and mystical insight (intuition). Both these modes of thinking are more primitive than the abstract understanding itself—therein lies the root of the irrationality of the modern subject, the subordination of the intellect to will. Harris's view in *The Restitution of Metaphysics* is that the looming ecological and political crisis we are experiencing "is the sorry aftermath of renaissance science and the Enlightenment, the deleterious consequences of an outmoded scientific paradigm" (Harris, 2000, viii). The atomism of the Newtonian picture of the universe, Harris argues, has been "superseded by the physics of relativity and quanta and an organismic biology, whose dominant concept is an all-embracing unity" (ibid.). "The new conceptual scheme has not yet borne fruit in philosophical thinking, nor has it permeated the social structure of our culture," Harris continues. "If it were to do so, the holism characteristic of the new physics would revolutionize all our thinking, would produce a new metaphysic and a new moral philosophy." The new global outlook will also encompass, he foresees, society and politics: "The social and political world, like the biosphere and the physical universe, must be seen as a single whole, and global solidarity has become the prerequisite of human salvation" (ibid.).

Harris's proposal for overcoming the modern worldview centers on the defining role of science in how we see the world. Once the flawed scientific paradigm is replaced by or transformed into a more adequate one, he argues, a new philosophical comprehension of morality, religion, and ultimately philosophy will follow, and a new worldview will emerge in its fullness, transforming human social practice on a planetary scale. "It is ... high time," he writes, "that [the influence of the older scientific outlook] began to wane, for the science that generated the metaphysical background has been superseded by a new physics and a new biology requiring a very different metaphysic" (Harris, 2000, 261). What follows is the crux of his entire argument in the book:

> What is ultimately desired is union with the absolute whole, which transcends the human intellect and the finite human will; although both of these can be cognizant of it, because its principle of unity and order is immanent in them both. Accordingly, humankind seeks, in religion that reveals a perfection transcending the merely human, the "at-one-ment" with the whole that cannot be achieved by unaided moral effort.
>
> (Harris, 2000, 263)

The resonances between Harris's new metaphysics and the Russian religious-philosophical tradition of All-Unity are so numerous and deep that one is astonished to find no references to Russian philosophers in his writings. We can recall, for example, Aleksei Losev's description of Vladimir Solovyov's philosophy as "a doctrine of life and being, including the entire human and the entire cosmic spheres, as an unbreakable and comprehensively unified (*vseedinoi*) wholeness." "[A]ll exists in all," sums up Losev. "And this *principle of all-unity* ... is nothing other than Vl. Solovyov's main principle—as well as that of classic philosophy" (Losev, 2000, 105 and 107-8). Among other examples, too numerous to mention, one can also recall Semyon Frank's view of cognition as "the comprehension of the notion of being as a *concrete-supratemporal* all-unity ... the excess of unity, of being self-affirmed, plenitude and concreteness, that distinguishes being from [abstract] knowledge of it" (Frank, 2000, 7). In Vladimir Solovyov's own words:

> The grand thought lying at the basis of any truth consists of the acknowledgement that in essence everything that is, is *one whole*, and that this whole does not represent some sort of existence or being but is deeper and higher than every kind of being; thus in general all being is only the surface, under which is concealed that which is truly existent as an absolute unity, and this unity comprises as well our own inner essence—in elevating ourselves above everything in daily life and existence, we directly experience this absolute substance, because at this point we become it.
>
> (Solovyov, 2008, 100)

The return of religion and theism in particular to the circle of legitimate domains of culture is doubtless one of the strongest contributions of Harris's doctrine. The modern outlook has denied religion legitimate existence and participation in the life of contemporary culture. This denial creates conditions for monstrous perversions of religious consciousness and religious practice. In the meantime, with the dismantling of the Western historiography of progress, the avowed moral superiority of the modern outlook over its premodern, religious counterparts has become ever more doubtful.

A holistic view of culture recognizes that religion is a necessary domain with its own, unique functions that cannot be reduced to any other activity. Art and philosophy, it should be noted, are identical in this regard: they each play a part without which culture becomes lopsided and its evolution stumped. The modern subject is incapable by its very nature of acknowledging religion's right to existence. It can only reduce religion to something else within its field of vision, and since all of its interests culminate in the will to power, it most often sees religion precisely as an instrument of power. As Vladimir Solovyov pithily observed, this outlook equates "gods with a person, a person with an animal, and an animal, with a machine" (Solovyov, 2008, 79). But religion begins where the quotidian and the sublunar appears in all its limited nature and human consciousness reaches farther, to broader horizons of being, and ultimately to the absolute principles of human and universal existence. Such was the religion of Socrates, Plato, and Aristotle for whom the living, beautiful, and rational cosmos was the ultimate horizon of all being. Such was the religion of Pseudo-Dionysius the Areopagite who belonged to a culture that had developed the idea of a transcendent Absolute. Such was the religion of Confucius, for whom the limit of the orderly nature of the world was embodied in the traditional Chinese myth and symbol of Heaven. Such was also the religion of his fellow countryman Lao Tzu who comprehended this ultimate horizon as the Way, a universal mystical-dialectical connectedness of all phenomena. The list can be continued, but it should be evident that the Absolute assumed various forms whose internal connection consists in human attempts to comprehend the nature of last beginnings—my oxymoron is fully intentional.

It is this great earnestness of religion that art subjects to a ludic negation—and therein lies their indestructible mutual relation and necessity. The modern subject has understood art only partially and is trying either to reduce religion to it or to reduce art to religion—or both. As I have argued above, neither the former nor that latter is possible, and the modern subject's attempts lead now to tragic, now to farcical results.

The liberation of art from the will to power consists in recognizing its rational-ludic nature. Art is the play of the free intellect and when alien, non-ludic tasks are imposed on it its nature is perverted. In such cases it is most often distorted into moral sermonizing or technical exercises. Both those activities are useful and necessary, but not in the sense in which art is. Art's utility, if I may put it this way, and necessity consist in developing our intelligence: it transforms our entire experience into an object of ludic manipulation whose purpose is to demonstrate the simultaneous freedom and unfreedom of human reason. Let us recall that the wisdom of Socrates, according to his own confession, consisted precisely in the awareness of his own ignorance. Art's business is ludic reflection, and it leads human consciousness up to the threshold of such Socratic awareness, the cradle of philosophy.

Concluding Thoughts

From the dialectical-holistic worldview there emerges the conviction that culture is the center of human interest and activity and that cultural perfection of human existence is the rational goal of history. The subordination of our economic and political activity to this goal flows directly from such a reorientation of thinking. Rational thought in pursuit of truth is in turn recognized as the highest form of cultural life. Art is the sphere that dialectically, through its ludic action, connects such cognition with humanity's vital interests and invigorates religious life. And, finally, through religion the ultimate goals are translated into moral (more narrowly, political) and economic life.

It seems that anyone who grasps the chief tasks of the current moment in these terms is bound to fall into despair rather than be filled with enthusiasm and hope. The forces opposing such a course are not merely formidable: they are overwhelming. A philosopher can at best say that, unless such a basic revaluation of values and transformation of concepts occurs, humanity will remain in the grips of cyclical progress and the irrationality of our condition will not abate. To show hope for the success of the revolution of consciousness that the toppling of the modern subject implies is tantamount to intellectual suicide today. Such an enthusiast most likely will be scornfully dismissed as yet another well-meaning, perhaps, but irredeemably naïve dreamer. To this, however, the dreamer can observe that those who mock them look with the eyes and speak the tongue of none other than the modern subject. There has never been a civilization in history that was based on reason. Those who consider the modern order of the world as rational are badly mistaken. True, modernity comes closer than its predecessors to such an ideal, but it falls short of it because it relies on a truncated form of rational thought. Pre-modern orders relied on faith and custom and, despite at times significant philosophical achievements, assigned subsidiary roles to reason. Rational thought was *ancilla fidei* or a Confucian guide of conduct in a given social order, but it was not recognized as that which *defined* both natural and social orders where the conduct was to be practiced. And yet, despite this history of submission, close philosophical scrutiny reveals that it is reason, after all, that ultimately determines the forms of faith, fills intuition with determinate content, and, generally, underlies cultural history, which, in turn, determines the various social, political, and economic orders that we observe in our past and present.

The modern civilization owes its remarkable successes to a partial acknowledgement of rational thought as central to our humanity. But the modern subject did not *transcend* its pre-modern rivals, it merely set itself in opposition to them and in the process rejected what was most rational in them: their holistic aspirations. Today we are reaping the fruit of its one-sidedness: all its achievements are turning into so many perils threatening us with extinction. When the modern subject first appeared on the historical scene, it looked like a creature woven of the inversions of its predecessors. It brought along an infinite inanimate universe instead of a living, integral cosmos or Creation; human society, the Leviathan, that established all truths as a matter of social convention instead of a transcendent Absolute; and a proud, isolated individual, consumed with its own, particular goals instead of a church congregation looking upward. The modern conquest of time and space is now filling the Earth's air with deadly gases and waters with equally deadly waste on a planetary scale, while the conquest of human polity, with liberal democracy at its peak, is secreting the poison of staggering inequality disguised by empty talk of equality and diversity, and permanent global-imperial war masked by the rhetoric of "a rules-based order" that deceives no one. Any one of these aspects of the modern world order can bury humanity; their joint action makes our survival virtually impossible—unless we manage rationally to resolve the screaming contradictions of the subject at the center of this "triple storm." This requires the modest feat of learning to think, not in an abstract-rationalistic, but rational-dialectical manner. Like Shakespeare's Macbeth, the modern subject is at the end of its journey and life appears to it as "a tale told by an idiot, signifying nothing." But we are not Macbeths, whose relentless pursuit of power brought him to this conclusion. Nor was Shakespeare.

Despite all misgivings, I believe we are on the cusp of recognizing, acknowledging, and following in practice the full, rather than partial, form of rational thought. There is no guarantee, of course, that this will indeed take place: we are not dealing with an inexorable law that imposes itself on our history *volens nolens*. We are, rather, at the moment of a truly authentic choice, that, unlike the existentialist act of will, can be informed by rational judgement. Whether we shall be able to make it and by what channels such a metanoia may reach a sufficient number of human beings to effect historical change remains to be seen. But the alternative—continued reliance on the modern world view—will bring cyclical progress to its logical conclusion: the point of our own vanishing.

Notes

1 Translation from Russian here and elsewhere is mine unless otherwise specified.
2 Mearsheimer defines liberal hegemony, which he views as the cause of the demise of the United State's unipolar power in the world, as an "ambitious strategy" aiming "to turn as many countries as possible into liberal democracies while also fostering an open international economy and building formidable international institutions. In essence, the United States has sought to remake the world in its own image" (2018, viii).

References

Afanas'ev, Aleksandr. 1979. *Narodnye russkie skazki. Iz sbornika A. N. Afanas'eva*. Moscow: Khudozhestvennaia literatura.
Agamben, Giorgio. 1999. *The Man without Content*. Trans. Georgia Albert. Stanford, CA: Stanford University Press.

Askol'dov, Sergei, et al. 1991. *Iz glubiny. Sbornik statei or russkoi revolutsii*. Moscow: Novosti. Original edition 1919, Moscow and Petrograd: Russkaia Mysl'.

Chomsky, Noam. 2020. *Internationalism or Extinction*. Eds. C. Derber, S. Moodlier, and P. Shannon. London: Routledge.

Coomaraswamy, Ananda. 2004. *The Essential Ananda K. Coomaraswamy*. Ed. Rama P. Coomaraswamy. Bloomington, IN: World Wisdom.

Dahl, Vladimir. 1935. *Tolkovyi slovar'*, vol. 4. Moscow: Khudozhestvennaia literatura. Original [second] edition 1882, Moscow–St. Petersburg: M. O. Vol'f.

Eliade, Mircea. 1954. *The Myth of the Eternal Return, or, Cosmos and History*., Trans. W. R. Trask. Princeton: Princeton University Press.

Eliade, Mircea. 1959. *The Sacred and the Profane: The Nature of Religion*. Trans. W. R. Trask. London: Harcourt Brace Jovanovich.

Frank, Semyon. 2000. *Predmet znaniia. Dusha cheloveka*. Minsk-Moscow: Harvest ACT.

Guriand, Félix (ed.). 1960. *Larousse Encyclopedia of Mythology*. Trans. Richard Aldington and Delano Ames. New York: Prometheus Press.

Harris, Errol E. 2000. *The Restitution of Metaphysics*. New York: Humanity Books.

Kant, Immanuel. 2000. *Critique of the Power of Judgment*. Trans. Paul Guyer and Eric Matthews. Cambridge: Cambridge University Press.

Kuznetsov, Aleksei. 2023. "*V gostiakh u liubimykh mifov*" channel *Diletant*. https://www.youtube.com/watch?v=8kHybrdsTmI&t=2565s

Losev, Aleksei. 2000. *Vladimir Solov'ev i ego vremia*. Moscow: Molodaia gvardiia.

Lyotard, Jean-François. 1993. *Postmodern Condition: A Report on Knowledge*. Trans. Geoff Bennington and Brian Massumi. Minneapolis, MN: University of Minnesota Press.

Mearsheimer, John. 2018. *The Great Delusion: Liberal Dreams and International Realities*. New Haven, CT: Yale University Press.

Sakharov, Sergei. 1968. *Progress, Coexistence, and Intellectual Freedom*. Trans. *The New York Times*, New York: W.W. Norton & Co.

Shakespeare, William. 1975. *The Complete Works of William Shakespeare*. New York: Avenel Books.

Solovyov, Vladimir. 2008. *The Philosophical Principles of Integral Knowledge*. Trans. Valeria Z. Nollan. Grand Rapids, MI: Wm. B. Eerdmans.

Solzhenitsyn, Alexander, et al. 1974. *From Under the Rubble*. Trans. A. M. Brock et al. Boston–Toronto: Little, Brown and Company.

Suleimenov, Olzhas. 1979. *Opredelenie berega: Izbrannye stikhi i poemy*. Alma-Ata: Zhazushy.

Žižek, Slavoj. 1989. *The Sublime Object of Ideology*. London: Verso.

12

Being Guilty, Feeling Guilty: Right and Morality in Russia in the Shadow of the Current War

Michail Maiatsky

Is there *philosophical* guilt? I must confess that my pain is only multiplied by the fact of my involvement with Russian-language philosophy. It is known that "Russia" is its central and self-sustaining theme. The endless discussions of Russia's "mission," "calling," "nature," "essence," and "particularity" have made up an enormous part of almost two centuries of Russian philosophical literature. In a marginal way, this age-old problem also serves as a target for the already traditional self-irony. At least since the revival of pre-revolutionary philosophy from 1980-1990, there was always a self-mocking component in the debate. And now, since February 24, 2022, the mask has been dropped: *this* is what Russia's mission, nature, essence, and particularity are all about. Any prevarication, disguise, or denial of this circumstance is merely an internal, naïve product of local debates incapable of convincing outsiders.

From the early days of the war, it also became apparent that many professional philosophers had been waiting for this event and welcomed it in one way or another. Not all of them explicitly supported aggression. Russians who were silent at the beginning now have even less of a desire to express themselves as the military fiasco continues. In the philosophical "party of war," all agents are equally virulent, even though some of them may be less militant. There are instigators and hawks, and there are passive bystanders. Although I left Russia a long time ago and defended my dissertation in philosophy twenty years past in the West, I never lost contact with the Russian philosophical community, which is the source of my shame today. It turns out that I misunderstood or misjudged many things.

I underestimated the seriousness with which some of my colleagues indulged in the chatter about a special civilizational code, a special (and, of course, "the best") civilization paradigm; the whole stream of raw resentment and pseudo-intellectual claims that has gradually become Putin's ideological position. I mistook this dialogue for a routine curtsy toward the authorities that had nothing to do with the real views of these philosophers. After all, I said to myself, in Soviet times, any philosophical text was accompanied (and often began) with a reference to Marx-Engels-Lenin (and, almost until the late 1950s, to Stalin), which the savvy reader would just skip knowing that the author was merely following the rules of the game. It was a large misjudgement on my part.

The various reactions to the outbreak of the war were telling. Some fellow philosophers would have preferred a peaceful outcome of events due to their pacifism. Therefore, they lament the Ukrainians for not behaving in a civilized manner (i.e., not surrendering), condemning both themselves and those who heroically impose the light of the *Pax Rossica* to death. Others, referred to or self-described as "leftists," believe that the main battle of the times is the fight against North American neo-imperialism, and that Russia is not fighting against Ukraine, but *in* Ukraine against the US to rid the whole world of the yoke of Western neo-imperialism. The third category is outraged not by Russian bombs, but by the inhumane sanctions of the pseudo-human West, which leave Russian patients without medicine and Russian children without their usual toys and dainties. The fourth category gloats about the manufacture of various crises (the energy crisis, famine, inflation, etc.) that will finally make the West collapse. The fifth category admits that the February invasion was a "mistake," but as citizens of this country, they will wish it a victorious outcome and, of course, in case it is achieved, enjoy its fruits. For example, some of my former colleagues expressed their willingness to head Ukrainian universities and faculties after Russia's victorious de-Nazification campaign and simultaneously de-Europeanize them, rid them of their slumbering peasant dialect, and allow them to flourish under the tutelage of the great and mighty Russian language, culture, and, of course, the great Russian idea. The sixth repeats the cheap ideological clichés of the Putin regime, such as the mantra that "we had no other choice," that the West provoked Russia and is therefore to blame. The seventh is pleased to find, in the unified response that Russian aggression was met with from the West, confirmation of Western Russophobia, which they have been searching for signs of for a long time. I have yet to mention the most rabid category: those who are happy about the deaths of civilians or the everyday hardships of the Ukrainian population.

It turns out that many philosophers understand their task not as a critique (in Kantian, Frankfurtian, or any other forms) of social institutions, ideology, dominant ideas, ordinary thinking, etc., but as preemptive loyalty. They have been ready and willing to provide "theoretical" assistance in the ideological legitimation of any leader's undertaking, however criminal and irrational it might be. Thousands of pages across the country have been devoted to the obsessive proclamation of a specific Russian "way" and its corresponding "values." All those texts have been written exclusively to please those in the corridors of power and are easily recognizable by this new-speak. After decades of communist ideological subjugation, and after a liberation that promised so much (but was so short-lived), the philosophical servility that increased between 2000 and 2010 is the most shameful feature of the post-Soviet period of Russian philosophy, a period that reached a long-awaited, yet unforeseen, end in February 2022.

But no matter the exclusive and particularistic tones in which the question of Russia and its inextinguishable uniqueness were discussed—for many Russians who were not so acquainted with the "Russian idea," a quite universalist question about guilt and responsibility arose immediately or soon after the beginning of the war. In the most conscientious part of the population (or even just the intelligentsia), moral reflection has found a clear model in the post-Nuremberg experience. From the very first days of the war, many people began to write on Russian-language social networks that they felt guilty about what had happened. For example, the artist Yuri Albert wrote on Facebook on May 19, 2022: "Strange. Everyone writes that collective guilt does not exist, but I feel it. Individually" (I cite only one testimony due to its brevity[1]). This and other similar confessions received comments ranging from expressions of solidarity to condemnation: from "I have nothing in common with this regime, why should I blame myself for it" to "these confessions won't wash us Russians clean." Another popular response was that we should reject or overcome this feeling because "guilt is not constructive."

It seems to me that there are several confusions here. The word "guilt" (*vina* in Russian) belongs to both the language of morality and the language of law, and has different meanings in them (and of course ordinary usage is not bound to distinguish between them). In the moral sense, "guilt" is often spoken of in a subjective way, as a moral feeling close to shame. Like other feelings, it is either there or it is not. It is therefore strange to demand an interlocutor not to feel guilty if they feel so, or to urge, much less force, them to feel guilty if they do not feel so. The first resembles folk-amateur psychotherapy: eliminate negative emotions, and everything will be fine; the second is similar to culpabilization, the imputation of guilt. Besides, "feeling guilty" and "telling someone that you feel guilty" are two different actions. But reproaching the interlocutor, for example, for the insincerity of his message is also hardly appropriate: how can I judge it to be insincere? As for legal language, guilt (fault, blame; *faute*; *Schuld*) has an objective meaning: the court establishes guilt in the sense of the measure of an individual's participation in unlawful actions and, therefore, the measure of his responsibility for them.

This confusion produces complex psychological effects: someone may forbid oneself and suppress a moral sense of guilt for fear of being blamed, this time quite in the legal sense. Such a denial is not devoid of purely legal connotations. Under Russian law (and I am not speaking of the current, deeply flawed justice system), a guilty plea ("confession," "active repentance") can spare the accused from trial, speed up and simplify the procedure, and reduce the sentence (no more than two-thirds of the maximum term) or penalty.

So Russian *vina*, "guilt," is vague and ambivalent. It is interesting and noteworthy that for all the discrepancy between the Russian and English vocabularies, the vagueness of terminology here is common. On the one hand, one might proclaim, as for the English usage: "Guilt, unlike shame, is a legal concept" (Taylor, 1985, 85). However, a few lines below show that the situation in English is not so simple: "He [*sc.* a guilty person] may of course be guilty and not feel guilty, for he may think the law in question bad and oppressive, or he may be quite indifferent towards the authority of the law" (Taylor, 1985, 85). The very possibility of feeling guilty implies that ordinary language does not distinguish between legal and moral-emotional meanings too strictly.

In some ideal sense, the legal and moral meanings should coincide: offenders should feel regret about their actions. In fact, however, and especially in the case of a collective trauma such as the one we are dealing with now, if there is any correlation between the moral and legal meanings of guilt, it is more the reverse, the chiastic meaning. It is very likely that the people who made the decision to start the war, and whose legal guilt can be (and hopefully will be) easily established, feel (at least for now) no guilt at all. Nor, conversely, can Yuri Albert and many of his like-minded fellows, under any circumstances, face any legal charges, no matter how acute the pains of conscience may gnaw at them.

The relationship between law and morality is one of the most complex topics in any society. In today's Russia, these two areas are in quite a harmonious relationship: the catastrophic situation in justice aligns with a colossal lag in the moral and ethical sphere. Morality and ethical thought have been replaced by moralization or even (with the effective abolition of the separation between church and state) by religious sanctimony. In Russia, there is practically no public discussion of the problems known to the world under the name of "Applied Ethics" or "Applied Philosophy." As a result of the ill-conceived nature of the ethical sphere here, it tends to go far beyond what is called "minimalist ethics"[2] and attempts to regulate the behavior of citizens in areas that are either morally irrelevant or belong to other realms, as, for example, economics or politics. This tendency is reflected in the inclination to resort to moral argument where it has no place at all. A couple of years before the war, I had a Facebook discussion with a former high school classmate who had since become an important regional official. Over a 40-year career, his views had undergone a major evolution toward monarchy. He threatened that he would fight the supporters of a legitimate rotation of power with arms in his hands. Why so? "For my right to take walks with my granddaughter." This argument should disarm any opponent: whose immoral hand would be raised against a touching, loving grandfather walking his sweet little progeny?

Naturally, the question of *national specificity* arises regarding the question of responsibility and guilt. With such a formulation of the problem, it is difficult to avoid essentialism. At the same time, it is difficult to deny a certain continuity and sustainability of the historical context. Recently, in his characteristically aphoristic vein, the philology scholar and political thinker Denis Dragunsky formulated three harms of Russian literature (Dragunsky, 2022). The first harm was noted by Vasily Rozanov: for an entire century (its great, "golden" nineteenth century), Russian literature was ridiculing and humiliating those people who form the pillars of normal society: the hardworking peasant, the honest merchant, the selfless doctor. Ivan Turgenev noted the second harm in Dostoevsky's work, speaking of the inverse commonplaces: the thief is inevitably honest, the murderer is a walking conscience, the drunkard or profligate is a philosopher (of course, the opposite also happens: the philosopher is a drunkard or profligate), the prostitute is a great soul, the idiot is smarter than anybody else. Yet from Russian literary-centric philosophy, what matters to us most is the third harm, named after Tyutchev[3]: according to Dragunsky, this is the persistent self-deceptive conviction that we are quite special, that we are above any possible law, neither European, nor Slavonic, nor Christian, nor, God forbid, anything common to all people like international law.

And why? Because we are so unique, so special, and unlike anyone else in the world. Russian literature has long cherished this old adolescent complex, and philosophy followed accordingly. I call this damage a *deficitary paradigm*: We are better than anybody else for no other reason than our shortcomings. Today this is clearer than ever because the year 2022 brought new clarity and new evidence. The shabby rags of the "Russian way"—of the Russian particularity that does not accept being the trivial uniqueness that makes any country and any person unique, but only our special, unique uniqueness—dictate that we are not just special: we are worse and therefore better. Concerning this "better," we can recall the dialectic of stigma by Irving

Goffmann, where stigma, a social disadvantage, can become a new privilege (Goffman, 1963).

This begins with Pyotr Chaadayev, with his first "philosophical letter" at the very end of the 1820s, which is unanimously considered to be the first text of Russian philosophy proper as well, although written in French. This letter is permeated by the very motive that was destined to have such a rich fate: we are defective, we have no history, tradition, laws, thinkers, or ideas—"and therefore we are privileged," as was added after Chaadayev. Russian philosophy is developing in this deficitary paradigm, as the poet Igor Irteniev parodically put it:

Oni[4] ustroeny inache v sviazi s otsutstviem korney, pust' v chëm-to nas oni bogache, no v chëm-to glavnom my bedney.	They are arranged differently due to the absence of roots, even if in some ways they are richer than us, but in some main things we are poorer.

A symptomatic example of this phenomenon is the relation between law and morality. I will refer here to an article written during the Soviet era, in the late eighties, during *perestroika*. It is a great text by the now living and vigorous Erikh Soloviev—one of the key moral philosophers and historians of ideas of the late-Soviet and post-Soviet philosophy, whom we all wish a long life and creativity—published in Russian under the title "The Deficit of Understanding of the Right in Russian Moral Philosophy." Soloviev writes:

> This deficit was expressed above all in a lack of respect for individual moral autonomy and in a stubborn resistance to the idea of the primacy of justice over compassion. Our high moral pretensions too often degenerated into moral intolerance. Its constant companions have been tactless benignity, communal inquisitorialism, and the urge to make people happy according to a common measure of coercive equalization. In times of sociocultural crisis, the deficit of legal consciousness has, it so happens, ruined morality as such. The deficit of legal consciousness in the national consciousness corresponded to a deficit of legal understanding in Russian philosophy, which was closely connected with its ethicocentrism and the preaching of an absolute moral approach to life.
>
> (Soloviev, 1991)

Soloviev then provides citations from Tolstoy and his own namesake, the Russian philosopher Vladimir Solovyov:

> The elevation of misfortune to virtue is the real curse of the philosophizing Russian mind. It comes as no surprise that Leo Tolstoy credits his countrymen with literally the following: 'Russians have always treated power differently from European nations. They have never fought against power and, most importantly, never participated in it. Russians have always looked upon power as an evil which one must avoid. The legend of the invocation of the Varangians perfectly expresses the attitude of the Russian people toward power. The Russian people have for the most part submitted to power because they have always preferred submission both to fighting it and to participating in it.' Vladimir Solovyov in "The Three Forces" argues even more surprisingly, even more audaciously: 'The supreme image of slavery in which the Russian people are, the miserable position of Russia in economic and other respects cannot serve as an objection to its higher mission, but rather confirms it. For that supreme power, which the Russian people must carry into mankind, is a power which is not of this world.'
> (Soloviev, 1991)

Erikh Soloviev concludes, "such is the paralogy of the absolute moral approach to life, a paralogy that must also be vanquished. Russian philosophy, on whose revival so many hopes are pinned today, is a dubious and unreliable ally in our current struggle for law and legal culture" (Soloviev, 1991).

The hypertrophy of morality to the detriment of elementary legal notions was also expressed in the condemnation of the West for excessively insensitive legalism. This is how virtue is derived from deficiency. The first thesis: we do not have developed law, while the West does. But in the absence of law, everything in our country is perfectly regulated by custom, morals, and our inherent morality. If so, then (the second thesis) our morals are highly developed. Hence, the conclusion that morality is underdeveloped in the West: the West is amoral. It is not a very convoluted syllogism.

It is worth recalling that this highly topical article was written thirty-five years ago, during *perestroika*. When the Soviet Communism collapsed a few years later, at the beginning of the 1990s, different scenarios of philosophical development emerged: what will happen next, where will philosophy go next? The first scenario argued for turning away from these misguided seventy years, returning to the reference point of 1913 or 1917 and to continue philosophizing as if this later mistake had never happened.

The second scenario called for a return to the authentic Marx: yes, Soviet philosophy was a dead end, but only because it had betrayed an authentic (pre-Stalinist or immediately post-Stalinist) Marx to whom it must now return. This trend was the fastest to be rolled back and was represented by the least amount of people and effort.

The third scenario insisted on a further development of the unofficial philosophy in use during the Soviet period, a philosophy that was not Marxist but covered itself with the label to avoid problems.

Another scenario proposed forgetting about the preceding seventy years and joining the normal world of philosophy, trying to catch up with it, of course, because it had not stood still during the Soviet period.

The fifth scenario warranted a simple concentration on the history of philosophy: to abandon philosophy in the traditional donnish-pedantic sense and systematic philosophy for the sake of its history, considering the great lateness and the huge gap in the development of the discipline.

And a sixth scenario was to think through and rethink Russia and Russianness from different perspectives: historiosophic, political-ideological, geopolitical, but still with the same sentimental notion that we are unique and that a universal law cannot apply to us.

If no scenario completely surpassed the others, it is the latter scenario that has received strong and growing government support in recent years. But even in this support, the modern Russian state has demonstrated its transgressive hubris. This can be seen in their recent attempt to interfere with the Institute of Philosophy of the Russian Academy of Sciences. The Institute was actually absolutely allegiant to the state. Of course, it employed hundreds of very different researchers who can hardly be united by any general tendency; but officially, on its website and throughout its publications, the Institute was demonstratively loyal, and no doubt hoped that this loyalty would ensure it relative freedom of research and creativity. Its website and program documents have always been full of formulas like the "Russian civilizational paradigm" or even "Russian genetic code." But this did not prevent the attempted brutal *Gleichschaltung* to which the Institute was subjected a couple of months before the war. The authorities found that its routine loyalty was not enough, so they tried to turn it into an ideological hit squad justifying the forthcoming aggression against a neighboring sovereign state under the propaganda slogans "the whole world is against us," "we are special, so everyone envies us," and "if we don't attack today, we will be attacked tomorrow." The cherry on the cake: one year later, at the end of 2022, Ruben Apresyan, the head of the ethics department at the Institute, who had worked extensively on non-violence and (un)just wars, was declared a foreign agent.

If we return from the narrow sense of professional, philosophical responsibility to the broader notion of guilt, then in essence we use abbreviations, referring every time to *collective* guilt, *collective* responsibility. Guilt as individually experienced may concern not only the acts of the person themself, but also the collective with which the individual identifies themself or which they are associated with by others, independently of their explicit will or even contrary to it. In this case, we can call it "collective guilt," bearing in mind the figurative, metaphorical character of this concept, and keeping in mind that guilt itself can only be experienced individually. In practice, because of the aforementioned inverse or chiastic correlation, experiencing collective guilt (that is, individually experiencing guilt for an action that is collective) tends to be experienced by people who not only disapproved and did not contribute, but who protested and resented, and exactly for the fact that maybe they did not resent and protest enough, and perhaps did not do *all* they could to avoid the disaster.

In discussions on Russian social networks, one often comes across the rejection of the very notion of collective guilt and/or responsibility as precisely a totalitarian prejudice. But this is, of course, only a symptom of the lag in the level of the ethical and legal debate. There is a vast literature on these issues, both ethical and legal (see, e.g., May and Hoffman, 1991; Branscombe and Doosje, 2004; Bazargan-Forward and Tollefsen, 2020).

The ethical and/or legal discussion of these issues in Russia has developed only semi-officially (i.e., on social networks) and only recently (but very vigorously), in connection with the aggression against Ukraine. Of course, the lag in ethical reflection is not the ultimate cause, but only a direct (and not even the gravest) consequence of the overall catastrophic destruction of civil society undertaken by the regime in recent decades. Economic initiative has been systematically suppressed for the benefit of monopolists close to the state. Any civic, grassroots participation in politics has been suppressed, often by the most brutal means. For years, the population has been accustomed to the idea that politics was not a matter for ordinary citizens, but for a special category of professionals, namely, politicians. Civic virtue was reduced to the ability to limit oneself to one's private affairs and concerns. To resist the herd instinct, to be in any way different from others became seen as a vice close to pride. The organicist notion of a single, monolithic collective subject, devoid of any expression of individuality, continues to be implicitly used, originating from Russian philosophy of the nineteenth century. Indistinguishable from Orthodox views of the dissolution of the individual in the body of the Church, the citizen must melt and merge within the common organism, where his personal will can take only one form, obedience. If, however, the citizen tends to distinguish his private interest from the common will (that of the state), he can and must be expelled from the body of society as an impure and foreign matter: to be declared a foreign agent[5] and a traitor.[6]

The extensive Western, primarily English-language research literature on collective guilt and responsibility is devoted for the most part to the situation in liberal democracies. On the one hand, this is understandable, as this literature discusses the *internal* situation; but, on the other hand, this state of affairs is seen in the literature itself as problematic and distorting. The problem of collective responsibility is by definition very different when comparing countries where the process of delegating decisions from the people to the executive is carefully prescribed in the constitution and closely monitored by the opposition and media, as opposed to those countries where power is monopolized by one party or clique and where regimes are described as authoritarian, despotic, tyrannical, or totalitarian. According to one scholar, e.g., "we should acknowledge that there may be cases where the state's responsibility is rightly left 'hanging in the air,' as in tyrannical or terroristic states. Here, citizens are the innocent victims of their regime, and they cannot be held responsible for its acts" (Stilz, 2011, 208).

In fact, there is a great mismatch between the statistical distribution of democracy in the world (according to the most optimistic estimate, no more than one third of the world's population lives in democracies today) and the developed reflection on citizens' responsibility (as noted earlier, the overwhelming majority of publications on this topic cover the reality of democracies). Thus, Holly Lawford-Smith admits that her book focuses in particular on *democratic* states. That is not because they are the easy case; rather the opposite, it is because they are the hard case. In a dictatorship or a monarchy, so long as the dictator or monarch is an agent (which they usually will be), we simply identify the state with that person and can be confident that they are an agent. The actions of the dictator represent the actions of the state, with the responsibility usually resting solely on the dictator. However, others may still be complicit based on their actions. Democracies are harder because there is obviously an explanatory relationship between what the citizenry votes for, and even what polling reveals about what the citizenry *wants*, and what the state does. However, this connection is not determinate; other factors are also relevant. Direct democracies are different from representative democracies, and ideal democracies (which do not exist) are different from actual (non-ideal) democracies (Lawford-Smith, 2019, 4). A Western observer should be aware of some local Russian peculiarities. Neither pre-Soviet, nor Soviet, nor post-Soviet Russia knew the separation of powers, the true be-all and end-all basis of any democracy. This was only natural for the Tsarist autocracy. In the

Soviet era, the primacy of the party over the constitution was practiced for the entire period and, since 1977, has been explicitly spelled out in the Constitution (its 6th article eliminated partisan opposition and division within government by granting to the unique and only party the power to lead and guide society). In the post-Soviet period, and especially in Putin's two decades, a constructed "power vertical" appeared, although not in the constitution, but in numerous official documents. The top decision-making "black box" consists presumably of the Security Council and the FSB, but also outside persons who have at the given moment achieved proximity and influence over the president. His own personal, more or less unpredictable interference is also, of course, an important factor in decision-making.

Directly derived from this state of affairs is the manual administration of justice and, as a consequence, its demonstratively political and arbitrary nature. It combines, on the one hand, the volitional imposition of unjustified (and often excessively harsh) punishments (Alexei Navalny's case can serve as a tragic illustration of this aspect) with, on the other hand, impunity for real offenses and crimes (we'll come back to this a little later).

Another specificity to keep in mind is that, in the West, responsibility is often quantified or monetized: accordingly, the Western literature usually refers to responsibility in the financial sense:

> [W]hen we hold the state responsible, its citizens will be affected. When West Germany, Iraq, Canada, Argentina and Chile discharged their compensatory liabilities to their victims, the large sums of money that were needed to finance these compensation schemes came from the public purse. Their responsibility to address their wrongdoing was distributed, *de facto*, to their populations. ... On the one hand, the reparation schemes ... are commonly regarded as laudable enterprises, despite their impact on the citizenry as a whole. ... But, on the other hand, another common intuition is that at least the oppressed subjects of dictatorial regimes should not be bearing the costs of their state's policies.
>
> (Pasternak, 2021, 3)

This kind of responsibility sounds abstract to the average citizen of an authoritarianism of the Russian type: their state already puts its hand into people's pockets whenever it sees fit. That this will be done by punitive organs of other states or international justice organs makes no essential difference. But even concentrating the financial burden on the political elite does not automatically solve the problem. After all, authoritarian regimes tend to be kleptocratic as well. Therefore, the finances with which the political elite will have to pay for their misdeeds are ultimately stolen from the people's purse by a variety of corrupt schemes designed, implemented, and thereby legitimized by the regime itself.

Finally, there is a huge topic that is still waiting in the wings—a specific (post-)Soviet cynicism. How, in the most preliminary way, can its causes be outlined? The underdevelopment of the legal system, a legacy of autocracy, was superimposed by the Marxist-Leninist conviction that law is an instrument of class rule (and therefore should be abolished), and morality is part of an ideological false consciousness which should also be criticized and rejected. The culture of the contract (*contrat social* à la Rousseau) is utterly alien to the so-called Russian civilization. The contract is treated here as a means of deceiving the counterparty. Thus, an important aspect of (post-)Soviet cynicism manifests itself in the distrust of treaties: they are concluded just to make-believe, not in earnest, right? That is why the USSR existed only for show: it was supposedly a voluntary union of fifteen equal and sovereign states, but as one can predict, the Russian Soviet Republic was central and dominant. Its collapse, therefore, was also for show, a make-believe scenario where the Russians allowed their younger brothers to pretend they were adults.

Specific *post*-Soviet cynicism is the revenge on the part of the "common man." During the long Soviet decades, this person was systematically weaned from any initiative, from any pursuit of his own interests (which were seen as "bourgeois values alien to our society"). This person was systematically coerced into the supposedly good communist values and ideas—asceticism (rejection of philistine consumerism), unselfishness, altruism, friendship of peoples, respect and trust in others … When the Soviet project collapsed, the common man had a natural desire to throw these imposed values away en masse. No matter how hard propaganda tries to make NATO the main enemy, the most hated in Russia is political correctness. The individual sees in it yet another (after communism) attempt to cheat him.

Much has been written (including by me) about the nature of the Soviet phenomenon as a historically contingent superposition of two initially disrupted and heterogeneous ideas: the idea of Russianness and the idea of communism. This superimposition resulted in the amalgam of, on the one hand, the idea of God's election ("We are Russians, God is with us"), and, on the other hand, the Hegelian-Marxian idea of World Reason, which, through the "cunning of reason" (*List der Vernunft*) is threading its way through contradictions and the divergent private wills of individual agents. Only, of course, the Russians began to identify themselves not with one of the private agents or one private will, but with the World Reason itself, or, in the secularized Marxist version, with the world law (*Gesetzmässigkeit*): we are always and by definition right, because the "laws of nature" themselves are on our side.

If one considers the Marxist definitive legalization of interests as driving motives (Marx was but the conclusion of a long thought evolution, magnificently expounded in Hirschman, 1977), one can understand the distrust that the Soviet leadership has traditionally felt toward other countries which (in its view, ostensibly or insidiously) base their line of behavior not on *interests*, but on *principles*.

Kissinger describes liberalism as a quintessentially American point of view, driven by a belief that American values are universally applicable and capable of forming the basis of an international polity motivated by principle rather than merely the balance of power. He notably chastises Stalin—a stateman for whom one might infer Kissinger otherwise has considerable respect—for underestimating the American tendency to make decisions in accordance with principle rather than national interests. Stalin's greatest foreign policy mistakes, he suggests, were to assume that every other foreign leader would act with such ruthlessly single-minded pursuit of his state's own self-interest as did Stalin himself [Kissinger, *Diplomacy*, ch. 13] (Parish, 2011, 12).

The 1975 Helsinki Accords are a vivid illustration of Soviet cynicism. Their goal was, as is widely known, détente—i.e., the reducing of international tensions and the establishment of a more democratic and humane political order in Europe and the world. Their signing was triumphantly celebrated in the USSR as a major achievement of Soviet diplomacy. Indeed, they declared European borders inviolable (including those established by overt or secret deals between Stalin and Hitler) and enabled the USSR to slow down in the exhausting and destructive arms race. It goes without saying that the Soviets never intended to take the agreement's chapters devoted to human rights and freedoms seriously. The Moscow Helsinki Group, established in 1976 to monitor these chapters of the Helsinki Accords, was subjected to brutal repression from the beginning. It logically ended in December 2022 with the de jure banning of the group.[7]

As for guilt in the legal sense, what are the prospects for justice in the case of Russian aggression against Ukraine? An important requirement in international law stipulates that the country itself, the author of the atrocities, must investigate and punish the perpetrators. Only if this requirement is not met does the international mechanism of justice come into play. Is there any reason to believe that this requirement has any chance of being realized in Russia? Recently, but before the war, an outstanding book (analytical report by genre) by Nikolai Bobrinsky and Stanislav Dmitrievsky, *Between Vengeance and Oblivion: The Concept of Transitional Justice for Russia* (Bobrinsky and

Dmitrievsky, 2021[8]), was published (partly eclipsed by the war and *in fine* remaining largely unnoticed by the public). This analysis came out well before the war, so the authors cannot be suspected of any "hindsight wisdom" or "hindsight bias." The authors begin the book with a statement of "systemic lawlessness," presenting "systemic impunity" as the main feature of Russian justice. In fact, the latter has been dismantled by the state itself. In its current condition, it is clearly incapable of raising the issue of crimes committed by the regime itself at its highest echelon. That is, one of the crimes of the Putin regime before the war or as its precursor consists of dismantling the legal system, which meanwhile will either someday have to pass judgment on Putin, his regime, and his entourage or yield this mission to the international court.

And there is reason to believe that Putin, as a trained lawyer, dismantled justice not only deliberately and incidentally, but rather with a certain expertise. Instead of being the guarantor of the constitution, he waged a consistent struggle against it. Part of this dismantling was Russia's self-removal from international law, particularly from the Rome Statute of the International Criminal Court (which aims to prosecute the most serious crimes of international concern and to end impunity), which came into force at the turn of the century. Russia signed it in 2000, then (in response to criticism over the seizure of Crimea) withdrew its participation in 2016. In general, against the background of the declared (in particular, by another lawyer-in-power, Dmitry Medvedev) battle against "legal nihilism," the latter is flourishing under the slogan: there is no benefit from obedience to the law; what we need, we will take by force, and what others need from us, let them try through their feckless and piffling law. Because of the successful construction of the above-mentioned "power vertical" in all its unaccountability to the people (if not to say: in all its adversary-to-the-people character), the responsibility for what is happening cannot be laid upon the citizens under the motto "the people's responsibility for their government." The Putin regime has consistently paralyzed, distorted and/or destroyed the very foundations of civil society and its basic institutions, which, in a democracy, are designed to keep the actions of the authorities within the framework of the constitution and the public good.

Of course, in January 2023, as I write these lines, the war still promises many military and diplomatic surprises. But so far, with each passing day, it looks more and more like Putin, the alleged chief culprit of the war, faces a fairly simple set of choices: a more or less natural death, or a trial. One can hardly imagine Putin at rest, lecturing at the world's best universities, as, say, Gorbachev or Obama did. Another instructive book on this subject is a collection of articles on the final phases of tyrannies in the twentieth and twenty-first centuries (Garibian,

2016). The authors distinguish three types of diverse endings for dictator-hangmen[9]: (1) death, natural or suspiciously similar to suicide and perceived as a way to dodge justice (Pol Pot, Pinochet, Milosevic), (2) a rarer type of court-ordered execution (the top Nazi leaders, Saddam Hussein); (3) extrajudicial reprisal (Mussolini, bin Laden, Gaddafi). The authors conclude that an open trial is the most enviable end that modern dictators can dream of.[10]

The author of one of the most important books on the history of the concept of tyranny (Turchetti, 2001), Mario Turchetti, has analyzed in a separate article the difference between despotism and tyranny to clarify the status and nature of the "right of resistance" (Turchetti, 2006). Why are there no known cases of "despoticide," in contrast to tyrannicide? The distinction here seems almost pedantic, if not artificial. But it is by no means idle: while the despot uses his *legitimate* power too extensively, with cruelty, arbitrariness, and abuse, the tyrant *usurps* power in an illegitimate way. Because of this distinction, according to Turchetti, despotism can and should be criticized, but the right of resistance is fully a right only in relation to tyranny. In the Russian case, if Putin could be considered a despot until 2008, then, starting with the reshuffle in 2012 and certainly after the "Tereshkova amendment" in March 2020, he should be treated as a tyrant, and resistance to him as a right.

The ghost of Nuremberg is never far away, and it is no wonder that Nazism (a concrete historical phenomenon of one of the two most sinister totalitarianisms of the twentieth century, transformed into a universal pejorative) is used as a prism of analysis and misused by propaganda. The legitimacy of applying this term to Putin's regime itself is *per se* interesting and deserves a separate examination. As was said even before the seizure of Crimea, the new totalitarianism of tomorrow will not wear a moustache and a long oblique scalp. It will certainly not be called "Nazism" or "fascism." But it will certainly boast about its strength. It will offer itself as an efficient remedy to curb the chaos of the world with one or two simple ideas ... And again, its seductiveness will be irresistible (De Smet, 2014, 157-8).

Notes

1 For further examples of the admitted guilt and an interesting analysis of them: see Serebryakov, 2022.
2 The reflection on this topic has been developed by the French ethician Ruwen Ogien, inspired by John Stuart Mill's *harm principle* (Ogien, 2007).
3 What is meant here, is his famous maxim
Who would grasp Russia with the mind?
For her no yardstick was created:

> Her soul is of a special kind,
> By faith alone appreciated.
> (translated by John Dewey)

4 The Americans are meant here.
5 This official status was introduced in 2012.
6 The implementation of this official status was proposed by the Human Rights Council (!) under the President of Russia in January 2023.
7 The example of the Helsinki Accords serves Jean-François Revel as crucial evidence in his long-standing engagement against the cynicism and depravity of communism and the self-defeating policies of the West toward it; see, e.g., Revel, 1983.
8 Another very important book is to be mentioned here: Lëzina, 2021.
9 It is the French word *"bourreau"* that is used in the title.
10 See also Borneman, 2004; Ducret and Hecht, 2012.

References

Bazargan-Forward, Saba, and Deborah Tollefsen, eds. 2020. *The Routledge Handbook of Collective Responsibility*. London: Routledge.

Bobrinsky, Nikolai, and Stanislav Dmitrievsky. 2021. *Mezdu mest'yu i zabveniem: koncepciya perekhodnogo pravosudiya dla Rossii* [*Between Vengeance and Oblivion: The Concept of Transitional Justice for Russia*]. Preface by B. Grozovsky. Moscow: Institute of Right and Public Policy.

Borneman, John, ed. 2004. *Death of the Father. An Anthropology of the End in Political Authority*. New York: Berghahn.

Branscombe Nyla, and Bertjan Doosje, eds. 2004. *Collective Guilt. International Perspectives*. Cambridge: Cambridge UP.

De Smet, François. 2014. *Reductio ad Hitlerum. Une théorie du point Godwin*. Paris: PUF.

Dragunsky, Denis. 2022. "Tri vreda Russkoi Literatury." *LiveJournal...* https://avderin.livejournal.com/2236775.html

Ducret, Diane, and Emmanuel Hecht, eds. 2012. *Les derniers jours des dictateurs*. Paris: Perrin.

Garibian, Sévane, ed. 2016. *La mort du bourreau. Réflexions interdisciplinaires sur le cadavre des criminels de masse*. Paris: Petra.

Goffman, Irving. 1963. *Stigma: Notes on the Management of Spoiled Identity*. Hoboken, NJ: Prentice-Hall.

Hirschman, Albert. 1977. *The Passions and the Interests. Political Arguments for Capitalism before its Triumph*. Princeton: Princeton University Press.

Lawford-Smith, Holly. 2019. *Not in Their Names. Are Citizens Culpable for Their States' Actions?* Oxford: Oxford University Press.

Lëzina, Evgenia. 2021. *Prorabotka proshlogo. Praktiki perekhodnogo pravosudiya i politika pamiati v byvshikh diktaturakh. Germania, Rossia, strany*

Tsentralnoi i Vostochnoy Evropy [*Working Through the Past. Practices of Transitional Justice and the Politics of Memory in Former Dictatorships. Germany, Russia, and Central and Eastern European Countries*]. Moscow: NLO.

May, Larry, and Stacey Hoffman, eds. 1991. *Collective Responsibility. Five Decades in Theoretical and Applied Ethics*. Lanham: Rowman & Littlefield.

Ogien, Ruwen. 2007. *L'éthique aujourd'hui. Maximalistes et minimalistes*. Paris: Gallimard.

Parish, Matthew. 2011. *Mirages of International Justice. The Elusive Pursuit of a Transnational Legal Order*. Cheltenham: Edward Elgar.

Pasternak, Avia. 2021. *Responsible Citizens, Irresponsible States: Should Citizens Pay for Their State's Wrongdoings?* New York, NY: Oxford University Press.

Revel, Jean-François. 1983. *Comment les démocratie finissent*. Paris: Grasset [the book was the same year published in English: *How Democracies Perish*. Trans. William Byron. New York: Doubleday].

Serebryakov, Artem. 2022. "On the Distorted Structure of Russian Guilt," *Studies in East European Thought* [Special Issue: Russia's War in Ukraine: When Barbarism Takes Over Civilization. Edited by Marina Bykova] 74: 585–92. https://doi.org/10.1007/s11212-022-09489-8

Soloviev, Erikh. 1991. "Defitsit pravoponimania v russkoy moral'noy filosofii" [The Deficiency of Understanding of Right/Law in Russian Moral Philosophy]. In *Proshloe tolkuet nas*. Moscow: Politizdat. https://scepsis.net/library/id_2659.html

Stilz, Anna. 2011. "Collective Responsibility and the State." *The Journal of Political Philosophy* 19 (2): 190–208.

Taylor, Gabriele. 1985. *Pride, Shame, and Guilt Emotions of Self-assessment*. Oxford: Clarendon Press.

Turchetti, Mario. 2001. *Tyrannie et tyrannicide de l'Antiquité à nos jours*. Paris: PUF.

Turchetti, Mario. 2006. "Droit de Résistance, à quoi? Démasquer aujourd'hui le despotisme et la tyrannie." *Revue historique* 4 (640): 831–78.

13

Russian Ouroboros

Mikhail P. Shishkin

N: You say that a new beginning is impossible in Russia—for this, Russia must first come to an end. Yet there is a strong argument that a social order based on freedom and democracy is possible, even in Russia: because it can't be otherwise. It's a law of nature, like "every river eventually flows into the ocean." Human development proceeds according to the rule of steadily increasing humanity. Long ago, people crushed the skulls of weak infants and the old were left to die from hunger when they could no longer feed themselves. That was the norm. But norms change. In the past, the weak made way for the strong. Now, the strong step aside for the weak. The arbitrary rule of dictators gives way to the rule of law. It's simpler and easier to live in a world where your rights are protected than it is to live in a society where, at any moment, they can take away everything and toss you in the shithole. The entire world progresses in the same direction. Why should Russia be any different?

bI: The quintessential Russian debate—begun by Gogol and Belinsky nearly two centuries ago—came to an end on February 24, 2022. Both sides lost. Faith in the Christian God has failed to resurrect the dead souls. Yet, just as surely, the achievements of European civilization, along with education and culture, have also failed to "save Russia." The original disagreement was over the exact same question: how do you change the norm, humanize the dead souls, turn slaves into citizens? The social norm is a reflection of the average minimum level of maliciousness. Life is mean everywhere. But in Russia you pay more for your lack of malice. Gogol made his covenant with a non-chosen nation: "people need to remember that they are not mundane beasts, but rather lofty citizens of a heavenly city on high. For as long as they continue to fail, in any degree, to lead the live of citizens of the heavens, there will be no order for us as citizens of the mundane world, either."[1] Gogol's dead souls were supposed to start living in Christ, to follow the way of Chichikov, who, in a Siberian prison camp in the third volume of *Dead Souls*, was supposed to achieve his Russo-heavenly citizenship, earned by suffering.[2] But Chichikov rebelled against his creator via self-immolation—not barricaded in a wooden church, but wrapped in a manuscript. And then there is Belinsky, writing his endless oppositional blog:

> Russia sees its salvation ... in the achievements of civilization, enlightenment, and humanity. Russia needs no sermons (she's heard enough of them), no prayers (she's repeated them enough). Instead, Russia needs the awakening among the people of the feeling of human dignity that's been lost in the mud and manure for so many centuries—of a sense of law and rights derived not from the teachings of the church, but rather from common sense and justice, along with their maximally strict observance. Yet instead, our country offers the awful spectacle of a land in which ... not only are there no protections for the individual, dignity, and property, but there isn't even police enforcement of social order. Instead, all we have are hulking conglomerates of bureaucratic thieves and bandits.
>
> (Belinsky, 1936)

This was a battle of the superheavyweights, Russian-lit edition: internal rebirth in Christ vs. social transformation. For his entire life, Dostoevsky labored toward completion of the third volume of *Dead Souls*. The result was a bloody nothingburger. Instead of following Alyosha Karamazov into the monastery, the country took the path of *Demons* into revolutionary terror.[3] The authors of *Landmarks* threw a white towel into the ring.[4] What came next was a bloody mess that we haven't seen the end of yet. In short, neither proposal worked out: Christ couldn't arrange heavenly citizenship for our compatriots. But universal education, with the internet and open borders thrown in for good measure, couldn't lead to a triumph of civilization, enlightenment, and humanity either. From the entirety of European civilization, the Russian people have gained nothing except for two letters: V and Z.[5]

N: Commonly accepted norms don't fall from the skies. People work to change them. Not everyone in Russia sees rulers as the source of all truth. People work to change themselves, set their own rules for life, and that's how they transform society as a whole. In August of '68, just a few people went out onto the square, knowing they could not win and that their sacrifice would achieve nothing.[6] But their bravery changed something in all of us. Remember this: you were a teacher, it was August, at the dacha. Suddenly: the Putsch.[7] You went in to the White House in Moscow and found thousands and thousands gathered at the barricades, and ran into students from class 9b, which you supervised. It occurred to you then that maybe you were not such a bad teacher, since you had seemingly managed to teach them something other than the *Plusquamperfekt*. Alongside those students, you transformed the country right then and there. Now, it is those who go out in the square with "No War" signs, only to wind up in prison, who are changing the world. Once upon a time, a Czech wrote about those who faced the Kremlin in 1968: "Seven people on Red Square—that's at least seven reasons why we can never hate Russians." Each person who demonstrates against the war now is one more reason not to hate Russians. Even if it is only isolated individuals, someone has to be first.

bI: Do you remember that teacher who read us the fable about the oak and the reed in primary school? For us, it was a fairy tale. For her, it was life experience. The entire world is in shock as the Russian state drives its "electorate" into Ukraine to kill and be slaughtered, while "the people stay silent."[8] Where are the millions of protestors from all across this enormous country? Where are the strikes? Are Russians really just a "nation of serfs"?[9] What the millions of others who are protesting against the war everywhere else in the world don't understand is that silence has been a Russian survival strategy for generations. You know how it works. In 1930, grandfather was declared a "*Kulak* underling" just because he spoke out when they took his cow into the *Kolkhoz*.[10] Everyone else stayed quiet and survived, but he was arrested and perished in the Gulag. In 1982, against everyone's advice that she should "stay silent," mama let the older students organize an evening of Vysotsky's guitar poetry.[11] They fired her as school principal after a show-trial-scandal. It literally killed her—she developed cancer right afterwards. Every family has stories like this. The state destroys anyone who refuses to give in and remain silent. That's the way it's always been here, from the very beginning, when Princess Olga "of the Varangian people" carried out the genocide of the Drevlians, and when Alexander Nevsky, acting in the name of his Khan overlord, gouged out the eyes of rebel Novgorodians— both Russian saints, by the way.[12] And following along all the intermediate points along the way, from Ivan the Terrible to Joseph Stalin, to punitive operations in Chechnya, right up to the present genocide of the Ukrainians, who dared to tell the Russian battleship "to go fuck itself." Russian history is an illustration of the principle of natural selection: the state has consistently eliminated or driven into emigration the most active and educated part of the population. The Russian state was from the start a creation of foreign conquerors—first the Varangians, then the Mongols. The people and the state are alien to one another. An alien is always the enemy, to be treated without pity. The population of Russia has been subjected to a monstrous experiment in artificial selection for centuries. The oaks have been torn up by the roots and the reeds have multiplied. That's how the traits necessary for life in the "ru" zone have developed over the generations.[13] Vital energy and the power of survival is concentrated in the Russian capacity to "stay silent."

N: But the country has also known freedom. Russia has experienced the fight for democracy—and sometimes victory in that fight. In spring, 1917, following a true revolution of the people, Russia became the freest country in the world. People gained rights beyond the dreams of other nations. Take the case of women, for example: Swiss women achieved that form of equality only a half-century later. There was freedom in the 1990s—and that's already within our, your, and my own experience. It's simply not true that Russians are too immature for democracy. Dictatorships all share a common enemy—free speech. And it eventually triumphs. In the Russian duel between Poet and Tsar, the latter does not stand a chance.[14] Russians are not serfs by birth—they've been made into serfs. It's possible to corrupt any nation—just think of the Germans. But the Germans lifted themselves out of their own past and underwent a purification. The Nazi state made Zyklon B gas the legal norm. Now, the struggle against anti-Semitism has become the legal norm of Germany. The state can degrade its people, or it can enlighten them. There's anti-Semitism everywhere, but the state can either encourage it or fight against it. From generation to generation, step by step, the Russian authorities have degraded the population, turning people into "orcs." Degradation has been the single recognized state policy over the past twenty years. Propaganda has done its job. All these years, the norm has been shifting before our eyes—in the direction of hundreds of thousands of new collaborators with the repressive authorities. In Russia, everything depends on the state—Russians become orcs if that's the state wants, but if the state wants something else, Russians can be more Swiss than the Swiss themselves. There is no nation of serfs. Consider the millions of emigrants who have not only adapted easily to democratic norms, but who've gone on to achieve success and respect across the world with the same qualities of "soul and talent"[15] that Russia has no use for. Gather all of them together and you get precisely the "beautiful Russia of the future"[16] that everyone hopes for.

bI: Propaganda takes root only in well-prepared soil. Market pseudo-democracy was not good for the majority of Russians. For generations, everything was taken from people and they were given "imperial greatness" in return. They were ruled and never allowed to think for themselves or make their own decisions. Dismissed from the army, professional soldiers feel enormous emptiness. Suddenly, you have to take responsibility for your own life, find your own way, and think for yourself. People longed for certainty, for order, for rulers. Having eaten its fill after the Soviet famine, the country gave in to melancholy—to Russian "*toska*."[17] *Toska* for a clear picture of the world. *Toska* for clear borders—for a battle front dividing friends from enemies. *Toska* for a wise father-commander. *Toska* for the great victory. *Toska* for the motherland's greatness. This kind of *toska* gives off a suffocating stench, like the smell of soldiers' boots. Two attempts to air out the fatherland, to make it possible to breathe, have ended instead with simply more suffocation. In 1917, freedom lasted just a few months. In the 1990s, it scraped by for a few years. Whenever Russia tries to introduce elections, a constitution, a parliament, it instead sinks into gangster anarchy and reemerges as a totalitarian empire. Russian history has bitten its own tail and just keeps swallowing it, deeper and deeper. Gogol showed us to our seats in his troika, flying like a bird into the future.[18] But his future is our monstrous past: the twentieth century, littered with corpses. Today, he would probably compare Russia to a subway train, running back and forth in the tunnel from "Dictatorial Order" at one end of the line to "Democratic Chaos" at the other, with only an occasional change of decrepit signs. We rode that train for a hundred years between "Tsarist Empire" and "Anarchy in 1917," back to "Stalinist Order," and then on to the "Roaring 90s." Now we've arrived once again at the other terminal station: "Z For Victory!" One can pretty much guess where the train will head next.

N: The next time around, the period when you can breathe freely may last even longer. You have to multiply forty years in the desert by the length of the Russian winter. Military victories have always strengthened the regime, whereas defeats have accelerated its downfall. What were the consequences of the Russo-Japanese War, World War I, the Afghanistan War? What will be the consequences of the so-called "special military operation"?

bI: World War II ended not with Hitler's suicide, but with the complete and total defeat of the German military and machine of state. The sparrow is a bird. Russia is our fatherland.[19] The man in question, who has a stool-sample kit brought around everywhere he goes, will inevitably die. De-Putinization will follow, without a doubt, but some new Putin will be there to implement it. It will lead not to peace, but to the "respite of some abominable Brest-Litovsk."[20] New Putins will need to prove their legitimacy with victories. If the fatherland is defeated, the tsar is false. In return for victory, Stalin was forgiven his millions of victims. Having lost Afghanistan and after being defeated by the West in the Cold War, Gorbachev was seen as a pretender to the throne. The HIMARS are now putting an end to Putin's Crimean legitimacy, and there's an open call for the role of new, *authentic* tsar. The new occupant of the throne must prove his right to the tsardom in the only manner recognized in the fatherland—by defeating the enemies, no matter what sacrifices are involved. War against Ukraine and the world is being waged not by Putin, but by the entire Russian system of power, which consistently regenerates after each defeat and collapse. The nature sanctuary of history has preserved a dragon that switches its avatars over the ages: from the Ulug Ulus,[21] to the Tsardom of Muscovy, the Romanov Empire, the Stalinist USSR, or "managed democracy." In the euphoria of August, 1991, it was believed that this "monster stout, wicked, huge, with a hundred maws, and barking" had vanished into the past.[22] We passed by "de-Stalinization station" without making a stop, skipped the Nuremberg trials against the CPSU, and the country failed to inject any form of antidote for the past. So rather than any new principle, the reappearance of the old one was just a matter of time. We failed to bury the drowned man—the system, that is—and it came back to life. The Ulus shed its skin one more time. The system needs enemies and war. So now our country is once again at war with the whole world—a war with no end.

N: I still don't understand the thesis that "after Putin will be another Putin." That has no precedent in history. Nikolai I was not followed by another Nikolai I, there was no new Stalin after Stalin.

bI: Dictatorship and the dictator give birth to a population of serfs; the population of serfs gives birth to a dictator and dictatorship. It's a *Megalosaurus*-egg problem. Where can any new principle, any new beginning, possibly emerge?

N: Germany was able to make a new beginning—why can't Russia? Russia is in critical need of a zero hour. Of course, the Germans justified themselves: "Sure, Hitler turned out to be criminally insane, but we didn't know anything about what was going on! We, *das deutsche Volk*, are just as much victims of the Nazi regime as everyone else!" But Roosevelt replied, "The German people as a whole must have it driven home to them that the whole nation has been engaged in a lawless conspiracy against the decencies of modern civilization" (Roosevelt, 1944). And the residents of Germany not only were taken on "tours" of the concentration camps, they also were forced to bury the bodies of the murdered and to exhume the mass graves. Posters were hung in German cities with horrific photographs of mountains of dead bodies and inscriptions like: "This city is guilty! You are guilty!" In the same way, the Russian population will need to dig up mass burial sites and gaze at posters: "You are guilty!" Everyone, every war criminal, must meet with a just punishment. Neither NATO nor Ukraine will carry out a real denazification of the country for Russians. We ourselves must cleanse Russia of rot. Without repentance and national recognition of guilt, no democratic new beginning is possible in Russia. In order to "rise from our knees," our country must kneel and repent. Every day, with every new destroyed life in Ukraine, it becomes more and more painful to be Russian. Bitterness and shame. On behalf of my own people, my own country, on my behalf, monstrous crimes are being committed.

bI: The principle of collective responsibility leads to decimation. We've already gone through bouts of collective guilt: the bourgeois are to blame; the Jews are to blame. Instead, each individual has to answer for crimes he or she personally committed or for personal inaction that contributed to crime. Ultimately, everyone must meet an individual judgement, addressing personal guilt. Not a Last Judgment—there are no such things—but actual judgement here on earth. Yet will this ever come to pass?

N: You can be innocent and still feel responsible for events, all the same—and even ask for forgiveness. At least on one's own behalf—I'm Russian, after all. But how can I ask Ukrainians for forgiveness on behalf of my own country and people, if these people themselves still have no comprehension of what they are doing? I ask for forgiveness, myself, while understanding full well that everything my country is doing cannot be forgiven. Father went to war when he was eighteen to avenge his older brother. For the rest of his life, he hated Germans and everything German. I tried to talk to him about the achievements of German literature, about this beautiful language I love so much, but it had no effect on him. What are we supposed to say to Ukrainians, whose loved ones are being murdered by Russian soldiers, whose homes are being destroyed by Grad and Caliber missiles—that Russian literature is wonderful; the Russian language is marvelous?

bI: Will anyone ever repent in Russia? Who would have repented in Germany, if there had been no total destruction of cities, no allied rule in place of the defeated Nazis, no fear of punishment? Is Russia capable of kneeling down in Irpin, Bucha, Kyiv, Prague, Budapest, Vilnius, or Tbilisi? Without a doubt, what we will hear in Russia is: "Well sure, it turned out that Putin was criminally insane. But ordinary Russians like us—we didn't know anything. We thought we were saving the Ukrainians from the fascists. We were the Putin regime's victims, too!" In short, we'll get the same old principle and nothing new. The main line of defense will be the same as usual: talk to the people in charge; it has nothing to do with us. These are proverbial Russian army commandments: take your time following orders, they'll be cancelled anyway; keep your distance from the authorities and stick to the kitchen instead; it's the guys at the top who are responsible for everything—not me. But let's be clear: Putin wasn't the one raping, torturing, and murdering in Ukraine; Putin wasn't the one who painted Z in all those apartment windows; Putin wasn't the one who taught kindergarteners to sing: "We stand with you, Uncle Vova!" Putin is the symptom, not the disease.

N: Taking responsibility for the crimes of your country is already a step towards a new beginning, and many have taken it. As Adam Michnik said, love for the homeland is defined by your degree of shame for crimes committed in the name of your nation. It's true that in Russia, people prepared to accept guilt and atone for it are in the minority. An utterly marginal minority. They are losing their fight. But one must not fear defeat. Tolstoy was defeated, as were Rachmaninov, Malevich, and the seven who went out on Red Square in 1968. There's no shame in being in their company. Of course, it's impossible to build democracy without a "critical mass" of conscientious citizens and a mature civil society. Change is impossible without mass protests. And there are incomparably fewer people ready to take to the streets and demand an end to war, obsession with victory, and state terror than there are sheeple— and those few are concentrated in the capitals. But it's a long-established truth that history is made not by the general population, but rather by the courageous vanguard at the head of the masses. At the least, the necessary critical mass of citizens can be gathered in Moscow and St. Petersburg, and that's already enough. The entry pass to the Russian future is issued in the capitals, where historic events have always taken place. And keep in mind the main law of all political transformations: it's impossible to predict which spark will set off the conflagration.

bI: Russia is a prison state with its own peculiar outlook on law and *Weltanschauung*. A quarter of the population has been imprisoned. The rest grew up among former convicts. When prison didn't finish the job, the army did. Prison argot, the criminal subculture, and prison "moral" norms are more than just an influence on modern Russian society—they have become its foundation, a more significant constitution than the one on paper. The prison mentality recognizes only one law—the law of brute force. The country has lived and lives according to this unwritten law. In Russia, even in the freest elections imaginable, Vaclav Havel wouldn't stand a chance.

N: But there is another Russia. Some have said that Peter opened a window to Europe, but in fact he cut a hole in the bottom of the Ulus ark.[23] People, ideas, and words poured through the gap, but there was nothing for them to catch hold of in the world of the Ulus: no dignity, respect for the individual, rights, humanity, the public, or literature. Within a few generations, words had carried out the crucial Russian revolution: they transformed the nation into Siamese twins, one body with two heads that no longer understand one another. Since that time, two nations have coexisted in Russia, both speaking Russian, but opposed to one another in mentality. In one head's imagination of the world, Holy Rus' is an island in an ocean of enemies and the country and its people can only be saved by the Father in the Kremlin. The other head has been crammed full of European education and liberal thoughts and ideas about how Russia belongs to a universal civilization. That one has no desire to live in a patriarchal dictatorship; it demands freedoms, rights, and a constitution. Two heads, one body, and they have to live together. They're doomed to keep searching for a common language, for mutual understanding. Sooner or later, they will have to come to agreement, to change, otherwise they simply won't survive.

bI: The country is perpetually at war with itself. Yes, there are two Russias, and each considers itself to be the real one. They share a language, territory, and past, yet have nothing else in common. Strike that. Even their pasts and languages are distinct—and now even their territories. In the endless civil war, one "real" Russia always loses to the other "real" one. And today, once again, one has lost and the winner takes all. But there can't be two different realities. One of them is the pretender-Russia. I think you know which. We must find the strength and courage to admit defeat.

N: Who can we admit it to? To the people who are ready to go out and protest? There are more of them than you think. There are tens, if not hundreds of thousands of them—people who never voted for Putin, who went to protest rallies and were thrown into the police vans. The main thing is for the protests to remain peaceful. Change must be non-violent. We must finally break free from the endless "red wheel."[24] Only peaceful protest can alter the paradigm of violence. Russia already knows where "the good by means of the fist" winds up.

bI: Peaceful protest is not for the "country of cotton-print birches."[25] Talk to the riot police about constitutional rights, and they'll pound you in the face. At best, they'll throw you into the vans. At worst, as it turns out, a "patriot" can slam your head with a pipe, or a "defender of the fatherland"—with a sapper shovel. Once again, we have the vicious circle: the only rational approach is peaceful protest, but it's powerless against violence. We saw this in Belarus, and we've seen it in Moscow and St. Petersburg. But to take up arms means to fall into the same "red wheel" one more time. What's left: emigration? The Russian exodus is already in full swing. There are millions of us. A new beginning on the other shore? "Russia's borders have no end"?[26]

N: Here we are talking about the preservation of Russian culture as such. In the country of origin of the Russian language, only officially permissible culture is possible now—which means there can be no culture at all, apart from in the underground. Art cannot live according to the principle "the hell with it, just go ahead and kiss the mobster's hand."[27] When a director, in order to save his theater, kisses the mobster's hand—or some other part of his body—he can no longer achieve his calling in the theater. It was the same in Nazi Germany, where there was nothing left but entertainment and propaganda by the end. In our understanding, culture is something else. For an artist, the only thing left in Russia is to sing patriotic songs or remain silent. Yet emigration is also resistance. It's an explosion of previously accumulated energy. As in the cases of Rachmaninov's *Symphonic Dances*, Chagall's stained-glass windows in the Reims Cathedral, Shmelyov's *The Year of Grace*, Bunin's *Dark Alleys*, and Nabokov's *Gift*. The people themselves never returned to their homeland, but their achievements did—Russian culture returned. And it will return again someday.

bI: But can Russian culture survive now "in foreign lands"? And for how long? We benefit from the experience of the first emigration. We know what they didn't know. They believed the downfall of Bolshevism was imminent and that they would be able to return to a free homeland. One way or another, that belief was a help to them. But we know there never was any return to a free Russia. They didn't know that although the second generation in emigration would still feel somehow Russian, the third would not. But we know it. Just as it was for Nabokov, it will be our lot to witness as the Russian language completely fades away in emigration and as readers fall away in Russia. Literature can't last long in isolation—one or two generations at most. So if you want to be read, you'll switch to English, German, or French. Everyone has been wondering what the end of the world will look like. Well, here it is: the end of the world for a distinct variety of Russian culture. This is to say: in Facebook, or whatever comes to take its place, cultural life will of course continue to smolder, but it will last only until we ourselves pass away.

N: Times have changed. This is emigration in the twenty-first century. Because we have something they didn't have: high tech. A hundred years ago, if you landed in Argentina, Harbin, or Serbia, you were cut off from the Russian émigré capitals in Berlin, Paris, and New York. Now, no matter where we are, electronic communication networks allow us to create a new, global, and independent Russian cultural space, free from the "hands of the barber."[28] We are together. The capital of Russian culture is the entire world, anywhere where we are—its bearers, consumers, and creators. Long ago, the American colonies rebelled against an empire and won their war for independence. Russian culture, dispersed across the modern world, has been ready to rebel against its own Mordor for a long time. By no means are we talking about some "united states of free Russian culture" or "republic of Russian culture." All words in Russian associated with statehood have a certain stink. Rather, this must be a declaration of independence of Russian culture from the jackboot. And that's already the beginning of a new Russia—it already exists, unconnected with geography, but linked to people—a Russia without a state.

bI: The war will spare no one. And Russian culture, too, is under fire from all sides. The main blow, of course, comes from the motherland itself: they'll strangle and trample everything in Russia. And what can you really say when they knock over a monument to Pushkin in Ukraine? All you can do is keep quiet and hope a Ukrainian poet will raise his voice to object. But in emigration, everything Russian is under attack—and they're using carpet bombs, not precision weaponry. A hundred years ago there was no shame in speaking Russian on the streets in Europe. Those Russians had been defeated in a civil war, but at least they fought. Now, all Russians are stigmatized—the "good" Russians along with the "bad" ones. Perhaps the "good" Russians are despised even more, because they saw what was coming and did nothing to prevent it. Our fatherland has rendered Russian a language of murderers, war criminals, and a fascistic regime. The stain of shame marks the entire country—everyone. People no longer associate Russia with its literature and music, but with bombs falling on children. Henceforth, the illustrations for any text written in Russian will be photographs of corpses on the streets of Bucha.

N: Russian culture has finally found its purpose: the goal is to survive, and survival depends on winning this war. We must help others survive and win together with them. Our state, a maniacal serial killer, wants to take away our language, just like it took away elections, freedom, and any possibility to feel that our own country belongs to us. Now it's up to us to prove to the whole world that one can speak Russian without shame. The survival of Russian culture depends on Ukrainian victory. And so, we must help Ukraine any way we can. We must atone, however possible, for the fact that we are Russian. Until Ukraine wins, we as Russians have no moral right to Pushkin, Tolstoy, Tchaikovsky, or Rachmaninov. Every sane person in the world today is on

Ukraine's side, and that has nothing to do with either language or passport. Now, everyone must declare like a catechism, a symbol of faith in the future of humanity: *Slava Ukraine*—Glory to Ukraine! Glory to its defenders and eternal memory to the fallen. The empire must be destroyed.

bI: A symbol of faith for whom? For the millions of people who are keeping their mouths shut or saluting the Z in Russia? You can take a Russian out of the empire, but you can't take the empire out of a Russian. Russian literature was written out of an imperial inkwell—there was no other. Let's not even get into such examples of "great" Russian writing as Pushkin's denial of the Polish right to liberty in "To the Slanderers of Russia" or Dostoevsky's repugnant anti-Polish and anti-Semitic caricatures and conception of Russians as "pan-humans." For Tolstoy, everything western was rotten and everything Russian was good. He sincerely believed that Russians have no need for European culture, because within himself, a peasant in a fur hat holds comprehension of God and virtue—all those delights that should be taught to others. Russians have no immunity against the virus of "patriotism" that all tyrants grow in their laboratories. Just as in Ionesco's play, when it comes to the boundaries of empire, an absolutely ordinary person turns into a rhinoceros. There are so many of these rhinoceroses now, running around in herds, trampling everything and everyone in their path—in Russian cities, on the internet, and in "contemporary Russian literature." In the Russian mind, it remains unclear to the present day where the fatherland ends and where the regime begins—everything has grown together. Remember: the children of the serial killer Chikatilo loved their father.[29]

N: There have always been some people who understood the difference between good reasons to love one's native land and bad ones. When the Poles rose up "for your freedom and ours,"[30] only to be massacred by Russian troops, Bakunin articulated the patriotism of a different, of a *real* Russia:

> With no concern for what those who see things from the perspective of a narrow, vainglorious patriotism might say or think, I—a Russian— resolutely protested and continue to protest against the very existence of the Russian Empire. I wish all possible humiliations and all possible defeats for the empire, in the conviction that its successes and glory are now and always have been in direct contradiction to the happiness and freedom of Russian and non-Russian peoples, who are currently its victims and slaves … Recognizing that the Russian army is the foundation of imperial power, I openly express the desire that it should suffer defeat in every war the Empire undertakes.[31]

bI: Schoolchildren don't study that in literature classes. In Russia, literature and writers are just another kind of army. There, even the most talented have demanded: "Let the pen be the equal of the bayonet."[32]

N: "Nobody even mentioned hatred of Russians. The emotion felt by all Ukrainians, young and old, was stronger than hatred. Instead of hatred, this was a refusal to recognize the Russian dogs as people, and such a degree of disgust, loathing, and amazement at the absurd cruelty of these creatures that the desire to exterminate them—like the desire to exterminate rats, poisonous spiders and wolves—was as natural as the sense of self-preservation."[33]

Today, Tolstoy would have written these lines not about Chechens, but about Ukrainians instead. Fascist regimes have always and everywhere draped themselves in the names of writers—for one regime it was Goethe and Nietzsche, for another, Tolstoy and Brodsky. It's nothing new. The dead cannot object. Suppose Brodsky were to rise from the dead—just let them try then to enlist him as "one of their own" or an admirer of empire. They'd get a response they wouldn't forget. Let alone Tolstoy—he'd give it to them in full form. On the subject of patriotism, Tolstoy said it all: "Patriotism is slavery." Culture is practically the only thing that has always stood up against this Moloch. By the very fact of its existence, true art and true culture is a protest against the omnipotence of the Ulus. All culture in Russia is just an element of global culture, imported once upon a time by *Gastarbeiters* from the banks of the Rhine. The Russian state wanted artillerists, but those who arrived from abroad brought their own cultural context with them— the context in which we have persisted for generations, despite centuries of efforts on the part of the authorities to strangle it. Only the word can stand against silence. That's why in Russia, poetry is more than poetry. That's why the state has always violated and suffocated culture, even while using it as its "human face"—as a disguise. And that's why Stalin needed Shostakovich. The present regime, however, doesn't even need the mask of culture—the *Lyube* rock band is enough for it.[34] The path to Bucha did not lay through Russian literature, but rather through its persecution, through the removal of books from libraries, secret repositories, the public persecution of Pasternak and Solzhenitsyn, the executions of Gumilyov and Babel, and tags on Mandelstam's and Gumilev's feet in the morgue. The path to this war lay not through Russian literature, but instead through centuries of desperate resistance and continuous failure as Russian culture has battled against a criminal state. That resistance will continue despite all defeats.

bI: And there will be defeat once more. Culture has no chance against the jackboot. And furthermore, culture will now be subject to the laws of war.

N: Pain and hatred can linger in the soul for a long time. Only art, literature, and culture can help to overcome trauma. Sooner or later, the dictator comes to the end of his vile, worthless life, but culture remains—that's how it's always been, and that's how it will be after Putin, or following whoever comes after him and continues this war. Literature shouldn't be about Putin, literature shouldn't try to explain the war. The war can't be explained: why do people order one nation to go and murder another? Literature is what stands in opposition to war. Real literature is always about the human need for love, not hate. Ukraine will triumph, in a victory of world culture over Russian fascism.

bI: The victorious Ukraine will have a future, but will Russia have one? The entire world will work to rebuild Ukraine, but from the center of Moscow to the limits of Russian geography, there will be nothing but ruins, in heads and in souls. A new Time of Troubles is knocking at the door.[35] With its jackboot. Very well, let's imagine a miracle—the opening of another historic window of opportunity. A new Russia must begin with elections. But who is there to conduct these fair elections? Those same hundreds of thousands of intimidated teachers who took part in the falsification of the last "free and fair" elections? And will the passion-bearing nation elect emigrant foreign agents? Or will it instead elect defenders of the Russian land? Who will carry out the reforms? Who will prosecute and judge the war criminals who supported and carried out the war against Ukraine—that is to say, the entirety of the police, military, judges, and officials. Will the war criminals send themselves to prison? You can replace the tsar, dissolve the government and the Duma, but how can you replace the population itself? We only have one population! The half-life decay of the empire will once again accelerate. Everyone else will chase close on the heels of Chechnya, through a hole in the barbed wire. The Russian Federation will fade from the map into oblivion.

N: Yes, imperial collapse will continue in accelerated fashion. Moscow will no longer be able to flood Chechnya with money, and the Chechens will claim their independence, followed by other regions and national republics. The Russian Federation will come to an end. But the centrifugal forces of regions and nations are not a destructive, but rather a creative energy. This is a force of healing and purification. The collapse of this last empire is a painful step, but a necessary one, without which it will be impossible to build a democratic society across a territory that is infected with megalomania as though it were some kind of radiation. The national consciousness must come to accept that there can be several countries with Russian as a state language, that it's possible to live without a tsar in charge. Empire must be excised from Russia's cranium like a malignant tumor. When this operation has been carried out, only then will it be possible to move on to reforms and to building a "beautiful Russia of the future" in the new states that will emerge.

bI: The grammar of Russian history has only one tense: the past future. Do you seriously think that states oriented towards democracy could emerge in the territories that achieve independence from Moscow? Among the population, Putin's regime of thieves has utterly discredited the idea of democracy: "You saw what the 'democraps' brought the country to!" You seem to have forgotten that we already had all those beautiful words—republic, constitution, elections. Take just the article on the rights and freedoms of citizens in Stalin's constitution—it's superb! As it is in Putin's! But the country will no longer be taken in by "constitutions." Instead, a struggle for power will begin. New formations will certainly appear on the map, but they will be sultanates in alternation with Donbas-style separatist enclaves. Even in Yugoslavia, the collapse immediately brought massacres and ethnic cleansing. Violence will throw Russia backwards by centuries once again. No one wants to live in chaos—and so the desire for a firm hand will increase. Even given the freest elections—if they come to pass—power will go to a new dictator. The muzzled population will again see its salvation only in an "iron hand" that promises order and stability, and one will be found without delay. It's not dictators who give birth to dictatorships, but instead the people's need for order. It's impossible to live in chaos, and in Russia the genetic memory drones on: even the most repulsive government is better than none at all. Totalitarianism is never simply imposed by decree—it's the result of the collective efforts of a whole society. In Putin's Russia, the people lost control of the authorities and their actions because they never had any control in the first place. The people have no idea what can and should be controlled—they have no historical memory of such a thing. It is impossible to transform a population that places faith in a good tsar into a democratic electorate overnight. And the West will extend a hand to the many-headed dragon in some new guise, because the dragon at least promises to control the rusty nuclear dump. Russian history will swallow its own tail even deeper. Pharmacy, lane, streetlight. Huge, a hundred maws, barking.[36]

N: Yes, Russia has become a giant abscess, but a breakthrough into the future is brewing within it. Revolutions happen because people need them in order to feel like human beings. Life demands such moments—moments when you can no longer endure endless humiliation and go out into the street. Even if you can't win, you can and must fight. On that day in August of '68, they went out into the square not for victory, but to defend their honor. Now, people are coming out into the square against the war, risking the total ruin of their lives, because they have no other way to defend their sense of dignity. Take Maria Ponomarenko, one of thousands of political prisoners, who has written from prison: "We are at the threshold of great changes, and therefore of grandiose labor. It's time to unite, to believe in ourselves, to believe in victory. We will soon meet again in the beautiful Russia (for the time being) of the future." Every generation breathes its own air of freedom. The young need the future, and in the name of that future, in order not to drown in Putin's vomit, they will go to peaceful protests and man the barricades. And one more argument: the young always triumph over the old. No dictatorship, even with all its policemen, riot police, and paddy wagons, can ban the future. By all the laws of political biology, the living grass must break through the asphalt.

bI: More than a century ago, too, wonderful young people took to the streets of Russian cities to struggle against the autocracy and injustice and to stand up for democracy, the people's will, a constitution, and a beautiful Russia of the future. If they had known then what their struggle would bring, if they could have looked into the future and seen the civil war, executions of prisoners, and the Gulag, if they had understood that they would themselves, in that future Russia, remember the era of "rotten autocracy" as the happiest of times—would they still have gone out into the streets? Today, people fear revolution like a plague. What, should we wash Russia with blood one more time and fill up all the ravines with corpses? Russians are immune from revolution. Folk wisdom wasn't written by authors: don't wish for the death of the tsar, even for a bad one.

N: You've said all this already.

bI: And you've said all this already. In general, everything that can be said about our fatherland has already been said many times. We're moving in a circle. Möbius has pasted Russian discussions into his strip, which has become sticky with time, so that ideas stick in it, like flies. It's better to just remain silent about Russia now. A new beginning is impossible in Russia— for this, Russia must first come to an end.

Notes

1   From a letter to Count A. P. Tolstoy that Nikolai Gogol planned to include in his *Selected Passages from Correspondence with Friends*, yet which was

excised by the censor. All translations in this essay are by Kevin M. F. Platt, unless otherwise noted.

2 Pavel Ivanovich Chichikov is the hero of Gogol's novel *Dead Souls*. Gogol completed and published the first part of his intended three-part work and burned the manuscript of the second part shortly before his death. In the later installments of the novel, Chichikov, a great sinner, was to find salvation.

3 Alyosha Karamazov, novice in an Orthodox monastery, is a character in Fyodor Dostoevsky's novel *The Brothers Karamazov*. *Demons* is Dostoevsky's satirical novel about revolutionary terrorism.

4 *Landmarks* is an important 1909 anthology of essays by Russian philosophers on the nature and fate of the intelligentsia.

5 The letter "V," standing for "victory," dating in use from the era of World War II, is now commonly used as a pro-war symbol in support of the Russian invasion of Ukraine. The letter "Z," emblazoned on military equipment, houses, banners, etc. appeared at the start of the invasion as another pro-war symbol. Its meaning and provenance are disputed.

6 On August 25, 1968, a handful of individuals went out on Red Square to protest the Soviet invasion of Czechoslovakia. They were promptly arrested, tried, and punished by the Soviet state.

7 The Putsch of 1991 was an attempted coup d'état by conservative forces in the Soviet leadership to seize control from Mikhail Gorbachev and reverse his reforms. Its failure accelerated the collapse of the USSR.

8 This is the final line of Alexander Pushkin's historical drama *Boris Godunov*.

9 A quotation from the nineteenth-century utopian socialist thinker and novelist Nikolay Chernyshevsky. His words echoed the line "country of serfs, country of masters" from Mikhail Lermontov's epigram "Farewell, unwashed Russia."

10 "*Kulak*" (lit. meaning "fist") was a term used prior to the Russian Revolution to refer to a (relatively) wealthy peasant and was taken up by the early Soviet and Stalinist state as a term of class warfare in the countryside. "Kulak underlings" ("*podkulachniki*") referred to anyone accused of being allied with the Kulaks against Soviet power.

11 Vladimir Vysotsky was a late Soviet actor and "guitar-poet" (or "bard") who frequently defied Soviet cultural and political authorities and whose work was often suppressed.

12 Olga was a princess of Kievan Rus' in the late tenth century and the first Rus'ian ruler to convert to Christianity. Alexander Nevsky was a thirteenth-century prince who is remembered for his victory against attempts by Swedes and the Livonian Order to subjugate Novgorod and its territories.

13 The "ru zone" refers to the Russian Internet, or Russian cultural space more broadly.

14 "Poet and Tsar" is a longstanding formula and motif in Russian politics and culture, the title of various works, including a poem by Marina Tsvetaeva, a Soviet film, and others.
15 A reference to a famous phrase of Pushkin, "It was the devil who fated me to be born with soul and talent in Russia."
16 A well-known phrase and slogan of the Russian oppositional politician Alexey Navalny (1976-2024), jailed by the Putin regime.
17 *Toska* is an untranslatable Russian term for intense melancholy and "spiritual anguish," in the words of Vladimir Nabokov.
18 The final passages of Gogol's *Dead Souls* include a lyrical evocation of Russia as a troika (a sleigh pulled by a traditional Russian harness combination of three horses) careening into an unknown future.
19 The sentence refers to the epigraph of Vladimir Nabokov's novel *The Gift*, drawn from a late nineteenth-century Russian grammar textbook by P. V. Smirnovsky, "The oak is a tree. The rose is a flower. The deer is an animal. The sparrow is a bird. Russia is our fatherland. Death is inevitable."
20 A quote from Vladimir Mayakovsky's long poem *Vladimir Il'ich Lenin*.
21 "Ulug Ulus," meaning "Great State" in Turkic, was a term for the Mongol Empire and later the Golden Horde, which held sway over medieval Rus'ian territories, including the principality of Muscovy, among other domains, from the thirteenth to the fifteenth centuries.
22 The epigraph to Radishchev's *Journey from St. Petersburg to Moscow*, drawn from Vasily Trediakovsky's translation into Russian of Fénelon's *Les aventures de Télémaque* (Radishchev, 2020).
23 Pushkin, in his long poem *The Bronze Horseman*, described Peter the Great as having "cut a window into Europe."
24 "Red Wheel" is the title of Alexander Solzhenitsyn's epic novel about the Russian experience of World War I and the Russian Revolutions of 1917.
25 A line from Sergey Esenin's poem "I don't regret, I don't call, I don't cry."
26 An assertion of Vladimir Putin at a public appearance in 2016.
27 A quotation from Pushkin's historical novel about the Pugachev Rebellion, *The Captain's Daughter*.
28 A reference to the line "power is revolting, like the hands of a barber," from Osip Mandelstam's poem "Ariosto."
29 Andrey R. Chikatilo was a serial killer in the late Soviet era.
30 This was the slogan first held aloft at a Polish demonstration in support of the Russian Decembrists in 1831. It subsequently became a long-standing Polish anti-imperial slogan that was eventually adopted by Russian dissidents and displayed on banners at the 1968 Red Square protest referenced above.
31 Quotation from Russian revolutionary Mikhail Bakunin's address to the congress of the *Ligue internationale de la paix et de la liberté* in 1867.
32 From Mayakovsky's poem "Homewards."
33 A quotation from Tolstoy's novella *Hadji Murat*, altered here to replace the word "Chechens" with "Ukrainians."

34 *Lyube* is a Russian rock group, founded in the last years of the USSR, that actively supports the Putin regime and the Russian war in Ukraine.
35 The Time of Troubles was a period of dynastic succession crisis in Muscovy marked by war and anarchy, lasting from 1598 until 1613.
36 The last two sentences of the paragraph are a mashup of Alexander Blok's poem about existential dread and fatalism, "Night, lane, streetlight, pharmacy … " and the epigraph from Radishchev, 2020 referenced above.

References

Belinsky, Vissarion G. 1936. *Pis'mo k Gogoliu* [*Letter to Gogol* of July 15, 1847]. Edited and introduced by N. F. Bel'chikova. Moscow: Gosudarstvennoe Izdatel'stvo "Khudozhestvennais Literatura." http://az.lib.ru/b/belinskij_w_g/text_3890.shtml

Radishchev, Alexander. 2020. *Journey from St. Petersburg to Moscow.* Translated by Andrew Khan and Irina Reyfman. New York: Columbia University Press.

Roosevelt, Franklin D. 1944. "Memorandum to Secretary of War [Henry L. Stimson]," August 26, 1944. Archived at the site of the US Office of the Historian. https://history.state.gov/historicaldocuments/frus1944v01/d311

14

Defederating Russia

Alexander Etkind

The Russian Empire disintegrated at the end of an imperialist war. The Soviet Union collapsed at the end of the Cold War. What will happen to the Russian Federation? The answer is obvious, even if it would sadden many.

I am not calling for the collapse of the Russian Federation. I am predicting it, which is by no means the same thing. Even for people like me, who looked forward to seeing Ukraine's total victory and Russia's rulers tried at an international court, it was not easy to admit that the Russo-Ukrainian War spelled the end of the country. The collapse of this composite state had long been feared, but Russia's rulers succeeded in perpetuating their domain for a while. Reflecting their central concern, the ruling party went by the name "United Russia," articulating the fear of disintegration and lack of other values that led Navalny to rebrand them "the party of crooks and thieves." They had a chance: a favorable economic situation and a competent government could have staved off the collapse. The party's failure was not the work of foreign peoples or governments; before the war, Western governments had been the best allies of a "United Russia."

What is a Federation?

The era of empires was long gone. Russia called itself a federation, like Germany or Switzerland, but behaved like an empire in decline. Confederal unions are defined by the free accession and secession of their members; Brexit is a good example. In contrast to historic empires such as Austria-Hungary, the USSR had a constitutional mechanism permitting its dissolution. The principle of self-determination was adopted by the Bolsheviks in November 1917 and enshrined in the Soviet constitution. The same formula of self-determination became the founding principle of the League of Nations, and later of the United Nations. But after the collapse of the Soviet Union, "the right of self-determination, including secession" disappeared from Russian constitutional texts. The principle, however, had not been forgotten.

Composite states and federations bring an added value to their peoples, a *federative premium*. Pursuing economy of scale and a politics of synergy, it is possible to keep this premium positive. This should be the central concern of any composite formation, such as the European Union, the United Kingdom, or Russia. In a parasitic petrostate that functions as a logistical hub for trading and redistributing its natural resources, the federative premium is negative. Political tradition, historical mythology, or the imperial domination of one ethnicity over others can defer the collapse of this unproductive formation. Empires and federations develop in peace, consolidate in war, and disintegrate after defeat. It would be better for them to remain pacifistic like Switzerland, but they tend to be aggressive like Russia. In the way of Nemesis, the wars they start are likely to be suicidal.

In describing this process, I prefer the term "defederation" to the more commonly used "decolonization," because the former implies a transformation of all parts of the composite state while the latter applies only to colonies and not the metropolitan core of the empire.[1] There was nothing predetermined in the process: if Russia had not invaded Ukraine it would have probably deferred or avoided its defederation. But revanchism proved stronger than caution, and fetishism stronger than reason.

Russian Imperialism

As an empire, Russia emerged on the international stage at the same time as the early Portuguese and Spanish Empires, grew in competition with great terrestrial powers such as Austria and China, matured in a race with the British and French maritime empires, and outlived most of them. In the seventeenth century, Moscow colonized the Urals and Siberia. In the eighteenth century, it annexed the Baltic lands, Crimea, parts of Poland, and Alaska. In the nineteenth century, it took Finland, the Caucasus, parts of the Balkans, and Central Asia. Externally aggressive, the Russian Empire was a threat to revolutionary France and enlightened Prussia, to British India and Spanish California. Internally oppressive, the Empire crushed a major mutiny in the Urals, sparked several revolts in Poland, unleashed a permanent rebellion in the Caucasus, and confronted violent revolutions in its capitals.

The Empire was deeply integrated in European politics. Russian soldiers took Berlin in 1760, Paris in 1814, and Budapest in 1848, but they did not do it alone; every time, the Russian Empire was part of an international coalition. Founded as a military capital, St. Petersburg was also a center of diplomacy. Famous diplomats served there—Joseph de Maistre, John Quincy Adams, Bismarck ... After the victory over Napoleon, Russian diplomats created the Holy Alliance, the first attempt to integrate Europe by marrying military prowess to conservative ideology. Always a hyperactive player, the Russian Empire extended its Great Games to Central Asia, North America, and the Middle East.

The closest historical analogy to the Russo-Ukrainian War of 2022 is the Crimean War of 1853–1856, which was lost by Russia. In his wartime dispatches to *The New-York Daily Tribune*, Karl Marx wrote that "a certain class of writers" attributed to the Emperor of Russia, Nicolas I, "extraordinary powers of mind, and especially of that far-reaching, comprehensive judgement which marks the really great statesman. It is difficult to see how such illusions could be derived" (Marx, 1897, 396). Russia was never as isolated in its fight against modernity as in these two wars. In both, the Russian army's logistics were poor, its weapons obsolete, its morale low, and the generational gap between its soldiers and their political masters tremendous. In both, the anti-Russian coalition was stronger, though its aims were vague. In both, Russia's disinformation split Western pundits. As Marx wrote, "a lot of reports, communications, etc., are nothing but ridiculous attempts on the part of the Russian agents to strike a wholesome terror into the Western world" (Marx, 1897, 367). Both wars challenged the internal structure of the Russian imperial state, and both led to a swift transition of power from the fathers to the sons, or even the granddaughters. In both, ethnic issues were important but not decisive. Close to the end of the Crimean War, the British government discussed a plan for a "war of nations," which would have involved supporting nationalist movements in the Caucasus and elsewhere so that the Russian Empire could be weakened and dismembered. The plan never came to fruition as the government in London fell, and Nicolas I died (or took his own life) at just the right time to not have to acknowledge his defeat. The new British government signed a toothless peace with the heir of the throne, Alexander II, but he launched the Great Reforms of the 1860s—still the most successful attempt at modernizing Russia.

All Russian and Soviet reincarnations of the ancient Muscovite state were imperialist, but their successes were not consistent. For every expansionist tsar or commissar like Catherine II or Putin, there was a leader who presided over the contraction of the Empire's domains: Alexander II sold Alaska, Lenin withdrew from Finland and Ukraine, and Gorbachev gave away much more. None of them liked this part of the job, but I am not sure that matters. While imperial victories consolidated the conservatism of the state, military defeats led to reforms and revolutions. The Great Reforms followed defeat in the

Crimean War; the revolution of 1905 followed defeat in the Russo-Japanese War; the two revolutions of 1917 responded to the catastrophe of World War I; and the dismembering of the Soviet Union in 1991 concluded the Cold War. The Soviet collapse led to the liberation of fifteen countries, including Ukraine and Russia. It was a great example of the peaceful transformation of an empire, and part of the success story of global decolonization. However, the Russian loss of territory was smaller than that experienced by the British or even the German empires when they lost their colonies. The large-scale violence that tends to accompany the end of empires was only deferred.

The word "Ukraine" means "the edge." Over the centuries, Ukraine's lands and peoples both absorbed Russian expansionism and limited it. A central target of Russia's colonizing efforts, Ukraine was forced to supply the Empire with its goods, services, and cadres. While the Ukrainian Cossacks rebelled against Russian rule, the Ukrainian nobility participated in running the Empire, and Cossack strongmen were included in the imperial elite. Ruled from its distant corner, St. Petersburg, the Empire was ambitious and unstable. Its new Crusades to capture Istanbul, Jerusalem, or Manchuria fueled Russia's military efforts up until World War I. With the Bolshevik revolution, the renamed empire lost some peripheral lands but preserved its core. The relocation of the capital to Moscow, the creation of the Soviet Union, and its victory in World War II gave new energies to imperial expansion. After the war, the Soviet Union annexed parts of Bukovina, Eastern Prussia, the Baltic countries, and Tuva. Parts of Ukraine and Moldova, and parts of the Pacific coast, changed their status more than once. Throughout the twentieth century, Russian borders shifted almost as often as the most unstable parts of the global South.

Revanchism

In 1991, as a newly independent country, Russia adopted a new constitution and dismantled old power structures. Like the metropolitan center of any collapsed empire, Moscow experienced massive problems, including the loss of traditional markets, the disruption of supply chains, and the frustration of the elite. At that point of bifurcation, Russia had two strategic options. The first was postcolonial development, which would have seen Russia bid a final farewell to the Soviet state in the same way the Ukrainians or Estonians did. A revolution had taken place and the new Russian laws, leaders, and institutions had nothing in common with their Soviet predecessors. In this narrative, Russia was a colony of the Soviet Union in the same way as

Latvia or Uzbekistan were. But this new country, post-Soviet Russia, was still a composite state. There was no reason to expect that, left to themselves, the constituent parts of the former empire such as Chechnya, Tatarstan, or the oil-rich parts of Western Siberia would maintain their loyalty to Moscow. Left with its postcolonial modesty, Russia would need to accept further splits and secessions. Indeed, local protests and rebellions began immediately after 1991. The other option was a continuation of the imperial narrative in which the Russian state was the exclusive heir to the Soviet Union: the survivor of a "geopolitical catastrophe," as Putin put it, the target of a global conspiracy and a bulwark against the apocalypse. One option was the decolonization of Russia, the other a reconquest of the original Soviet space. The former would promise peace and prosperity, the latter war and revanchism.

The choice was soon made. Vladimir Putin came to power in 2000 with the promise of suppressing a major rebellion in the Caucasus. Two bloody and wasteful Chechen wars (1994–1996 and 1999–2009) undermined the project of democracy-building in Russia. Putin pressed further, depriving the constituent parts of the Federation of their sovereign powers (2013), and then invading and annexing Ukrainian Crimea (2014). With every imperial endeavor, Putin consolidated his personal rule. A basic truth of imperialism is that external expansion and internal oppression are connected like two sides of a coin.

In 1993, Galina Starovoitova warned about the dangers of a "Weimar Russia"—defeated, revanchist, and crumbling. Her analysis was sharp and instructive:

> The Soviet empire had some peculiarities that distinguished it from its Western counterparts. First of all, the colonies of this empire were situated not overseas but in neighboring territories, which resulted in a great intermingling of ethnic groups. A second peculiarity is that the metropole had a lower standard of living than some of its colonies.
> (Starovoitova, 1993, 108)

Having left 25 million Russians living outside Russia, the former metropole was doomed to revanchism. But there were, Starovoitova counted, 126 different peoples living in the Russian Federation—almost as many as there were in the old Soviet Union. She paid much attention to religious differences.

> Secession may be tried by some of those republics within the Russian Federation where most people have Buddhist or Islamic ties. Secessionist tendencies are already evident in Tatarstan and Chechnya, and may

develop in the recently created Ingush Republic as well as in Buddhist Tuva. Claims for greater economic and political sovereignty will probably come from other republics, as well as from the large historic economic regions of Russian 'proper'.

(Starovoitova, 1993, 108)

Better than anybody else then, and several decades after, Starovoitova understood the dialectical relation between the domestic policies of the metropole and its outward revanchism. She saw how the Caucasian wars undermined the initial liberalism of the Russian reformers. And she predicted that waging a new war of imperial revenge would bury the Russian Federation. Still, she hoped that "the secession of smaller republics would be less problematic for Russia than any attempt to keep such lands by force" (Starovoitova, 1993, 108). Five years later, Starovoitova, a brilliant ethnographer and arguably the most successful female politician in post-Soviet Russia, was murdered by a political assassin.

According to later scholars, the Russian Federation was "the subaltern empire" (Morozov, 2015), the "red mirror" of global troubles (Sharafutdinova, 2020), a "failed state" on the brink of rupture (Bugajski, 2022). Reconquering the Caucasus and Crimea that had belonged to the Soviet Union, the new Russia increasingly identified with Soviet might and glory. Each step towards reconquering Ukraine was a major step towards reconquering Russia. Unlike classical imperialism, which sought new lands and markets, Putinism was a revanchism—a less common but particularly toxic kind of imperialism.

The Russian Federation included an enormous territory that was populated sparsely and unevenly. Its population density, nine persons per square kilometer, was comparable to that of Finland or Canada. In these vast northern countries, people congregate in a small number of habitable nooks, leaving other areas thinly settled (Vishnevsky and Shcherbakova, 2018). In the post-Soviet era of expensive transportation and relatively open borders, people toured and traded in adjacent lands more than in national centers. The men and women of Kaliningrad had better opportunities for studying, working, or finding a partner in Poland or Germany than in central Russia. The same was true for the millions living in the agglomerations of Southern Siberia: they had better chances of getting on in life in China or Mongolia than in Russia. The Caucasus traded and prayed with Turkey, the White Sea coast traded with Norway, and St. Petersburg with Finland and northern Europe. Moscow was booming while the provinces were looking elsewhere. The very size of the country facilitated its disintegration.

In May 2022, during the third month of the full-scale Russian invasion in Ukraine, the BBC Russian service produced an instructive study. Exploring data from eleven cemeteries with fresh military graves, the journalists identified more than 3,000 Russian soldiers killed in Ukraine and listed their hometowns. The results were stunning: the soldiers came from distant regions of Russia, and a majority of them were of non-Russian ethnicity. Dagestan suffered most of the losses, Buryatia ranked second, the Volgograd region third, followed by Bashkortostan and Southern Siberia. These were the poorest areas of the Russian Federation, plagued with high unemployment. The locals either volunteered to serve in the army or were unable to bribe their way out of obligatory service. Among the dead, there were only six (0.2 percent) from Moscow, even though the capital's residents accounted for 9 percent of Russia's population (Ivshina and Prosvirina, 2022). Putin was wary of declaring general conscription, fearing it would lead to mass protests in the capital. Partial mobilization was declared only in September, and it confronted the demographic and healthcare problems that Russia had suffered for decades. No province lost more from the war than Donbas, which consisted of two Ukrainian regions that had been controlled by Russian-sponsored separatists since 2014: their men were conscripted, and women fled to Russia having no support there.

Towards the beginning of his reign, Putin was asked what had happened to the Russian submarine *Kursk*, which perished in the Arctic in August 2000. "It sank," he said, with a cynical smile. The tautology of his response masked the shocking catastrophe. In trying to rescue the legacies of the Russian past—Orthodoxy, imperialism, and Soviet collectivism—Putin wished to melt them into a new substance that could only be referred to as Putinism. But there was no melting pot for the task. It melted.

Ethnicity or Politics?

The Russian economist Natalya Zubarevich spoke of the four belts of Russia: the first was made up of a dozen big cities, each with a population of more than a million; the second consisted of the decaying industrial belt of the Volga and the Urals; the third was the enormous agrarian heartland stretching from the Ukrainian border to the Pacific coast; and the fourth included the poor areas of the Caucasus and Southern Siberia, most of which were ethnically non-Russian (Zubarevich, 2011). The government redistributed revenues, and all four belts were beneficiaries of the transfers that came from a small number of internal colonies—the oil-pumping and gas-trading regions at the center of the Eurasian continent. The biggest donors were two "autonomous districts" named after their largely extinct indigenous populations: the Khanty-Mansi District and the Yamalo-Nenets region—a vast land of empty marshes and migrating reindeers in Western Siberia. Another donor was

Moscow, the official residence of many extractive corporations that were drilling and mining in Siberia but paying taxes in the capital. Nevertheless, Khanty-Mansi delivered so much and consumed so little that this region contributed two times more to the Russian budget than Moscow (Tsyprin and Anisimova, 2021).

Tatarstan was another breadwinner in the post-Soviet empire. Settled on the banks of the Volga River, this booming community possessed its own oil fields and industrial facilities. Speaking in Kazan, the capital of Tatarstan, in 1990, Boris Yeltsin offered the locals "as much sovereignty as you can swallow." Tatarstan held a referendum, and the citizens voted for sovereignty. Many debates about the elusive meaning of this word followed. In 1992, Moscow and Kazan signed a treaty, and Tatarstan became a "state united with the Russian Federation." However, its economic growth was faster than the rest of Russia's, and in many respects it acted like an independent state (Graney, 2009). On coming to power, Putin declared an end to this "parade of sovereignties." In 2001, Tatarstan's referendum was retrospectively declared unconstitutional. Having already lost billions of dollars to Moscow, Tatarstan had now lost its political autonomy as well.

In 2017, this attack on Tatar sovereignty, or what remained of it, resumed. This time the target was culture and language rights: Kazan lost its power to teach the Tatar language in local schools. The number of people who identified themselves as Tatars decreased with every new poll: many felt it safer to declare a Russian identity. But in contrast to Chechnya, Tatarstan retained a relative prosperity and peace. Moreover, its officials supported the war in Ukraine and recruited ethnic troops to fight there. Other "republics" such as Bashkortostan, Chuvashia, and Chechnya also created ethnic battalions with ethnic commanders. In the nineteenth century, the Russian Empire had supported such formations, but the Soviet Union shunned the practice on the grounds that it would feed nationalist violence and lead to the risk of new internal conflicts. In March 2022, émigré Tatar activists published an appeal urging the people of Tatarstan to separate from Russia (Radio Azatlyk, 2022). Eventually, the fate of the Russian Federation would be decided in Kazan and the other capitals of the Eurasian republics, rather than in Moscow.

From Karelia to Chukotka, self-identified Russians had a numerical majority in many ethnic regions of Russia. However, confrontations between Moscow and the provinces concerned social and environmental justice issues as well as language and cultural policies. In this maze, Russians and non-Russians had many overlapping interests. The Russo-Ukrainian War demonstrated that, in the modern world, it is not ethnicity or identity that define people's choices but politics. Before 2014, Ukraine was a land of ethnic peace like Tatarstan, but it was forced to fight for its freedom like Chechnya. Many of those who fought in the Ukrainian army in 2022 spoke better Russian than their Russian foes, and made better use of their Soviet-manufactured weapons. Unlike homogeneous Chechnya, which is culturally distant from Russia but lost its war against the overwhelming force of Russian weapons and money, heterogeneous and culturally similar Ukraine was able to confront Russia vigorously.

The mass migration of Russians, Ukrainians and many others to Europe, Israel, and the United States showed that these people could quickly become responsible citizens. As the Soviet saying put it, in their homeland they "pretended to work while their employers pretended to pay." In the US, ethnic Russians boasted median incomes that were higher than those of Chinese, Italian, or even Swiss migrants. One in four faculty members at Israel's universities were native Russian speakers. The first generation of post-Soviet Russians who arrived in Israel surprised the locals with their right-wing views, but research showed that the voting preferences of the second generation were indistinguishable from those of the general population (Tabarovsky, 2019). Multiple waves of Russian emigrants, including those who fled Putin's war in 2022, were natural experiments in causality. It was the Russian state that made its citizens of any ethnicity unproductive and frustrated, not the other way around.

Indigenous Rights

Various nations in Russian territory had been impatient with Putin's state. In 2019 in Izhevsk, the capital of the Udmurt Republic, Albert Razin set himself alight in protest at the suppression of his native Udmurt language. A banner found next to his body read "If my language disappears tomorrow, I am ready to die today"—a quote from the Dagestan poet Rasul Gamzatov (Edwards, 2019). Earlier, in 2013, Ivan Moseev, a leader of the Pomory (Seasiders), was arrested for "inciting hatred against Russians" and collaborating with the Norwegian intelligence services. Almost nine years later, the European Court in Strasbourg ruled against Russia, declaring Moseev the victim of an illegal verdict. The Pomory—an ethnic minority in the Russian North with a distinct identity and culture—spoke a dialect of the Russian language and had never experienced serfdom. Led by the Pomory, massive protests shook Shiyes, a village in the Arkhangelsk region, in 2018–2020. This barely populated area had already been crisscrossed by eight gas and oil pipelines. Moscow planned to construct a monstrous landfill there, destroying the woods that the locals used for hunting and berry-picking. It would have been Europe's largest garbage dump, with waste delivered from Moscow, located 1,200 kilometers away (Tereshina, 2019). The mass protests, in which locals blocked the railway line with tents, lasted two years. The project was cancelled in 2020. It was the biggest victory of the environmental movement in contemporary Russia.

During the 1990s, indigenous rights were included in the new Russian constitution. The Russian Federation accepted responsibility for the "defense of age-old environments of habitation and traditional ways of life" (Article 72). The American political philosopher Leif Wenar argued that respecting the rights of indigenous peoples was the only way out of the oil curse: if hydrocarbons are to be mined and burned at all, the profits should go to the locals, and especially to those who have been discriminated against in previous periods (Wenar, 2015). As Wenar observed, the constitutions of almost all nations proclaim that local mineral treasures belong to the people. This formula was present in the Soviet constitutions, but it never appeared in the constitution of the Russian Federation. The habitats of the Khanty, Mansi, Yakuts, and other indigenous peoples of Northern Eurasia were circumscribed to facilitate the extraction of oil, gas, coal, and diamonds. Drillers destroyed even the national parks that had been created for these peoples in the 1990s. In 2017, Russian oil workers beat up Sergei Kechimov, a Khanty herder and shaman who tried to defend the holy Lake Numto from their invasion. Citing four oil spills that threatened local fish and birds, Kechimov tried to sue the powerful oil and gas company Surgutneftegaz but was unsuccessful. Federal legislation passed in December 2013 removed the protected status of lands on which indigenous people hunted, fished, and herded (Luhn, 2017). In 2019, Alexander Gabyshev, a Yakut shaman, set out for Moscow on foot, "to drive President Vladimir Putin out of the Kremlin"; he was arrested on the way and subjected to forced psychiatric treatment, a form of torture (Amnesty International, 2021). Even before the war, Marjorie Balzer, an American anthropologist who spent years in Yakutia, Buryatia, and Tuva, believed in the potential of their emancipatory movements (Balzer, 2021). Intense discontent had been growing in the major cities of Siberia (Hill and Gaddy, 2003). Booming industrial centers, they experienced a sharp decline when the military orders dried up, as had happened after the Cold War and as will happen again after the Russo-Ukrainian War. In September 2022, mass anti-government protests occurred in Dagestan, against both conscription and the war itself.

Having visited St. Petersburg in 1839, in the wake of the Russian army's brutal suppression of yet another Polish uprising, the French author the Marquis de Custine wrote that the Russian Empire was an "enormous prison, and only its emperor had the keys." In 1914, Lenin called the Russian Empire "a prison of nations." This cyclical narrative was to be disrupted.

Bullitt's Attempt

A hundred years before the Russo-Ukrainian War, two revolutions and a bloody civil war plunged the Russian Empire into chaos. In March 1918, the Bolsheviks exited World War I, signing a separate peace treaty with the Central Powers at Brest-Litovsk, in which Russia pledged to supply oil, gold, timber, and other commodities to Germany. The Allies were worried that the Germans would take over parts of Russia and seize resources in the Urals. To preempt this, Japan proposed to invade Russia before the German army did. Moving along the Trans-Siberian Railway, the Japanese troops would make their way up through Siberia to the Urals. The Americans opposed the plan. Nurturing a romantic affinity for Russia, Woodrow Wilson's administration feared a stronger Japan. If Japan occupied Siberia, what guarantee would there be that its troops would ever leave? The future showed that Japan was indeed an unreliable ally of America.

Negotiations on the issue were led by Edward House, Wilson's chief advisor on European politics during World War I and at the Paris Peace Conference. A Southerner who owned plantations and wrote novels, House was a permanent presence in Democratic administrations up until the eve of World War II. In 1918, Wilson and House diluted the Japanese invasion plan by limiting its force to 10,000 men. Ultimately, largely thanks to the US president and his advisor, the Japanese invasion never happened.

World War I ended a few months later but chaos continued to reign in Russia. Wilson had led his country into war in order to establish a perpetual peace. The Versailles Peace Treaty reshaped Europe, but the fire continued to blaze in Russia. The various combatants in the Russian Civil War sent their representatives to the Paris Peace Conference. Their reports contradicted one another on each and every point. To clarify the situation, Wilson dispatched a reconnaissance mission to Russia.

William Bullitt, a young diplomat and journalist, led the mission, which also included two spies and a poet. The delegation was received in Moscow by Lenin, who enchanted Bullitt; as it happened, the sympathy was reciprocal. It was April 1919, when the Bolsheviks were at their most vulnerable: retreating, they controlled the least territory of all the combatants in the Civil War. Bullitt drew up a plan for reconciling all the belligerents. The former Russian Empire would be divided into twenty-three parts; each combatant would get the territory it controlled at that moment. Finland, Ukraine, and the Baltic countries had already been recognized by the international community. Southern Russia, the Urals, Siberia, and Tatarstan would also become independent states. The Bolsheviks would be left with Moscow,

Petrograd, and eight provinces surrounding these cities. The project fit with Wilson's concept of the self-determination of peoples. In a similar way, the Balkan states were created on the ruins of the Austro-Hungarian Empire. The arbiter would be a new international organization, the League of Nations, which would recognize the new independent states at a special conference in Oslo.

Lenin agreed to Bullitt's proposal and confirmed his participation in the planned conference. Now, Bullitt and House had only to convince the remaining combatants. But first the plan had to be approved by Woodrow Wilson. Bullitt rushed from Moscow to Paris, where House was preparing for a meeting with Wilson. The meeting never took place. The president was tired and had heart problems; he had probably had his first stroke. But it is also possible that Wilson's hesitation was linked to his attitude towards Russia: he did not want to be responsible for its dismantlement (Etkind, 2017).

For Bullitt, this was a severe disappointment, and he resigned. He later went on to testify against Wilson in the Senate. House was also upset. He proposed as an alternative that Russia should be divided into five parts, with Siberia independent and European Russia split. Wilson was not convinced, and the peace plan failed again. Bullitt later wrote a psychobiography of Wilson, co-authored with Sigmund Freud. In it, he claimed with bitterness that Wilson's rejection of the plan to split Russia was "the most important single decision that he made in Paris" (Bullitt, 1966). Indeed, Wilson saved Russia twice—the first time from Japanese invasion, and the second time from internal secession.

On December 23, 2021, Putin reiterated his suspicion of American intentions towards Russia. He recalled that "one of President Woodrow Wilson's advisors" had endorsed the partition of Russia into five parts and cited an entry in House's personal diary from September 1918. The Russian president did not, however, thank his American counterpart for having preserved a united Russia.

Who Needed This Federation?

Much had changed in Eurasia since the era of Wilson and Lenin. Russia's military and economic power had impressed its neighbors for decades. Two key factors ensured this might: nuclear weapons, which provided security, and fossil fuel exports, which generated the enormous revenues that stabilized the local currency and enriched the rulers.

Neither was produced by the living generations. Oil was not created by labor; some places had it, but many others did not, which was why it was so expensive. Russia's nuclear weapons had been built by the fathers or grandfathers of those in power. Relying on their pipelines and inherited nuclear umbrella, the Russian leaders appropriated the nation's wealth without lifting a finger. Embezzlement created record inequalities not seen even under the tsars. Two unearned privileges, wealth and security, shaped the elite that started the war. Well-paid propagandists assured the people that peace, tranquility, and a stable currency were being secured through the hard work of this elite. The people believed this for as long as they experienced these benefits. They thanked their leaders, and for a while it seemed as if these rulers would rule forever.

But for decades, nothing was produced in the Federation. The pipes continued to pump oil and the nuclear weapons continued to protect. The rulers got older and richer, and the people went on with their lives more or less without complaint. The Federation consisted of many regions, large and small, and they didn't complain either. Thanks to the oil, the money the elite received was convertible and could be used to buy nice cars or villas abroad. Thanks to the nuclear weapons, the Federation protected all its regions from their enemies and from each other. As long as there was peace and oil in the Federation, everyone could hope that this would always be the case. The oil would flow out through the pipes and the money would flow back in. The formidable weapons would continue to protect while remaining unused. There would be more and more villas and yachts to purchase overseas. And nothing too bad would happen to the ordinary folk.

The best-kept secret of the Federation was why its rulers decided to start their war. Explanations ranged from boredom to despair, realism to fetishism. More significant was the fact that the rulers had never waged such a war and were not expecting it to be a long and difficult endeavor. They did not know that during it their oil would no longer be purchased, that goods would stop flowing into the country, or that people accustomed to having money would stop working if they were left unpaid. Confronting such difficulties, the rulers now had to decide whether to use their nuclear weapons.

On the one hand, if they were not used, the Federation would lose the war. There were many explanations for why they couldn't win without using these weapons: their commanders were incompetent, their missiles were imprecise, their soldiers were hungry. The fecklessness of the rulers was matched by the impotence of the people; both had been numbed by the constant flow of oil and the awesome power of their weapons. Now that the oil was no longer flowing, the weapons would have their say.

On the other hand, these ancient weapons of the ancestors had never been used. For decades they had sat in storage, their use-by dates extended many times. Of course, they had been tested, but over the months of war the rulers realized that drills were one thing and combat quite another. In short, using the nuclear weapons was a difficult decision to make. The Federation's rulers were not prepared to make it, or maybe their weapons were not in good shape. The soldiers fought to the bitter end until they lost the war.

Well, they lost and that's all there is to it. The rulers will have to move on. But first they will have to pay for the colossal damage they had done to their neighbor, and this used up all the reserves they had not already wasted. They were left with a lot of oil they couldn't sell and a lot of weapons they couldn't use. Discontent will spread throughout the Federation.

The rulers' villas and yachts were gone. Their nuclear weapons had been feared only for as long as others thought they could be used against them. But since the Federation had lost its most important war without using its most important weapons, that meant it would never use them. And it would never sell oil again either: people abroad had somehow learned to live without oil. So, who now needed this Federation?

Oil that could not be sold and weapons that could not be used will turn the center of the country into an enormous warehouse for the dirtiest scum on earth. But in many other regions of the Federation, a new life will begin. Not immediately, but they will learn how to earn their own living and defend themselves. Some will trade in the scraps the Federation had left them, but each will eventually come up with their own ways to prosper: some will sell grain, others cars; some will teach students and others will invite tourists. Relieved of the combined curse of oil and weapons, these will be beautiful countries.

It will be the peoples who will decide which countries will emerge on the ruins of the Federation. Ethnic tensions will play their role, but events will be triggered by the exhaustion of the subsidies and protection the regions had received from Moscow. Some of these "provinces" and "republics" already had their borders and leaders in place, others did not. New borders and authorities will be contested, and violence will follow. But it could not be worse than what the Federation had unleashed with its nuclear threats, global blackmail, and transcontinental famine.

The new states will be diverse—some democratic, others authoritarian. Their bigger neighbors will be their main partners in trade and security. New tensions and dilemmas will emerge. Would China shift its focus from Taiwan to Siberia? Would Eastern Prussia be viable as an independent state, or would it merge with one of its neighbors? How would the poor, overpopulated republics of the Caucasus sustain themselves? And how would the reparations to Ukraine be divided?

The Federation's dismemberment will throw up an enormous number of legal, strategic, and economic questions. Settling borders, rebuilding trade, and negotiating security arrangements will take decades. Dealing with the legacy of the heinous war and creating new statehoods will not happen immediately. But the peoples of the former Federation will learn how to make their own way. History will continue, and the international community will take note of the changes.

A peace conference will be held, modeled after the Paris Peace Conference of 1918–19. A new Eurasian Treaty will complete the work begun at Versailles a century earlier. From Ukraine to Mongolia, the neighbors of the new countries will mediate the negotiations. More successful confederations and federations such as the European Union and the United States will also play a part. The new countries will remember their long period of subservience to the Federation with contempt. Above all, they will be grateful to the country that defeated the Federation in the war.

Note

1 For recent statements on this issue, see Etkind, 2022; Casey, 2022.

References

Amnesty International. 2021. "Russia: Siberian shaman who marched against Putin is indefinitely confined to a psychiatric hospital." *Amnesty International*, September 23. https://www.amnesty.org/en/latest/news/2021/09/russia-siberian-shaman-who-marched-against-putin-is-indefinitely-confined-to-a-psychiatric-hospital

Balzer, Marjorie Mandelstam. 2021. *The Tenacity of Ethnicity*. Princeton: Princeton University Press.

Bugajski, Janusz. 2022. *Failed State: A Guide to Russia's Rupture*. Washington, DC: The Jamestown Foundation.

Bullitt, William C. 1966. "Foreword," in Sigmund Freud and William C. Bullitt, *Thomas Woodrow Wilson: A Psychological Study*. Boston: Houghton Mifflin.

Casey, Michael. 2022. "Decolonize Russia." *The Atlantic*, May 27, 2022.

Edwards, Maxim. 2019. "A professor's self-immolation puts the spotlight on the fragile future of Russia's minority languages." *Global Voices*. https://

globalvoices.org/2019/09/16/a-professors-self-immolation-puts-the-spotlight-on-the-fragile-future-of-russias-minority-languages

Etkind, Alexander. 2017. *Roads Not Taken: An Intellectual Biography of William C. Bullitt*. Pittsburgh: University of Pittsburgh Press.

Etkind, Alexander. 2022. "Defederating Russia." *Desk Russia*. https://en.desk-russie.eu/2022/04/18/defederating-russia.html

Graney, Katherine E. 2009. *Of Khans and Kremlins: Tatarstan and the Future of Ethno-Federalism in Russia*. Lanham, MD: Lexington Books.

Hill, Fiona, and Clifford G. Gaddy. 2003. *The Siberian Curse: How Communist Planners Left Russia Out in the Cold*. Washington DC: Brookings Institution Press.

Ivshina, Olga, and Olga Prosvirina. 2022. "Ot Generalov do Dobrovol'tsev: Poteri Rossii v Ukraine k Nachalu Iiunia." *BBC News. Russian Service*. https://www.bbc.com/russian/features-61638530

Luhn, Alec. 2017. "The reindeer herder struggling to take on oil excavators in Siberia." *The Guardian*. https://www.theguardian.com/world/2017/mar/17/reindeer-herder-oil-excavators-siberia

Marx, Karl. 1897. *The Eastern Question*. London: Sonnenchein.

Morozov, Viatcheslav. 2015. *Russia's Postcolonial Identity: A Subaltern Empire in a Eurocentric World*. London: Palgrave Macmillan.

Radio Azatlyk. 2022. https://www.idelreal.org/a/31748114.html

Richard, Carl J. 2012. *When the United States Invaded Russia: Woodrow Wilson's Siberian Disaster*. London: Rowman & Littlefield.

Sharafutdinova, Gulnaz. 2020. *The Red Mirror: Putin's Leadership and Russia's Insecure Identity*. Oxford: Oxford University Press.

Starovoitova, Galina. 1993. "Politics After Communism: Weimar Russias?" *Journal of Democracy* 4 (3): 106-109.

Tabarovsky, Isabella. 2019. "Israel's Russian Speaking Minority: Political Force in the Knesset?" *Riddle*. https://ridl.io/israel-s-russian-speaking-minority-political-force-in-the-knesset

Tereshina, Daria. 2019. "'Shiyes Is Our Stalingrad': Garbage Riots and Moral Outrage in Northwest Russia." *Max Planck Institute for Social Anthropology*. https://www.eth.mpg.de/5353781/blog_2019_12_10_01

Tsypkin, Ilya, and Elena Anisimova. 2021. "Donory v Defitsitakh. Analiz Dinamiki Nalogovykh Postupleny v Federal'ny Biudzhet s Territory Sub'ektov RF." *Akra*. https://www.acra-ratings.ru/research/2302

Vishnevsky, Anatoly, and Ekaterina Shcherbakova. 2018. "A new stage of demographic change: A warning for economists." *Russian Journal of Economics* 4 (3): 229-48. https://rujec.org/articles.php?id=30166

Wenar, Leif. 2015. *Blood Oil: Tyrants, Violence, and the Rules That Run the World*. Oxford: Oxford University Press.

Zubarevich, Natalya. 2011. "Chetyre Rossii." *Vedomosti*. https://www.vedomosti.ru/opinion/articles/2011/12/30/chetyre_rossii

Index

absolutism, the 50-7, 119, 224
   Enlightened 50
activism 87, 213-16
   philosophical 87
   trickster 216
affairs, the
   church 66, 139
   communal 129
   domestic 48
   educational 52
   foreign 131, 183-5
   human 177
   international 177-8
agenda, the
   anti-progressivist 46
   authoritarian 70
   imperial 63
   traditionalist 64-71
Antichrist, the 15, 18-28, 88-9, 109-10
apocalypticism 15-18, 22-7, 33-4, 37, 116
art, the 213, 257, 259-61, 267-8, 300, 304
Article 6 (of the Constitution) 151, 283
atheism 18-20, 89, 101
attitude, the
   anti-rational 71-2
   cynical 135, 214
   ethical 257
   power 279 (*see also* power, the)
   resentment 194, 226
   universal responsiveness 244-5
authoritarianism
   Enlightenment 50
   post-historical 173, 175
   post-Soviet 183, 224
   responsibility and 282-3
   threat of 183-4
   Weimar Russia 156

Bakunin, Mikhail 196, 302, *see also* Bolshevism; Slavophilism, revolutionary
barbarity 110, 170-2, 196-7
Berdyaev, Nikolai 60-1, 89-90, 251, 253
   apocalyptic vision of 15, 60
   on Bolsheviks/Bolshevism 107-10
   on communism 89-90
   on Dostoyevsky vs. Tolstoy 259
   on Slavophilism 119-20
Blok, Alexander 26-8, 89, 112-14
Bolshevism
   eschatology 25-6, 31-3 (*see also* Dugin, Alexander)
   and Eurasianism 84, 89-91, 151
   and Germany 161
   and imperialism 62, 79
   response to 107-23
   rise to power 159, 321 (*see also* the October Revolution)
bourgeoisie 99, 110, 113-15, 159
Brodsky, Joseph 303
Bulgakov, Sergei 115-16, 119, 253

capital
   cultural 179
   private 96, 263-4
capitalism 101, 114-15, 173, 199
   global 214, 225
   Russian 202-4
chauvinism 59-60, *see also* patriotism
   militant 223
   national 92
Christianity, *see also* church, the
   Enlightenment 49, 52-7, 182
   revival of 16-21, 182-3 (*see also* Antichrist, the; Dostoevsky, Fyodor)

Russian Orthodox 15–17, 65–71,
        81–3, 281
    universal 61, 82–9, 100–3, 139
        (*see also* church, the;
        common faith; political
        theology; Solovyov,
        Vladimir Sergeyevich)
    values (*see* values)
church, the 81–8, 107, 139, 269, 292,
        see also Christianity
    authority of 52, 73
    Christian 18–20
    churchmen 23, 49, 52
    false 38–9
    language of 37
    Roman Catholic 83, 87–8, 91,
        100–1
    Russian Orthodox 16–17, 22,
        26, 37–8, 46, 49, 52–6, 62,
        65–6, 81–3, 88, 127, 182,
        224, 281
        failure of 88
        vs. Ukrainian Orthodox 16
    -state 19, 38, 49, 66, 73, 88,
        276
    Universal Christian 83–4, 86,
        89 (*see also* Solovyov,
        Vladimir Sergeyevich)
civilization
    anti-civilization 27
    vs. barbarism 169–71
    vs. culture 175–9
    ethno- 238
    European 91–4, 291–2 (*see also*
        colonization)
    modern 269
    purpose of 98, 175–7
    Russia as 68, 273–5 (*see also*
        Russian, world, the)
    war on 115 (*see also* Bolshevism;
        revolution, the)
    Western 180–7, 263 (*see also*
        Westernization; politics,
        global)

colonialism
    decolonization 314–15
    economic 101–2
    Russian 240, 312–20
    Western 91, 263
communism
    fall of 154–6, 214, 279–80
    German 157–8, 161
    post-Soviet 162
    Soviet 62, 151, 284
    Stalinist 98–9
    universal 83, 89
consciousness
    collective 72, 194–5, 225–30,
        244
    false 225, 284
    legal 223, 278–9
    modern 261–3
    mythological 231–2
    national 264
    progressivist 255–8, 261–3 (*see
        also* cyclical progress;
        progressivism)
    religious 267–8
    self- 171–2
    tribal 197–8
    unconscious 242
cosmopolitanism 92, 96–98, *see also*
        chauvinism; nationalism
Crimea 29, 31, 63, 126, 202, 286–7,
        295–6, 312, 315–6, *see also*
        Crimean War, the
chthonism 17, 242–4
cult
    Bolshevik 108, 121
    of death 222
    Khlysty 109
    of the state 224
    of transgression 208 (*see also*
        transgression)
culture
    crisis of 196
    European 91–5, 239 (*see also*
        Europeanization)

history of 256
holistic 267–8
identity 68–9, 90–2, 98, 178
legal 279, 284
modern 257
multiculturalism 169, 179, 317–20
national 98
post-historic 174 (*see also* Fukuyama, Francis)
post-Soviet 183, 201–8, 214 (*see also* cynicism, post-Soviet)
preservation of 300–1
prison 62, 298, 320 (*see also* prison)
replacement of 227
resistance 303–4
Russian 54–7, 242–5
sovereign 66–8
specificity 95, 98, 242, 283
traditionalist 68–72
universal 81, 96, 103
values 102–3
vs. civilization 175–9
Western 182

cynicism
post-Soviet 204–16, 284 (*see also* trickster)
pragmatism 127, 134–5 (*see also* pragmatism)
Soviet 203, 285

democracy
Athenian 86
vs. authoritarianism 183–4, 253
export of 263–4
and ideocracy 96 (*see also* Trubetzkoy, Nikolai)
liberal 169–75, 186–7, 263
and liberalism 153
and pragmatism 128–9, 132, 141
responsibility 282
Russian 126, 154–63, 285, 294–8, 304–6
Weimar German 152–63

de-Stalinization 296
determination
historical 117, 120
natural 102
self- 83, 90, 230
act of 223
formula of/concept of 311, 322
national/of nations 80–1, 90
people's 111
religious/spiritual 111, 223
dictator/dictatorship, the 6, 122, 140, 159, 179, 232, 253, 263, 282, 291, 294–96, 304–6
communist 154, 156
–hangmen 287
modern 213–14, 287
party 232
patriarchal 299
of the public realm 128 (*see also* Heidegger, Martin)
regime 62, 149, 282–3
undeclared 150
Dostoevsky, Fyodor
and Antichrist 18–21
and intersubjectivity 228–30
and Russian exceptionalism 277
and universal responsiveness 244
vs. Tolstoy 259
Dugin, Alexander 31–5, 153–4, 163

economics
capitalist 173
Chinese 184
economic independence 90–1
neoliberal 214, 263
of scale 312 (*see also* federation)
state-monopolistic 225, 317–18
of thought 231 (*see also* consciousness, mythological)

education
    cultural 93–4
    Enlightenment reform(s) of 52–6, 59, 182 (*see also* reform)
    political 221
    Western 82–3, 94, 291–2, 299 (*see also* Europeanization; Westernization)
elite(s), the 122, 153, 177, 314, 323
    financial 264
    ruling/political 54, 64, 198, 208, 221–2, 255, 283–4
        overthrown of 157–60
    Western educated 82, 95
empire, the
    Christian 84–9 (*see also* political theology; Solovyov, Vladimir Sergeyevich; church, the, Universal Christian)
    collapse of 184, 191–3, 304–5, 311, 313–16, 321–2
    and democracy 264, 295
    Eurasian 185–6
    European 80
    idea of 192, 302
    ideocratic 96 (*see also* Trubetzkoy, Nikolai)
    Latin 97–102 (*see also* Kojève, Alexandre)
    Mongol 185 (*see also* Golden Horde)
    post-national 103–4
    post-Soviet (*see* Russian Federation)
    Russian 52, 61–3, 74, 79, 81–4, 89, 99–102, 141, 154, 186, 237–38, 302, 311–13, 318–21
        as a prison of nations 320 (*see also* prison)
        disintegration of 311
        territory of 96, 311–12
        restoration of 154
    Soviet 89–90, 150–1, 315
    Tsarist 56, 60–2, 79, 182, 312–14
    universal 81–4 (*see also* universal state)
Enlightenment, the
    counter- 71–2
    critique of 87, 265
    European 47–8
    positive legacy of 171, 186–7
    Russian 48–57, 292
eschatology, the
    Bolshevik 26, 116
    Christian 89
    communist 89–90
    Eurasian 34
    necro- 34
    Russian Orthodox 37
ethics
    ethicotheology 259 (*see also* Kant)
    modern 257
    and patriotism 222
    pragmatist 131, 135–7 (*see also* pragmatism)
    Russian 276–81 (*see also* law, the, and morality; Solovyov, Vladimir Sergeyevich)
    traditional 220
    trickster 214–16 (*see also* tricksterism)
Eurasianism 31–4, 83–4, 89–91, 97–8, 151, 184–6, 228, 230, *see also* Dugin, Alexander
Europeanization 81, 91, 94–6, *see also* Trubetzkoy, Nikolai; Westernization
exceptionality/exceptionalism, the 55–72, 80–1, 91, 270, *see also* Slavophilism

fascism 18, 96, 162, 193, 303–4, *see also* Nazism

faith, the
    blind 197
    and Bolshevism 115
    common 139 (*see also* church, the, Universal Christian; Solovyov, Vladimir Sergeyevich)
    ideological tool 16–17
    and modern subject 256–8
    Orthodox 55, 60 (*see also* Orthodoxy; *sobornost'*)
    pride of 29–30
    in progress 255, 265
    and reason 269
    resurgence of 187
    Soviet 151, 162
federation, the 304, 311–25
    de- 312
Frank, Semyon 108–9, 116, 120, 266
Frankfurt School, the 128–9
freedom
    ecclesiastical 88
    Hegelian 172
    intersubjective 228–9 (*see also* Dostoevsky, Fyodor)
    liberal-democratic 127–9, 263
    moral 117–20, 172, 229–30
    and patriotism 223, 302
    Russian 60, 70, 156, 224–6, 285, 294–5, 306
    trickster 203, 214–15
    Weimar Germany 155–6
Fukuyama, Francis 169–75, 179–81, 186–7, 252

Galich, Alexander 7
geopolitics
    cultural-civilizational 177–8
    Eurasian 16, 31, 185–6 (*see also* Dugin, Alexander)
    Russian 64, 237–9
glasnost' 151, *see also* Gorbachev, Mikhail; *perestroika*

God
    death of 182, 197
    kingdom of 37
    love of/for 84–5, 228
    overthrow of 19–26, 195
    relationship with 187, 227–8
    revenge of 182
    and sanctimony 28–30 (*see also* theocracy)
    and the state 80 (*see also* theology, political)
Gogol, Nikolai 291, 295
Golden Horde (*Ulus Ulug*) 68, 185, 193, 296, 303
Gorbachev, Mikhail 143, 151, 160, 193, 286, 295, 307, 313, *see also perestroika*; *glasnost'*
government 140, 154, 219, 280
    absolutist/authoritarian 51, 119, 184, 224
    Athenian 86
    Bolshevik 90
    communal 171
    institutions 51, 264
    Kyiv 264
    limited 135
    parliamentary 150
    Putin's 75, 204, 220–1, 225, 286, 304–5
        reins of 125
        unrestricted role of 70
    republican 184
    Russian imperial 82
    social-democratic (in Germany) 157–8
    Soviet 73, 198
    Western 311
        British 313
    world 192
    Yeltsin's 159
grandeur
    Russia's 244–5
    historical 72
    imperial 181

guilt, *see also* responsibility
   collective 281–2
   legal vs. moral 275–6
   political vs. moral 138–9
   recognition of 296–7
GULAG (*Glavnoye Upravleniye LAGerey*) 226, 293
Gumilev, Lev N. 31, 303

hatred 26, 31, 195–8, 222, 303
Hegel, Georg Wilhelm Friedrich 86, 98, 171–2, 186–7, 251, 256–7, 259, 262, 284
   his notion of
      desire for desire 171–2, 186–7
      modernity 262
      reason 86, 284
      religion 259
      world spirit (*Weltgeist*) 98–100
Heidegger, Martin 128, 260
hero, the
   cultural 214 (*see also* tricksterism)
   heroization of death 222
   Sharov's 23–7
historiosophy 115, 122
history
   angel of 202
   Christian 18–19
   civilizational 176–9
   common 103
   cyclical 192, 251–6 (*see also* cyclical progress)
   end of 15, 34, 100, 169, 172–4 (*see also* Fukuyama, Francis)
   Enlightenment, the (*see* Enlightenment, the, Russian)
   German 155–161 (*see also* Russia, Weimar)
   instrumentalization of 67–72
   modern 257–9, 262–3
   philosophy of 120–1, 172, 187, 191–2, 256, 259, 262, 268–70 (*see also* Hegel, Georg Wilhelm Friedrich; Karsavin, Lev)
   revolutionary 114, 118
   Russian 25, 59, 65–6, 139–40, 156–163, 293–6, 305
   trickster 214–16
   universal 83, 171–3

idea
   Bolshevik 116–9
   Christian 67
   communitarian 69–70
   democratic 161, 305
   empire (*see* empire the, idea of)
   Enlightenment 47–8, 50–4, 171
   Eurasian 151, 225
   European 96–7
   pragmatic 132
   Russian 16, 55, 58, 60–2, 68, 95 (*see also* exceptionalism; Slavophilism; traditionalism)
   Soviet 151, 284
   vs. pontocracy 35
ideal, the
   Enlightenment 46–7, 50–3, 56–8, 186
   of ideocracy (*see* ideocracy)
   rational 269
   Romantic 262
   Slavophile 120
   socialist 108, 113
   traditional 61–2, 69, 220 (*see also* traditionalism)
identity, the
   collective 227–9
   crisis 160–1
   cultural 90–1, 98, 170, 178
   geopolitical 238
   personal 131, 223
   politics 136, 209–11, 318–20
   Russian national 58–63, 67–72, 81, 90, 193, 221
   Soviet 183, 193
   Western 182
ideocracy 35, 62, 96–7, 103

ideology
    and cynicism 205–6, 211, 214
        (*see also* cynicism)
    Eurasian 17, 22, 83–4 (*see also*
        Eurasianism)
    liberal (*see* liberalism)
    pragmatic 126
    progressive 253–61, 264–5
        (*see also* progressivism)
    Slavophile 82
    Soviet 63, 151, 198, 202–4
    state 55–7, 64–5, 224–5, 273–5
    universalist 90
imagination, civic 136
imperialism, *see* empire, the
    anti- 91, 95
    Christian 100–1
    militaristic 263–4
    neo–imperialism 84, 274
    Russian 63, 79, 180–1, 238–40,
        312–17
    sovereignty 80, 83
    Soviet 99–100
intelligentsia
    and Bolshevism (*see* Bolshevism,
        response to)
    intelligentnost' 133, 140
    legacy 251
    non-European 95
    post-Soviet 193
    responsibility 137–8, 140
internationalism 98, 116, 119, 151
irrationality, the
    of [human] condition 269
    of modern subject 265
irreligion, humanist 101
Iz glubiny (*Out of the Depths*) 115, 119

Kant, Immanuel 48, 191, 259
Karsavin, Lev 97, 120–1, 228
Kojève, Alexandre 97–104, 171–3, 186

law, the
    constitutional 47, 51, 171, 220
    exception to 80
    historical 162
    international 277, 285–6
    lawlessness 72, 108–10, 215–16,
        226–7, 286
    Magna Carta (*Magna Carta
        Libertatum*) 185
    and morality 276
    Russian 275–80, 284–5, 298
    structural 242–3
left, the 57–8, 161–3, 173
Lenin, Vladimir 109–10, 118–19,
    156, 220, 321–2
liberalism
    American 285
    critique of 96, 98–9, 174
    democracy (*see* democracy,
        liberal)
    Enlightenment 47
    neoliberalism 214, 252
    post-Soviet 207, 214
    rejection of 57–9, 65–72, 152–3
literature 227, 232–3, 259, 277,
    300–4
logic
    duel logique 95 (*see also*
        Trubetzkoy, Nikolai)
    ethical 131 (*see also* pragmatism)
    French revolutionary 117–18
    mythological 231
    progressive 254–5, 265
    of the "red wheel" 26–7
    of resentment 194 (*see also*
        resentment)
    structural 244 (*see also*
        universal responsiveness,
        universal)
    totalitarian 221

Mandelstam, Osip 303, 308
Marx, Karl 87, 101, 280, 313
Marxism 62, 284–5
messianism 60–1, 207–8, *see
        also* exceptionality/
        exceptionalism;
        Slavophilism

militarism
    apocalyptic 17
    imperial 80, 99, 102–4, 263–4
    patriotic 221
    Russian, causes 142, 313–14
    Western 142, 181–2, 263
modernity
    anti- 45, 70, 313
    critique of 176, 256–70 (*see also* modern subject)
    nature of 47, 97
    postmodernist (*see* postmodernism)
    Soviet 202–3
modernization 56, 178, 182, 238–9
monarchy 49–56, 86–8, 114, 158, 282
morality
    amorality 205–6, 214, 227, 284 (*see also* cynicism)
    freedom (*see* moral freedom)
    and guilt 275–6 (*see also* guilt)
    and law 276–9 (*see also* law, the)
    and patriotism 222–3
    pragmatic 137–40
    progressive 263
    revolutionary 108–12, 116–17, 119–20
    secular 47–8, 258–61
    spiritual 186–7, 265–8
    traditional 65–71, 220 (*see also* traditionalism)
    and war 81
    Western immorality 60–5, 152, 208
mysticism 223, 258–9, 265, 267–8
mythology
    and art 260
    consciousness 231–2 (*see* consciousness, mythological)
    of the earth 241–3 (*see also* cthonism, structure)
    geopolitical 239
    Greek 32
    and ideology 254–5, 257–8
    national 68, 193, 225
    trickster 214

Nabokov, Vladimir 300, 308
narodnost' (nationality) 62, 74, 224
nation
    brotherly 29
    European 91, 94–5 (*see also* Europeanization)
    liberal-democratic 96, 152, 183, 264
    modern 103–4, 258
    notion of 80–3, 85–6, 120
    Russian 63–4, 81–3, 89–90, 180, 253, 299
    of serfs 293–4
nationalism 59, 82, 96–7, 209, 222, *see also* patriotism
    egoistic 99
    ethnic 57, 61–2, 71, 264
    European 82, 91
    French 99
    German 152–4
    imperial 216
    post-nationalism 102–3
    rejection of 99
    Russian 5–6, 17, 57, 79, 180
    zoological 96
NATO, *see* North Atlantic Treaty Organization
naturalism, affective 222
Nazism 209, 287, *see also* fascism
    German 16, 131, 211
nihilism
    European 153
    legal 183, 286
    Russian 15
norms 55–6, 65–6, 68, 135, 230, 291–2
    civilizational 4
    cultural 56, 71
    democratic 74, 294

moral 64, 258, 298
Western 126
North Atlantic Treaty Organization (NATO) 126, 134–5, 142, 209, 297
nostalgia 154, 201, 262

order, the 57, 61, 156, 215, 220, 226–7, 244, 307, *see also* government
　authoritarian/autocratic 74
　bloody 225
　constitutional 136
　democratic 156, 173
　European 152
　just 49
　military 320
　modern 266–9
　of nature 80
　political 3, 80, 98, 207, 263, 285
　republican 158
　ruling 161–2
　social 61, 71, 87, 269, 291–2
　Stalinist 295
　world 5, 63, 127, 142, 266–7, 270
Orthodoxy 183, 224, *see also* Orthodox church
　Christian 183, 243
　Russian 15–17, 38, 52–60, 317

Pasternak, Boris 283, 303
patriotism 94, 129–30, 158
　as a value 68
　imperial 59
　instinctive vs. spiritual (Ivan Ilyin) 223
　lack of 154
　modern 221–2
　Russian 221, 302–3
　virus of 302
perestroika, the 150–1, 156, 159, 193, 214, 232, 236, 278–9
　reforms 137, 141

Peter the Great/Peter I 27, 48, 50–2, 56, 60, 73, 81, 182, 239, 298, 308
Philistinism 122
　positivist 110
　spiritual 107–8
philosophy
　applied 276
　classic 266
　Hegel's 262 (*see also* Hegel, Georg Wilhelm Friedrich)
　of hope 108
　Institute of 280
　literary-centric 277
　moral 266, 278
　political 171
　Russian 59, 194, 275, 278–81
　religious 97, 227, 253
　Soviet/post-Soviet 278–80
　Western 53, 172
Plato 17, 33, 86, 171–4, 186, 231, 260, 267
Platonov, Andrei 17, 27, 31–3
poetry, the 74, 113, 260, 293, 303, *see also* Blok, Alexander; Pushkin, Alexander Sergeevich
politics 23–5, 46–8, 51, 72, 130, 136, 139–40
　anti-Western 90, 103, 127, 171, 173, 251, 264–8
　cynical 303, 308
　democratic 128
　of emancipation 83
　European 321
　global vs. local 178
　identity 136, 318
　participation in 281
　Putin's (aggressive) 142, 225, 261
　Russian 155, 308, 312
　world 127, 182, 185, 242, 247
population, the 6, 48, 54, 81, 151, 243–5
　Armenian 199
　control over 51, 53, 70

educated part of 293
indigenous 317
oppressed 252, 281, 298
passive 224, 226
non-Christian 89, 101
of Russian Empire 87, 89–90, 92, 94, 97
Russia's/Russian 81, 83, 224, 293–6, 304–5, 317
Russian-speaking 134
Soviet 156, 158, 161
Ukrainian 274
postmodernism, authoritarian 205
power(s), the 17–20, 25–6, 30, 35–7, 48, 65, 86–8, 109–10, 117–19, 132–3, 142
attitude 279
authoritarian 5, 9, 12
destructive 15
imperial 80, 83
leader's absolute 121
military 102–3, 150
nature of 4
Russian monarchs' 48–51
self-legislative 48
Soviet 143
syndrome 8
Western 91–2, 142
pragmatism 10
American 128–9, 141
disdain for 127–8, 130, 133–4
philosophical 128
principled 135
Putin's 125–7, 129
prison 62, 138, 226, 298, 320, *see also* GULAG; culture, prison
camp 291
culture 62
of nations 320 (*see also* Empire, Russian)
state 298
progress 63, 70, 72, 80–4, 265
anti- 10, 45–6, 71
civilizational 72

cyclical 254, 265, 269–70
faith in 162
historiography of 263, 267
historical 60, 256
humanity's 47, 92, 170, 193, 259, 263
ideology of 162, 254–8, 262, 264–5
infinite 255, 265
modern 254–5
resistance to 45, 52, 57–8, 62, 71–2, 253, 255
social 56, 72, 162, 175, 180
spiritual 177
technological 94, 265
world 92, 291
progressivism 121, 172, 179, 186, 252–3, 255–7
anti- 10, 45–6, 71, 258
propaganda 287
anti-modern 45
Bolshevist 114
cynical 208
machine 6, 294
Moscow/Putin's/Russian 10, 67, 72, 130
anti-Western 280, 284
nationalist 180
of national superiority 131
and Nazis Germany 287, 294, 300
power of 245
state 219, 294
TV 210
of Roman-Germanic chauvinists 92
pacifist 153
Soviet
atheist 183
vs. post-Soviet 212
Western 252
protest(s), the
anti-government (in Russia) 302–3, 307

defeat of 207
lack of 11, 161, 293
local 315, 319–20
mass 203, 299, 317
global 3
peaceful 299, 302, 306
social, forms of 11, 209, 293
(*see also* cynicism)
psychoanalysis 32, 232, 242
Pushkin, Alexander Sergeevich 30, 170, 196, 244, 246, 301–2, 307–8

rationalism 53, 55, 60, 131
rationality 133, *see also* irrationality
enlightened 47
modern 257, 262 (*see also* ideology)
scientific 241, 265
reason/reasoning 47–8, 61, 86–7, 100, 112, 128, 132–4, 171–2, 174, 206, 211, 222, 252, 255, 257, 261–2, 269, 312
cold 133
cunning of 284
human 48, 186, 268
logic of 231
paralyzed 11
primacy of will over 257, 261
pure 128, 133, 258
reduction of, the 128
self-criticism of 48
Shmat- 255
state of 86, 98 (*see also* state)
and sympathy 133, 186
transformation of 261
universality of 87 (*see also* universalism; Enlightenment, the)
victory of 100
world- 284 (*see also* Hegel, Georg Wilhelm Friedrich; Marx, Karl)

reform 49–50, 52, 137, 206, 304–5
Church 16, 49, 52
educational 52, 55–6, 59, 182
Enlightenment 52, 56
period of 159, 307, 313 (*see also perestroika*)
political 50, 71, 75, 81, 142, 159
social 50, 73, 186
religion, the 19, 22, 51–2, 64, 73, 89, 178, 187, 245, 258–60, 266–8
Bolshevism 109–11
Common 182
enlightened 258
instrumentalization of 66–7
of the masses 87
negation of 260, 267–8 (*see also* art)
philosophical 86
resurgence of 182
return of 267
of revolutionary socialism 109
and [the] state 17, 66, 96
true 67, 89
of war 17
republic(s), the 142, 235, 301, 304–5, 318–19, 324–5
democratic 184
Federal 155
Greek 86
parliamentary 157
The Republic 171, 260 (*see also* Plato)
Soviet 119, 151, 193, 284, 315–16, 318
Weimar 149, 155–8, 160, 163, 199
resentment 45, 71, 142, 209, 273
attitude of 226–7
feeling of 194
logic of 194
reaction of 195
vengeful 29

responsibility, the 110, 131, 138, 150, 205, 207, 276, 281–3, *see also* guilt
  citizen's 9, 282, 286
  collective/shared 11, 120, 138, 198, 281–2, 297
  and guilt 275, 277, 281–2, 298, 320
  individual/personal 70, 109, 130, 294
  [of] intellectuals 7–8, 129
  legal 141
  moral 205
  philosophical 281
  political 138, 197
  state's 282
retrotopia 202–3
revanche 152
  bureaucratic 160
revanchism 312, 314–16
revolution, the 26, 31, 73, 80–1, 102, 107–12 114–18, 122, 126, 139–40, 153–5, 161, 251, 305–6, 312–13, 321
  1905/1905–1907 9, 108, 314
  1917/October/Bolshevik 16, 73, 83, 89–90, 108–9, 114, 116, 120, 232, 314
  1991 159
  American 79, 184
  anti-communist 202
  apocalyptic 33
  autocratic 184
  Christian 89
  of consciousness 269
  Conservative 152–3
  eschatological meaning of, the 116
  European 114
  failed (of 2011–12) 208
  February 108, 113, 120, 156–7
  French 47, 52, 79, 84, 86–7, 117, 157, 184
  German 157
    of 1848 155–6
    of 1918 153, 156, 158–9
  global/world 90, 116
  industrial 150
  morally just 109
  music of, the 112–13
  of the people 294
  post- 114, 156, 159–60
  religious 113
  Russian 89, 113–20, 157, 259, 299, 307–8
  social 114–15
  theory of 219
  top-down 114
right(s) 30, 36, 82, 86, 119, 131, 154, 160, 240, 267, 292–4, 296
  constitutional 299
  and freedom 70, 72, 220–5, 285, 299, 302, 305
  human 47, 57, 84, 97, 127, 179–81, 285, 288
    violation 141
  indigenous 319–20
  individual 6, 46–8, 51, 57, 69–72, 206
  language 318
  of minorities 211
  and morality 277–8, 301
  natural 73, 80
  of resistance 287
  of self-determination 80, 312 (*see also* self-determination)
  protected 291
  reproductive 136
  to power 229
  traditional 83
  Weimar 152–4, 163
right, the 79, 157–8, 180
  extreme/radical- 16, 57, 157, 162, 173
  -wing 69, 119, 161–4, 319
Russian question, the 57–8, 62–3, 81, 94
Russophilism 60, *see also* Slavophilism

Satanism 109
    Western 64
Scheler, Max 128, 227
schism/shismatic 15–17, 26, 28
    beliefs 15
    policy 17
Schmitt, Carl 80–1, 85, 88–9, 153
sectarianism 23
    apocalyptic 17
    necro- 37
serf(s) 50, 293–6
    nation of 293–4, 296, 307
    serfdom 57, 121, 243, 319
Slavophile, the 55, 59–61, 82–3, 91, 118–20, 170, 224, *see also* Westernizers
    later-generation 118
    revolutionary 116
Slavophilism 55, 60, 120, *see also* Russian idea, Russian nationalism
sobornost' 38, 60–1, 227
socialism 35, 90, 95, 108–9, 113–16, 122, 194, 205
    communitarian 227
    idea of 108
    imperial 99
    late 202
    pseudo- 201
    revolutionary 109
    Russian 110
    Soviet 9
    State 207
    Western 90, 110
Solovyov, Vladimir Sergeyevich 61, 83–91, 96–7, 100–3, 210, 266–7, 289
Solzhenitsyn, Alexander Isayevich 63–4, 227, 252, 257, 303, 308
sovereignty 82–3, 102–3, 129, 244
    cultural 66–7
    God-given 79
    national vs. imperial 80
    of the people 79
    political 98, 316
    Russia's 74
    source of 82–3
    spiritual 220
    state 80
    Tatar 318
    true 83
Soviet
    collapse 45, 180, 314
    constitution 311, 320
    doublethink 206
    legacy 201, 203, 214
    man 191, 193, 198, 203, 226
    past 201–2
    period 79, 203, 206, 280
    philosophy 280
    post- 205–7, 319
        capitalism 204
        cultural identity 183
        democracy 164
        empire 318
        era/period 15, 18–19, 22, 66, 72, 149–53, 158, 160, 283–4, 316
        neoliberalism 214
        philosophy (Russian) 275, 278
        power 207
        Russia 19, 149–53, 158, 160, 162, 179, 181, 186, 282, 315–16
        trickster(s) 204, 212
    power 143, 307
    predecessors 314
    regime 9, 62, 156, 160–1, 203–4
    republic(s), the 119, 163, 284
    Russia 62, 91, 118, 137
    Society 203, 205
    State 100, 307, 314
    system, the 202, 206, 253
    trickster, the 203, 213–14 (*see also* trickster)
    Union, the 3, 5, 58, 63, 89, 127, 150–1, 155–6, 184, 198, 221, 230–2, 314–18

disintegration/collapse of 68,
142, 162, 169, 178, 180–1,
185, 191–3, 238, 311
dismembering of 314
nostalgia for 201
"special military operation," the 8, 58,
64, 127, 129, 131, 134, 180,
219, 244, 295
Spinoza, Baruch 133, 223
Stalin, Josef Vissarionovich 23–4, 99,
134, 156, 160–1, 201, 224,
226, 257, 274, 280, 283,
293–6, 303, 305
Stalinism 118
state(s), the 6, 16–20, 50–3, 58, 60–8,
73–5, 80–91, 96, 98–103,
150–2, 155–62, 180–5,
203–4, 207, 220–1, 224–6,
230–2, 238–40, 280–6,
301–8
  authoritarian 173, 224
  Balkan 322
  capitalism 203
  censorship 232
  Christian 19, 85, 88–9
  church– 19, 38
  church and 73, 276
  city– 184
  communist 89
  composite 311–12, 315
  democratic 282
  European 87, 142
  failed 316
  godless 20
  ideocratic 96–7, 103
  imperial 80, 85, 88, 99, 313
  independent 62, 184, 219, 318,
321–2, 324
  Islamic 182, 184
  law-based 160
  modern 103, 264
  nation 80, 85, 91, 103, 173, 178
  national 80–1, 88, 97
    post– 102
  Nazi 294

  political 173
  prison 298
  Putin's 319
  religion 17 (*see also* religion)
  revolutionary 111
  Russian 26, 58, 61–6, 68, 73, 82–3,
116, 120, 123, 176, 240,
280, 293, 303, 315, 319
  socialist 198, 214
  sovereign 81, 280, 284
  Soviet 100, 307, 314
  totalitarian 156
  transcontinental 237
  Tsarist 61
  universal 82–3, 86–7, 90, 100, 178
  Western 152
statehood, Russian 116, 120, 163, 238
subject 120
  collective 131, 221, 224–7, 281–2,
297, 305
  divine 31
  ethical 215
  modern 256–62, 265, 267–70
(*see also* modern subject,
irrationality of)
  mythical 257–60
  neoliberal 214, 263
  oppressed 83, 118, 152, 192, 252,
283

theocracy 19, 30
theology 21, 49
  Christian 31, 37
  ethico– 259
  political 80–4, 88–9, 100
  of terror 22–5
Tolstoy, Leo 103, 121, 228, 259, 279,
298, 301–3, 308
toska 226, 295, 308
totalitarianism 62, 227, 305
  political 220, 225
  resurgence of 45
  tendency to 224
  twentieth century 45, 287
  value-based 220

tradition
    anti- 153
    Christian 84
    cultural 92, 95, 97
    emancipatory 84
    Eurasian 102
    German 128
    historical 58, 96
    intellectual
        Anglo-American 177
        Russian 9, 60, 93
    Orthodox 98
    philosophical 262
        Russian 266
    political 79, 312
    worldwide 253
traditionalism 64–5
    Russian 10, 46, 55–62, 65–6, 71–2, 74
transgression/transgressivity 202, 204, 206, 214–15, 280
    cult of 208
trauma 18, 156, 235, 304
    collective 156, 193, 276
    national 130, 193
    social 232
    of the Soviet collapse 45
treason 132, 150
trickster 203–17
    Eugene Shvarts's 212–13
    failed 208
    omnipresent 213
    post-Soviet 204–6, 212
    Soviet 203, 214
tricksterism 208–10, 212
Trubetzkoy, Nikolai 91–6, 99, 102–3

Ukraine
    aggression against 3–5, 11, 211, 219, 281, 285
    conflict 4–6, 264 (*see also* the "special military operation")
    invasion of 3–4, 130, 175, 180, 307
    people of 3, 58, 135

victorious 304
war in 5, 10–11, 62, 67, 127, 137, 141–2, 233, 264, 309, 318
    (*see also* Russo-Ukrainian, war, the)
Union of Soviet Socialist Republics (USSR) 35–6, 58, 96, 141, 181, 193, 212, 217, 238, 284–5, 307, 309, *see also* Soviet Union, the
    Stalinist 36, 285, 296
United Nations (UN), the 311
United States of America 20, 67, 126, 128, 141, 169, 180–2, 185, 194, 225, 258, 264, 270, 319, 325
universalism 72, 154, 169
    Christian 89

values 5, 15, 34, 55, 60–1, 114–17, 172, 177, 179, 198, 207, 269, 284, 311–12
    battle for 196
    Christian 61, 70
    competing 136–7, 143
    cultural 11, 45–6, 81, 95–6, 102–3
    democratic 8, 47, 126, 152–3, 196
        (*see also* values, Western)
    denial of 15, 39, 215, 311
    dominant 134–5
    European 45–7, 52–3, 63, 96, 99
        (*see also* values, Western)
    liberal 8, 52, 58, 208, 230
    moral 187, 208
    naturalized 225
    social 219–21, 284
    surplus 101
    traditional 45–6, 54–7, 64–71, 74, 127, 130, 181, 219–22, 225, 275
    truth 129
    universal 71, 81, 179, 253
    Western 64, 95, 153, 170, 182, 263, 285 (*see also* values, European)

Vekhi (*The Signposts/Milestones/Landmarks*) 8–9, 108, 251–3, 292, 307
Victory Day 194, 221
viscosity 237–8, 243
voluntarism 121, 257

war, the 21, 80–2, 98, 115, 138–9, 156, 170, 174–6, 183–4, 198, 201, 207–8, 232, 235, 258, 262–3, 298–9, 301–4, 306, 309, 323–4
    Chechen (1994–1996 and 1999–2009) 198, 315
    Cold War 3, 155, 178, 182, 295, 311, 320
    Crimean (of 1853–1856) 313–15
    cult of 15
    history of 102–3
    holy/just 39, 280
    nuclear 23, 27
    religion of 17
    Russian Civil War 79, 83–4, 108, 113–15, 156, 321
    Russo-Ukrainian 3–5, 6–11, 17, 29, 34, 45, 57, 62–3, 67, 127, 130, 132, 137, 139–42, 154, 163, 180, 186, 191–7, 201, 209–12, 233, 242–4, 253, 264, 270, 273–7, 296, 303–4, 311–13, 317–21, 323
weapon, the 38, 229, 260–1, 301, 313, 319–24
    geopolitical 64
    nuclear 15, 20–1, 23, 36–7, 180, 183, 322–4
Weimar
    complex 193–4, 199
    Constitution 158
    democracy 158, 161
    Germany 152, 155–7, 160, 162, 207
    Republic 149, 155–8, 160, 199
    right 152, 154, 163
    Russia 149, 315
    scenario 181
    syndrome 10, 149
Westernization 51–2, 67, 90, 178, 182, *see also* Peter the Great
Westernizers, the 59–60, 82–3, 154–5, 170, 239, 244
    extremist 119
will, the
    act of 270
    Christ's 26
    free 111
    of the majority 157
    of the nations 80
    people's 121, 230, 306
    personal 281
    political 252
    primacy of the 257, 262
    rational 252
world, the 35, 83, 116, 122, 181
    Russian 6, 17, 26, 38, 68, 129–31, 136, 222
World War I 141, 150, 152–3, 156, 184, 199, 308, 314, 321
World War II (the Great Patriotic War), the 3, 36, 97, 125, 128, 184, 221, 231–2, 295, 307, 314, 321

Yanov, Alexander 149, 180–1, 193
Yeltsin, Boris 126, 142, 154–5, 159–60, 163, 193, 231, 318